THE UNPUBLISHED OPINIONS OF
Mr. Justice Brandeis
THE SUPREME COURT AT WORK

THE COURT AND THE CONSTITUTION

A SERIES EDITED BY

Philip B. Kurland

THE UNPUBLISHED OPINIONS OF

Mr. Justice Brandeis

THE SUPREME COURT AT WORK

ALEXANDER M. BICKEL

With an Introduction by PAUL A. FREUND

PHOENIX BOOKS

The University of Chicago Press

CHICAGO AND LONDON

Library of Congress Catalog Card Number: 67-12001

THE UNIVERSITY OF CHICAGO PRESS, CHICAGO & LONDON

The University of Toronto Press, Toronto 5, Canada

© *1957, by the President and Fellows of Harvard College*

First Phoenix Edition 1967

Printed in the United States of America

Preface

This book derives from the private papers of Louis D. Brandeis relating to his service as a Justice of the Supreme Court of the United States from June 1916 to February 1939.

Before President Wilson appointed him to the Court, Brandeis, though he had held no office save, briefly, that of ad hoc special counsel to the Interstate Commerce Commission, had had a great public career. He had, with unsurpassed courage, dedication, and effectiveness, engaged in the private practice of the public profession of the law. Perhaps the best concise estimate of Brandeis' achievement at the Bar — from which it is illuminating to quote — is found in an unpublished letter of his junior but close friend, Professor Felix Frankfurter of the Harvard Law School. Dated January 19, 1915, and addressed — how these ironies recur in the lives of great men — to one of those seats of ephemeral judgment, in this instance the Committee on Admissions of the Cosmos Club in Washington, the letter contained this passage: "As only two or three other men in this country he [Brandeis] has affected the thought of the nation. He has profoundly affected our national ideals. He has been a leader who has influenced other leaders, and his power has thus penetrated far beyond the reach of his own personality. Mr. Brandeis has been an inventor of ideas propelled by a great moral force."

A career such as these lines suggest would, of course, be of great interest to the historian and the biographer, and it would be attended by the accumulation of a substantial written record. Brandeis gave the papers touching his activities while at the Bar to the Library of the Law School of the University of Louisville, an institution in his native city whose development he had done much to foster. Among these papers are also some items dating from the period of Brandeis' service on the Bench, but having no close relation to his judicial work, as well as a few notes bearing on judicial matters. The Louisville papers have proved of great usefulness to scholars. Alpheus Thomas Mason drew on them, of course, for his *Brandeis — A Free Man's Life*. They are the starting point for any understanding of Brandeis and of his achievement. But the systematic files concerning Supreme Court cases on which Brandeis did any written work as a Justice — files maintained in his office for the twenty years from 1919 till his retirement — were not included in the gift to the Law Library in Louisville. On February 12, 1939, the day before the effective date of his retirement, Brandeis gave these files, some scattered papers of a similar nature, and most importantly, full discretion to determine their further disposition, to his friend of many years and colleague of two weeks, Mr. Justice Frankfurter. The files remained closed and in Justice Frankfurter's keeping until August 1954. At that time, they were transferred to the Harvard Law School, the Justice having granted access to them for study to Professors Paul A. Freund and Mark DeWolfe Howe of that school and to myself. I should say immediately and plainly what is obviously implicit: that in surrendering the papers the Justice surrendered also any duty to decide what specific use those to whom he had granted access might make of them; hence be must be absolved of responsibility for the use that is being or may be made. And I should, as regards Messrs. Freund and Howe, add that, of course, the responsibility for the present publication is wholly mine.

The papers remained at the Harvard Law School for two years. I was enabled to study them there by a generous financial grant from the Jacob Brenner Memorial Foundation and the Philadelphia Community Foundation, Inc., arranged through the good offices of Arthur W. A. Cowan, Harry A. Kalish, and Richard L. Levy of the Philadelphia Bar. The papers are now temporarily on loan to me at the Yale Law School. I have, however, in my notes, referred to them as being in the Library of the Harvard Law School, since they are ultimately to be placed on permanent deposit there.

The papers may be characterized as generally falling under four heads: notes and other evidence of the sources of information Brandeis canvassed for purposes of deciding cases and of documenting his opinions; memoranda and drafts submitted to him by his law clerks; Brandeis' successive drafts and revisions of his opinions; and the comments of other Justices on copies of opinions circulated to them by Brandeis — comments, usually penciled on the back of an opinion, which in the parlance of the Court are called "returns." Not every file is complete under all four heads, of course, if for no other reason than that, even though Brandeis often bestowed enormous labors on relatively unimportant decisions, not every case required the same amount of fresh, independent research, and some opinions wrote more easily than others. On the whole, however, the files constitute a remarkable revelation of the workings of a judicial mind — one, surely, of the half-dozen most influential ones in our history — and of the evolution

of judicial utterance. They provide, therefore, insight into the process
of decision; and they do so in an additional way, as well; for in bearing
witness to the interplay between Brandeis and other judges they enable
us to penetrate further behind what Thomas Reed Powell called the
"unwarranted animism" latent in references to "the Supreme Court,"
and to gain understanding of the alignments of some of the Court's
members and occasionally of why and how "swing-men" swing.

To surmise, as professional opinion must and does, about pulling and
hauling within the Court is inevitably to seem, at least, to trivialize
the process. To see the process in operation as these files reveal it —
they provide an important and substantial, though of course a partial,
view — is not to be disabused of the sound notion that judges are
human; but it is to be salutarily reassured that within their limitations
of intellect and experience, subject each to his failings and to the
finite human capacity to govern emotional biases, judges practice state-
craft, which is an art, but also an intellectual discipline.

Nine of the eleven unpublished opinions printed in this book were
found in files such as I have described. Indeed, since each was written
under unusual circumstances — in cases, one might say, which show the
judicial process in a heightened state — they come from particularly rich
files. Two of them date from the first three years of Brandeis' tenure,
before systematic files were started. Brandeis preserved them, though
without attendant drafts and other papers. All eleven — and I say
this on the basis of familiarity with the entire mass of files — are finished opinions, opinions that Brandeis, a consummate craftsman, would
almost certainly have been prepared to publish but for circumstances,
unrelated to their quality, which made it unnecessary or unwise to do
so at the time. They are to be distinguished from a number of other
unpublished writings originating in generally similar situations but
differing in that they remained in varying stages of relative undress.

The reason for building a book around these eleven opinions and
thus singling them out from the many materials in the Brandeis judicial papers which deserve to be brought to light is essentially this:
since they are, as much as Brandeis' opinions in the official reports of
the Supreme Court, the finished work of a great judge, they should
be in print in their entirety, to be placed where they belong, on the
shelf next to the work published in his lifetime. Once the decision to
publish the opinions had been made, it seemed appropriate to undertake at the same time and between the same covers the attempt to
derive from them and from the circumstances surrounding them such
new or confirmatory insight into the Court's process and into Brandeis'
thought as they might yield.

In preparing this book, I have made use, at relevant places, of materials in the Brandeis judicial papers relating to other cases than the eleven in which the unpublished opinions were written. Through the courtesy of Professor Mark DeWolfe Howe and of Mr. Justice Frankfurter, I have had access also to the papers of Mr. Justice Holmes and to the Holmes-Frankfurter correspondence. I have drawn on the Brandeis papers at the Law School of the University of Louisville, and through the kindness of my colleague, Professor Joseph Goldstein, on some recently discovered letters from Brandeis to Harold J. Laski. Finally, and most importantly, I have relied on contemporaneous notes of conversations with Brandeis which were made available by Mr. Justice Frankfurter as part of the Brandeis collection ultimately to go on permanent deposit at the Harvard Law School.

Of course, an initial judgment I have had to make in planning and preparing this book has been that none of the "disclosures" it contains violates proprieties. I use the word "disclosures" because its connotations suggest the problem; I have put it in quotes because those connotations are inapplicable. The problem of how much the historian should know and should tell of the inner life of going institutions of government is not one peculiar to the Supreme Court. It is in part — and, I am persuaded, in the largest part — a problem of which time is the solvent. More harm than good may be done by disclosing that which, because men and issues are still alive, may inhibit, or indeed, affect in whatever way, the current functioning of the institution. To be sure, the large issues the Court deals with are in a sense never dead because they never change. But their form and their historical setting live and die. This book — to the extent that I have been successful — sheds light on issues which are of interest because issues endure, but which in their form and setting are dead, because their form and setting are those of twenty-five, and for the most part, thirty and thirty-five years ago. The book, by the same token, sheds light on judges who are of interest because the process they engaged in abides, but the last of whom departed from the Court more than ten years ago, and none of whom survives.

There is a further dimension to the problem. Other men now sit in the places of those who were the Court of the twenties. May not the knowledge that their actions and words, their chits to each other, will perhaps be public after they are gone inhibit them today? The answer I have found satisfactory is twofold. First, what we know, we know because Brandeis thought it useful that we know it; else he would not have seen to the preservation of these files. There are no trivia preserved here, no casual gossip or malice; only that is here which is relevant to a fair appraisal of the performance of public men. To the extent that the judgment of the future influences the deliberate actions and words of men anxious for their reputations, the influence is, I should think, a highly beneficial one. Second, while we are deficient, by and large, in judicial biographies, enough has long since been gleaned from the private correspondence of some past Justices, so that, if there is danger that free intercourse among present ones may be inhibited by "disclosures" about their predecessors, free intercourse must already be severely inhibited. Actually, there is no ground whatever for believing that it is.

Without overestimating the value of this precedent, or of precedent in general on such a matter as this, I may in concluding appropriately indulge a well-known lawyer's predilection and note that an unpublished opinion by Chief Justice Roger B. Taney was printed by the Court's official Reporter in Volume 117 of the Reports, which appeared in 1886, twenty-two years after Taney's death. The opinion was made available by Taney's executor, and the Reporter, in introducing it, briefly told its story. It was written in a case that was reargued and decided after Taney's death, although Taney had heard the first argument. (The case was *Gordon v. United States*, reported in 2 Wallace 561.) But the judges who decided the case had seen Taney's opinion, and "the surviving members of the court" (in 1886) recalled that Taney's views had been carefully considered by them. The fact that publication met with no disapproval, but indeed served a good purpose is indicated in *Muskrat v. United States*, in which Justice Day, disposing of an important jurisdictional issue for a unanimous Court, discussed at some length the conclusions expressed by Taney in this opinion. The *Muskrat* case was decided in 1911, and is reported in 219 U.S. 346.

I wish to record my grateful acknowledgement of support and assistance I have received in preparing this volume. It is for once literally true that there is someone without whom this work would not have been possible. That someone is Mr. Justice Frankfurter, who, as I have explained, made available the materials on which the book is based. In addition, the Justice has been a never-flagging source of encouragement, and if I may use a blushing sort of word, since my intellectual debt to him is immense, inspiration. Yet, of course, it would be exceedingly unfair to tax him with what I have done. As will be evident, and as is inevitable for one concerned with the Court of the twenties, I have leaned heavily on the writings of the late Thomas Reed Powell and on those of Professor Felix Frankfurter. I have learned a great deal, and but for my own limitations would have learned more, from Professor Paul A. Freund, both in days when I was formally his student and more recently when I sat more informally at his feet. Professor Mark DeWolfe Howe is also my teacher, and he has been unfailingly kind and helpful. Arthur W. A. Cowan, of the Philadelphia Bar, not only was instrumental in obtaining the financial assistance that enabled me to study the Brandeis papers at Harvard, but also extended a most welcome hand of friendship. Judge Calvert Magruder, the Hon. Dean Acheson, and Professor William G. Rice of the University of Wisconsin Law School, all former law clerks of Justice Brandeis, were good enough to read early drafts of portions of the manuscript. Mr. Acheson has enhanced one of the chapters by graciously troubling to set out, and permitting me to quote, his recollections of *United Mine Workers v. Coronado Co.* Earl C. Borgeson, Librarian of the Harvard Law School, and his staff extended countless courtesies. Dean A. C. Russell, Mrs. Pearl W. Von Allmen, Librarian, and Professor Carl A. Warns, Jr., of the Law School of the University of Louisville were most hospitable and ever ready to help, when I examined the Brandeis collection at their school. David Bronheim, of the Harvard Law School class of 1956, and Robert Kunkel and Jay W. Dushoff, of the class of 1957, assisted me most ably in gathering relevant published materials and in checking the opinions themselves. Mrs. James E. Duffy of the Harvard University Press saved me from many infelicities of style, though I daresay many remain through no fault of hers. Mrs. Charlotte Dvoretzky typed and retyped the manuscript with good cheer and without ever inserting any errors of her own. The editors of the *Harvard Law Review* granted permission to include here a chapter that previously appeared in their publication.

A word about the form in which the eleven unpublished opinions are presented. I have, with the assistance of the gentlemen I have named, who are to be credited but not held responsible, endeavored to check all of Brandeis' references to his sources. With very few and minor exceptions, I have been able to do so. I have corrected only the obvious. Other questions and corrections appear in, I trust, self-explanatory brackets; and I may add that most of the brackets contain dates of cases and the like, which I thought it useful to insert, even though they may sometimes mar the surface of the printed page.

                                                                A.M.B.

Yale Law School

CONTENTS

Illustrations

Following page 118

Introduction

When, after his retirement from the Supreme Court, Justice Brandeis was asked whether he was writing his memoirs, he gave a characteristic answer. "I think you will find," he said, "that my memoirs have already been written." And so, surely, they had been; for in a life whose impulsion was the duty of public persuasion the record is as open, in the main, as a book. Such a life is measured out in words: not words that are recollections in tranquillity, not inert counters with which to symbolize experience, but words that are the actual signs of living encounters, fragments of fleece, in Holmes' phrase, left on the hedges of life.

The words gathered in this volume are the record of a powerful mind in the act of thinking and persuading. To call them fragments is in a sense misleading, since they are in every case a rounded and completed expression prepared for delivery as a judicial opinion. Why the opinions were nevertheless undelivered is itself not the least absorbing feature of their presentation and analysis here.

The opinions have, in fact, a threefold interest. They are intrinsically important as expositions, now patient, now percussive, of major themes which recur in other forms in the body of Justice Brandeis' judicial work. When they are examined, moreover, in the context of the working papers which underlay them, they reveal to a rare degree the creative process of judicial judgment. And finally, when the events surrounding their preparation and withholding are reconstructed, they throw fresh light on the processes of collective decision-making in our highest Court.

This very catalogue of values may raise in some minds a question of the propriety of the present enterprise. There will be no doubt, to be sure, on the first count — that it is right to enlarge the body of published writings of one of the most influential figures of the century, provided the new accretions are not second-rate, as they assuredly are not. If the trunks and scrapbooks of an Emily Dickinson or an A. E. Housman are ransacked for fugitive pieces, shall the carefully wrought and preserved handiwork of a preëminent judicial craftsman be kept shut off from view? It is not likely, either, that objection will be taken to the glimpses of the judicial workshop itself, and of the art of opinion-writing as it was practiced there by a Justice laboring necessarily in isolation, save as he was aided or hindered, as the case might be, by the services of his law clerk. What was done for the inner mysteries of the poetic process in John Livingston Lowes' *The Road to Xanadu* surely deserves to be emulated in approaching the arcana of the judicial process; but this will be possible only as papers like those left by Justice Brandeis are made available to be studied with a sympathetic and knowledgeable eye. It is the third aspect of this work — the intimate disclosure of the pulls and tugs that make up the process of collective decision — that may give concern.

It is certainly true that privacy is essential in the consultative phase of a court's work, and no one was more sensitive to this need than Justice Brandeis, or more scrupulous in its observance. But there are also the claims of history, the interest of a succeeding generation in understanding, judging, and profiting from the deliberations of their predecessors which for valid reasons were veiled when they occurred. What is wanted is an accommodation between two truths: that perfect candor in the conferences preceding judgment requires secrecy and that, in Lord Acton's phrase, whatever is secret degenerates. The problem of reconciliation has been met satisfactorily in other contexts: diplomatic correspondence is made public after an interval; Madison's notes of the debates in the Constitutional Convention were published a generation after the event. If, as these examples suggest, a major key to the solution is the passage of time, it is to be noted that all of the cases presented in this collection are more than twenty-five years old. Moreover, the intimacies here described are not aimless or malicious disclosures; they are relevant to understanding, and so, to use a favorite word of Justice Brandeis, they are instructive. The fact that the Justice preserved his working papers and entrusted them without restriction to one in whose judgment he had perfect confidence, as explained in the editor's Preface, should be sufficient warrant that in the use which has been made of them there is no breach of his own rigorous standards of propriety.

To return to the documents themselves. They contain, as I have said, most of the dominant themes in Justice Brandeis' judicial philosophy. Among these an absolutely basic one was self-restraint, the avoidance of a "great" constitutional decision if a case could be disposed of on a lesser ground, the observance of every jurisdictional and procedural limitation on the Court's authority. Some observers, puzzled by this regard for technicalities on the part of a judge whose constitutional outlook was spacious and who pierced to the heart of the matter in viewing social legislation, have been led to conclude, with a touch of cynicism, that the raising of technical bars to a decision on the merits was simply a useful expedient to prevent an unenlightened court from reaching a deplorable result. The very first chapter in the present collection should give an embarrassed pause to any such interpretation. For there, in a striking episode, it appears that Brandeis' insistence on avoiding a great decision may have been pressed despite the readiness of a majority to sustain a tax on child labor, and in fact, through the consequent delay and a change in the Court's membership, it resulted in an adverse decision at a later term of court. Surely there could have been no more dramatic test of the Justice's faithfulness to his self-denying ordinance.

In truth this ordinance was central to the Justice's thinking. The other major themes in the unpublished opinions — devotion to the federal balance and recognition of the evils of bigness — were of a piece with the canon of judicial self-restraint. All proceeded fundamentally from his awareness of the limits of human capacity, the fallibility of judgment, the need for diffusion of power and responsibility, the indispensability of husbanding what powers one had, of keeping within bounds if action is not to outrun wisdom.

In considering these papers, next, as a study in the art of opinion-writing, it is easy to see, therefore, why the sense of craftsmanship was so deeply respected and cultivated by the Justice. More than a matter of style was involved; it was, at the risk of putting it pretentiously, a matter of morality. The opportunity to reach a multitude of minds from the eminence of the judicial office imposed its corresponding obligations, to plumb a problem to its depths, to sheath a hard-won judgment in the toughest fiber, to shun the facile and shoddy argument as a sin against the power of communication.

But before a judge can undertake to educate others he faces the problem of self-education. These papers show how Brandeis coped with that problem. The briefs and arguments of counsel were generally quite inadequate, especially on the part of counsel for states and municipalities, the very interests that stood in need of the strongest representation before the Court as legislation was being put to the test. Justice Brandeis felt this deficiency keenly, the more so because his devotion to the federal principle assumed a diffusion of talent from the center to the extremities. Once when he was asked what sort of argument had been made to the Court by a county solicitor in an important case, the Justice answered drily, "He seems to be a very *virtuous* man." Even when the briefs and arguments were more responsive to the demands of the case, Brandeis treated them as only a starting-point for investigation. In that enterprise a judge draws necessarily on what he has brought with him to the Bench — a knowledge of techniques and principles, an outlook toward problems of government, and experience in the world of affairs.

Brandeis' experience had been uncommonly wide although he had held no public office. Two of the cases reproduced here are examples of the direct educational effect of prior experience — one dealing with seamen's legislation, the background of which he knew intimately through his friendship with the elder La Follette, the other involving regulation of the grain trade, which in Kentucky had been the family business. Other cases drew in a more general way on his body of experience; for example, the celebrated Coronado Coal case, on the issue of the responsibility of a labor union under the Sherman Act, in which Brandeis' draft opinion, here reproduced, throws fresh light on his approach to organized labor as well as to the powers of the national government. At another extreme is a case raising a vexed question of state taxation of goods shipped in from another state; on this problem Brandeis had not had occasion to ponder in his pre-judicial career. Addressing himself to it with energetic inquisitiveness, he ended by changing some of his own preconceptions and some of the Court's as well.

In the process of continuing self-education a judge is restrained by his official position from the kind of consultation and free-ranging interchange that are the life-blood of ordinary scholarship. Modern science, one of its most eminent practitioners has remarked, is based on international gossip. The judge is perforce a more solitary inquirer. Brandeis exploited to the full the resources available to a judge. The bibliographical services of the Library of Congress were heavily drawn on, and librarians of more specialized collections in government departments were cultivated. The librarian of the Department of Labor was for some years a regular guest at Thanksgiving dinner. Reading not directed at specific cases was highly selective, and often depended for its value on the prepared mind which interpreted it. Thus two of the principal journals to which he gave special attention were the *Federal Reserve Bulletin* and *Labor*, the publication of the railroad brotherhoods.

But the two chief reliances of Brandeis in acquiring information and testing ideas were time and his law clerk. The use he made of both of these appears plainly enough in these papers. He was not an addict of speed in the work of the Supreme Court. Unlike a Holmes or a Cardozo, he was not impatient to turn off an opinion while the frenzy was on him so much as he was anxious that it persuade and instruct. Time for research, documentation, reflection, and the architecture of an opinion was indispensable. As he silently resented being rushed when opinions of colleagues were circulated for approval on the very eve of the Saturday conference, so he made a practice of distributing his own drafts early in the week, holding them over if necessary lest they reach the brethren too near the time for decision.

In all of this enterprise the law clerk played a not inconsiderable role. Changing each year, and only a year or two out of the academic halls, the law clerks served to channel the ideas of the law-school world to the Justice's study, and at the same time to reach out to the documentary resources of Washington for facts. The law clerk was investigator (most of them came to know intimately the labyrinths of the Library of Congress), critic, and foil. Not infrequently the fresh breeze of doctrine brought in by the law clerk proved too strong a draft for the Justice, and he would turn up his intellectual collar against it. Two instances are shown in this collection: one the case on state taxation of imports from other states, the second the case on the responsibility of labor under the Sherman Act. The law clerk argued valiantly but to no avail for a clean break with traditional doctrine; but the Justice chose to arrive at the result by finding a more traveled route and extending it to his objective. It may be significant that in each case the Justice was faced with a probably hostile majority, and in each he was able to carry the Court, though to another Justice went the writing of the Court's opinion. It is only fair to add that in the labor case the view of Dean Acheson, the law clerk, was proved in time to be the law of the future, which has scarcely ever been more effectively put than in his eloquent memorandum. What emerges from all this is the image of a judge whose strength lay in his power to blend tradition and change, to find in the heritage of the law resources adequate to the needs of the new day, if only there is imagination to see the resources and understanding to see the needs.

The willingness, indeed the termperamental inclination, of Brandeis to work within the received framework of the law, is a clue to his effectiveness in the collective task of decision-making. It is this aspect of the unpublished opinions that remains now to be touched upon. When William Howard Taft was appointed Chief Justice in 1921, his brother Horace wrote him a letter of congratulation which contained a remarkably perceptive reference to Brandeis, who on his nomination five years earlier had been called unfit to serve as a Justice by seven ex-presidents of the American Bar Association, including William H. Taft. In his letter Horace wrote: "As for the other members of the court, you will be thrown in with them so intimately that I have no doubt that you will take them into camp. I expect to see you and Brandeis hobnobbing together with the utmost good will. The truth is that, while Brandeis has been on the New Republic side, so to call it, in some cases, he has not put radical stump speeches into his opinions or done anything else to make him seem dangerous." In point of fact, as these unpublished opinions reveal, Brandeis and Taft were able to work together harmoniously; more than that, Brandeis was able to persuade Taft to modify his views, and through Taft the views of the Court. Whether through Taft in some cases or more directly in others, at least four of the opinions here reproduced were successful in altering the decision of the Court and for that reason were undelivered; another resulted in a material change in the scope of the decision and a transfer of the opinion of the Court from McReynolds to Taft. Still another was a rescue operation, involving the validity of a state workmen's compensation law, as a result of which a broadly philosophical opinion of Holmes, in danger of losing its majority, was made more acceptable by being made more circumspect.

For Brandeis almost the paramount quality of a good judge was the capacity to be reached by reason, the freedom from self-pride that without embarrassment permits a change of mind. It was this quality of open-mindedness which made Justice Pitney, who was in many respects poles apart from Brandeis, an especially respected colleague. The constructive influence of Brandeis in the councils of the Court owed much to his high boiling point, his self-control which, when excessively taxed, was able to convert the fire within him into the heat of dry ice. Above all he had the temperament of a teacher, whose classroom was first of all the Court, and failing that, the profession and the future. There is something grand and a little pathetic, too, in the story of his arrangement for a special all-day conference of the Court to be devoted entirely to a discussion of some complex issues of utility rates, and to center on an extensive study which he prepared and circulated in advance. The conference was held and was of some value, he acknowledged, but its full possibilities were not achieved because some of the brethren had not mastered their homework.

These papers are, then, rich for an understanding of both individual and institutional lives. A word of caution must nevertheless be introduced. Not all the themes of Justice Brandeis' judicial career are here represented; in particular, none of the opinions deals with a civil liberties case. Moreover, on the institutional side, the very fact that every one of the opinions was fully prepared and yet undelivered suggests that the web of circumstances was more than ordinarily complex and the involvements of the Justices — what modern psychology would call barbarously their interpersonal relations — were uncommonly prominent in the process of decision. A more rounded picture of the Court during this period requires a study of materials more extensive than these. The complete working papers of Justice Brandeis will, it is hoped, furnish a basis for a more generalized analysis, to which the present study may stand as a prologue.

The task of the editor has been the most difficult kind of historical reconstruction — the recreation of a mind at work. That task Alexander Bickel has accomplished with fidelity, insight, and disciplined imagination, — in a word, with artistry.

PAUL A. FREUND

Harvard Law School

Chronology

Louis Dembitz Brandeis, born in Louisville, Kentucky, on November 13, 1856, the son of Bohemian-Jewish pilgrims of 1848, was educated in private and high schools in Louisville; at Annen Realschule, Dresden (1874–75); and at Harvard Law School (LL.B., 1877). He married Alice Goldmark of New York on March 23, 1891. Brandeis was admitted to the Bar in St. Louis in 1878. But he soon moved to Boston, where he practiced from 1879 to 1916. It was a part of practice for Brandeis to lend his legal talents to the advancement of public purposes. Soon after the turn of the century, "the people's lawyer," as he was often called, emerged on the national scene. He was counsel for *Collier's Weekly* in the Ballinger-Pinchot investigation of conservation policy in 1910, and for the shippers in a freight-rates investigation before the Interstate Commerce Commission in 1910–11; later he was special counsel for the Commission in a second freight-rates case in 1913–14. He acted also as counsel for the states, in the years 1907–1914, in defending the constitutionality of Oregon and Illinois ten-hour laws, of similar Ohio and California statutes, and of an Oregon minimum-wage law. In representing private parties in matters of public concern in these and other instances Brandeis accepted no fees. He served without fee also in 1910 as chairman of an arbitration board in connection with a New York garment workers' strike, and later served as arbitrator under a protocol he had devised. Throughout this period, Brandeis took an active interest in state and national politics. He played a major role as an adviser to Woodrow Wilson, both before and after the election of 1912. Having joined the Zionist movement in 1912, Brandeis was chairman of the Provisional Committee for General Zionist Affairs from 1914 to 1916. He was appointed Associate Justice of the Supreme Court of the United States by President Wilson on January 28, 1916, and after an epic battle for confirmation in the Senate, took his seat on June 5, 1916. Brandeis retired February 13, 1939, and died in his house in Washington on October 5, 1941.

THE UNPUBLISHED OPINIONS OF

MR. JUSTICE BRANDEIS

I

"The Most Important Thing
We Do Is Not Doing"

One of the chief humanitarian objectives of the progressive movement which, before Brandeis' accession to the Bench, had looked to him as one of its leaders, and which achieved a national victory in the election of Woodrow Wilson in 1912, was abolition of the evil of child labor. Agitation concerning this issue, like advocacy of workmen's compensation laws and of minimum wage and hour laws, was carried principally to state legislatures, and it achieved there a good measure of success. Owing to the increasingly integrated nature of the American national economy, however, the effectiveness of state statutes regulating conditions of labor was subject to distinct limitations. A kind of Gresham's law operated in favor of states, no matter if few, which elected to stand pat. Moreover, there were enforcement difficulties in those jurisdictions in which corrective legislation had been obtained. The total result with respect to child labor was that the evil persisted. And the reformers turned to the federal government.[1]

But Congress has no power to deal with such a matter as child labor directly, as a practice affecting the health and well-being of the nation's young. If it was to act at all, Congress had to do so under one of the heads of authority specifically delegated to the general government by the Constitution. Among these, one of the broadest is the power over interstate commerce, which Congress, beginning at a relatively early date, has more than once exerted for the purpose of achieving indirect results. And so in 1916 Congress was persuaded to pass a statute excluding from shipment in interstate commerce articles manufactured, under certain circumstances, with the aid of child labor.[2] Litigation promptly resulted, and within two years, in the case of *Hammer v. Dagenhart*,[3] the Supreme Court declared the Act unconstitutional. Congress had overreached, the Court said, in trying through exercise of one of its admitted powers to attain ends which were none of its concern. Justice Holmes, joined by Justices McKenna, Brandeis, and Clarke, dissented.

Three years later, Congress tried again. Striking with another weapon but aiming at the same target, it imposed a special tax on the product of child labor. The Court's response this time was less prompt, the process of litigation having been more extended, but the Congressional attempt ended in failure just the same. The tax power proved no more serviceable than the Commerce Clause. The Child Labor Tax Act of 1919[4] was declared unconstitutional in 1922 in *The Child Labor Tax Case*,[5] as it is called. On this occasion, there was only one dissenter — Clarke — and he wrote no opinion. The decision put an end for nearly a generation, until late in the New Deal,[6] to federal efforts to help abolish child labor. Before announcing it, Chief Justice Taft, the Court's spokesman in the case, disposed of an earlier attempt to put in issue the constitutionality of the Act. This was *Atherton Mills v. Johnston*,[7] which the Court had held, without deciding, for two terms. Its history throws some new light on the *Child Labor Tax Case*, and particularly on the position of Brandeis, one of the dissenters in *Hammer v. Dagenhart* who remained silent in the later case.

Atherton Mills v. Johnston came about in this fashion: The father of a minor employed by the mills, setting forth the fact that the Child Labor Tax Act imposed the heavy tax of 10 per cent of annual profits on businesses which employed minors under sixteen in circumstances applicable to his son, complained that because of this provision of law the mill was about to discharge the boy, thus depriving the father of his earnings. The Act, the father averred further, was unconstitutional; accordingly, the impending discharge of his son and resultant injury to himself were illegal. On these grounds, he asked a federal district court to enjoin the mill from proceeding with the discharge. The mill admitted everything except the unconstitutionality of the Act. Thus the issue was framed, and the district court, holding the Child Labor Tax Act unconstitutional, granted the injunction prayed for. The case was brought to the Supreme Court on appeal.

In now disposing of the case, Taft suggested that it might at one time have involved a serious jurisdictional question. But, he went on, there was no longer any need to worry about that. For the plaintiff's son, heedless of the larger issue involved, had since turned sixteen. The Act was not now applicable to him, and his father no longer had cause to fear his discharge. The case was happily and indisputably moot. The boy had outgrown the judicial process.

In his celebrated special concurrence in *Ashwander v. Tennessee Valley Authority*,[8] Brandeis gives a citation to *Atherton Mills v. Johnston* which is somewhat puzzling on its face. The *Ashwander* concurring opinion is generally and justly regarded as the crowning statement of one of the truly major themes in Brandeis' judicial work: the conviction that the Court must take the utmost pains to avoid precipitate decision of constitutional issues, and that it must above all decide such issues only when it is absolutely unable otherwise to dispose of a case properly before it. In elaborating on this theme in the *Ashwander* opinion, Brandeis formulated a number of rules. The first of these he put as follows:

1. The Court will not pass upon the constitutionality of legislation in a friendly, non-adversary, proceeding, declining because to decide such questions "is legitimate only in the last resort, and as a necessity in the determination of real, earnest and vital controversy between individuals. It never was the thought that, by means of a friendly suit, a party beaten in the legislature could transfer to the courts an inquiry as to the constitutionality of the legislative act." [9]

Among other cases *Atherton Mills v. Johnston*, though prefixed with a cautionary "compare," is cited in support of this statement. But we have seen what *Atherton Mills v. Johnston* held. It was, when decided on May 15, 1922, a case of quite conventional mootness, hardly apt as an illustration of judicial self-restraint in constitutional litigation. The page which Brandeis cited is the place where Taft put to one side doubts concerning the genuineness of the controversy presented by the record. "These are serious questions," Taft said, "requiring full consideration. We only state them in order that it may not be thought by our conclusion that we here decide them." [10]

Yet by the time he wrote the *Ashwander* opinion, Brandeis had twice before cited the *Atherton Mills* case in the same way he did there.[11] And members of the Court in more recent years have taken up the habit.[12] Thus it can happen — and it not infrequently does — that in the course of being transcribed into lawyers' shorthand, a case comes to stand for more than it actually decided. *Atherton Mills v. Johnston* was identified in Brandeis' mind with the problem of collusive suits arranged to obtain quick and convenient adjudication of constitutional issues, because before it became moot it presented the Court with that problem and kept it naggingly before the Court for two years. The case was the occasion for Brandeis' first statement of the theme which he developed more comprehensively in *Ashwander*.

Atherton Mills v. Johnston was first argued on December 10, 1919. Within a month and a half Brandeis had prepared the opinion printed below, which he labeled a Memorandum to the Court. He urged dismissal for lack of jurisdiction. The controversy between the parties, he argued, was fictitious; the suit was collusive. The federal courts had no authority to entertain such cases. Moreover, the plaintiff would have had no standing to raise the issue of constitutionality even in a bona fide suit. For, whether or not it felt impelled to act because of the Child Labor law, the employer had a legal right to discharge the plaintiff's son anyway, on whatever ground it chose. Even assuming that the Child Labor Tax Act was unconstitutional, therefore, the fact remained that the father was not aggrieved by it; the statute had not worked the deprivation of any legal right he otherwise had. And the federal courts may not pass on constitutional issues at the instance of persons having no immediate, palpable stake in their adjudication. As he was to do in his unpublished opinion in *United Mine Workers v. Coronado Co.*, Brandeis here also taunted the majority with its holdings in a series of labor cases in which the Court, while striking down legislation aimed at bettering the workingman's bargaining position, had erected the employer's liberty to hire and fire into a practically absolute constitutional guaranty. Could it be, Brandeis asked in effect, that now that the shoe was in a sense on the other foot, the guaranty had suddenly sprung an exception? It was true that *Truax v. Raich*,[13] in which an Arizona statute regulating the employment of aliens was declared unconstitutional, and *Hammer v. Dagenhart*, the earlier child labor case, had, like *Atherton Mills*, been suits to enjoin an impending discharge from private employment, and that the Court had in both readily assumed jurisdiction. But in both those cases government officials threatening to enforce the allegedly unconstitutional statute, in obedience to which the employer was about to act, were joined as parties defendant; and while an employee may have no legal right to stay the hand of an employer proposing to fire him, he is entitled to protection against third parties who without good cause attempt to interfere with his advantageous condition of employment. On that ground those cases were distinguishable. *Atherton Mills* was a suit against the employer alone, and the resultant jurisdictional defect could not be cured by joining the federal collector of revenue as a party defendant, because Congress had forbidden suits brought to restrain the collection of a tax. The constitutionality of taxes was to be litigated by paying them and suing for a refund.

SUPREME COURT OF THE UNITED STATES

No. 406. — October Term, 1919.

The Atherton Mills, Appellant, vs. Eugene T. Johnston and John W. Johnston, by Eugene T. Johnston, his Prochein Ami.	Appeal from the District Court of the United States for the Western Dis- trict of North Carolina.

[January 26, 1920]

Memorandum by Mr. Justice BRANDEIS.

In my opinion, the action of the District Court in entertaining the bill in equity herein and issuing an injunction on the ground that section 1200 of the Revenue Act of 1918 (approved Feb. 24, 1919, c. 18, 40 Stat., p. 1138) is invalid, was a clear usurpation of power; and the jurisdiction of this court is limited to reversing the decree below and directing that the bill be dismissed by the District Court for want of jurisdiction.

For nearly a century after the adoption of the Constitution federal courts approached with great reluctance the exercise of their high prerogative of declaring invalid an act of Congress.[1] This

---

[1] "It is but a decent respect due to the wisdom, the integrity, and the patriotism of the legislative body, by which any law is passed, to presume in favor of its validity, until its violation of the Constitution is proved beyond all reasonable doubt. This has always been the language of this court, when that subject has called for its decision; . . ." Ogden v. Saunders, 12 Wheat. 213, 270 (1827).

"It is our duty, when required in the regular course of judicial proceedings, to declare an act of Congress void if not within the legislative power of the United States; but this declaration should never be made except in a clear case. Every possible presumption is in favor of the validity of a statute, and this continues until the contrary is shown beyond a rational doubt. One branch of the Government cannot encroach on the domain of another without danger. The safety of our institutions depends in no small degree on a strict observance of this salutary rule." The Sinking Fund Cases, 99 U.S. 700, 718 (1878). See also Legal Tender Cases, 12 Wall. 457, 531 (1871); Trade Mark Cases, 100 U.S. 82, 96 (1879). See American Doctrine of Constitutional Law by James B. Thayer, 7 Harvard Law Review, 129, 142 [1893].

"With the exception of the extraordinary decree rendered in the Dred Scott Case, . . . all of the acts or the portions of the acts of Congress invalidated by the courts before 1868 related to the organization of courts. Denying the power of Congress to make notes legal tender seems to be the first departure from this rule." Haines, American Doctrine of Judicial Supremacy, p. 289 [1st ed. 1914]. The first

reluctance was finally overcome; and then there was manifested a disposition, encouraged by the acquiescence or active co-operation of the Department of Justice, to facilitate the efforts of litigants to secure decisions on the validity of statutes of wide public interest, when their constitutionality was questioned.[2] Latterly single judges sitting alone in trial courts have declared acts of Congress invalid without even stating the reasons for their decisions.[3] But hitherto the limitation upon the exercise of this power by the federal courts, expressly imposed by the Constitution, has been universally recognized and consistently observed.

The Constitution, Article III, section 2, limits their jurisdiction to "cases in law and equity" and to cases "of admiralty and maritime jurisdiction." No federal court has jurisdiction of a proceeding brought specifically to have an act of Congress declared unconstitutional, because such a proceeding is not a "case" within the meaning of the Constitution; and even Congress and the President acting together cannot confer upon it jurisdiction in any proceeding which is not a "case." In *Muskrat v. United States*, 219 U.S. 346, 356 [1911], this court adopted as authoritative the definition of a "case" given by Mr. Justice Field in *In re Pacific Railway Commission*, 32 Fed. 241, 255 [1887]: "By cases . . . are intended the claims of litigants brought before the courts for determination by such regular proceedings as are established by law or custom for the protection or enforcement of rights, or the prevention, redress, or punishment of wrongs. Whenever the claim of a party under the constitution, laws, or treaties of the United States takes such form that judicial power is capable of acting upon it, then it has become a case. The term implies the existence of present or possible adverse parties whose contentions are submitted to the court for adjudication." And the *Muskrat* case (p.

---

legal tender decision was overruled in part two years later (1871), Legal Tender Cases, 12 Wall. 457; and again in 1883, Legal Tender Case, 110 U.S. 421.

[2] See opinion of Hook, C. J., in New et al. v. Wilson, Nov. 22, 1916 (Adamson Law); reversed, 243 U.S. 332 [1917]; opinion of Van Valkenburg, D. J., U.S. District Court for Western District of Missouri in Smith v. Kansas City Title & Trust Co., Oct. 31, 1919 (Federal Farm Loan Act).

[3] See decree Dagenhart v. Hammer, U.S. District Court for the Western District of North Carolina, May, 1919 (first Federal Child Labor Law), affirmed by this court, 247 U.S. 251 [1918]; also decree of U.S. District Court for Western District of Kentucky, October 27, 1919 (War-time Prohibition Act), reversed by this court, December 15, 1919 in Hamilton, Collector v. Kentucky Distilleries and Warehouse Company [251 U.S. 146].

359) by quoting the words of Mr. Justice Brewer in *Chicago and Grand Trunk Railway Company v. Wellman*, 143 U.S. 339, 345 [1892], shows also what is meant by the existence of adverse parties: "Whenever in pursuance of an honest and actual antagonistic assertion of rights by one individual against another, there is presented a question involving the validity of any act of any legislature, State or Federal, and the decision necessarily rests on the competency of the legislature so to enact, the court must, in the exercise of its solemn duties, determine whether the act be constitutional or not; but such an exercise of power is the ultimate and supreme function of courts. It is legitimate only in the last resort, and as a necessity in the determination of real, earnest and vital controversy between individuals. It never was the thought that, by means of a friendly suit, a party beaten in the legislature could transfer to the courts an inquiry as to the constitutionality of the legislative act."

Here, in my opinion, it is clear that the alleged controversy between the parties to the suit is not actual; that it is a fiction; that this proceeding, however high the motives of the parties, is a device to secure an adjudication of an important question of constitutional law, — in short, the fruit of collusion, to which this court should not, and under ordinary circumstances would not shut its eyes;[4] and that the infirmity of the proceeding is not overcome by the acquiescence of the Department of Justice. Surely this is not "a real, earnest and vital controversy between individuals."

But the main objection to the jurisdiction is far more serious. The proceeding below was not a "case" within the meaning of the Constitution. To use it as an instrument for declaring an act of Congress void was a usurpation of power by the court. The proceeding was in form a suit in equity to protect a right of the plaintiffs from violation by a wrong threatened by the defendant; but it was a suit in form only. For it is clear beyond possible doubt that under our system of law the bill set up no right of the plaintiffs as against the defendant and that the act threatened is not a wrong as against the plaintiffs or as against anyone else in the present case. Plaintiffs' claim, as set forth in the bill, is this: They,

[4] Compare Miller & Lux v. East Side Canal Co., 211 U.S. 293 [1908]; Cerri v. Akron-Peoples Telephone Co., 219 Fed. 285 [1914]; Phoenix-Buttes Gold Mining Co. v. Winstead, 226 Fed. 855 [1915]

father and son, are employed at defendant's mill, the employment being terminable at the will of either party at any moment. The son's employment is on piece work. Solely because of the provisions of the Act of Congress of February 24, 1919, c. 18, Sec. 1200 [40 Stat. 1138], concerning child labor, which plaintiffs allege is unconstitutional, the defendant proposes to discharge the minor. If it does so, the minor will be deprived of employment in defendant's factory, and the father of the wages which the minor would otherwise earn there. The bill prays (1) that the act be declared unconstitutional; (2) that defendant be enjoined "from in any way or manner by reason of the apparent force of said act of Congress, discharging the minor . . . from its services or curtailing his employment to eight hours a day." The sole defendant, which is the employer, admits by its answer all the facts, including the fact "that in obedience to the law of the United States unless enforcement of the said law is forbidden, it will discharge the minor plaintiff . . . from its employ . . . ," but it "denies that said Statute is not in truth and in fact law, and denies that [the] said law is unconstitutional."

No principle is more firmly established in English and American law than the right of an employer to discharge the employee forthwith, if there is no agreement express or implied for a definite period of service or for notice before termination.[5] Where the employment is terminable at will the employer may terminate it for any cause or without cause.[6] This right of discharge has been

---

[5] See, for instance, Howard v. East Tennessee Ry. Co., 91 Ala. 268 [1890]; St. Louis, &c., Ry. Co. v. Mathews, 64 Ark. 398 [1897]; In re McPhee, 156 Cal. 335, 340 [1909]; Savannah Ry. Co. v. Willett, 43 Fla. 311 [1901]; Griffin v. Domas, 22 Ill. App. 203 [1887]; Blaisdell v. Lewis, 32 Me. 515 [1851]; Harper v. Hassard, 113 Mass. 187 [1873] [employee under contract for term "not exceeding three years" entitled only to reasonable notice before discharge]; Harrington v. Brockman, 107 Mo. App. 418 [1904]; Jersey City Printing Co. v. Cassidy, 63 N.J. Eq. 759 [1902; dictum]; Douglass v. Merchants Insurance Co., 118 N.Y. 484 [1890]; Currier v. Ritter Co., 150 N.C. 694 [1909]; Bowman v. Bradley, 151 Pa. St. 351 [1892]; Gould v. McCrae, 14 Ont. L. Rep. 194 [1907] [? English view: contract for indefinite term presumed to be for one year; employee discharged sooner entitled to damages; see note 6 *infra*]; Boyer v. Western Union Tel. Co., 124 Fed. 246 [1903].

[6] "Where no right of contract is involved, an employer may lawfully discharge an employee at what time he pleases and for what causes he chooses." 16 Ruling Case Law, p. 417 [1917]. See Freund, Standards of American Legislation, p. 243 [1917].

"A contract of employment for an indefinite term may, in the United States, be terminated at the will of either party." 26 Cyc. 981 [1907].

"On the other hand an employer has the equal right to employ, continue in or discharge from his employment, whom he pleases. . ." 24 Cyc. 819 [1907].

deemed by this court so fundamental that it held unconstitutional both an act of Congress and a state statute which would have had the effect to limit the employer's exercise of it, *Adair v. United States,* 208 U.S. 161 [1908]; *Coppage v. Kansas,* 236 U.S. 1 [1915]. Can it be that there exists a hitherto unnoticed exception to this universal right; an exception which provides that the employer may not discharge to escape taxation under an act of Congress which he believes to be valid, but which the employee assails as unconstitutional? If no such exception exists, what right can the plaintiff conceivably have against the defendant to remain in its employ; and what wrong to the plaintiffs does the defendant threaten by admitting that it purposes to discharge the minor?

It is important, in this connection, not to confuse the absence of a right in an employee at will as against his employer to remain in his service, with the well recognized right of an employee at will that third persons shall not unjustifiably interfere with his employment by illegally interfering with the exercise of the employer's judgment. *Truax v. Raich,* 239 U.S. 33, 38 [1915]. The failure to make this distinction doubtless led the lower court to erroneously rely upon that case as a precedent justifying it in taking jurisdiction. In fact the case is authority to the contrary. Unlike the present case, *Truax v. Raich* was a suit against third persons, and as this court said there (p. 37), was "framed on the theory that the act is unconstitutional, and that the defendants who are public officers concerned with the enforcement of the laws of the State are about to proceed wrongfully to the complainant's injury through interference with his employment." The fact that the right enforced was one against third persons and not against the employer, and that the wrongdoing complained of was that of third persons is emphasized in the following passage of the opinion (p. 38): "It is said that the bill does not show an employment for a term, and that under an employment at will the complainant could be discharged at any time for any reason or for no reason,

---

"In England, a domestic servant who is turned away without notice, and without fault, is entitled to one month's wages, although there be no agreement to that effect. We are not aware that a similar rule exists in this country." Parsons on Contracts, Vol. 2, p. 32 [9th ed. 1904].

The doctrine of the English decisions is that there is a presumption of fact that a hiring under a contract containing no express provisions as to length of engagement is a hiring for a year. See Labatt, Master and Servant, Vol. 1, p. 504 [1913].

But in the United States there is a presumption of a hiring at will. Id., p. 516.

the motive of the employer being immaterial. The conclusion, however, that is sought to be drawn is too broad. The fact that the employment is at the will of the parties, respectively, does not make it one at the will of others. The employee has manifest interest in the freedom of the employer to exercise his judgment without illegal interference or compulsion, and, by the weight of authority, the unjustified interference of third persons is actionable although the employment is at will." The opinion shows that the employer, Truax, was joined with the public officers as party defendant; but it does not show whether or not any relief was sought against him. An examination of the record discloses that the bill sought relief also against the employer, praying "That the defendant, Truax, be temporarily and permanently enjoined from in any way or manner, by reason of the apparent force of said law, discharging this complainant from his service, and from carrying out his intention and threat so to do, already made as in this bill alleged." The relief sought against the employer was denied, and the injunction was limited to enjoining the Attorney General and the county attorney from enforcing the law against Truax. This, as the opinion shows (p. 36), they had already attempted to do by arresting him for alleged violation of the statute.

The bill in the present case was framed in analogy to *Hammer v. Dagenhart*, 247 U.S. 251 [1918]. But there as in *Truax v. Raich* the bill set forth a right of the employee as against third persons and a wrong threatened by a third person — the United States Attorney, Hammer — who was made a defendant. An examination of the record discloses that the employer was also joined as defendant below and that it filed an answer admitting the facts alleged in the bill. Again, as in *Truax v. Raich*, the bill sought an injunction against the employer, and the injunction issued included a clause restraining the employer "from in any way or manner by reason of the force of said act of Congress discharging the minor plaintiff, John Dagenhart, from its services or curtailing the employment of the minor plaintiff Reuben Dagenhart to eight hours [per day]." But so far as appears from the record the employer did not resist and took no active part in the proceedings. No opinion was delivered below. Hammer alone appealed to this court. The fact that the employing corporation had been joined as defendant and that an injunction had been issued against it, was not in any way referred to in the report of the case in this court, nor was the question in any way referred to in our opinion.

The bill in the present case not only fails to set forth a cause of action, but it is fatally defective also, specifically for want of equity.[7] It is believed that no case can be found in which an employer was enjoined from discharging an employee for wages, even where there was a valid unexpired contract of service for a definite period.[8] Equity refuses under such circumstances to interfere either by injunction or by way of specific performance, both because of the peculiar relation of employer and employee and also because damages at law for breach of contract by the employer would afford an adequate remedy. The bill here lacks even the usual allegations of irreparable injury. There is no statement that the minor plaintiff could not find other employment or that the amount of loss in wages could not be ascertained at law. The bill does contain the general allegation that "Plaintiffs are without adequate remedy at law and only in an action of this nature, and by injunctive process of this court can they be fully protected in the enjoyment of their property and rights as aforesaid; the granting of the injunctive process as hereinafter prayed will prevent a multiplicity of suits and prosecution, and the questions here involved can be adequately determined only in a suit of this nature."

[7] The present case is not legally distinguishable from Boyer v. Western Union Tel. Co., 124 Fed. 246 [1903]. In that case a Lodge of the Commercial Telegraphers Union brought a bill for an injunction against the Western Union Company to prevent it from discharging "without notice or other cause" than membership in the union those among its employees who it discovered were members of the plaintiff union. The bill also alleged a conspiracy to destroy the union. The court sustained a demurrer for want of equity in the bill, saying:

". . . the answer to that complaint is that in a free country like ours every employee, in the absence of contractual relations binding him to work for his employer a given length of time, has the legal right to quit the service of his employer without notice, and either with or without cause, at any time; and in the absence of such contractual relations, any employer may legally discharge his employee with or without notice, at any time.

.   .   .   .

"If the last allegation means anything, it is that the defendant, its officers and agents, have conspired to destroy the union by discharging all its members in its employ, and refusing to employ others, solely for the reason that they were members of the union. But it is not unlawful, in the absence of contractual relations to the contrary, to discharge them for that or for any other reason, or for no reason at all." [124 Fed. at 248.]

[8] "It is held that an employee cannot restrain his employer from discharging him." Pomeroy, Equitable Jurisdiction, Fourth Ed., sec. 1713 [1919]; see also secs. 1343, 2181, 1710–1721, and cases cited.

But the bill alleges no facts on which these allegations can legally rest. It is true that plaintiffs have no remedy at law; but it is because, and only because, they have no legal or equitable right as against the defendant. If plaintiffs had a cause of action against this employer because of the minor's discharge, it would not require a "multiplicity of suits" to afford them an adequate remedy. Plaintiffs do not even purport to sue on behalf of others similarly situated; nor do they purport to invoke the aid of equity to protect their employer from that "multiplicity of suits" which they perhaps think will follow if it persists in the folly of acting "in obedience to the law of the United States" (Rec. p. 10) which it believes to be constitutional. Moreover the dismissal of this bill because it did not state a cause of action at law or in equity would effectively eliminate all danger of "multiplicity of suits." The sole purpose of the bill is frankly disclosed in the further allegation that "the question here involved can be adequately determined only in a suit of this nature." But that purpose cannot legally be accomplished; because such a proceeding is not a "case," and to entertain it transcends the power conferred upon this court by the Constitution.

As it is clear that there is no legal basis for the claim that the bill sets forth a legal or equitable right of the plaintiffs against the defendant which the latter threatens to violate; that there is no legal or equitable cause of action to protect, and no legal or equitable wrong threatened, the bill should have been dismissed below for want of jurisdiction. For neither this, nor any lower Federal court, acquires jurisdiction through the making in legal form of an obviously frivolous claim. Compare *Equitable Life Insurance Society v. Brown*, 187 U.S. 308, 311 [1902]; *Newburyport Water Company v. Newburyport*, 193 U.S. 561 [1904]; *Sugarman v. United States*, 249 U.S. 182, 184 [1919]. Here, it was not even contended in argument or brief that plaintiffs had any legal or equitable right as against the defendant, the employer. The alleged cause of action is a fiction. The well established rule that a plaintiff must show that he would personally suffer an injury by application of a law before he can institute a bill for relief to test its constitutionality demands that the bill be dismissed. *Tyler v. The Judges*, 179 U.S. 405 [1900]; *Turpin v. Lemon*, 187 U.S. 51 [1902]; *Hooker v. Burr*, 194 U.S. 415 [1904]; *Missouri, Kansas & Texas Ry. v. Cade*, 233 U.S. 642, 648 [1914].

The reversal of the decree of the District Court should be with directions to dismiss the bill. By no conceivable amendments can it be made to state a good cause of action in equity. If it were attempted to reframe the bill in analogy to that in *Truax v. Raich* by joining as defendants the Collector of Internal Revenue and the United States Attorney with a view to restraining enforcement of the act alleged to be invalid, the plaintiffs would be confronted by two insurmountable obstacles. The first is that there could be no occasion to enjoin enforcement unless the minor plaintiff or others like him were retained as employees, so that the contested tax became payable; in which event plaintiffs would have no ground for apprehending the minor's discharge. The second is that under Revised Statutes 3224, no suit may be brought for the purpose of restraining the assessment or collection of a revenue tax, *Dodge v. Osborn*, 240 U.S. 118 [1916]. In the present case there is no such relation between the parties as to make it possible to overcome the latter obstacle. In *Pollock v. Farmers' Loan & Trust Co.*, 157 U.S. 429 [1895]; *Brushaber v. Union Pacific Railroad*, 240 U.S. 1 [1916], and *Stanton v. Baltic Mining Company*, 240 U.S. 103 [1916], no official of the Government was made party defendant. The injunction sought was not against the assessment or collection of the tax, but against its payment under supposed compulsion of law. Payment was restrained on behalf of a stockholder to prevent a breach of trust. The same is true also of *Flint v. Stone-Tracy Company*, 220 U.S. 107 [1911], where the question of jurisdiction was not referred to. A bill in equity by an employee to enjoin his employer from terminating an employment at will cannot conceivably be amended into a bill by a stockholder to enjoin directors from committing a breach of trust.

For nearly a century and a quarter Federal courts, as an incident to deciding cases rightfully before them, have necessarily exercised at times the solemn duty of declaring acts of Congress void. But the long continued, uninterrupted exercise of this power has not sufficed to silence the doubt originally expressed whether the framers of the Constitution intended to confer it. On the contrary, the popular protest against its exercise has never been as vehement, nor has it ever secured the support of so many political thinkers and writers, as in the last decade. At a time like the present, when the fundamental principles upon which our institutions rest are being seriously questioned, those who have faith in their wisdom and desire to preserve them unimpaired, can best uphold the Constitution by careful observance of the limitations which it imposes. As this court declared in the *Sinking Fund Cases, supra* (p. 718): "One branch of the Government cannot encroach upon the domain of another without danger. The safety of our institutions depends in no small degree on a strict observance of this salutary rule."

It seems more than likely that this opinion was circulated to the Court. But the only return that has been preserved is Holmes', and it is possible that Brandeis sent him the opinion privately, at least at first. Holmes said: "I don't see the answer to this. Count me with you unless discussion discloses some reason I have not thought of. pp. 5, 7." On page 5 Holmes wondered whether the reference made to *Truax v. Raich* as a suit against third persons was not confusing. Third persons "other than the employer?" he asked. "The employer is a third person and this phrase puzzles as one reads." Brandeis' reference, of course, was to the state government official as a third person and party defendant. On page 7, Holmes underlined the phrase "injunctive process," which appeared in a quotation from the bill of complaint. "Horrid phrase," he muttered in the margin. Then — perhaps on the occasion of general circulation, following an initial private circulation to Holmes and possibly one or two others — the same copy was evidently sent to Holmes a second time. He returned: "This is a powerful discourse and I agree with it. I don't know why you sent it again. Yes."

The case remained undecided through the 1919 term, and through the next, toward the end of which Chief Justice White died. On the last day of the 1920 term it was set down for reargument, and it was reargued at the following term, together with the *Child Labor Tax Case*, after William Howard Taft, White's successor, had taken his seat. Throughout this time, Brandeis' opinion lay on the table, reproaching the jurisdictional conscience of the brethren. They never agreed to it, though as a holding action Brandeis' effort was successful. But success was achieved at a cost; the cost, very probably, of silence for tactical reasons when it came time, in the *Child Labor Tax Case*, to decide the merits; and, quite possibly, the cost of preventing an earlier decision, dealing with the merits and upholding the constitutionality of the Child Labor Tax Act.

After the *Child Labor Tax Case* had been decided, Brandeis, in a letter to his friend Norman Hapgood, pointed out that Taft's opinion, which to the liberal Hapgood surely looked like a very black cloud, might after all have a silver lining. Perhaps, he wrote, the decision would someday be recognized as "the beginning of an epoch, the epoch of State Duties" as opposed to State Rights. When "State Duties were ignored . . . state functions atrophied" — a consequence Brandeis, who was deeply attached to the values of federalism, deplored. The Court had just made an end — an unmistakable, final end — to efforts to obtain federal action against child labor. Was it too much to hope that the states, realizing this, would now concentrate on a more responsible and effective approach of their own? As it turned out, it was too much to hope. But Brandeis was telling Hapgood that if, in the long run, the *Child Labor Tax Case* were to provoke a new attack on the problem at the local level and were thus generally to serve to invigorate state government, then the larger good the decision would ultimately produce would far outweigh its immediate effect. "The new Progressivism," Brandeis wrote, "requires local development — quality not quantity."[14] In this fashion, accepting it and consoling himself and his friend with its potential for the achievement of broader purposes, Brandeis put the best possible face on the decision in the *Child Labor Tax Case*. Nevertheless, his failure to register a dissent from it requires explanation. For his silence is not easily reconciled with views to which he subscribed before and after.

In *Hammer v. Dagenhart*, the Commerce Clause child labor case decided three years earlier, Brandeis, with McKenna and Clarke, joined in the dissent in which Holmes argued that Congress had acted under a head of legislative power expressly conferred by the Constitution, and that its motive in doing so and the indirect effect of its action were not for the Court to consider. Among precedents Holmes adduced in support of this view were cases in which Congress had achieved similar indirect effects (on oleomargarine production, state banks, food and drug processing) by use both of the taxing and interstate commerce powers. Holmes cited the tax and commerce cases on a parity. Despite the tenor of this dissent, it would be possible that, on the facts of the *Child Labor Tax Case*, the use by Congress of the power to tax should have seemed to Holmes, to McKenna, and to Brandeis (but not to Clarke, for he dissented again) more disingenuous than was tolerable. Holmes, McKenna, and Brandeis could also simply have had a change of heart and have come to regard the taxing power as a more dubious and dangerous tool for the achievement of indirect results than the commerce power. This could well be true of McKenna who, at the term following the decision in *Hammer v. Dagenhart*, dissented in *United*

States v. Doremus,[15] in which the Court upheld a close federal regulatory scheme imposed by a taxing statute on manufacturers and distributors of narcotics. But Holmes and Brandeis were with the majority in *Doremus*, and they went along as well in *Nigro v. United States*,[16] a similar case decided after McKenna had gone. And, after Holmes had gone, Brandeis, with Stone and Cardozo, dissented when a special tax on liquor dealers who violated local prohibition laws [17] and the "processing tax" laid by the Agricultural Adjustments Act of 1933 [18] were declared unconstitutional. And he was with the Court in upholding a special tax on dealers in firearms.[19]

To be sure, distinctions can be and have been taken between these cases and the *Child Labor Tax Case*. But they are very slender, and they tend to fade in the face of such statements as the following ones by Cardozo, in a dissent in which Brandeis joined: "The underlying principle in all these cases is as clear as it is just. A business that is a nuisance, like any other business that is socially undesirable, may be taxed at a higher rate than one legitimate and useful. By classifying in such a mode Congress is not punishing for a crime against another government. It is not punishing at all." And: "Thus the process of psychoanalysis has spread to unaccustomed fields. There is a wise and ancient doctrine that a court will not inquire into the motives of a legislative body or assume them to be wrongful." [20]

An early, incomplete draft of his opinion in *Atherton Mills v. Johnston* makes it plain that Brandeis, no matter how reconciled he may eventually have become to the opposite result, would in that case have upheld the Child Labor Tax Act, had he been prepared to reach the merits. In fact, this draft carries the startling suggestion that when *Atherton Mills* was first argued, there was a majority so inclined.

In writing his opinion in this case, Brandeis did not employ his usual snowballing method of drafting. He would most frequently write out a few pages, have them printed, revise them, add a few more pages, have the whole printed again, and so forth. This time he sent the printer a complete long-hand draft, which needed but few changes and additions to become the final opinion of January 26, 1920. The only thing that preceded this complete draft was a partial one of a few paragraphs, which Brandeis heavily corrected as he went along, until, out of (unaccustomed) charity to the printer, he abandoned it in favor of a fresh beginning. The new start was largely a matter of making a clean copy. But Brandeis did drop an initial sentence from the earlier draft, which holds much interest. As he had corrected it, that sentence read: "If I believed that this Court had jurisdiction to pass in this proceeding upon the constitutionality of Section 1200 of the Revenue Act of 1918 (approved Feb. 24, 1919, C. 18, 40 Stat. p. 1138) [the Child Labor Tax Act], I should have no difficulty in holding the act valid, on the authority of Veazie Bank v. Fenno, 8 Wall. 533, and McCray v. United States, 195 U.S. 27, and for the reason expressed in the dissent by Mr. Justice Holmes in Hammer v. Dagenhart, 247 U.S. 251, 277, in which I joined." But, he went on to say, as he did in the final version of the opinion, it was a usurpation of power for the district court to assume jurisdiction. Brandeis had originally led into the passage just quoted with these two opening sentences, which he had then struck out: "I agree that the decree entered below by the District Court [declaring the Child Labor Tax Act unconstitutional] must be reversed with directions to dismiss the bill. But in my opinion the dismissal should be for want of jurisdiction."

There is no blinking the fact that these passages — and especially the two sentences last quoted — sound as if it had been decided at conference to ignore the jurisdictional difficulties in *Atherton Mills v. Johnston* and to hold the Child Labor Tax Act constitutional. No doubt one can force the language — though it takes quite a little forcing — and surmise that Brandeis was addressing himself not to what he expected to emerge as the majority opinion, but to what he thought would be a colleague's — perhaps Clarke's — dissent on the merits. That could account as well for his eventually dropping these sentences as inappropriate to a memorandum directed at the entire Court and meant to convince all, regardless of their views on the merits. But the other possibility cannot be ignored. In any event, we have here early evidence, confirmed later, notably in the great free-speech case of *Whitney v. California* [21] and in *Ashwander v. Tennessee Valley Authority* itself, of the rigid integrity with which Brandeis adhered to his jurisdictional scruples, no matter if to do so was to oppose a substantive result he himself desired. In this instance, he may have actually defeated such a result, thus demonstrating conclusively that he was not indulging in the coinage of idle epigrams when he said: "The most important thing we do is not doing." [22]

If there was a majority for upholding the Child Labor Tax Act in *Atherton Mills v. Johnston*, it was surely a narrow and a shaky one. The case may have stood four-to-one-to-four, with Brandeis in the middle, or four (wanting to strike down the Act) to three (believing it constitutional) to one (leaning with the three) to one (Brandeis). The members of the majority in *Hammer v. Dagenhart* had been Justice Day, who wrote, Chief Justice White and Justices Van Devanter, Pitney, and McReynolds. To produce the stalemate in *Atherton Mills v. Johnston* which has just been suggested, there would have to have been at least a tentative defection from this group, while McKenna, whose course in this area as in other ones was so often erratic, stayed with the *Hammer v. Dagenhart* dissenters. The defector might have been White, who in 1904, when he was an Associate Justice, had vigorously upheld the power of Congress to tax colored oleomargarine out of the market. It is perhaps significant that Brandeis cited this opinion of White's — *McCray v. United States* [23] — in the passage in which he agreed that the Child Labor Tax Act was constitutional. But White had not maintained a wholly consistent position since writing the *McCray* case. He had dissented, as had McKenna, from a later decision, holding constitutional an exercise by Congress of the same taxing power for the purpose of controlling traffic in narcotics. [24] He might well have thought that the Child Labor Tax Act was more like the narcotics than the oleomargarine legislation. Nevertheless, it seems more probable that White was the defector than that another possibility, Day, who wrote for the Court in the narcotics case — but who was also the author of *Hammer v. Dagenhart* — should have been the one. Be that as it may, by the time the *Child Labor Tax Case* was decided, White was dead, and there was no hint of a closely divided Court. But if the indications that there had been one earlier are to be credited, Brandeis was more than likely the hinge on which the heavy gate of the Court, groaning and seemingly about to open, in the end clanged shut for a generation against federal efforts to root out child labor.

Whichever way the Court may have divided on the merits of the Child Labor Tax Act when *Atherton Mills v. Johnston* was first argued, Brandeis' own view is clear. In the *Atherton Mills* case it was, according to his lights, dwarfed in importance by the jurisdictional issue. But why did he later maintain silence in the *Child Labor Tax Case*, which was free of jurisdictional difficulties?

Brandeis once remarked that the "great difficulty of all group action, of course, is when and what concession to make." There is no doubt that Brandeis sometimes suppressed dissents for tactical reasons. "Can't always dissent," he said. And: "I sometimes endorse an opinion with which I do not agree. I acquiesce." He also referred to Holmes' reluctance to dissent again after he had once had his say on a subject. [25] (We have seen that Holmes' opinion in *Hammer v. Dagenhart* speaks at least implicitly to the issue of the *Child Labor Tax Case*.) *Atherton Mills*, in its way, was a victory on the issue which for Brandeis was of overriding importance. Most of the Justices were no doubt anxious to decide and be done with it. It is noteworthy in this connection that the Solicitor General, who intervened as *amicus* in behalf of the United States to urge the constitutionality of the Act, commented on the jurisdictional point, but out of a "desire for a prompt determination of the question involved" indulgently declined to press it.[26]

So this was victory against odds; a considerable achievement. At the same time, another long battle, stretching over two years, was culminating in success for Brandeis. This was *United Mine Workers v. Coronado Co.*, which was to be decided unanimously on June 5, some two weeks after the *Child Labor Tax Case*. Victory brings let-down, and a desire for pacification. It might have seemed to Brandeis churlish, and a disservice in the long run to his effectiveness in the cause of jurisdictional observance and to his future relations with the new Chief Justice, Taft, to turn around at this juncture and register a dissent. No doubt he had, while the jurisdictional issue was alive, sincerely professed his comparative lack of interest in the merits. It was in order to maintain this neutrality that he had struck the sentences dealing with the merits from the draft of his opinion, and he may have felt that he was now required in good faith to continue to maintain it. In somewhat similar circumstances, in *Hill v. Wallace*,[27] which was decided on the same day as *Atherton Mills* and the *Child Labor Tax Case*, Brandeis took pains to avoid giving cause for the suspicion that he used "technicalities" as a screen for convictions on the merits. In the *Hill* case, the Court also upset a federal taxing and regulatory statute. Brandeis prefaced an opinion *dubitante* on a jurisdictional issue with an otherwise unnecessary concession on the substantive one.

The question of Brandeis' position in the *Child Labor Tax Case* is of more than simply academic interest. For while *Hammer v. Dagenhart* has long since been resoundingly overruled,[28] and Congressional power to affect conditions of labor by Commerce Clause measures is now very broad indeed and quite secure, the *Child Labor Tax Case* retains influence. The problem of the manipulation of the federal taxing power for the achievement of indirect and otherwise unattainable ends arises in new contexts and remains baffling. And the authority of the *Child Labor Tax Case* is not a little enhanced by the fact that of the dissenters in *Hammer v. Dagenhart*, three, among them Holmes and Brandeis, were silent in the later case. Thus in his dissent from a recent judgment upholding a federal tax statute, which forced gamblers to register and disclose themselves to state authorities or incur the risk of federal as well as state criminal prosecution, Mr. Justice Frankfurter emphasized the significance of the Holmes-McKenna-Brandeis concurrence in the *Child Labor Tax Case*.[29] Surely the history of *Atherton Mills v. Johnston* detracts from that significance.

It remains to say a word about the place of the *Atherton Mills* opinion in the imposing body of Brandeis' jurisdictional writings. In the discussion of standing, the opinion may be thought to emit some dubious implications akin to the contention, of which so much is heard these days, that one who is an applicant for a privilege rather than the claimant of a right (the candidate for a government job, the petitioner for a passport or for a mailing permit) is not entitled to object to the grounds, be they irrelevant or unjust, on which denial of the privilege is rested. It may be safely assumed that Brandeis intended no such generalization. Actually, he had occasion once to reject it as applied to mailing privileges.[30] This feature of the opinion to the side, it is fair to say that *Atherton Mills* ranks with, though after, the famous concurrence in *Ashwander v. Tennessee Valley Authority*. The opinion here lacks the completeness of *Ashwander*, of course. But in laying bare the first principles upon which the legalism of jurisdiction rests, it strikes a note of fervor, almost of passion, which is in turn lacking in *Ashwander*. That opinion is rich and weighty with the experience of twenty years on the Bench. *Atherton Mills* is urgent with a sense of the truly fundamental issue of the division of powers between those organs of the government which are responsible to the electorate, and the judiciary, which is not. A sedate, technical tone overlies the immediacy of the issue in *Ashwander*. The newer, fresher judge who spoke in *Atherton Mills* faced the task of constitutional adjudication with no greater feeling of self-restraint than the Brandeis of *Ashwander*; but he felt more awe.

II

Dissenter's Dilemma

About half-way through the very first term of his service on the Court, Brandeis had his initial confrontation with an especially perturbing aspect of that "great difficulty of all group action" — when to dissent, and when to concede and be silent. The problem arose in connection with a jurisdictional issue.

St. Louis, Iron Mountain & Southern Ry. v. Starbird [1] was a suit brought by a shipper in the Arkansas state courts to recover from the railroad for damage to ten carloads of fruit. The bill of lading required, as a condition precedent to the railroad's liability, that claims for damage to goods in transit be reported in writing to the railroad within thirty-six hours after arrival of the goods. There had been no report in writing in this case, and the railroad defended on that ground. The Supreme Court of Arkansas held that the bill-of-lading provision was not binding on the shipper, and that an oral report to the railroad's agent was sufficient; and it granted recovery for five carloads with respect to which there had been such an oral report, and denied it for the other five on account of the lack of a report of any kind, oral or written. Seeking review of this judgment, the railroad sued out a writ of error to the Supreme Court of the United States.

The Supreme Court of the United States had jurisdiction to entertain a writ of error in a case decided by the highest court of a state only if the state court had denied a right especially asserted by one of the parties under a statute or the Constitution of the United States. And so the railroad argued that the Arkansas decision had denied its rights under the Carmack Amendment,[2] a federal statute which, in the exercise of the Congressional power over commerce, regulated the liability of interstate railroads for damage to goods in transit.

The shipper's response to the writ of error took the form of a motion to dismiss on the ground that the federal right the railroad was now asserting had not been invoked, or, indeed, so much as mentioned, in the state courts; consequently it had not been denied there, and the basis on which the railroad was attempting to rest the jurisdiction of the United States Supreme Court failed. However, not wishing to put all his eggs in one motion, the shipper also filed a cross-writ, asking for review to the extent that he himself had lost in the Arkansas courts. This cross-writ presupposed the existence of jurisdiction, being thus inconsistent with the motion to dismiss.

The opinion of the Supreme Court, delivered by Justice Day, was unanimous. There was jurisdiction, Day said, of both the railroad's writ of error and the shipper's cross-writ. The railroad's reliance on the bill of lading was a sufficiently explicit assertion in the state court of the federal right established by the Carmack Amendment. No express citation of the statute was necessary. And the requirement for written notice set up by the bill of lading, being reasonable and conformable to the Carmack Amendment, could not be overridden. The Arkansas Supreme Court had, therefore, committed error to the extent that it had granted recovery, although its judgment in favor of the railroad with respect to half the carloads was to be affirmed. As for the cross-writ, Day said (and he dealt with it just this off-handedly), it also "involves the liability of the carrier under the bill of lading," since it proceeded on the theory that the bill's provision for reporting claims in writing violated the Carmack Amendment. "This court has jurisdiction upon the cross-writ." [3]

This unanimous opinion was delivered on April 30, 1917. However, following the argument of the case nearly five months earlier, in December 1916, the opinion of the Court had been assigned not to Day, but to Brandeis, and Brandeis had written the opinion printed below. It was dated for delivery on March 6, 1917, almost two months before the date of ultimate decision. Brandeis' result was dismissal of both the writ and the cross-writ for lack of jurisdiction. We do not know whether this was the outcome agreed upon at conference prior to the assignment to Brandeis, or whether Brandeis, having initially taken the same view as Day and the others, found upon study that he was unable to write it that way. In later years, it was Brandeis' custom, when he changed his mind in a case in which he had the assignment of the majority opinion, to label the statement of his position a Memorandum to the Court rather than, as he did in this instance, an Opinion of the Court. But that is far from conclusive.

Brandeis had little quarrel with the doctrinal propositions which Day was to set forth in his opinion. To be sure, Brandeis' formulations differed somewhat from Day's, but he allowed that a defense based solely on the bill of lading could assert a right under the Carmack Amendment. And he agreed that the precise mode in which such a right was asserted in a state court was of minor importance, so long as it appeared that the court had been made aware of the alleged right and had passed upon it. There, however, was the rub. To Brandeis, the record in this

Bronze head of Justice Brandeis by Eleanor Platt, presented to the Harvard Law School in 1943 by a group of Brandeis' former law clerks.

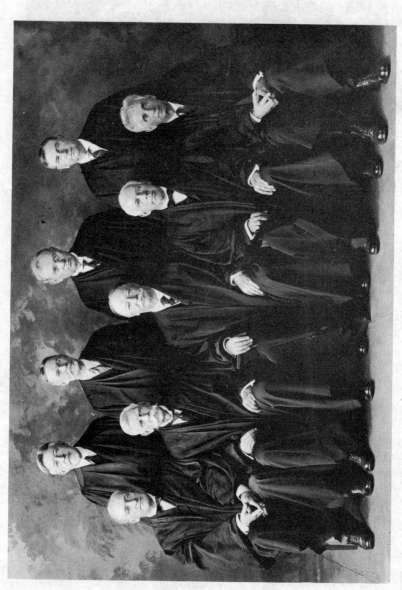

The Supreme Court, 1928. Seated, left to right: Justices McReynolds and Holmes, Chief Justice Taft, Justices Van Devanter and Brandeis. Standing: Justices Sanford, Sutherland, Butler, and Stone.

case affirmatively showed the contrary. It was plain that the Arkansas court had dealt with the case wholly in terms of Arkansas law, without reference to the federal statute, and that so had the parties, before attempting to obtain review of the decision by means of their writs of error.

SUPREME COURT OF THE UNITED STATES

Nos. 275 and 796. — October Term, 1916.

St. Louis, Iron Mountain & Southern Railway Company, Plaintiff in Error,	
275 vs.	
C. A. Starbird, Administrator of the Estate of Adam Miller, deceased.	In Error to the Supreme Court of Arkansas.
C. A. Starbird, Administrator of the Estate of Adam Miller, deceased, Plaintiff in Error,	
796 vs.	
St. Louis, Iron Mountain & Southern Railway Company.	

[March 6, 1917]

Mr. Justice BRANDEIS delivered the opinion of the Court.

Prior to the Act of September 6, 1916 [39 Stat. 726], the right to have this court review on writ of error decisions of the highest court of a State denying a title, right, privilege or immunity claimed under a statute of the United States, was granted by Section 237 of the Judicial Code, in those cases where "the title, right, privilege or immunity [was] especially set up or claimed, by either party." In No. 275 the assignment of errors in this court presents two questions arising under the Act to Regulate Commerce. A motion to dismiss challenges the right to review, on the ground that the claim was not duly made below. No. 796 is a cross writ of error. The proceedings were as follows:

In July, 1907, Miller shipped from Greenwood, Arkansas, to New York City, by the St. Louis, Iron Mountain & Southern Railway and connecting lines, on a through bill of lading, ten carloads of peaches which were damaged while in carriers' possession. Alleging that the damage was due to negligence in failing to carry promptly and ice properly, Miller brought this action for damages against the initial carrier in a state court of Arkansas. He died before final judgment and his administrator revived the action. The Railway Company relied in defense mainly upon failure to make claim for damages, as provided in the following clause of the bill of lading:

"Claims for damages must be reported by consignee, in writing, to the delivering line within thirty-six hours after the consignee has been notified of the arrival of the freight at the place of delivery. If such notice is not there given, neither this Company nor any of the connecting or intermediate carriers shall be liable."

The case was tried before a judge without a jury. Plaintiff did not prove written notice of the claim for damages; but introduced evidence tending to show knowledge of condition on the part of employees of the Pennsylvania Railroad, the delivering carrier; and contended that, under the circumstances, notice in writing was not essential. The judge found for the plaintiff in respect to each of the ten cars. No request for findings of fact or rulings of law was made by defendant until a motion to set aside the judgment and for a new trial was filed. The court declined to pass upon them then "because not presented or asked during the trial of the cause" and denied the motion. Upon appeal the Supreme Court of Arkansas held that the terms of the bill of lading could be complied with, although written notice had not been given, if "personal notice be given to that employee or agent of the company whose duty it would be, if written notice had been received, to make the inspection to ascertain the nature and extent of the damage, if such employee or agent does not already possess this knowledge." It further found that such notice had been given as to five of the ten cars, but not as to the other five; and accordingly affirmed the judgment as to five cars, and reversed the judgment as to the other five cars. (118 Arkansas 485 [1915]). Each party then filed a petition for rehearing, which was denied without stating reasons; whereupon each sued out a writ of error from this court. The plaintiff below duly moved to dismiss the Railway Company's writ of error, on the ground that no Federal question had been raised below; and the consideration of the motion was postponed until the argument on the merits.

The two questions presented by the Railway Company's assignment of errors in this court are these:

First. That "said shipments being interstate and governed by an Act of Congress, known as an 'Act to Regulate Commerce'" the Supreme Court of Arkansas erred in holding that "it is unnecessary . . . . to show that the consignee had complied with the provisions of the bill of lading, which required written notice of an intention to claim damages," and in holding that "knowledge of the dock foreman of the damaged condition of the peaches upon arrival at destination" dispensed with the necessity of giving written notice, "said provision of the bill of lading being reasonable under the provision of the Act of Congress, known as an 'Act to Regulate Commerce.'"

Second. That the Supreme Court of Arkansas erred in not holding that the action was barred by Section 16 of the Act to Regulate Commerce, it not having been brought until more than two years after the cause of action accrued.

The shipment was an interstate shipment made upon a through bill of lading after the passage of the Carmack Amendment (Act of June 29, 1906, c. 3591, sec. 7, 34 Stat. 584, 593) and long before the Act of March 4, 1915, c. 176, 38 Stat. 1196, dispensing with the necessity of notice of claim in certain cases. The rights and obligations under the bill of lading were governed by the Federal law; and the objections recited in the assignment of errors clearly state a Federal question, which, if presented to the state courts at the proper time and in the proper way, would have given this court jurisdiction to review their judgment. *Northern Pacific Ry. Co. v. Wall,* 241 U.S. 87, 91 [1916]; *Georgia, Florida & Alabama Ry. Co. v. Blish Milling Co.,* 241 U.S. 190, 195 [1916]; *Cincinnati, New Orleans & Texas Pacific Ry. Co. v. Rankin,* 241 U.S. 319, 326 [1916]; *Southern Ry. Co. v. Prescott,* 240 U.S. 632, 636 [1916]. But this claim of "title, right, privilege or immunity" under the Act of Congress was not "especially set up or claimed." There was, possibly, a blind reference in the motion to set aside the judgment. But the claim was not made in any manner until it was included in

the assignment of errors in this court, more than five years after
the commencement of the action and more than three months
after denial by the Supreme Court of Arkansas of the petition for
rehearing. Obviously the objection comes too late, when first raised
in this court. *Maxwell v. Newbold,* 18 How. 511, 515 [1955];
Butler v. Gage, 138 U.S. 52 [1891]; *Chicago & Northwestern Ry.
Co. v. Chicago,* 164 U.S. 454 [1896]; *Appleby v. Buffalo,* 221 U.S.
524, 529 [1911]. Even if the Federal question had been raised in
the petition for rehearing, it would not have been open to review
in this court, since that petition was denied without passing upon
any Federal question. *St. Louis & San Francisco R.R. Co. v. Shep-
herd,* 240 U.S. 240 [1916]. And the requests for rulings made in
the motion to set aside the judgment were rejected by the court as
having been presented too late. *Mutual Life Ins. Co. v. McGrew,*
188 U.S. 291, 308 [1903].

Where it appears from the record, by clear and necessary in-
tendment, that a definite issue as to a matter of Federal right was
raised, so that the court could not have given judgment without
deciding it, the precise mode in which it was raised is of minor
importance. *Powell v. Brunswick County,* 150 U.S. 433, 439, 440
[1893]; *Sayward v. Denny,* 158 U.S. 180, 184 [1895]. And where
the state court either holds or assumes that a question of Federal
right is raised for its decision, and proceeds to dispose of it as a
Federal question, and such decision is essential to the judgment
rendered, this court has jurisdiction to reëxamine the question on
writ of error. *Haire v. Rice,* 204 U.S. 291, 299 [1907]; *Chambers
v. Baltimore & Ohio R.R.,* 207 U.S. 142, 148 [1907]; *Miedreich v.
Lauenstein,* 232 U.S. 236, 242 [1914]; *North Carolina R.R. Co. v.
Zachary,* 232 U.S. 248, 257 [1914].

In the present case the contrary clearly appears. Not only is
there no mention of any such Federal question in the record or in
the opinions of the trial judge or of the Supreme Court of Arkansas,
but the latter, by reference to *Cumbie v. St. Louis, Iron Mountain
& Southern,* 105 Ark. 406 [1912] (and on a second appeal in 118
Arkansas 478 [1915]), shows affirmatively that it was applying
the common law of Arkansas. In those decisions, the latter of which
was handed down on the same day as the decision presented for
review here, that court, citing only Arkansas cases, assumed that
the initial carrier would, under the common law as administered

in that State, be liable for negligence of connecting lines (see *Kansas City, Fort Scott & Memphis R. Co. v. Washington*, 74 Arkansas 9 [1905]), and declared the provision of the bill of lading in question to be reasonable; but construed it as not requiring notice, where the delivering carrier had knowledge of the damage.

The Railway Company did raise the other Federal question in its answer and set it up specially in the petition for rehearing in the Supreme Court of Arkansas as well as in the assignments of errors in this court, namely:

"that the shipment involved herein was an interstate shipment, as alleged in the complaint, and that the complaint herein was not filed within two years from the accrual of the cause of action; that said shipment was governed by the rules of the Interstate Commerce Commission which requires that all complaints for the recovery of damages must be filed within two years from the time the cause of action accrued."

The rule referred to (Sec. 16 of the Act to Regulate Commerce concerning reparation proceedings) declares that "All complaints for the recovery of damages shall be filed with the Commission within two years from the time the cause of action accrues" (34 Stat. 590). This defense appears not to have been pressed at the trial or in the motion for a new trial. It was therefore not open to defendant in the Supreme Court of Arkansas; was not mentioned by that court in its opinion; and is not open for review in this court. We are thus relieved from considering whether this assignment of error is not so obviously unfounded as to be deemed frivolous.

Counsel for Starbird did not seriously contend that there was jurisdiction here on his cross writ of error. Both writs of error are

Dismissed.

Brandeis circulated this opinion, but only one return has been preserved. It was from Justice Van Devanter, who agreed, adding: "There probably will be earnest dissent." Van Devanter also had a suggestion. It concerned the paragraph near the end in which Brandeis conceded that, everything else being equal, it mattered little what form the invocation of a federal right in a state court had taken. Van Devanter, though he hastened to say that this was "only a suggestion," thought "it would be well" to add: But, as was said in *Maxwell v. Newbold* [4] [a case earlier cited by Brandeis], "to bring that question [of a federal right] for decision in this court, it is not sufficient to raise the objection here, and to show that it was involved in the controversy in the state court, and might, and ought, to have been considered by it when making its decision. It must appear on the face of the record that it was in fact raised; that the judicial mind of the court was exercised upon it; and their decision against the right claimed under it." Van Devanter's care in reading the opinions circulated by his brethren never flagged, and his understanding of jurisdictional issues was first rate. "Good suggestion," Brandeis noted, doubtless intending to adopt it. But he never had a chance to do so.

The opinion was greeted with more than the "earnest dissent" which the shrewd and knowledgeable Van Devanter had foreseen. Brandeis lost his court. The brethren were unable to resist the temptation to grapple with the issue on the merits, and get it over with. The question is, why did Brandeis then silently go along with the majority? Day's opinion did not meet his points. It ignored them by gathering this case in under the cover of general principles, and simply suppressing the particular facts which caused it not to fit. This is perhaps plainest with respect to the cross-writ. The shipper, in his motion to dismiss the railroad's writ, alleged specifically that no federal statutory right was "set up or claimed, *by either party*" (italics supplied) in the Arkansas court.[5] This obviously included himself, and was a bald admission of lack of jurisdiction on the cross-writ. And the shipper's brief in support of the cross-writ made no attempt to show that vindication of a federal statutory right had been contended for in the State court; rather it simply ignored the jurisdictional issue.[6] Yet Day blandly assumed jurisdiction of the cross-writ.

We know that in later years Brandeis at times suppressed his dissenting views on questions which he considered to be of no great consequence. As he said, apropos of a subsequent case [7] that involved no jurisdictional question but dealt with a similar point on the merits, such cases were not important enough to warrant dissent.[8] But it is equally true that Brandeis was very far from deeming the requirement that federal questions be timely brought to the attention of state courts a trivial one. From the first, and very consistently, he laid much stress on the scrupulous observance of all sorts of jurisdictional niceties.[9] This was, for Brandeis, not a matter of *elegantia juris* but of first principles. Jurisdictional technicalities, as they might appear, in fact served ends of the greatest importance. Properly applied in a case such as this, they furthered the perfection of a balanced federal system by giving state

courts a chance for voluntary compliance with federal law before they
were coerced into obedience. Thus such "technicalities" tended to induce a responsible regard for federal law through the simple and cour-
teous expedient of assuming respect for it whenever the contrary did
not appear. On more than one occasion, Brandeis found the issue of
the timely raising of federal questions in state courts to be decisive, and
found it a worthy ground for dissent.[10]

It may be that Brandeis' failure to register a dissent in *Starbird* is attributable to the special circumstances of his first term of service on the
Bench. At the time this case came down, Brandeis had not yet announced his first dissenting opinion. Doing that is, inevitably, an event
in a judge's career; and in the perhaps somewhat anxious choice of the
fitting occasion, he cannot help but have an eye for factors which may
be irrelevant with respect to subsequent dissents. Brandeis had, in three
earlier instances, joined in dissenting opinions written by others.[11] In
this case, neither Van Devanter nor anyone else presumably cared to
write. And neither Van Devanter nor anyone else may have been prepared to join in a dissent by Brandeis. Brandeis may very well have
felt that it would be unseemly to come forth, probably alone, with a
first dissenting opinion pitched on what his senior colleagues considered
a side issue, in a case which otherwise involved only a minor statutory
point. (Congress, by amending the statute in question, had, for the future, already largely abrogated the substantive rule the Court was laying down.) [12] This feeling may have been the stronger since a clearly
fitting occasion for a first dissent was in the offing. Brandeis had in
preparation an opinion in an argued case, in which the Court forbade
application of the New York Workmen's Compensation Act to interstate railroads; he differed on the merits, and was joined by Clarke.[13]
(Brandeis' only other dissent of the term, coming later yet, was also in
a case in which the constitutionality of a state statute was in question.
Here too he was not alone.) [14]

Quite likely, it made a difference that a dissent in *St. Louis, Iron
Mountain & Southern Ry. v. Starbird* would have been not just another
one but the first of Brandeis' career. But, in conjunction with this factor,
Brandeis' silence may also be attributable to a reason of broader application, equally plausible in this case, and consistent with his practice
of later years.

In discussing in a book published in 1937 the landmark case of *Pensacola Telegraph Co. v. Western Union Telegraph Co.*,[15] Felix Frankfurter, then Byrne Professor of Administrative Law at the Harvard Law
School, remarked: "The scope of a Supreme Court decision is not infrequently revealed by the candor of dissent." [16] This undoubted fact pre-

sents a Supreme Court judge with a subtle and recurring dilemma, which was present for Brandeis in the *Starbird* case. In the majority opinion in the *Pensacola* case, decided in 1877, the Court for the first time adumbrated the doctrine that a state might be without power to exclude corporations engaged in interstate commerce from doing business within its borders.[17] But Chief Justice Waite, who wrote for the Court, "almost ostentatiously" avoided any explicit statement of the new doctrine. A dissent by Justice Field, however, addressed itself boldly to the implications of the Court's opinion. For that reason, as Professor Frankfurter pointed out, "the general emphasis which he [Field] placed upon the meaning of Waite's opinion in the *Pensacola* case is much more revealing of its dynamic significance than Waite's shrouded exposition." [18]

Thus the dilemma. To remain silent, not drawing attention to a possibly nascent doctrine which one deems pernicious, not assisting, despite oneself, in its birth; or to speak out. Silence under such circumstances is a gamble taken in the hope of a stillbirth. The risk is that if the birth is successful, silence will handicap one's future opposition. For one is then chargeable with parenthood. Yet dissent may serve only to delineate clearly what the majority was diffident itself to say. Field in the *Pensacola* case made one choice. In years to come Brandeis was to face the dilemma more than once. Instinct, a craftsman's inarticulable feel, which must largely govern action in such a matter, dictated now one choice, now the other.

An interesting instance of Brandeis' taking the same course as did Field in *Pensacola* — without, however, incurring the consequences which attended Field's choice in that case — is *Barnette v. Wells Fargo National Bank*.[19] Like *Starbird*, this case is a striking illustration of the operation among the brethren of the urge to decide substantive issues and get them over with despite jurisdictional difficulties, and of Brandeis' resistance to it. *Barnette v. Wells Fargo National Bank* came up through the federal courts. As the late Alfred McCormack, Stone's law clerk at the time, recalled, it was at first unanimously decided on the merits and was assigned to Stone. The opinion which Stone circulated made no mention of any jurisdictional irregularity. It happened, however, that the papers which would normally set forth the basis for jurisdiction were not included in the record, and such facts as did appear indicated the absence of federal jurisdiction. Counsel, perhaps through oversight, perhaps for other reasons, had failed to argue the point. But the lack of jurisdiction became evident to Brandeis upon study, and he circulated an opinion urging that the case either be dismissed on the record as it stood, or else be held while the Court ordered the appropriate papers filed on the chance that possibly they might spell out a proper jurisdictional basis.

As McCormack remarked, "it became clear, after long nights of research, that the position of Brandeis was virtually impregnable." In a brief memorandum to the Court, Stone admitted as much. There was no diversity of citizenship, on which jurisdiction could rest. The only semblance of a federal question — an alternative ground for jurisdiction — derived from the fact that the plaintiff was trying to recover a fund in the hands of a receiver appointed by the United States District Court for the District of Alaska. But Stone admitted: "This, as a ground of jurisdiction in the Federal Courts, would seem to be unsubstantial." He went on to suggest, in a somewhat ambiguous passage, that what he had just said might not be entirely free from doubt. In any event, he concluded: "Under all the circumstances, it would seem advisable to terminate this long drawn-out litigation by decision on the merits." McCormack further recalled: "Van Devanter, master of formulas that decided cases without creating precedents, was called in, and with much travail a form of words was devised that asserted jurisdiction without too great risk of future embarrassment." The form of words was that the Court would indulge a presumption of jurisdiction, where, as here, the record, while not substantiating it, did not expressly negative it, and where the appellee had abandoned in the Supreme Court any effort to attack jurisdiction. This was not unlike Day's technique in the *Starbird* case. This time, however, Brandeis did not pass the matter over in silence. He published his dissent, in which Justice Sanford joined. Stone, McCormack said, "was human enough to like Brandeis no better for this incident." [20] While this dissent highlighted the holding Brandeis deplored, it did not, as things turned out, further the future development of a disagreeable doctrine.

Holmes' books of returns contain two apt illustrations of Brandeis' taking the other way out of the dissenter's dilemma, the way he also took in *Starbird*. In *Central of Georgia Ry. v. Wright*,[21] the state of Georgia had imposed a tax on the railroad which, the latter contended, the state had by contractual agreement, contained in the railroad's charter, agreed never to impose. In an earlier case, reported in 236 U.S. 674,[22] the Court had upheld the same contention against a similar tax. Now Holmes, in a very brief opinion, again decided in favor of the railroad. Brandeis' return read: "I think this case, like 236 U.S. 674, is wrongly decided — and have no sympathy with any of the cases bartering away the right of taxation. But you have restricted the opinion so closely to the facts of this case, that I am inclined to think it will do less harm to let it pass unnoticed by dissent." [23] In a more celebrated

set of cases, *Western Union Telegraph Co. v. Foster,* [24] called the *Ticker
Cases,* Holmes, for the Court, held that the transmission of stock exchange quotations constituted interstate commerce until completed in
subscribers' offices and was at no point subject to state regulation.
Brandeis' first return was: "Please note my dissent." A few days later,
however, on May 20, 1918, Brandeis wrote: "Dear Judge Holmes, In
your Ticker cases I have concluded that dissent would only aggravate
the harm. Hence shall not dissent. L.D.B." [25]

Day's opinion in the *Starbird* case made, on its face, no radical new
departure. Its error, as Brandeis deemed it, became obvious only in
light of the record, and the facts which emphasized it remained buried
there; Day made no reference to them. For the reader ignorant of those
facts, no startling new jurisdictional rule was announced. To the extent that Brandeis remained silent in order not to "aggravate the harm"
by endowing the opinion with a potential for future jurisdictional mis-
chief which it might not otherwise carry, his gamble turned out well; as
well as the opposite course he took in the *Barnette* case. *Starbird* was
in future occasionally cited for its substantive holding.[26] On the jurisdictional issue, its relatively innocuous pronouncements have from time
to time been referred to.[27] But nothing Brandeis would have regarded
as an alarming jurisdictional aberration can be charged to its influence.
Indeed, within three years, in a very similar situation, Brandeis, with
Van Devanter's aid this time actively enlisted on his side, succeeded in
getting the majority he had failed to hold in *Starbird.*

Hiawassee Power Co. v. Carolina-Tennessee Co.,[28] the case in which
this happened, was a suit brought in the North Carolina state courts by
a power company against a competitor to establish its exclusive right
to develop certain lands and streams in the state. This right was upheld in the state Supreme Court pursuant to a special North Carolina
statute which conferred it on the plaintiff company. The losing company now claimed that the state's grant of such a right to a single concern amounted to a denial of the equal protection of the laws guaranteed by the Fourteenth Amendment of the federal Constitution. This
point had been raised on a motion to exclude evidence in the trial court,
but it had subsequently been abandoned in the state Supreme
Court, from which the case came on writ of error to the United States
Supreme Court.

Brandeis, to whom the opinion was assigned, held that there was no
jurisdiction to pass upon the equal-protection claim because it had not
been especially set up in the highest court of the state, and had consequently not been decided there. This was the very holding he had
advocated in *Starbird,* which was, if anything, a stronger case for it. On

this occasion, Brandeis got returns expressing unqualified agreement from Chief Justice White, and Justices Van Devanter, McReynolds, and Clarke. That made a court. But there were those who had misgivings. Not least among them Holmes, who returned: "I have a little hesitation over the precise mode of reaching the result as the record discloses the question, and I am not quite clear that even if the objection is raised in the wrong place it ought not to be considered. I should feel a little happier if you added that there was nothing in it [on the merits]. I shall say no more." McKenna returned: "I voted the other way but — ." And Pitney: "I still think there should be an affirmance, not a dismissal." That left Day, and Van Devanter — the subtle, indefatigable Van Devanter — took charge of Day. Brandeis, no doubt forseeing the difficulty, had sent Van Devanter an advance draft of his opinion. "I saw Justice Day," Van Devanter wrote, "and think this will be satisfactory — am sure it will." Day had asked for a small change. He wanted the citation of certain cases to be prefixed with a "see" rather than "compare." Brandeis acceded. Day returned, "Yes," and the opinion came down unanimously.[29]

III

The Simple Service of Statutory Interpretation

When in 1927 Augustus N. Hand was elevated from the district
court, where he had already earned an enviable reputation, and began
his great career on the United States Court of Appeals for the Second
Circuit, Brandeis wrote him a congratulatory note. Hand's gracious
reply contained these two sentences: "However much some of your as-
sociates may differ with your general point of view, I believe they appreciate the light you bring to many cases from sources they would never
and by their training and education could never explore. The thing
which impresses the average lawyer and the law professors about your
work is the thoroughness with which you proceed so that everything is
tied up before your opinion ends." Four years later, on the occasion of
Brandeis' seventy-fifth birthday, Augustus Hand, who was not given to
lightly bandying compliments, expanded on this thought. "I confess,"
he wrote then, "that the 'judicial hunch' is to me a terrible thing. If I
by mistake employ it I don't believe in any such nebulous stuff and I
think it at present a special danger. The worst literalist and case judge
is better than one who thinks he has everything in his own hands. By
it we should lose the only sanction for our decisions. I have been particularly impressed by the care with which you justify and fortify your
conclusions in all the opinions you write." [1]

Augustus Hand's remarks are a fair assessment of the Brandeis method, of the rules by which Brandeis abided in the practice of his craft.
And the unpublished opinion here printed is a representative example.
Facts and understanding — so Brandeis preached and so, almost always, he practiced — must precede judgment, and they must be un-
folded in the opinion at whatever length necessary, to explain judgment, to justify it, and to gain acceptance for it. This was the proper
way in which a decision was made and announced. Its wellspring was
principle, a coherent philosophy of life and of government; in this, as
in so many instances, the conviction — generally accepted as doctrine
but much honored in the breach by Brandeis' colleagues — that social
and economic policy formulated by legislatures should, within wide
and infrequently invoked limits, have the freest range. Whether a policy
was novel, experimental, unwise — all that was not the Court's concern;

when called upon to do so in the course of litigation, it was for the Court faithfully to give effect to the legislative will. But only one in command of all the facts, the history of a statute, the needs that evoked it, the agitation out of which it grew, the choices it embodies, can truly apply such a principle. For on the surface — and to hindsight — the capricious is often indistinguishable from the merely foolish. And the frailties of legislators and of language are such that a statute may not, on its face, give the relevant indication of purpose; thus it may leave a judge who looks no further with little recourse but to construe its ambiguities on the basis of "hunch" — whether or not he acknowledges it even to himself.

There are opinions by Brandeis more strikingly illustrative of the method which Augustus Hand admired, and of the guiding principle it implemented. And there are other cases in which the contrast between Brandeis and the "literalist" and the "hunch" judge is vivid. But the contrast is seldom so salient as in this case, where, in the end, Brandeis and the brethren, in their different ways, came to the same result.

SUPREME COURT OF THE UNITED STATES

Nos. 373 and 391. — October Term, 1919.

Strathearn Steamship Company, Limited, Petitioner, 373 vs. John Dillon.	On Writ of Certiorari to the United States Circuit Court of Appeals for the Fifth Circuit.
J. M. Thompson, Master and Claimant of the Steamship "Westmeath," etc., Petitioner, 391 vs. Peter Lucas and Gustav Blixt.	On Writ of Certiorari to the United States Circuit Court of Appeals for the Second Circuit.

[March —, 1920]

Memorandum by Mr. Justice BRANDEIS.

The two cases present this question: Does Section 4 of the so-called La Follette Act of March 4, 1915 (c. 153, 38 Stat. 1164, 1165) confer upon seamen of foreign vessels loading or unloading in a port of the United States the right to demand while there payment of one-half of all wages theretofore earned under their shipping articles, although these were made abroad and provided, consistently with the law of the vessel, the place, and their own nation, that payment of the wages should be deferred until the termination of the contract? The foreign vessel owners and the British Embassy contend both that Congress is without power to confer such right and that it did not by the Seamen's Act attempt to do so. It will aid in determining the validity of these contentions to consider first the nature, the occasion, and the purpose of the provision in question.

First: The provision is primarily a regulation of the relation of master and servant, similar in character to many which the States have enacted in the exercise of their police power. It resembles most closely weekly and fortnightly payment laws, like that sustained in *Erie Railroad Co. v. Williams*, 233 U.S. 685 [1914]. But it is a modification of our shipping laws made by Congress in the exercise of its power over admiralty and interstate and foreign commerce.

The act of which it is a part contains twenty sections, the whole being designed to complete the emancipation of American seamen and to make possible the participation of the United States in the foreign carrying trade. The status of servitude, fastened upon American seamen by the Act of July 20, 1790, c. 29, 1 Stat. 131, was held not to have been affected by the Thirteenth Amendment, *Robertson v. Baldwin*, 165 U.S. 275 [1897], and had become ever more galling by comparison with the increasing liberties, the growing comforts, and the improved conditions enjoyed by workingmen on land. As a result, relatively few American citizens were willing to enter upon service at sea. Efforts to ameliorate the condition of seamen were continually engaging the attention of Congress. In the twenty years preceding 1915 ten acts were passed to that end.[1] Flogging was abolished in 1850; corporal punishment in 1898; and, in the same year, the right to arrest seamen on American vessels for desertion in American ports. The grosser incidents of servitude had thus been largely overcome, and in the coastwise carrying trade conditions for seamen greatly improved. Congress had re-

[1] February 18, 1895, c. 97, 28 Stat. 667; March 2, 1895, c. 173, 28 Stat. 741; March 3, 1897, c. 389, 29 Stat. 687; December 21, 1898, c. 28, 30 Stat. 755; April 11, 1904, c. 1140, 33 Stat. 168; April 13, 1904, c. 1252, 33 Stat. 174; April 26, 1904, c. 1603, 33 Stat. 308; June 28, 1906, c. 3583, 34 Stat. 551; March 2, 1907, c. 2539, 34 Stat. 1233; April 2, 1908, c. 123, 35 Stat. 55.

served that trade exclusively to vessels built and owned in the
United States;[2] and suppression through control by competing
railroads was guarded against.[3] Fair wages and working conditions
prevailed. The industry developed.

In the foreign carrying trade American seamen remained liable
to arrest for desertion abroad. That was believed to be necessary
for the operation of our vessels. But vessels of the United States
had almost ceased to engage in that trade. There had been a con-
tinuous decline for nearly three-quarters of a century. Between
our ports and those of other countries, as well as in the carrying
trade wholly between foreign countries, our vessels were subjected
to the unrestricted competition of foreigners; for Congress had not
afforded either to American capital or to labor engaged in such
trade protection like that given under the tariff to our manufacturing industries.[4] It had not even been found feasible to reserve the
trade between the Philippines and the United States to vessels of
American registry.[5] Americans were practically barred from entering the mercantile marine (otherwise than in the coastwise trade),
except as employees of foreign vessels; and this entailed temporary
allegiance to the foreign flag, *In re Ross*, 140 U.S. 453 [1891], and
subjection to wages and a standard of living lower than those prevailing in the United States.[6] The Act of March 3, 1813, c. 42, 2

[2] Act of September 1, 1789, c. 11, 1 Stat. 55; December 31, 1792, c. 1, 1 Stat.
287; February 18, 1793, c. 8, 1 Stat. 305; March 1, 1817, c. 31, 3 Stat. 351; Revised
Statutes, Section 4131; Act of May 28, 1896, c. 255, 29 Stat. 188.

[3] Report of Commissioner of Corporations on "Transportation by Water in the
United States," July 12, 1909; December 23, 1912; Panama Canal Act, August 24,
1912, c. 390, section 11, 37 Stat. 560, 566.

[4] "From 1789 until shortly before our civil war American shipping in the foreign
trade was in some form or degree protected, first by discriminating duties and tonnage taxes, and later by mail subventions. It is a matter of record that so long as it
was protected it prospered. But, for some unconscionable reason, when the protective policy in general was strengthened and broadened by the political party which
came into full power in 1861, adequate encouragement was denied to this one industry out of all our industries, and has been denied to the present time." Report of
Joint Commission on Merchant Marine, December 6, 1905, 59th Congress, 1st Session, Report No. 1, p. 6.

[5] Act of April 29, 1908, c. 152, 35 Stat. 70, amending Act of April 15, 1904,
c. 1314, 33 Stat. 181.

[6] "Ninety-three per cent of our foreign trade is carried in foreign ships manned
by foreign sailors. Of the few ships that carry the 7 per cent of our foreign trade
not 10 per cent of their crews are American citizens. Of this very small number of
American sailors in the foreign trade practically all of them are . . . running under
the subsidy act of 1891. . . ." Report of Minority of House Committee on Merchant
Marine and Fisheries, May 22, 1912, 62d Congress, 2d Session, Report 645, Part 2,
pp. 1–2.

Stat. 809, had made it unlawful to employ on board any public or private vessel of the United States any person except a citizen thereof or a native colored person. This act and supplementary legislation were repealed by Act of June 28, 1864, c. 170, 13 Stat. 201, so far as concerned employment of the crew. The number of American citizens engaged in sea-faring grew steadily less; and in 1914, when our mercantile marine was increased by admission of foreign-built ships to American registry, Congress deemed it necessary (Act of August 18, 1914, c. 256, 38 Stat. 698), to authorize the President in aid of foreign commerce to suspend the requirement that watch-officers be citizens of the United States.

Congress investigated from time to time the causes of this decline of the American mercantile marine and many bills were introduced proposing remedies.[7] Some minor measures designed to remove provisions in then existing laws believed to be unnecessarily burdensome and some to lessen otherwise the cost of building, equipping and repairing and operating vessels engaged in the foreign carrying trade and to promote their entrance into it, were enacted from time to time;[8] but they had proved ineffective. Proposals repeatedly made for general bounties, subventions, and subsidies and for discriminating duties and discriminating tonnage

[7] 41st Congress, 2d Session, Report from the Committee on the Causes of the Reduction of American Tonnage, February 17, 1870, Report No. 28; 47th Congress, 2d Session, Report of Joint Select Committee on American Shipping, December 15, 1882, Report No. 1827; 58th Congress, 3d Session, Report of American Merchant Marine Commission, January 4, 1905, Report No. 2755, and No. 2755, Part 2; 61st Congress, 2d Session, Report of House Committee on Merchant Marine and Fisheries, February 21, 1910, Report No. 502; 61st Congress, 3d Session, Report of said committee, February 24, 1911, Report No. 2253.

[8] The Act of June 26, 1884, c. 121, 23 Stat. 53, contained many such minor provisions including one (section 16) permitting the importation of supplies free of duty; thus supplementing Section 10 of the Act of June 6, 1872, c. 315, sec. 10, 17 Stat. 230, 238, which placed on the free list certain material for building, equipping, and repairing wooden vessels built in the United States for foreign trade. By the McKinley Tariff Act of October 1, 1890, c. 1244, sections 8 and 9, 26 Stat. 567, 613–14, free entry was granted also to material used for building, equipping, or repairing steel vessels engaged in the foreign carrying trade; and the privilege was extended by later acts. See Act of August 27, 1894, c. 349, Section 7, 28 Stat. 509, 548; Act of August 5, 1909, c. 6, Sections 19, 20, 36 Stat. 11, 88. By Act of March 3, 1891, c. 519, 26 Stat. 830, limited provision was made for aiding American ships in the foreign trade by mail subsidies. By Act of May 10, 1892, c. 63, 27 Stat. 27, a limited provision was made for American registry of foreign-built vessels to be so engaged. And some aid was given to the ocean merchant marine by the extension of the American monopoly in the coasting trade to Alaska, Act of July 27, 1868, c. 273, 15 Stat. 240; Hawaiian Act of April 30, 1900, c. 339, sec. 98, 31 Stat. 161, and Huus v. New York and Porto Rico Steamship Co., 182 U.S. 392 [1901].

taxes, had all been rejected. The proposal of Government ownership and operation of vessels in the foreign trade was not then
accepted.[9] Committees of Congress concluded that the decline of
the American merchant marine was the result of lower costs in
building, equipping, and operating foreign vessels; and that the
lower cost of operation was due mainly to their lower wage scale
and the inferior living conditions of their crews; and that equalization of operating costs in this respect would be an indispensable
factor in reestablishing our mercantile marine. With this general
end in view Congress had provided a generation earlier (by Act of
June 26, 1884, c. 121, section 20, 23 Stat. 58), that American vessels
could engage seamen in foreign ports to serve for round trips without being required to reship them in ports of the United States.
Thus equalization with foreign operating costs was sought to be
attained by reducing the standard of American wages to that of
the foreign competitors. The provision failed to accomplish its
purpose. The committees of Congress in reporting the La Follette
bill recommended trial of a new method. It was to overcome the
reluctance of Americans to engage in sea-faring by completing the
emancipation of seamen; and to equalize operating expenses by
raising to the American standard the wages and conditions of seamen on foreign vessels. To accomplish this, the committees proposed, among other things, to abrogate the existing right of arresting American seamen for desertion abroad and to emancipate all
seamen on foreign vessels entering ports of the United States for
the following reason.

It had been the common practice of such foreign vessels to engage their seamen abroad for long periods of service, or, at least,
for a period covering the return or outgoing voyage from the
United States. It was also the common practice of such foreign
vessels to make to seamen an advance payment at the signing of
the shipping articles, and to provide in the articles for deferring
payment of substantially the balance of the wages earned until the
termination of the shipping contract. Prior to the passage of the
Act of March 4, 1915, seamen on foreign merchant vessels who
deserted while in American ports were liable to arrest; and by many
treaties American magistrates and courts were bound to lend aid

[9] See Act of Sept. 7, 1916, c. 451, 39 Stat. 728.

in arresting and returning them to their ships. See *Dallemagne v. Moisan*, 197 U.S. 169 [1905]; compare *Tucker v. Alexandroff*, 183 U.S. 424 [1902]. The committees of Congress concluded that if seamen on foreign vessels were freed from liability to arrest in our ports for desertion, and this exemption from arrest were coupled with a provision enabling the seaman to obtain here payment of a substantial part of all wages theretofore earned and remaining unpaid, foreign vessels engaged in the American trade would be compelled to raise wages and working conditions to practically the standard prevailing in our coastwise trade. For otherwise they would lose many seamen whenever they entered a port of the United States, and they would be unable to ship new crews except at the rate of wages prevailing in America. As a very large part of the world's shipping was required to carry America's exports and imports,[10] some believed this equalization of operating expenses would extend gradually to vessels engaged in the carrying trade wholly between foreign countries; and, if the initial cost of the vessels should also be equalized, America would be able to compete for the foreign carrying trade. To equalize the initial cost of vessels, Congress had already provided in 1912 for American registry of foreign-built cargo vessels not more than five years old, and in 1914 had removed the age limit.[11] The purpose to effect such equalization of costs was clearly set forth in reporting the measure to Congress as will be hereafter shown.[12] Such is the nature of the measure in question; such the evils against which it was aimed and the means by which it was proposed to overcome them. Was it within the power of Congress to employ these means and did Congress express its intention to do so?

Second: The foreign vessel owners and the British Embassy

[10] It was said in 1906 that 500,000 sailors enter the port of New York each year. Hearing, 59th Congress, 1st Session, on H.R. 383, before Committee on Merchant Marine and Fisheries, February 2, 1906. In 1914 the number of masters, officers and men employed in Great Britain's merchant marine (20,300,000 gross tons) being one-half the world's tonnage, was only 295,652. Commerce Reports, January 26, 1920, p. 507. [World tonnage in 1914 was 49,089,552 gross tons, according to Commerce Reports, April 13, 1920, p. 242.]

[11] Act of August 24, 1912, c. 390, Section 5, 37 Stat. 560, 562; Act of August 18, 1914, c. 256, 38 Stat. 698; Letter of Acting Secretary of Commerce, December 12, 1914, 63d Congress, 3d Session, Sen. Doc. No. 640; Foreign Vessels Admitted to American Registry, 63d Congress, 3d Session, H. Doc. No. 1664, March 2, 1915.

[12] Reports of House Committee on Merchant Marine and Fisheries, 62d Congress, 2d Session, May 2, 1912, No. 645; 63d Congress, 2d Session, June 19, 1914, No. 852.

contend that Congress is without power to confer upon foreign seamen of a foreign vessel the right to demand while in our ports and to recover here wages earned abroad under a contract made abroad and valid where made, if the contract specifically provides that the payment of the wages shall be deferred and be made abroad. They say that this want of power is apparent where, as in these cases, the vessel, the seaman, the place of contract and the agreed place of payment are all of the same foreign country. But the contention will not bear analysis. Such legislation, it is argued, impairs the obligation of contracts. The constitutional inhibition against impairing the obligation of contracts does not apply to acts of Congress. Furthermore, the contract of the Strathearn was made after the La Follette Act became operative, and those of the Westmeath after the date of its enactment. Compare *Diamond Glue Co. v. United States Glue Co.*, 187 U.S. 611, 615 [1903]; *Louisville & Nashville R.R. Co. v. Mottley*, 219 U.S. 467, 482 [1911]. No treaty presents any obstacle; for the Act by its terms provides for the abrogation of all treaties inconsistent with it. (Sections 16 and 17.) The objection to the validity of the provision must rest, therefore, wholly on supposed rules of admiralty or of international law.

It is urged that, by general consent of the nations, the regulation of the rights and duties of officers and crew are, like matters of internal discipline, to be determined by the law of the country to which the vessel belongs — and not by the law of the place where she may, from time to time, happen to be. This undoubtedly is the general rule. But it is such only because of the consent of each nation affected and to the extent to which such consent has been given either by implication from prevailing custom or expressly by treaty or legislation. Without such consent no nation can legally possess extraterritorial rights within the territory of another. As said in *Schooner Exchange v. M'Faddon*, 7 Cranch 116, 136 [1812]: "The jurisdiction of the nation within its own territory is necessarily exclusive and . . . is susceptible of no limitation not imposed by itself. . . . All exceptions, therefore, to the full and complete power of a nation within its own territories, must be traced up to the consent of the nation itself." In the absence of such consent, express or implied, every foreign vessel owes temporary and local allegiance to the country whose port she enters and becomes amenable to the jurisdiction and laws of that country. See *United States v. Diekelman*, 92 U.S. 520 [1876].

The decided cases illustrate how narrow are the extraterritorial rights conceded by the United States to foreign merchant vessels; and the tendency to restrict them further is indicated by our legislation. Thus in *Wildenhus's Case*, 120 U.S. 1 [1887], despite the common treaty provision conferring upon the Belgian consul cognizance of differences between captains, officers and crews of Belgian merchant vessels in our ports, a felonious homicide committed on such a vessel in a New Jersey port was held to be within the jurisdiction of the State although committed by one Belgian upon another Belgian, both members of the crew, and although the affray occurred and ended wholly below the vessel's decks and the tranquility of the port was in no wise disturbed or endangered thereby. In *Patterson v. Bark Eudora*, 190 U.S. 169 [1903], the Act of December 21, 1898 prohibiting payment in advance of seamen's wages was held applicable to foreign merchant vessels in our ports, even if the seamen engaged were also foreigners. In *Bucker v. Klorkgeter*, Fed. Case 2083 [1849], it was held that our admiralty courts would take jurisdiction of a suit for wages by a foreign seaman against the vessel of his nationality where the interests of justice appeared to demand it, although the shipping articles entered into abroad provided that the seaman could seek redress only in the courts of his country. Compare *The Belgenland*, 114 U.S. 355, 364 [1885]. In *Knott v. Botany Mills*, 179 U.S. 69 [1900], a provision in a bill of lading limiting liability for negligence, given in a foreign port by a British vessel covering a shipment to this country, was held void because in violation of our statutory law; and in *The Kensington*, 183 U.S. 263 [1902], a similar provision relating to baggage, in a ticket sold abroad by a foreign vessel to a passenger bound for this country, was held void because not in harmony with our public policy as interpreted by the courts. In *The Titanic*, 233 U.S. 718 [1914], the limitation of liability under the Harter Act [February 13, 1893, c. 105, 27 Stat. 445] (to the benefit of which foreign vessels had been declared entitled in *The Scotland*, 105 U.S. 24 [1882]; *The Chattahoochee*, 173 U.S. 540 [1899], *The Germanic*, 196 U.S. 589 [1905]; and *La Bourgogne*, 210 U.S. 95 [1908] [*The Scotland* and *La Bourgogne* were decided under a related statute, the Limited Liability Act,

Revised Statutes, Sections 4282–87]), was held to be applicable to a liability arising out of a contract made in England by a British ship with a British citizen, although the British law on the subject differs from our own.

It is insisted that while one country may decline to enforce in its courts a cause of action arising abroad, if the foreign law from which it springs contravenes the public policy of the forum, it may not create a liability out of acts occurring abroad, which do not, by the foreign law, give rise to a cause of action. Compare *Slater v. Mexican National R.R. Co.*, 194 U.S. 120, 126 [1904]; *American Banana Co. v. United Fruit Co.*, 213 U.S. 347, 356 [1909]; *Cuba Railroad Co. v. Crosby*, 222 U.S. 473, 478 [1912]. The general principle may be admitted; but it has no application here. The liability for wages arises when they are earned. There is *debitum in praesenti, solvendum in futuro*. The wages earned abroad are, therefore, owing though not due. See Bouvier's Law Dictionary: "Owing." The rule is applied in the attachment and the bankruptcy laws, which permit proceedings to be brought before the maturity of the claims of complainants. Compare *Schunk v. Moline, Milburn & Stoddart Co.*, 147 U.S. 500 [1893]; *F. L. Grant Shoe Co. v. Laird Co.*, 212 U.S. 445 [1909]. Refusal to give full effect to the provision in the foreign shipping articles deferring payment of wages earned may rest, also, on the general rule that where illegal conditions or clauses in a contract do not go to the whole consideration or where they are severable, they may be ignored and the contract enforced as if the invalid provision had never been inserted therein. Thus in *Knott v. Botany Mills, supra*, and *The Kensington, supra*, defenses based upon clauses in contracts made abroad which unquestionably go to the liability — like that limiting the carriers' liability for negligence — were disregarded because contrary to our law; and the contracts were enforced as if these clauses had not been inserted therein. The provision deferring payment may also be likened to clauses in contracts made abroad restricting suit to courts of the foreign country, or to clauses by which the parties bind themselves to submit any controversy to arbitration. In such cases it is held that the provision, although binding by the law of the foreign country, goes only to the remedy and that the suit will be entertained by our courts, although both parties are subjects of the country in which the contract was made.

The Eros, 241 Fed. 186, 191 [1916]; 251 Fed. 45 [1918]; certiorari denied, 247 U.S. 509 [1918].

Congress having absolute power over foreign commerce, *Buttfield v. Stranahan,* 192 U.S. 470 [1904]; *Oceanic Steam Navigation Co. v. Stranahan,* 214 U.S. 320 [1909]; *Weber v. Freed,* 239 U.S. 325 [1915], may prescribe the conditions under which it will admit foreign vessels; and it may express the condition in the form of a pecuniary obligation to its seamen inconsistent with the shipping articles. *Patterson v. Bark Eudora, supra,* p. 178. It is clear, therefore, that Congress possesses the power to confer upon foreign seamen on foreign vessels coming into our ports the right to demand payment of half the wages earned, even though by contract made abroad and valid where made, payment was to be deferred. The question remains however: Did Congress express its intention to confer such right?

Third: Section 4 closes with the following clause: "This section shall apply to seamen on foreign vessels while in harbors of the United States, and the courts of the United States shall be open to such seamen for its enforcement." The main provision of the section is this:

"Every seaman on a vessel of the United States shall be entitled to receive on demand from the master of the vessel to which he belongs one-half part of the wages which he shall have then earned at every port where such vessel, after the voyage has been commenced, shall load or deliver cargo before the voyage is ended and all stipulations in the contract to the contrary shall be void; *Provided,* Such a demand shall not be made before the expiration of, nor oftener than once in five days. Any failure on the part of the master to comply with this demand shall release the seaman from his contract and he shall be entitled to full payment of wages earned."

Thereby section 4 amended the then existing law (section 6 of the Act of July 20, 1790, c. 29, 1 Stat. 133, incorporated in the Revised Statutes as section 4530, and amended by section 5 of the Act of December 21, 1898, c. 28, 30 Stat. 755, 756), in the following particulars:

1. The half-wages made demandable are those "earned" instead of those "due."

2. The half-wages are made demandable notwithstanding any

"stipulations in the contract to the contrary." The then existing law had denied the right to payment if "the contrary be expressly stipulated in the contract."

3. The half-wages earned are made demandable only after "the expiration of, nor oftener than once in five days." There was no such limitation in the then existing law.

4. Failure to comply with the demand releases "the seaman from his contract and he shall be entitled to full payment of wages earned." There was no such provision in the then existing law.[13]

5. The section is made to apply to foreign vessels as above set forth. There was no such provision in the then existing law.

The contention that section 4 should not be construed as conferring upon foreign seamen on foreign vessels the right to half-wages earned is urged upon several distinct grounds. In the first place it is said that the provision should be limited to American seamen on foreign vessels. The second construction suggested is that the provision should be held to apply only to such seamen on foreign vessels as had been shipped in American ports. A third construction offered is that the provision be held to apply to all seamen on foreign vessels wherever shipped, but that the extent of the recovery be limited to wages earned in American ports; and, as a further limitation upon its application, it is asserted that no right to demand even these wages arises until the vessel has been in the American port for five days. Compare *The Ixion*, 237 Fed. 142, 144 [1916]; *The Italier*, 257 Fed. 712, 714 [1919]; *The Delagoa*, 244 Fed. 835 [1917].

The argument that the proviso should be limited to American seamen on foreign vessels rests mainly upon the fact that the Act is entitled "to promote the welfare of American seamen," etc. This argument may be answered by reference to the familiar rule of construction, that the title forms no part of an act, and is not to be resorted to in order to create an ambiguity. *United States v. Fisher*, 2 Cranch 358, 386 [1805]; *United States v. O. & C. R. Co.*, 164 U.S. 526, 541 [1896]; *Cornell v. Coyne*, 192 U.S. 418, 430 [1904]. For the natural meaning of "seamen on foreign vessels" is all sea-

---

[13] There was added by section 4 the further proviso: "That notwithstanding any release signed by any seaman under section forty-five hundred and fifty-two of the Revised Statutes any court having jurisdiction may upon good cause shown set aside such release and take such action as justice shall require."

men; and no reason appears for narrowing that meaning here. The Act of December 21, 1898, 30 Stat. 755, 763, construed in *Patterson v. Bark Eudora, supra,* was entitled "An Act To amend the laws relating to American seamen, for the protection of such seamen, etc."; and the clause there in question, which provided in almost identical terms that it should apply to foreign vessels, was held to be applicable to foreign as well as to American seamen thereon. Compare *United States v. McArdle,* 2 Sawyer 367 [1873]; *United States v. Sullivan,* 43 Fed. 602 [1890]; *United States v. Anderson,* 10 Blatchf. 226, 228 [1872]. If, however, the title is to be considered, it should be noted that it is "to promote the welfare of American seamen in the merchant marine of the United States. . . ." The title affords, therefore, no basis for the contention that the proviso in question related to American seamen on foreign vessels. But the title further declares it is an act "to abolish arrest and imprisonment as a penalty for desertion and to secure the abrogation of treaty provisions in relation thereto . . . ," a purpose obviously referring mainly to foreign seamen on foreign vessels. And would it not promote the welfare of the American seamen in the American merchant marine to equalize conditions and operating costs and make employment therein possible? Furthermore, the last clause of the proviso, in declaring our courts open to such seamen, makes clear that the proviso applies to foreign seamen. Americans shipped as seamen on foreign vessels were already entitled to resort to our courts to enforce rights against the vessel. *The Falls of Keltie,* 114 Fed. 357 [1902]; *The Neck,* 138 Fed. 144 [1905]; *The Epsom,* 227 Fed. 158 [1915]. Our courts of admiralty possessed, in the absence of treaty provisions to the contrary, jurisdiction also in controversies between a foreign vessel and her officers or crew; but our courts usually decline, as a matter of discretion, to entertain law suits by foreign seamen; *The Belgenland, supra.* By treaties with some countries, our courts were precluded from doing so. *The Salomoni,* 29 Fed. 534 [1886]; *The Burchard,* 42 Fed. 608 [1890]; *The Koenigin Luise,* 184 Fed. 170 [1910]. Consequently foreign seamen needed a grant of the right to sue.

Like the first construction suggested, both the second and third empty the proviso of substantially all effect, as applied to foreign vessels. To limit the application of the section to seamen shipped in an American port would so narrow its scope as to make it inefficacious. To give seamen the right to demand half the wages earned during the days that a foreign vessel is loading or unloading in an American port, and then only after she had been there at least five days, holds out no grant of freedom, even when coupled with the right to enforce payment in our courts. It reminds of the bondage-provision in section 4 of the Act of July 20, 1790, c. 29, 1 Stat. 133, which declared that "no sum exeeding one dollar, shall be recoverable from any seaman or mariner by any one person, for any debt contracted during the time such seaman or mariner shall actually belong to any ship or vessel, until the voyage for which such seaman or mariner engaged shall be ended."

If, as the contentions made here and decisions below indicate (see, also, *The Sutherland*, 260 Fed. 247 [1919]), the words of the Act standing alone leave a doubt as to the intention of Congress, we may resort to the reports of the committees of Congress to aid in ascertaining its intention. *Oceanic Steam Navigation Co. v. Stranahan*, 214 U.S. 320, 333 [1909]; *American Net & Twine Co. v. Worthington*, 141 U.S. 468, 473–74 [1891]. And the following passages from their reports, together with facts recited above, show conclusively that the several constructions suggested by the foreign vessel owners and the British Embassy are each contrary to the intention of Congress and that the section was properly construed by the Circuit Courts of Appeals.

The La Follette Act originated in the Senate (S. 136). When the bill reached the House, it was referred to the Committee on Merchant Marine and Fisheries which at this and previous sessions of Congress had considered a similar measure.[14] In recommending important amendments to the section under consideration, which were accepted by the Senate conferees (House Report 1439, 63d Congress, 3d Session [February 24, 1915]), and later enacted into law, the committee reported as follows (House Report 852, p. 19, 63d Congress, 2d Session, June 19, 1914):

". . . It is claimed that by making the provisions of section 3 of the Senate bill and section 4 of the committee substitute apply to foreign ships it will tend to equalize the operating expenses of vessels. It is also claimed that the provisions of this bill abolishing arrest for desertion would be largely annulled if the foreign ship-

---

[14] 62d Congress, 2d Session, H.R. 23673; Report from House Committee on the Merchant Marine and Fisheries, May 2, 1912, 62d Cong., 2d Sess., Report No. 645.

owner may by the terms of his contract deny the seaman the right to receive in our ports any part of the wages earned by him; that while the deserting seaman would not be subject to arrest, he would be compelled, if he deserted, to do so without a penny in hand to buy bread or procure a night's lodging; and it is claimed also that if American vessels are subject to the provision allowing seamen to demand half their wages earned, while foreign vessels are not, the shipowner might and probably would put his ship under a foreign flag to avoid this obligation.

"Quoting from the report on H.R. 23673, known as the seamen's bill, made to the House of Representatives in the Sixty-second Congress, second session, May 2, 1912:

" 'Under existing laws men may be and are employed at the ports where the lowest standard of living and wages obtain. The wages in foreign ports are lower than they are in the ports of the United States; hence the operating expenses of a foreign vessel are lower than the operating expenses of an American vessel. It is not proposed to prevent vessels from employing seamen in ports where they can secure them cheapest, but it is proposed by this bill to give the seamen the right to leave the ship when in a safe harbor, and in time this will result in foreign seamen engaged on vessels coming into ports of the United States being paid the same wages as obtain here, as a means of retaining their crews for the return voyage. That will equalize the cost of operation, so that vessels of the United States will not be placed at a disadvantage.'

". . . If, however, giving greater freedom to the seaman shall operate not only to equalize wages, but to elevate and better the conditions and service of the seaman, which is its purpose, then the provision will justify itself and be of benefit to the American merchant marine in equalizing the cost of operation as between our ships and those of other nations.

"It should be stated that the committee are not unanimous in making this provision apply to foreign ships.

"Some members of the committee doubt our right and the wisdom of making it apply to foreign ships and question its value to our merchant marine."

The report of May 2, 1912, had declared in introducing the passage quoted above (p. 7):

"Two things are essential to the building up of our merchant marine; one is the creating of a condition where the initial cost of the vessel is as low as that of the foreign vessel and the other is an equalization of the operating expenses.

"This bill will tend to equalize the operating expenses."

And on the following page (8), the report of May 2, 1912 gave the further explanation:

"The section thus amended gives the seaman the right to demand one-half the wages due him in any port, notwithstanding any contract to the contrary, and extends its application to seamen on foreign vessels while in American harbors, and the whole section becomes part of the means by which the cost of operation of all vessels taking cargo out of any American port may be equalized." [15]

Senator Fletcher in reporting to the Senate the Seamen's Bill, enacted March 4, 1915, said (50 Cong. Record, 5748–9):

"The three main purposes were: First, to give freedom to seamen and improve their condition; second, to promote safety of life at sea; third, to equalize the wage cost of operating vessels, foreign and domestic, taking cargoes or passengers from ports of the United States. It is very generally acknowledged that the bill will accomplish those three purposes . . . .

"First, Senate bill 136 permits seamen on foreign vessels to leave their vessels in ports of the United States; that was one great thing to be worked out; second, it permits seamen to draw one-half of the pay due them in any port where the vessel lies or delivers cargo, making this section applicable to foreign vessels while they are within the jurisdiction of our laws; . . .

"The right to one-half the earned wages at a stopping place on a voyage would seem to be reasonable. It would not induce a sailor to leave a ship when he was being decently treated and fairly compensated to have the privilege of quitting and collecting only one-half of what he had earned. On the other hand, if the sailor is maltreated, or for sufficient reason he quits the vessel, perhaps in a strange land, he should at least have half the wages he has earned in cash. The forfeiture of the other half would seem to be ample allowance by way of liquidated damages for breach of his contract . . . ."

---

[15] For vigorous dissent see the Minority Report, 62d Congress, 2d Session, May 22, 1912, Report 645, Part 2.

The enactment of the provision had been recommended by the Secretary of Commerce and the Secretary of Labor in a joint communication to the Senate committee ([May 6, 1913], 63d Congress, 1st Session, Senate Document No. 211, p. 6) which said: "The section thus amended gives the seaman the right to demand one-half the wages due him in any port, notwithstanding any contract to the contrary, and extends its application to seamen on foreign vessels while in American harbors, and the whole section becomes a part of the means by which the cost of operation of all vessels taking cargo out of any American port may be equalized."

The Senate bill had used the expression "one-half part of the wages which shall be due him at every port." To make certain that half the wages earned were to become payable Congress adopted upon recommendation of the House committee, as a substitute, the language: "One-half part of the wages which he shall have then earned." Whatever doubt might otherwise have existed, the reports of Congress made it clear that Congress intended that seamen on foreign vessels should be entitled to receive at every port an amount up to one-half of the wages earned then remaining unpaid under the shipping contract.

The foreign vessel owners and the British Embassy urge that the decisions below are inconsistent with the decision of this court in *Sandberg v. McDonald* (*The Talus*), 248 U.S. 185 [1918]; *Neilson v. Rhine Shipping Co.* (*The Rhine*); and *Hardy v. Shepard and Morse Lumber Company* (*The Windrush*), 248 U.S. 205 [1918]. The contention rests upon misapprehension. The precise question there involved was not whether the provision concerning advances applied to foreign vessels but whether it applied to advances made abroad. Because the place of the advance was deemed decisive, it was held inapplicable there to both the American and the foreign vessels. On the other hand the provision conferring the right to demand half-wages is confessedly applicable to American vessels wherever the wages were earned, whatever the nationality of the seamen, and wherever the demand may be made; and the United States gives this right to seamen on foreign vessels when they enter our ports; and that is practically the extent of our sovereign power. In reaching the conclusion that Section 10 of the Act did not apply to advances made abroad this court deemed the provision for criminal liability of "great importance as evidencing the legislative intent to deal civilly" as well as criminally only with matters in our own jurisdiction. No such criminal provision is attached to Section 4. Furthermore the court, having examined the "reports and proceedings in Congress there referred to" found in them "nothing which requires a different meaning to be given the statute." Here the opposite is true.

The contention that Dillon's demand was premature because made within three days after the arrival of the ship at Pensacola is also shown by its history and the report of the Committee on Merchant Marine and Fisheries [House Report 852, 63d Congress, 2d Session, June 19, 1914] (p. 18) to be wholly unfounded. The bill, as it came from the Senate, contained no such provision. It was inserted by the House Committee which said: "to prevent any unnecessary annoyance to the captain of the ship on voyages where the vessel may call at ports oftener than once in five days, it is provided that the demand for wages shall not be made more than once in five days." As was stated by the Court of Appeals in the *Strathearn* case [256 F. 631, 632 (5th Cir. 1919)]: "Evidently the intention was that such a demand should not have the effect given to it by the statute, if it is made within five days 'after the voyage has commenced,' or if made sooner than five days after the making of a previous demand contemplated by the statute."

The history of *Strathearn S.S. Co. v. Dillon* [2] in the Supreme Court goes back to November 1918, more than a year before the date of Brandeis' opinion. At that time the case was first argued together with *Sandberg v. McDonald*,[3] which involved a closely related issue. The section of the La Follette Act on which Dillon's claim depended provided for the payment to seamen, upon demand, of one-half of the wages earned when the vessel reached a safe port; anything to the contrary in the contract of employment notwithstanding. The *Sandberg* case turned on another section of the same Act, which rendered unlawful the payment of advance wages at the time of hiring, either to a seaman or, as was more usual, to an agent who had acted for him in arranging his employment. Violation of this section was made a misdemeanor punishable by a fine and a prison term. It was also provided that the payment of advance wages could not avail as a defense to a later suit for recovery of wages otherwise due. Like the provision which

Dillon invoked, this section was made applicable to foreign vessels while in waters of the United States.

Sandberg, not a United States national, had signed for a voyage on a British ship in Liverpool, and as was customary and legal in Britain, had received an advance payment on account of wages. When the ship put in at Mobile, Alabama, Sandberg asked for payment of one-half of the wages then earned. This was the same demand that Dillon made. Sandberg's master, unlike Dillon's, tendered payment in response to the demand, but in reckoning what was due he deducted the amount advanced in Liverpool. It was Sandberg's position that this deduction was inconsistent with the provision of the La Follette Act declaring advance payments unlawful. He quit the ship, being logged as a deserter, and brought his libel.

In both the *Dillon* and *Sandberg* cases, the seamen urged the Court to construe the La Follette Act as reaching out beyond the customary province of national legislation. Maritime law — admiralty, as this head of jurisdiction is called — normally regards a ship as an extension of the territory of the nation of its flag and holds that questions relating to the internal economy and discipline of a ship, to the conditions of seamen's employment, are governed by the law of that nation. Moreover, it is a maxim of private international law that the validity of contracts, such as the articles signed by both Dillon and Sandberg, and the legality of most acts undertaken pursuant to the terms of a contract, such as the refusal to pay half-wages to Dillon and the tender of an advance to Sandberg, are governed by the law of the place where the contract was concluded.

These and like rules of international courtesy and convenience are of long standing, and it is the natural and on the whole beneficial impulse of courts to resist their casual abrogation. To some extent, doctrines of private international law placing limits on national legislative power are held to be incorporated in the Constitution.[4] In both these cases, therefore, as Brandeis pointed out in his *Dillon* opinion, the Court was faced with two questions. First, did Congress have the power to reach out in the fashion in which the seamen claimed it had done, and second, had Congress done so, had it truly intended to disregard the laws of other nations and impose its own will to the limit of its power, or had it meant its enactment to be construed in light of traditional rules?

Though it was argued in both cases, the issue of power was in neither one very difficult. For the imposition of our will occurred within American waters. Compliance with the provisions of the La Follette Act was a condition attached to permission to enter our ports, which it is plainly within national power to deny. The effect of this condition, if any, on transactions taking place abroad was indirect. The second question was the difficult and the decisive one. For a judge who simply took the advance-payments and the half-wages sections of the Act at face value and read them separately, the question of Congressional purpose was baffling.

The drafting of the two sections was inartistic. With respect to each, for every exegetical argument which pointed one way, there was another tending in the opposite direction. Thus, Congress could not have intended to punish the making of advances abroad, where its jurisdiction did not extend. That would have been a futile purpose. Hence the section must have been meant to outlaw only advances to a seaman hired in an American port. But Congress had said that a seaman suing here might recover wages otherwise due, despite the fact that he had already been paid them by way of an advance. That was a perfectly enforceable purpose, as applied to advances made both here and abroad. Or Congress would not have expressly provided, as it did in the half-wages section, that our courts should be open to seamen for its enforcement, if it had not meant the section to apply to foreign seamen, for our courts are necessarily open to our own citizens. But our courts had also for more than a century been hearing suits for wages by foreign seamen, although in doing so they generally applied the law of the flag and exercised, at least in theory, discretion to dismiss such suits on the ground that another forum would be the more convenient one.[5] And the question was not whether a foreign seaman might, everything else being equal, sue for half-wages, but whether he was entitled to them when his contract of employment, providing otherwise, was concluded abroad. If it was necessary to open the courts to foreigners at all, it could have been thought necessary to do so for the case where the contract was made here.

The ease with which exegesis could lead to opposite but on the whole equally plausible results is demonstrated by the *Sandberg* case, which a majority of five decided adversely to the seaman a month and a half after the argument. Day spoke for the Court. The advance payment of wages was legal where made, he held. Conceding that the United States might disregard it with respect to foreign vessels seeking to enter our ports, Congress had manifested no intention to do so. "How far was [the advance-payments section] . . . intended to apply to foreign vessels?" Day asked. "We find the answer if we look to the language of the act itself. It reads that this section shall apply to foreign vessels 'while in waters of the United States.'"[6] Moreover, the fact that criminal sanctions were imposed made it doubly plain that advances paid abroad were not affected.

Proceeding in exactly the same fashion, McKenna, who (joined by Holmes, Brandeis, and Clarke) wrote the dissent, arrived at the contrary conclusion. On its face, he said, the section was clearly applicable. The Court was not "called upon to assign the genesis of the policy or trace the evolution of its remedy . . . ." "Ours," McKenna declaimed, "is the simple service of interpretation, and there is no reason to hesitate in its exercise because of supposed consequences." The statute was unambiguous. To depart from the grammatical meaning of the language, to qualify it, to wander from its "certainty" to "the uncertainties of construction," would "take us from the deck to the sea, if we may use a metaphor suggested by our subject." [7]

At the same time, Day, again speaking for the majority, held that advances on account of wages made by an American ship on the occasion of hiring seamen in Buenos Aires were also not affected by the Act. More in sorrow than in anger, Day remarked that the advances in this case were actually paid not to the seamen but to an agent without whose intervention seamen's services could not be obtained in Buenos Aires — a custom "which works much hardship to a worthy class." [8]

The *Dillon* case, though it had been argued together with *Sandberg*, was not disposed of at this time. A technical and remediable jurisdictional flaw necessitated its return to the lower court.[9] But the *Sandberg* decision augured ill for Dillon's chances when his case should come back to the Supreme Court. Distinctions were possible; yet the outlook was poor, considering the ready answer which, in *Sandberg*, the Court had sought and found in the language of the Act. If the legality of advances made abroad was respected, why should not the same courtesy be extended to contracts made there and providing, as Dillon's did, for payment of wages only at the conclusion of the voyage? It was no doubt just as well for Dillon that an incidental jurisdictional error delayed the judgment in his case. That this is more than idle speculation is indicated by the events which took place a year later, after the case had been argued once more. It was at this time that Brandeis wrote his opinion. His law clerk, Dean Acheson, made a somewhat rueful memorandum, telling what happened, which he filed with the Justice's papers in the case. The memorandum wastes no words and reads as follows:

This opinion was prepared at a time when it appeared that the decision might have gone against the interpretation of the act which is here advocated. The Chief Justice was wavering, Pitney, Van Devanter, Day and McKenna were contra. I don't remember whether a copy was sent to the Chief or not. But eventually it was decided according to this view and Judge Day wrote a poor opinion.

This took the Justice two weeks of hard work while court was sitting. D.G.A.

Justice Brandeis at the White House, 1932

Justices Stone, Holmes, and Brandeis

Chief Justice White and Justices Pitney and Van Devanter had been with Day in the *Sandberg* case. It had been Day's rather than McKenna's literalism that had convinced them then, and the conviction very likely lingered. McKenna himself may well have thought that *Sandberg* — a decision he had contested and lost — ruled this case, and that that ended the matter; or in the performance, on the deck, of the simple service of literal interpretation, he may have seen differences between the advance-payments and half-wages sections which enabled him to hold the second inapplicable where he had applied the first.

The facts that Brandeis set forth as decisive in his *Dillon* opinion cut through the inartistic drafting of the La Follette Act and dissipated the bafflement to which it gave rise. Indeed, these facts decided more than the *Dillon* case; they were sufficient also to resolve in favor of the seaman the ambiguities of the advance-payments section involved in the *Sandberg* case. In the light of the rational purpose central to the entire statute, verbal distinctions between the advance-payments and half-wages sections evaporated. Congress, it became clear, wanted to force the payment by foreign masters to foreign seamen of a substantial portion of their wages upon demand, in order to make it possible for such seamen to jump ship — as Sandberg did — and in order thus to cause foreign owners, if they wished to retain their employees, to raise their wage and other standards to those Congress required on American ships. Advances made abroad were not punished, to be sure, although advance payments in American ports were rigorously outlawed. Yet the making of advances abroad could be discouraged; and this the two sections, read together so as to prevent advances previously made from being reckoned in the calculation of half wages due in American ports, could accomplish. In this way the American seaman's lot could be bettered without weakening the competitive position of American shipping. Pressure was applied to improve conditions on foreign ships as well, thus affirmatively bolstering the American competitive position, which had long been on the decline, in part at least because American labor costs were high.

There can be little doubt that these considerations, and not McKenna's touching verbal certainties, determined the result for Brandeis in *Sandberg* as well as in *Dillon*. Yet Brandeis signed McKenna's dissent, in which none of this emerges. We do not know why Brandeis failed to write in the *Sandberg* case, nor, of course, whether if he had written there would have been a chance of gaining a court for his result. In the month and a half between the argument of *Sandberg* and its decision, Brandeis delivered six opinions. Five of these were opinions of the Court, and he may well have felt that disposing of them should take precedence over the writing of dissents.[10] Of the five, one had been held over from the previous term, and Brandeis doubtless considered it particularly urgent.[11] Another, though decided unanimously in the end, had been troublesome, becoming the subject of a debate with Pitney which occasioned an exchange of special memoranda.[12] The sixth, delivered on the day the *Sandberg* case itself came down, was Brandeis' massive and important dissent in *International News Service v. Associated Press*,[13] also a case pending from the previous term. In the same six-week period, Brandeis received as well the assignment of at least one other opinion of the Court. This was a case argued after *Sandberg*. It may also have had priority, and it came down two weeks after *Sandberg*.[14] It is thus likely that in the relatively short time Day took to write the majority opinion, Brandeis simply had no chance himself to write. He might of course have held up disposition of the case, had it been up to him to speak for the dissenters. But McKenna, next to Holmes, was the quickest producer on the Court. His dissent was most likely written and circulated in ample time to be delivered when the majority was ready. It is quite a different matter to hold up decision of a case for the purpose of writing another, rather than the only, dissent.

Of one thing we may be certain, and that is that what Brandeis wrote in the *Dillon* case, which is so different from what he signed in *Sandberg*, did not come as an afterthought. The history of seamen's legislation and the legislative history of the La Follette Act itself had been argued in the briefs for Sandberg, earnestly if not as exhaustively as Brandeis himself was to discuss them. Moreover, Brandeis did not need counsel to draw his attention to these matters. His awareness of them is shown by the manner of his drafting of the *Dillon* opinion. It was the law clerk who collected the comprehensive list of statutes going back to the earliest days. But Brandeis had started writing before he had the citations, and he referred to the subject matter of a number of the statutes, leaving blank spaces to be filled in when specific references became available.

Brandeis' general familiarity with seamen's legislation may be traceable to his close friendship with one of the sponsors of the Seamen's Act of 1915, the elder Robert M. La Follette.[15] Before coming to the Court, Brandeis had often acted as a sort of unofficial legislative counsel to La Follette.[16] There is no evidence whatever that Brandeis helped draft this statute, but he must have been familiar with La Follette's activities in its behalf. Moreover, La Follette was its chief legislative promoter. But the principal motive force behind the Act was another man whom Brandeis befriended, and whom he had heard speak about seamen's problems. This was a remarkable humanitarian figure, Andrew

Furuseth, the president of the International Seamen's Union of America. The passionate and dedicated Furuseth, born in Norway, had been to sea as a boy and young man and, battered but neither broken nor bent by life before the mast, had formed, as La Follette wrote, the deliberate purpose "to get one great nation to provide by law a haven where seamen could escape tyranny and maltreatment aboard ship. One country where a sailor could lawfully leave his ship would serve to elevate the condition of labor at sea throughout the world." Furuseth selected the United States as his battleground, jumping ship here and taking up residence early in the 1880's. From then on his campaign was unrelenting and effective. He called on leading men, preaching his cause, "a great soul speaking through his face, the set purpose of his life shining in his eyes." [17]

It was Furuseth's unshakable purpose, communicated to more than one Congressman, which, wedded to a policy of restoring the competitive position of American bottoms in international trade, informed the La Follette Act of 1915. Among the members of Congress whom Furuseth approached and converted was none other than the future Mr. Justice Sutherland, then in the Senate.[18] An echo of Furuseth's fervor resounds in these words (perhaps Furuseth wrote them; he took an active interest in the preparation of seamen's cases, often working with counsel) from one of the briefs filed in behalf of Sandberg: "This 'Seamen's' Act is no ordinary act of the Congress! . . . The pages of the Federal Reporter . . . are full of stories of how, under the cloak of the advance, had hidden the assassins of his [the seaman's] character and his wages. Societies sprang up in the name of humanity to protect him. Years pass and at last through the long night there flashes for the seaman the light of the 'Seaman's' Act!" [19]

When Brandeis came to write in the *Dillon* case, which had been fortuitously saved for another day, it was not enough, however, to set out the considerations that he deemed decisive. For *Sandberg* was by then on the books, and it had to be dealt with if a majority, let alone a unanimous Court, were to be obtained for a result favorable to the seaman's claim. It is almost certain that overruling so recent a precedent as *Sandberg* would have been out of the question for most of the Justices. And so Brandeis' opinion suggested unconvincing verbal distinctions and refrained from pointing out that, in light of the materials it discussed, the *Sandberg* case had been wrongly decided.

As Mr. Acheson's contemporaneous note suggests, and as appears from a brief notation in Brandeis' hand on a copy of his opinion, there was no general circulation of it. It is nevertheless possible that Brandeis showed the opinion privately to a few of his colleagues (he had the final draft printed in ten copies), and he certainly made its contents known in conference. The assignment to Day, once Brandeis' result was accepted, may be attributable to the situation created by *Sandberg*. That case and the decision in *Dillon* had to be reconciled. Nothing could leave a stronger impression of conflict than if *Dillon* were written by one of the *Sandberg* dissenters. Nor could anything give a greater appearance of consistency — for the benefit of wavering brethren and afterward of the Bar — than that the same judge should write both cases. Moreover, it is in any event quite doubtful that in the spring of 1920 a majority of the Justices would have signed an opinion such as Brandeis' in the *Dillon* case. Their attitude toward historical and legislative materials is indicated by a remark of Day's at the end of his *Sandberg* opinion. He alluded there to "the reports and proceedings in Congress during the progress of this legislation," to which counsel had drawn attention. He held them up at a distance, gingerly and uncertainly, his face partly averted, as if they were something he had picked out of a bundle of laundry. We have examined counsel's references, he said, "so far as the same may have weight in determining the construction of this section of the act. We find nothing in them, so far as entitled to consideration . . . ." [20] Perhaps, as Augustus Hand surmised, the light Brandeis shed was appreciated. But it had — for Day and his colleagues — to remain decently under a bushel.

In writing what became the unanimous opinion in *Dillon*, delivered in March 1920, Day went about his business as he and McKenna had done in the *Sandberg* case. The statute was by its terms applicable to seamen on foreign vessels putting in at American ports. It was manifest on its face that it was meant to be so applicable, since provision was made to open the courts to seamen with claims under the statute. Then, still dealing with the words of the statute only, Day made the following assertion, similar to the one at the heart of Brandeis' opinion. It was stated without documentation by Day:

Apart from the text, which we think plain, it is by no means clear that, if the act were given a construction to limit its application to American seamen only, the purposes of Congress would be subserved, for such limited construction would have a tendency to prevent the employment of American seamen, and to promote the engagement of those who were not entitled to sue for one-half wages. . . . But, taking the provisions of the act as the same are written, we think it plain that it manifests the purpose of Congress to place American and foreign seamen on an equality of right in so far as the privileges of this section are concerned. . . . In the case of *Sandberg v. McDonald*, 248 U.S. *supra*, we found no purpose manifested by Congress . . . to interfere with wages advanced in foreign ports under contracts legal where made.[21]

By way of support for this argument, Day mentioned that a predecessor statute, in also creating a right to half wages, had limited it to cases in which the articles did not provide to the contrary. In the La Follette Act, this proviso had fallen. Hence it was plain that Congress wanted half wages to be recoverable, no matter what had been agreed to in the articles. But it is, of course, on this basis alone, anything but plain that Congress was thinking of articles signed between foreigners abroad as well as contracts made here.

Eight years after the *Dillon* case had been decided, the issue of *Sandberg v. McDonald* was before the Court once more. The advance-payments section had since been amended slightly, and it was argued for the seaman, with much force, that the Congressional purpose had been to overrule the *Sandberg* result. But once more the statutory language harbored ambiguities (if, like McKenna, one may use a nautical turn of speech suggested by the subject). A unanimous Court dealt with it on its face. The distinctions made in *Dillon* came home to roost, and *Sandberg* was reaffirmed. Brandeis was silent.[22]

Nevertheless, in the generation since *Strathearn S.S. Co. v. Dillon*, Brandeis' method of ascertaining legislative purpose, for which he gained no acceptance in that case, has made much headway. It is as normal today as it was unusual then for the Court to look to legislative materials for indications of basic purpose and then to apply broadly or poorly worded statutes in conformity with that purpose. The method is today almost a matter of course; so much so that it has at times been abused; so much so also that there is evidence of reaction setting in against it. There are those who feel that to speak of a legislative intent is theoretically untenable and too often unrealistic. And there are those who fear that the prevalence of this method promotes irresponsibility in Congress, manifested by an unhealthy tendency to legislate by committee report.[23] Much — though not all — of this current of doubt, of second thought is directed only at abuses of the method, which cannot be charged to Brandeis. Among those whose misgivings went the whole way was the late Mr. Justice Jackson. He expressed them both judicially and in extra-judicial writings.[24]

In his last full year on the Bench, before his illness, Jackson dealt in an elaborate opinion with a problem not unlike that presented by the *Dillon* case. A successor statute to the La Follette Act of 1915, the Jones Act of 1920, creates a cause of action at law, with right to trial by jury, in favor of seamen injured in the course of their employment. The Act applies in this respect to "any seaman." [25] The suit in question was by a Danish seaman employed on a Danish ship, who was injured in Havana, Cuba. Jackson, for the Court, held the Jones Act inapplicable.[26] Without suggesting that Congress would have had no power to make the Act applicable, but also without seeking such light as the legislative and historical materials might have supplied, he concluded that Congress had not intended to give a remedy in a situation such as this. The normal doctrines of private international law showed what an extraordinary thing it would have been for Congress to have so intended. At the end there is this passage:

> In apparent recognition of the weakness of the legal argument, a candid and brash appeal is made by respondent and by *amicus* briefs to extend the law to this situation as a means of benefiting seamen and enhancing the costs of foreign ship operation for the competitive advantage of our own. . . . The argument is misaddressed. It would be within the proprieties if addressed to Congress. Counsel familiar with the traditional attitude of this Court in maritime matters could not have intended it for us.[27]

It may well be that the argument was indeed not tenable with respect to this provision of the Jones Act. Just the same, one cannot help being struck by Jackson's tone of dignified outrage. It recalls the Day and McKenna opinions in *Sandberg*. Precisely this sort of contention was decisive for Brandeis in *Dillon*. The briefs in Jackson's case, including one filed in behalf of the Friends of Andrew Furuseth Legislative Association, though not exhaustive, buttressed the argument with references to historical and legislative materials. Brandeis would certainly have wanted to meet it factually.

IV

Real Life and the Upper Conceptual Chambers

It is an oft-told tale how, during much the better part of Brandeis' judicial career, a self-willed Supreme Court generally opposed and often defeated the concerted drive to better the conditions of labor in which Brandeis, while in practice, had himself been active, and which was increasingly successful in state legislatures and in Congress. The activities of organized labor and the favorable legislation that labor was sometimes able to obtain amounted, of course, to intrusions upon the process by which the individual employer and the individual worker defined their relationship. This the Court viewed as an infringement of the ancient liberty of each; the liberty of the one, in the management of his property, to offer wages and conditions of employment, and of the other to accept or reject. "In some upper conceptual chamber," wrote Thomas Reed Powell in 1918, "these two common-law liberties may dwell together in amity. In actual life they conflict." [1] But the Court would not see this, or in any event, would not concede it to be remediable under the Constitution. The consequences Brandeis himself recited strikingly and not without some bitterness in his unpublished opinion in *United Mine Workers v. Coronado Co.* As he had told a Senate committee investigating business practices in 1911, there was serious danger of social unrest in "letting the people learn that our sacred Constitution protects not only vested rights but vested wrongs." [2]

There were of course dissenters against the course pursued by the majority in labor cases. Brandeis often led them. There were also instances of escape from the conceptual compression chamber. But such instances had a way of remaining discrete exceptions. If, rarely and grudgingly, the Court permitted an impairment of the theoretical liberties of the individual employer and employee, it did not subsequently draw the logical consequences of its action. The exceptions were left, perversely, to prove the rule. When next it returned to the subject, the Court would purport to find, and would again leave, the abstract liberties upon which it generally based its decisions, unmarred in their perfection.

One exception was *Muller v. Oregon*, [3] a case which Brandeis had

argued for the state before his accession. Here the Court upheld a statute decreeing the novelty of a ten-hour day for women employed in
laundries. This decision resulted in the later approval of a similar statute applicable to all persons employed "in any mill, factory or manufacturing establishment." [4] The ten-hour laws were upheld as health
measures, traditionally within the purview of State authority. But the
Court failed to see statutes providing minimum wages for women in
the same light, although their supporters very plausibly justified them
on the same ground.[5]

Another exception concerned state workmen's compensation and
employers' liability laws. Such statutes force employers to bear more
of the burden of industrial accidents than was placed on them by the
common law. The risk of injury would, at common law, often be said
to have been assumed by the employee, as when he knowingly continued to use defective machinery; and recovery would be barred as
well, even though the employer had been at fault, if the negligence of
the injured employee or of a fellow worker could be said to have also
contributed to the accident.[6] Although it required Congress to try
twice, the Court in the end sustained federal legislation easing the situation for employees of interstate railroads.[7] In a series of decisions culminating in the *Arizona Employers' Liability Cases*, the Court upheld
State statutes embodying much more drastic departures from the common law. These cases illustrate what a precarious and painful task it
was in those years to extract from the Court an exception to the doctrine it customarily applied in labor matters. The *Arizona Employers'
Liability Cases*,[8] the last in the line, teetered on the brink for a year and
a half, as Day and Pitney apparently fought down their fears that the
basic doctrine itself was in danger. There was a struggle for their souls,
and Brandeis in this instance won it.

The first of the state workmen's compensation cases was *New York
Central R.R. v. White*.[9] The New York statute attacked in this case was
applicable to employees engaged in so-called hazardous occupations,
of which the statute listed a very large number. Whether or not their
injury was by common law standards attributable to the fault of the
employer, such employees, or in the event of death their families, were
entitled to an award compensating them for medical expenses and loss
of earning power. The awards were to be made by an administrative
board according to a predetermined scale, and the remedy so provided
was exclusive; employees were not free to take a chance on trial by
jury in lieu of it. The state offered employers insurance against the liability created by this statute, but left them the option of seeking private
insurance or of not insuring at all; in the latter event, however, they

might be required to deposit securities as a guaranty of payment of possible future awards.

"The scheme of the act is so wide a departure from common-law standards respecting the responsibility of employer to employee," Pitney said in the unanimous opinion he wrote for the Court, "that doubts naturally have been raised respecting its constitutional validity." For one thing, he continued, stating the doctrine to which he and his brethren normally adhered, it was objected that under the statute "both employer and employee are deprived of their liberty to acquire property by being prevented from making such agreements as they choose respecting the terms of the employment." But the states should be free, Pitney held, to change the standards of responsibility imposed by the common law, if they provided "a reasonably just substitute." What New York had provided here was fair enough; it conformed to "natural justice." A new kind of liability had been imposed on the employer, to be sure, but it was limited and predictable in amount; and the statute, on the other hand, freed the employer from the risk of large verdicts, not so limited, to which he was subject at common law upon a finding of negligence. The new liability was not dependent on fault, but "the act in effect [thus] disregards the proximate cause and looks to one more remote — the primary cause, as it may be deemed — and that is, the employment itself." [10]

On the same day on which this case was decided, Pitney, for the Court, also upheld the workmen's compensation systems enacted by Iowa and the state of Washington. The Iowa statute hardly differed from the New York one, and it also passed muster unanimously.[11] Not so, however, the Washington law. It exacted from employers compulsory contributions to a state liability insurance fund, with no option not to insure. Pitney noted that this meant the imposition of an expense on an employer regardless of whether injuries had befallen his own employees, an expense he had to meet no matter how prudently he might manage his own business, and which might be increased because a competitor was managing his less prudently. Nevertheless, Pitney held that the compulsory contributions were in this case not excessive, amounting at worst to an occupation tax of the sort which would very likely have been upheld if the state had chosen to levy it for some other reasonable purpose. However, Chief Justice White and Justices McKenna, Van Devanter, and McReynolds evidently thought otherwise. Without writing an opinion, they registered dissent.[12]

How the four dissenters reconciled their approval of the New York and Iowa statutes with disapproval of the Washington law is not easy to see. Thomas Reed Powell, writing in 1917, pointed out that while

it was true that the New York law left employers the option of not insuring, this was a distinction without much difference. If New York
employers elected to insure, they were in the same position as employers under the Washington statute. If they elected not to insure, they
could be required to deposit securities, and thus also incur an expense.
And the fact of the matter was that it was the commonest sort of business practice to insure against liability in any event. Hence, "it is but a
slight step further to compel him [the employer] to join in a co-operative plan for providing payment, so long as the plan corresponds with
the business practices followed by sensible men." [13] But a slight step
further can be impossible if the first one was difficult and distasteful.

Such was the situation in January 1918, when the *Arizona Employers'
Liability Cases* were first argued. Arizona's way of dealing with the
problem of industrial accidents differed from the New York, Iowa, and
Washington schemes in that, while Arizona compelled employers to offer compensation under a statute much like the ones the Court had
earlier considered, it also preserved for the employee the alternative
right to trial by jury and to recovery of damages in amounts not limited
by a prescribed scale. The employee's choice was restricted to the extent that, if he elected trial by jury, his recovery might be barred should
the employer be able to prove that the injury was in fact due to the
employee's own negligence. But whichever of the alternative remedies
he chose, an injured worker could recover regardless of whether his
employer had been at fault, provided only that he was engaged in one
of the large number of occupations which the legislature had classed
as hazardous or dangerous.

Pitney, in the *White* case, had made a good deal of the fact that while
the New York statute created a new head of liability, it also conferred
upon the employer a compensating benefit by freeing him from the risk
of large verdicts in cases in which, at common law, he had been subject to suit. Plainly this was not true under the Arizona scheme; indeed,
Arizona had extended the risk of large verdicts to a new class of cases.
Hence it was argued that Pitney's earlier opinions not only were no
precedent for upholding this statute, but required that the decision
here go against the state. Nevertheless, the five-man majority Pitney
had led when the Court divided in the Washington case held together
again. Moreover, it apparently gained, at first, at least one recruit. At
conference following the argument, a decision was reached in favor of
the validity of the Arizona statute, and Chief Justice White assigned
the writing of the majority opinion to Holmes. This would indicate that
at this stage, White, who had dissented earlier and who in the end was
to dissent here too, was prepared to go along, since the Chief Justice

does not make assignments in cases in which he disagrees with the majority.

Holmes wrote and circulated the opinion that now appears as a special concurrence, joined in by Brandeis and Clarke. It was winningly titled with the name of one of the cases, *Inspiration Consolidated Copper v. Ceferino Mendez*, and disposed of the issue on the basis of the following generalization: If a business is successful, Holmes reasoned, "the public pays its expenses and something more. It is reasonable that the public should pay the whole cost of producing what it wants and a part of that cost is the pain and mutilation incident to production. By throwing that loss upon the employer in the first instance we throw it upon the public in the long run and that is just." [14] The question of whether liability may be imposed without fault, Holmes said, was disposed of by the New York and Washington cases decided earlier. But in stating this undoubted fact, Holmes took occasion to rephrase the holding of those cases without indulging any of Pitney's cautious qualifications. As for the specific objection based on the difference between the Arizona system and the ones involved in the earlier cases — Holmes considered that the generalization quoted above disposed of it.

After the decision had been finally handed down, Holmes, in a letter to Sir Frederick Pollock, noted what had happened: "My last opinion was in favor of the constitutionality of a state law throwing all the risks of damage to employees on the employers in hazardous businesses. To my wonder four were the other way, and my opinion was thought too strong by some of the majority, so that Pitney spoke for the Court and I concurred, with what I had to say — Brandeis and Clarke only with me. I pointed out that even in what was supposed to be the Constitutional principle of basing liability on fault it meant that a man had to take the risk of deciding the way the jury would decide — in doubtful cases." [15] On a slipsheet of his opinion, Holmes made a notation to the same effect: "This case originally was written by me as assigned by the C.J. D[ay] and P[itney] thought there was danger in this op. and P. wrote what none of his majority could disagree with and so I suggested that his op. should be the op. of the Court to avoid a majority with one op. by 3 JJ. and another by 2." [16]

It is not difficult to see how Day and Pitney might have become alarmed at the boldness of Holmes' logic. Holmes was launching not another discrete exception, but a general principle, capable of life and growth and application to other instances, and he was stating it without fear of its implications. This could scarcely have been palatable to Day. He had been known to sponsor an exception or two to the doctrine the Court normally applied in labor matters. But when he defended that doctrine, he did so passionately; with a feeling rendered, perhaps, the more intense by his own occasional waywardness.[17] And there was the factor of Day's temperament; he was, Brandeis said, a "hot little gent," "a fighter, a regular game cock," and "fierce" about his views.[18] As Brandeis saw it, most of the labor cases touched, in a man like Day, a deep prejudice, a fear that organized labor threatened the existing social and economic order. Day was hardly the man, then, to agree to a statement such as Holmes', which, at least in its radiations, undermined the position he and the Court had so often taken.

Pitney was a different sort from Day, but he also presented a problem with respect to Holmes' opinion. Of Day Brandeis said that he "couldn't be persuaded by anybody but himself." And one readily concludes that the process of self-persuasion was not a solely, and perhaps not even a largely, intellectual one. This was not true of Pitney. There was, no doubt, much that Pitney could not see. But, Brandeis once remarked, he had "real conscience and steady growth." His was a case of the "triumph of conscience over experience and brains." [19] Holmes, who had at first been irritated by Pitney's personal mannerisms, wrote Pollock in 1923, when Pitney was ill: ". . . I came to appreciate his great faithfulness to duty, his industry and his candor. He had not wings and was not a thunderbolt, but he was a very honest hard working Judge and a useful critic." And, nearly two years later, after Pitney's death: "He could not touch the superlative, and when he first came on the bench riled me by excessive discourse. But he took his work seriously, was untiring in industry, had had some experience of life, and as Brandeis always said and, I came to think, truly had intellectual honesty that sometimes brought him out against his prejudices and first judgment." [20] Pitney was thus open to persuasion — by others, not wholly and mysteriously by himself, like Day. But it was highly doubtful that the persuasion of Pitney could be accomplished by Holmes' soaring, though of course quite valid generalization. For Pitney's commitment to views of a different kind in labor matters was as thorough and extensive as that of any member of the usual majority on the Court.

As a state judge in New Jersey, Pitney had made what the Senate opposition to his confirmation as Supreme Court Justice not unfairly considered an anti-labor record. And it was Pitney who, writing for the majority in the notorious case of *Coppage v. Kansas*,[21] struck down as unconstitutional a statute outlawing "yellow-dog" contracts, by which workers agreed, as a condition of their employment, not to join unions. Such statutes, Pitney held, were an intolerable interference with individual freedom of contract. (It is notable that this holding was too much even for Day; he, Holmes, and Hughes dissented.) It was Pitney also who wrote for the majority in *Hitchman Coal & Coke Co. v. Mitchell*,[22] enjoining as an unlawful interference with contractual relations efforts of the United Mine Workers to organize a mine that had extracted from its employees yellow-dog agreements. And it was Pitney finally who, in *Duplex Printing Co. v. Deering*,[23] held that the Clayton Anti-Trust Act was not the Magna Carta labor had thought it was upon its enactment, but rather permitted issuance of an injunction against a union boycott. This was Pitney.[24] In the two cases last mentioned, he stood firm under the attack of two powerful Brandeis dissents. It would have been natural for Pitney to believe that workmen's compensation laws were also unconstitutional. And, in fact, such appears to have been his initial reaction when *New York Central R.R. v. White*, the first workmen's compensation case, was argued. "He came around," Brandeis said, "upon study, though he had been the other way." [25]

That Pitney was capable both of meaningful "study" and of "coming around" is demonstrated by *Truax v. Corrigan*.[26] The case shows also that when he did come around, Pitney, as one might expect, did so on narrow grounds rather than on the basis of broad, decisive first principles. First principles were exactly what he and a Brandeis or a Holmes differed about. If their minds met, it had to be in spite of this. *Truax v. Corrigan* was argued at the term after the *Arizona Employers' Liability Cases* had finally been decided. It also involved an Arizona statute, one which forbade the state courts to issue injunctions against strikes or against peaceful picketing. In pursuance of this statute, the Arizona court had declined to enjoin certain picketing. The Supreme Court, by a five-to-four majority, held that Arizona had thus perpetrated an unconstitutional deprivation of property without due process of law, the property in question being business good will. Pitney at first was with the majority and received the assignment of the opinion. As was not infrequently his way, Brandeis wrote and circulated the mighty dissent which he eventually published, before there was any majority opinion. He received from Pitney this note, dated November 3, 1920: "Thanks for your memorandum in number 72, which I have read with interest. I have not yet seriously tackled the opinion in that case, but when I do I of course will give full consideration to what you have written." Before the end of the term, "being unable," as he said, "on further examination, to write in accordance with the vote," Pitney circulated what later became his own dissent.[27] He changed nobody's mind, although the case was held for another term and reargued, and so he dissented; but he did it alone, on his own narrow grounds, not joining either Brandeis or Holmes, who also wrote. Shortly after *Truax v. Corrigan* was decided, Holmes briefly alluded to this course of events in a letter to Laski, quoting Brandeis as saying that "it was a proof of Pitney's intellectual honesty." [28] The *Arizona Employers' Liability Cases* are an earlier and similar instance of the workings of Pitney's mental processes.

It would seem that Holmes' opinion in the *Arizona Cases*, with its breadth and vigor of statement, not only did not gain the assent of Day and Pitney, but lost the previously given assent of at least one of them to the result itself. For the next thing that happened, under date of October 1918, was an opinion by Brandeis reaching the same result as Holmes', but labeled a dissent. It is printed below. As will be evident, it is quite a different paper from Holmes'. Brandeis addressed himself to the problems that Pitney and Day, given their premises and their anxieties, might well have. To begin with, Brandeis conceded that one could entertain serious doubts about the wisdom of Arizona's policy in permitting the continuation of "unprofitable and demoralizing law suits," rather than entrusting solely to an administrative tribunal the task of compensating the injured worker. He then modestly stated the holding of the earlier cases by quoting from them, and dealt with the difficulty of the employees' option to seek trial by jury by citing a few reassuring analogies and stressing the continuing power of judges to control excessive verdicts.

SUPREME COURT OF THE UNITED STATES

Nos. 20, 21, 232. — October Term, 1918.

The Arizona Copper Company, Limited,
Plaintiff in Error,
20　　　　　vs.
Joseph B. Hammer.

The Arizona Copper Company, Limited,
Plaintiff in Error,
21　　　　　vs.
Richard Bray.

Ray Consolidated Copper Company,
Plaintiff in Error,
232　　　　　vs.
Dan Veazey.

In Error to the District
Court of the United States
for the District of Arizona.

[October —, 1918]

Mr. Justice BRANDEIS, dissenting.

By an employers' liability act, which is peculiar in its provisions, Arizona provides a remedy for personal injuries received by employees in occupations "especially dangerous and hazardous to the workmen therein, because of risks and hazards which are inherent in such occupations and which are unavoidable by the workmen therein." The statute declares that "all work in or about quarries, open pits, open cuts, mines, ore reduction works and smelters" shall be deemed to be hazardous occupations. The statute differs from other employers' liability acts, in that it makes the employer liable, although himself without fault, except where the injury was caused by the negligence of the employee. It differs from workman's compensation laws, in that it denies the employee recovery, if the accident was caused by his own negligence and was not partially due to a risk or danger inherent in the employment; and also in that it leaves the amount payable to be fixed by court and jury, instead of limiting the amount, to be determined on a prescribed scale by an administrative tribunal. Unlike both workman's compensation laws and some employers' liability acts, this statute does not, in case of injury resulting in death, confine the benefit of the recovery to those who were dependent upon the deceased for support. Furthermore, workmen injured while engaged in hazardous occupations are, under the several Arizona statutes, given the election to pursue this or one of two other remedies, namely, either a proceeding under the workman's compensation law or an action for negligence, in which the fellow-servant rule has been abolished and issues of contributory negligence and assumption of risk are declared to be questions of fact to be determined by the jury. The employee need not elect, until after the accident, which of three remedies he will pursue and the election is made by commencing the suit or other proceeding for compensation. When so made the election is irrevocable. Constitution of Arizona, Article XVIII, Sections 4–8. Revised Statutes of Arizona (1913) Sections 3153–3169, 3176. *Consolidated Arizona Smelting Co. v. Ujack*, 15 Ariz. 382 [1914].

These three cases were argued together and present the same question. Each is an action under the Arizona employers' liability law. Hammer, an employee of the Arizona Copper Company, was injured while making repairs and improvements on a hopper on the feed floor, a large quantity of hot calcine having been discharged upon him from a loaded car operated above the hopper. In the District Court of the United States for the District of Arizona, he sought to recover $50,000 damages. The jury rendered a verdict for $12,000. Bray, another employee of that company, was injured in one of its mines, by rock and earth falling upon him from the roof of the tunnel in which he was engaged. He sued in the same court for $50,000. The jury rendered a verdict in his favor for $9,000. Veazey, an employee of the Ray Consolidated Copper Company, while engaged in fastening timbers at an elevation in its reduction works, fell a distance of 10 feet to the concrete floor. He sued in the same court to recover $10,000. The jury rendered a verdict for $3,000. In each case judgment was entered upon the verdict; and the cases come here under Section 238 of the Judicial Code. It is contended, in each, that the Arizona statute violates the Fourteenth Amendment, in that it deprives the employer of its property without due process of law and denies equal protection of the laws.

The feature which is mainly relied upon as rendering the Arizona statute obnoxious to the Federal Constitution is this: It makes the employer, who is without fault, absolutely liable unless the wrong resulted from the employee's negligence or willful act; and it makes this liability unlimited in amount and recoverable by ordinary legal proceedings. If we were permitted to express an opinion upon the wisdom of the statute, the arguments urged against it might prove persuasive. The right of the employee to litigate is preserved. Consequently there remains the temptation to waste the time of employer and employee and their and the State's money in unprofitable and demoralizing law suits; with the possibility to the individual workingman of a broken life, to the employer of bankruptcy, and to the State of heavy burdens, social and financial. But with the wisdom or expediency of the act, we have no concern. Our duty is confined to determining whether the Federal Constitution is violated when a State imposes upon employers the obligation of making such compensation as court and jury may decide to be reasonable for accidental injuries to employees which are due, at least in part, to the conditions of the occupation and not wholly to the negligence of the employee.

First: If such a statute denies to the employer due process of law, it must be because it creates unlimited liability without fault, leaving the amount of compensation to be fixed by court and jury instead of an administrative tribunal. The mere fact that the statute creates liability without fault is not fatal to its validity. As stated in *New York Central Railroad Company v. White*, 243 U.S. 188, 204 [1914]: "The common-law liability of the carrier, of the inn-keeper, of him who employed fire or other dangerous agency or harbored a mischievous animal, was not dependent altogether upon questions of fault or negligence." Statutes imposing liability without fault have been repeatedly sustained by this Court. *St. Louis & San Francisco Ry. Co. v. Mathews*, 165 U.S. 1, 22 [1897]; *Chicago, Rock Island and Pacific Ry. Co. v. Zernecke*, 183 U.S. 582, 586 [1902]. The liability enforced in the *Mathews* case was that of a railroad for fire communicated from its locomotive. The liability enforced in the *Zernecke* case was that for injury to a passenger. If statutes creating liability without fault under such circumstances are held not to be arbitrary or unreasonable, clearly an act should not be held to be so which imposes upon employers engaged in hazardous occupations the duty of making compensation to workmen for personal injuries unavoidably suffered therein. As stated in the *White* case (p. 203): "This is a loss arising out of the business, and, however it may be charged up, is an expense of the operation, as truly as the cost of repairing broken machinery or any other expense that ordinarily is paid by the employer."

Nor can we say that the statute is arbitrary and unreasonable in that it leaves the amount of the compensation recoverable to be determined by the jury. While the liability thus created is not limited in amount, and is to be fixed by a jury as in common law actions for personal injuries, the verdict, like others, is subject to the power of the court to set it aside as excessive, or, in the alternative, to compel its reduction to such amount as the court may deem reasonable compensation for the injuries suffered. Under the Arizona statute, as in cases of common law liability for negligence, the damages recoverable are limited to reasonable compensation for the injuries suffered. It does not provide for punitive damages in any case; and we can no more assume here, than in a common law action for negligence, that the jury will assess, or the court permit to be entered, a judgment for more than reasonable compensation. In the instances of common law and of statutory liability without

fault referred to in the *White* case (p. 204) the damages recoverable were also unlimited and were determinable, as here, by the
jury, under the control of the court. The liability created by the
Safety Appliance Acts, which apply also where the carrier may not
have failed to exercise reasonable care, *St. Louis, Iron Mountain
& Southern Ry. Co. v. Taylor*, 210 U.S. 281, 295 [1908], is likewise
unlimited.

In support of the contention that the act is arbitrary and unreasonable, the plaintiff in error refers to *Superior & Pittsburg Copper Co. v. Tomich*, 165 Pacific 1101, 1185, 1186, 19 Ariz. 182, 191,
192 [1917], where Judge Ross, in his dissenting opinion, calls attention to a provision of the statute by which, as he says, an employer wholly free from negligence is subjected to greater liability
than one whose negligence contributes to an injury, since in the
latter case (but not in the former) the damages are diminished if
the employee is guilty of negligence contributing to the injury.
The alleged difference in result, if it exists, is far from arbitrary.
The legislature might reasonably believe that plaintiff's contributory negligence should constitute a ground for reducing the
amount recoverable when the cause of action arises out of the employer's negligence, but shall not be a ground for such reduction
where the cause of action arises from conditions inherent in a
hazardous employment. However, it does not appear that the alleged difference actually exists. Section 3159 of the Revised Statutes of Arizona (1913) expressly provides that in a suit under the
statute in question, "the fact that the employee may have been
guilty of contributory negligence shall not bar a recovery, but the
damages shall be diminished by the jury in proportion to the
amount of negligence attributable to such employee." This seems
clearly to provide that the amount of recovery shall be diminished
when the injury is due partially to the negligence of the employee,
no matter whether the employer is negligent or not. The declaration of the majority of the court in the *Tomich* case is not to the
contrary.

As showing that the act is arbitrary and unreasonable, attention
is also called to the fact that in case of death recovery may be for
the benefit of decedent's estate, although he left no dependents.
We have no occasion to pass upon this contention; as the actions
here under consideration are not for injuries resulting in death; and

that provision of the statute is clearly severable from those involved in the case at bar.

Second: The statute does not deny to employers equal protection of the law in that it gives to the employee the option to determine which of three remedies for injury he shall pursue. It does give to the injured employee the right to elect between: (1) The enlarged common law remedy for damages, unlimited in amount, under which he must establish negligence on the part of the employer, but the fellow-servant doctrine cannot be pleaded as a defence. (2) The remedy under the statute in question, also for damages unlimited in amount, where he need not prove negligence on the part of the employer, but will fail if the injury was proximately due solely to his own fault; and (3) The remedy under the Workman's Compulsory Compensation law, where he may recover a limited amount, although his employer was not negligent and the injury was due wholly to his own negligence. The common law frequently grants to him who is injured, the option to select one of several remedies. Thus, a party to a contract may, sometimes, elect whether he will sue for specific performance or for damages; likewise whether he will rescind or seek damages for misrepresentation or fraud. The owner of a patent may elect between seeking damages or profits. The owner of personal property, wrongfully taken, may elect whether to sue in replevin or for conversion. And the legislature frequently grants alternative remedies. Such options commonly enjoyed by the plaintiff in a litigation, may be likened to the option which he so frequently enjoys in selecting the forum in which the controversy shall be conducted. A law which grants to the one who institutes adversary proceedings, the right to determine by which of several possible remedies the alleged claims shall be determined, necessarily denies to the other party the choice of remedies. But this is not a denial of equal protection of the laws within the meaning of the Fourteenth Amendment. Compare *Missouri, Kansas & Texas Ry. Co. v. Cade*, 233 U.S. 642, 650 [1914]; *Standard Oil Co. v. Tennessee*, 217 U.S. 413, 420 [1910].

In my opinion, all of the objections urged against the statute are unsound and the judgments of the District Court should be affirmed.

Brandeis' approach was evidently convincing. We do not know whether he circulated his dissent. It seems likely that Pitney, at least, saw it. In any event, there was a reargument, and then Pitney wrote the prevailing opinion, which he delivered in June 1919. It was long and rambling. Holmes called it, "but a flabby performance." [29] Yet it served the immediate purpose, and it shows quite clearly the influence of what Brandeis had written.

"But for Pitney," Brandeis once said, "we would have had no workmen's compensation laws." [30] The *Arizona Cases* settled the matter, the Court taking a benign view of a few other statutes which were attacked as extending the earlier holdings.[31] Brandeis, much better than Holmes, could understand and deal with considerations that were decisive to a Pitney. Holmes had little patience with them. It seems not unlikely, therefore, that but for Brandeis there might have been a different outcome in the *Arizona Employers' Liability Cases*, with the ultimate result that the Court would have taken a hand in shaping workmen's compensation systems rather than leaving that task to the legislatures with whom it properly belonged.

The two expressions of dissent from Pitney's opinion indicate the pull to which he was subject from the other side. The first of the dissents was by McKenna, joined in by Chief Justice White and Justices Van Devanter and McReynolds, and it is a remarkable document. The earlier workmen's compensation cases — McKenna had dissented in the third one — had not been easy to decide, he said, "against the contentions and conservatism which opposed them," and "to me the present case is a step beyond them. I hope it is something more than timidity, dread of the new, that makes me fear that it is a step from the deck to the sea — the metaphor suggests a peril in the consequences." (The metaphor was a favorite of McKenna's.) [32] The Arizona statute, he continued, could be upheld only on the basis of a generalization such as Holmes had formulated. "Of this there can be no disguise. It may be confused by argument and attempt at historical analogies and deductions, but to that comprehensive principle the case must come at last." The statute was an interference with the rights of employers, with "precepts of constitutional law," and "precepts of moral law." "I say this, not in dogmatism, but in expression of my vision of things . . . ." Once launched, where would such interference stop, and was there any hope that it would? The "drift of opinion and legislation" currently favored labor and set it apart so as to withdraw it from the action of economic forces and their consequences, giving it "immunity from the pitilessness of life." Holmes' argument that the cost of industrial accidents, being imposed upon the employer, was passed on to the consumer had an "attractive speciousness" about it. If valid it could justify the imposition of any and all burdens upon employers.[33]

McKenna was an intriguing, highly erratic figure. He could come forward, as he did here, in the role of champion of a set of utterly sterile, theoretical liberties, upon which society had to rest if it was to endure in freedom. In his knotty style he would develop the logic of these liberties, carrying them relentlessly to their driest extremes and giving the impression that he realized well enough the drawbacks of his result, but could not help himself; he appeared almost in a state of self-hypnosis, of unwilling fascination by, and submission to, the consequences of the concepts he marshaled. Thus he confessed in this opinion that he found "appealing considerations" in favor of protecting the laboring man from what he called the pitilessness of life. But principle stood in the way. Similarly in the *Pipe Line Cases*,[34] McKenna, dissenting alone, protested against the Court's upholding of the Hepburn Act, which declared interstate pipe lines common carriers and forced them to convey the oil of minor producers who had hitherto been cut off from markets. McKenna saw in this statute a taking of property without just compensation, and, in much the same tones he used here, wondered where it would all stop. "Every once in a while McKenna sends up a balloon just to show that he is there," [35] Brandeis once remarked of this sort of opinion. Yet McKenna never lacked a certain grace, and he had the charm of candor. He might parade irrelevant formulas, but they somehow escaped being clichés. And he was not given simply to venting bad temper, as, for example, McReynolds took to doing in later years. Moreover, McKenna did at times show a sensible, indeed a quite modern, understanding of the proper role of the Court in applying the Due Process Clause of the Constitution, as well as a grasp of the realities underlying legislative policies.[36] As an unkind verse said of Wordsworth, two voices of wildly differing accents were both his.

McReynolds also dissented at some length. He thought the majority was undermining freedom of contract, a principle "fundamental and vital," and he cited Pitney's own opinion in *Coppage v. Kansas*. One can imagine that this citation was not without effect. Rights guaranteed by the Constitution were endangered, McReynolds wrote, by a new doctrine which "is revolutionary and leads straight towards destruction of our well-tried and successful system of government. Perhaps another system may be better — I do not happen to think so — but it is the duty of the court to uphold the old one unless and until superseded through orderly methods." And: "As a measure to stifle enterprise, produce discontent, strife, idleness and pauperism the outlook for the enactment seems much too good." [37]

The alarms raised by the dissenters were reflected on the outside. Whatever legislation the current drift in favor of the laboring class might culminate in, McKenna said, "cannot now be predicted, but it is very certain that, whatever it be, the judgment now delivered will be cited to justify it." Taking the cue, a writer for a law journal who discussed the case in September 1919 under the heading, "Collectivism Supplanting Individualism," declared that a new day had dawned. He greeted it with resignation but little joy: "The old conservatism has departed even from the halls of justice. Old principles of law, thought to be forever true, are thrown into the junk pile . . . ." [38] But — partly, no doubt, because of the alarms expressed in dissent, which must have shaken Day and Pitney and had their share in preventing Holmes' opinion from speaking for the Court — the predictions of doom remained wrong for nearly two more decades. The new day had not quite dawned as yet.

Although by then the time of decisive change was not far off, as late as June 1936, only two and a half years before Brandeis' retirement, the Court was still declaring minimum wage legislation unconstitutional, over Stone's protest (joined by Brandeis and Cardozo, Hughes also dissenting) that there could be no more objection to "requiring an industry to bear the subsistence cost of the labor which it employs, than to the imposition upon it of the cost of its industrial accidents" through workmen's compensation statutes. [39] No great principle of general application, such as Holmes had enunciated, had radiated forth from the decision of the *Arizona Employers' Liability Cases*.

V

"A Union Man's Country"

The Supreme Court — as the discussion of the *Arizona Employers' Liability Cases* has suggested — for many years maintained a generally inhospitable attitude toward both private and governmental efforts to improve conditions of labor. Shaped chiefly by preconceptions which had little relation to the facts of industrial life, this attitude manifested itself, for example, in decisions frustrating minimum wage laws. It found expression also, for some forty years ending in the thirties of this century, in the Court's intervention as arbiter of the trial of economic strength between employers and incipient organizations of labor.

The labor relations of interstate railroads, which Congress and the Executive took in hand during and after the First World War, were an exception.[1] Otherwise, however, both before and following that war, it was the courts, under the leadership of the Supreme Court, which, drawing on common law rules for the protection of property against maliciously inflicted harm, undertook "to deal with the conflicts of interest between employers and employees by defining: (1) the occasions on which employees might engage in concerted activities in pursuit of their interest, (2) the objectives which employees might lawfully pursue by concerted action, and (3) the tactics which employees might lawfully use."[2] The prohibitions laid down by the courts, though they varied somewhat from time to time and place to place, and though their common law rigor was occasionally tempered by a recognition that employees acted not out of malice or caprice but in the attempt to protect an identifiable economic interest of their own, left organized labor with little room for maneuver. These prohibitions were enforced in the main by exercise of the ancient equity power to issue injunctions, whose violation constituted contempt of court and was punishable by fine or imprisonment imposed without trial by jury.

State courts needed to look no further than the common law for their authority to act. Nor did federal courts, in the many cases in which their jurisdiction could be rested on the parties' diversity of citizenship; that is, on the fact that the employer and the employees or labor officials to be enjoined were citizens of different states. And the federal courts, coming more and more to take charge, were able also to rely on a statute which, though till 1914 it did not authorize the issuance of injunctions at the behest of private parties, proved quite serviceable just the same, since it made possible the award of whopping punitive damages. This was the Sherman Anti-Trust Act, forbidding combinations ("in the form of a trust or otherwise") and conspiracies in restraint of interstate commerce.[3] The Sherman Act is — and was apparently meant to be — a very broadly worded statute, expressing only the most general objectives and trusting to the courts to endow it with concrete meaning. Whether or not it was so intended, labor organizations and their activities could plainly be brought within the terms of the Act. And so they were.[4]

Two landmark cases will serve to convey the flavor of the federal judicial stewardship of labor relations in the United States. These cases are *Loewe v. Lawlor*,[5] and *Hitchman Coal & Coke Co. v. Mitchell*.[6] The first, known to fame as the *Danbury Hatters'* case, was a suit for triple damages, allowed by the Sherman Act to the victim of an illegal combination in restraint of trade. The plaintiffs manufactured hats in Connecticut and sold them nationally. Deeming it, as they said in their complaint, "their right to manage and conduct their business without interference from individuals or associations not connected therewith," they did so "upon the broad and patriotic principle of not discriminating against any person seeking employment because of his being or not being connected with any labor or other organization"; and they "refused to enter into agreement with any person or organization whereby the rights and privileges, either of themselves or any employé, would be jeopardized, surrendered to or controlled by said person or organization . . . ." [7]

The defendants in their turn were, to quote Chief Justice Fuller, who spoke for the Court in *Loewe v. Lawlor*, "members of a vast combination called The United Hatters of North America, comprising about 9,000 members and including a large number of subordinate unions . . . combined with some 1,400,000 others into another association known as The American Federation of Labor, of which they were members, whose members resided in all the places of the several States where the wholesale dealers in hats and their customers resided and did business . . . ." [8] The defendants being, if one may borrow an irony of Holmes in a not entirely unrelated case, "in this ominous attitude," [9] they endeavored to unionize plaintiffs' employees, and failing to achieve their end by more direct methods, instituted a national boycott against plaintiffs' product. On these facts, a unanimous Court, of which Holmes was a member, found the defendants guilty of conspiring to restrain interstate commerce in violation of the Sherman Act.

In the *Hitchman Coal & Coke Company* case, the United Mine Workers had had a contract with the plaintiff. However, having broken a strike by employing nonunion labor, the plaintiff had then exacted from each of his new employees an agreement, widely if indelicately known as a yellow-dog contract, not to join the union while in plaintiff's employ. Without resorting to violence, the union tried to organize the company's new employees. This activity was the subject of an injunction issued by a federal district court on the ground that the union was a conspiratorial organization whose very existence was outlawed by the Sherman Act, since its aim was to restrain, indeed to destroy, free trade in coal among the states. The Supreme Court, to which the case was brought for review, also held that the union's actions were illegal and should be enjoined, but it did not rely on the Sherman Act, nor did it declare the union an outlaw organization. The Court held only that the union was engaged in an effort to induce plaintiff's employees to break their agreement with him; for it was urging them both to join the union and to stay on their jobs. This was forbidden conduct. It might very well be that men should be permitted to band together for purposes of improving the conditions of their employment, but they could not lawfully be induced to do so when they had contracted not to. It should be noted that in this case Holmes joined Brandeis and Clarke in dissent.

Needless to say, it was not universally conceded that the struggle between employer and employee was unequal on the side on which Chief Justice Fuller, referring with a tremor to the "vast combination" of 9,000 members, implied that it was. A considerable body of opinion, including some men of a conservative cast of mind,[10] would have subscribed to the view, expressed by Brandeis in a dissent in 1921, that the real motive of employers in seeking injunctions and initiating actions for damages under the Sherman Act was "not ordinarily to prevent property from being injured nor to protect the owner in its use, but to endow property with active, militant power, which would make it dominant over men. In other words, that, under the guise of protecting property rights, the employer was seeking sovereign power." Many disinterested men, "solicitous only for the public welfare," believed, as Brandeis went on to say, "that the law of property was not appropriate for dealing with the forces beneath social unrest; that in this vast struggle it was unwise to throw the power of the State on one side or the other according to principles deduced from that law; that the problem of control and conduct of industry demanded a solution of its own; and that, pending the ascertainment of new principles to govern industry, it was wiser for the State not to interfere in industrial struggles by the issuance of an injunction." [11]

The issue, signaled by the phrase "Government by Injunction," was featured in a number of political campaigns.[12] In that of 1912, promises were made which Congress was prevailed upon to redeem by the Clayton Act of 1914.[13] Section 6 of that statute began with a ringing declaration: "That the labor of a human being is not a commodity or article of commerce." It legalized the existence of labor organizations, and went on to say that nothing in the Sherman Act should be construed to "restrain individual members of such organizations from lawfully carrying out the legitimate objects thereof." Section 20 of the Act provided that no injunctions should issue "in a case between an employer and employees . . . unless necessary to prevent irreparable injury to property . . . ." Moreover, no "such" injunctions were to issue prohibiting anyone "from terminating any relation of employment, or from ceasing to perform any work or labor, or from recommending, advising, or persuading others by peaceful means so to do [striking]; or from attending at any place where any such person or persons may lawfully be, for the purpose of peacefully obtaining or communicating information [picketing] . . . or from ceasing to patronize or to employ any party to such dispute, or from recommending, advising, or persuading others by peaceful and lawful means so to do [boycotting] . . . or from doing any act or thing which might lawfully be done in the absence of such dispute by any party thereto; nor shall any of the acts specified in this paragraph be considered or held to be violations of any law of the United States."

Upon passage of this legislation, Samuel Gompers, founder and president of the American Federation of Labor, was pleased to say: "This declaration is the industrial magna charta upon which the working people will rear their construction of industrial freedom." And: "This declaration removes all possibility of interpreting trust legislation to apply to organizations of the workers, and their legitimate associated activities." [14] These famous remarks have come down in history as a classic expression of feckless optimism. The Clayton Act appears to have been the product of mixed Congressional motives, which it reflected in its many ambiguities. It was studded, at decisive places, with words such as "lawful" and "legitimate," and it gave them no explicit new content. Other crucial terms were also lacking in precision, though Section 16, which was to prove a boon to employers, provided with all due clarity that private parties could — as they had not previously been authorized to do — seek injunctive relief under the Sherman Act. Left with this much leeway, a sympathetic court might actually have found labor's Magna Charta in the Clayton Act. An unsympathetic one was free not to do so — and that without overtaxing its ingenuity. The majority on the Supreme Court of these years was decidedly unsympathetic and adequately ingenious.

The ineffectiveness of the Clayton Act was conclusively established by *Duplex Printing Press Co. v. Deering.*[15] In connection with an otherwise unsuccessful strike against the Duplex Company in Michigan — that company being one of only four concerns manufacturing printing presses in the United States, of which the other three had been organized — the union and its affiliates in New York refused to work on the installation of presses made by Duplex in Michigan and delivered in New York. This refusal the Court declared unlawful, calling it a secondary boycott. An injunction, the Court held, could issue despite the Clayton Act, for that statute merely legalized what had been considered legal before it was passed, and, in any event, it did not apply to a boycott of an employer by others than his own employees.

Soon after the *Duplex* decision, the Court held also that mass picketing of a struck plant could be enjoined and that the injunction should not be restricted only to picketing "in a threatening or unlawful manner." For "the sinister name of picketing" itself implied intimidation and hence illegality. However, the Court, speaking through Chief Justice Taft, did in this case recognize that an entire union, rather than merely the employees of the struck plant, had a legitimate interest in the controversy; and it indicated that the union — but the emphasis was on the *local* union, as distinguished from the national one involved in the *Duplex* case — might engage in reasonable "persuasion" in order to try to make the strike effective.[16] A few years later, in *Bedford Cut Stone Co. v. Stonecutter's Association,*[17] the Court held that a concerted refusal by all members of a small national union to work on stone produced by firms which refused to bargain with the union was an illegal conspiracy to restrain trade in violation of the Sherman Act. Again nothing was found in the Clayton Act to prevent issuance of an injunction.

In summary of this experience, Frankfurter and Greene concluded, in their comprehensive and justly influential study, *The Labor Injunction,* published in 1930: "Surely . . . the position of labor before the law has been altered, if at all, imperceptibly. Common law doctrines of conspiracy and restraint of trade still hold sway; activities widely cherished as indispensible assertions of trade union life continue to be outlawed. Statutes designed to contract equity jurisdiction have been construed merely as endorsements of the jurisdiction theretofore exercised. Even the procedural incidents of the equity process which make it so dangerous a device in labor controversies have not been systematically adjusted to modern needs; safeguards are all too much dependent on the wisdom and rigorous fair dealing of occasional judges . . . ."[18]

Agitation continued, and finally, in 1932, it culminated in the enactment by Congress of the Norris–La Guardia Anti-Injunction Act.[19] This statute was a very different legislative article from the Clayton Act. In crisp terms, it defined a broadened class of industrial combatants whose self-interest entitled them to engage in activities frowned upon at common law and under the Sherman Act. It then described such activities and generally forbade the courts to interfere by injunction except as fraud or violence might be involved.

Although the Norris–La Guardia Act was framed as an exercise of the settled power of Congress to regulate the jurisdiction of the federal courts, there was some doubt about its constitutionality, since the Supreme Court had in 1921, in *Truax v. Corrigan*,[20] held it to be a violation of the Due Process Clause for a state to forbid its courts to issue injunctions against nonviolent picketing and similar union tactics. But in 1937 a decision by Brandeis stilled doubts about the Norris–La Guardia Act, though that statute was not directly involved.[21] In that same year of grace and fast-moving change, the Court, speaking through Chief Justice Hughes, also upheld the constitutionality of the Wagner National Labor Relations Act of 1935.[22]

When the Congress took a firm hold on the problem of industrial relations, the Court thus acquiesced. In 1940, the Court did more. It executed a somewhat distracted retreat from the old Sherman Act precedents, abandoning them in considerable disorder. Without expressly overruling any cases, the Court held — or so it seemed — that the Sherman Act was directed chiefly at commercial practices tending toward monopolization and that it did not authorize the judiciary to deal with incidental obstructions of commerce resulting from industrial strife.[23] A few months later, taking another course, and using the Norris–La Guardia Act for cover, the Court continued its withdrawal from the forward positions of old.[24] The Court's new and present position is that organized labor is to all intents and purposes quite immune from Sherman Act restraints, so long as it behaves in furtherance of its own interests and does not concert with employers toward ends the latter are forbidden to pursue alone.[25] Of course, labor may still be visited with injunctions — in state courts;[26] perhaps, as the inconclusive flurry involving the Truman Administration and John L. Lewis in 1946–47 may indicate, at the instance, under certain conditions, of the federal Executive, despite the Norris–La Guardia Act;[27] and pursuant to some provisions of the Taft-Hartley Act.[28] But the reign supreme, such as it was, of the Court as discretionary umpire of labor relations is happily over.

Such, in sketchy outline, is an exciting chapter in American social, economic, political, and legal history. It forms the setting of Brandeis' unpublished opinion in *United Mine Workers v. Coronado Co.*, called the *First Coronado* case,[29] which is here printed. The *Coronado* case was the aftermath of a lockout, followed by a bitter and bloody struggle in the mining country of western Arkansas. In order to cut costs, the management, breaking a contract with the union, closed one of its mines, fortified it in frank preparation for battle, and reopened with imported nonunion labor as an "open shop." The plan was to do the same in other mines. Fighting followed as expected. Eventually one and then another of the company's mines were destroyed by union crowds. The company sued the national and local unions for triple damages under the Sherman Act, charging that its mines had been destroyed in pursuance of a conspiracy to restrain interstate commerce.

There was a jury trial, marked, when the jury appeared unable to agree and came back to advise with the court, by strong, and scarcely proper, instructions from the judge, amounting to a direction of a verdict for the company.[30] Such a verdict was then returned. It was affirmed with a minor modification by the Circuit Court of Appeals, one judge dissenting.[31] The case was argued in the Supreme Court on October 15, 1920. At this stage, the union was able to secure the services of Charles Evans Hughes.[32] "Since I've been on the Bench," Brandeis remarked the summer after *First Coronado* had been decided, "only one labor case has been well argued — Hughes' argument on the first hearing of the *Coronado* case." [33] Nevertheless, the decision at conference went against the union, and within a few months Brandeis had prepared the dissent printed below.

Brandeis described in some detail the events which took place "in the mountains of western Arkansas, near the village of Frogtown." He conceded, of course, that the destruction of the mines had been illegal, indeed criminal, action. And he conceded that labor unions, though they were unincorporated associations, should be suable, just as corporations and other juridical entities were suable. This, it should be noted, had not been held before. Earlier suits had named union officers and other individuals as defendants. But, Brandeis went on, whatever else might be said about the union's and the workers' actions, they could not be deemed a conspiracy in restraint of interstate commerce. Brandeis quoted from *Hammer v. Dagenhart*,[34] where, over his own and Holmes' dissents, the Court had held that Congress could not control the employment of child labor in manufacturing, because manufacturing was not interstate commerce. By the same token, he said, mining of coal was not interstate commerce, and could not be protected by the Sherman Act. Such restraint as had resulted from the workers' violent behavior was of intrastate commerce. To be sure, the purpose of the union was to organize all coal miners in the United States, and to this end to seek to prevent the operation of any nonunion mine. But this purpose and the action taken to carry it out would even if successful still restrain only the mining of coal — an intrastate activity. Interstate trade would be restrained only if the purpose of the union and the effect of its action were to monopolize or control the production, distribution, or price of coal moving in interstate commerce. Nothing of the sort was shown in this case. A boycott case, such as *Loewe v. Lawlor*, was quite different. Would anyone contend that if the Federal Council of the Churches of Christ combined with citizens of various states to prevent the employment of child labor in the manufacture of goods intended for sale in interstate commerce, an action would lie under the Sherman Act?

SUPREME COURT OF THE UNITED STATES

No. 31. — October Term, 1921.

| United Mine Workers of America et al., Plaintiffs in Error, vs. Coronado Coal Company et al. | In Error to the United States Circuit Court of Appeals for the Eighth Circuit. |

[   ]

Mr. Justice BRANDEIS, dissenting.

That the acts testified to constitute wanton destruction of plaintiff's property for which the perpetrators are liable, under the law of Arkansas, civilly as well as criminally, is undoubted. That labor unions, if guilty of participating in such acts cannot escape liability on the ground that they are unincorporated, I agree. That there was evidence on which the jury would have been justified in holding that at least District 21, as well as the local unions, did so participate, I also agree. But the wrongs committed were violations of the law of Arkansas, not of any federal law. The laws of that state offer not only full compensation, but punitive damages. The plaintiffs did not, however, seek the aid of the courts of Arkansas. Nor do they seek the aid of the federal court to enforce the laws of

Arkansas; which, in so far as there is diversity of citizenship, they might have done. Instead they entered the federal court with a suit under the Sherman Law, claiming that the injury suffered was inflicted in pursuance of a conspiracy to restrain interstate commerce. To support that claim there is, in my opinion, not a shred of legal evidence. As the Court said in *Hammer v. Dagenhart*, 247 U.S. 251, 272 [1918]: "The making of goods and the mining of coal are not commerce, nor does the fact that these things are to be afterwards shipped or used in interstate commerce, make their production a part thereof." The wrongdoers conspired to prevent the operation of the plaintiffs' mines and in large part destroyed them. But their conspiracy was not to restrain interstate commerce.

In the mountains of western Arkansas, near the village of Frogtown, were nine small coal mines which Bache and Denman managed as a business unit. Arkansas was "organized territory." That is, all the mines there were operated as union shops under agreements with the United Mine Workers of America. See *Hitchman Coal & Coke Co. v. Mitchell*, 245 U.S. 229, 236–37 [1917]. The Bache-Denman mines had been so operated since 1903, when the first of them was opened. In 1913 (or before) the business became unprofitable. Bache and Denman were led to believe that this was due to union exactions and restrictions. The superintendent proposed operation on the open shop basis; but he advised that the change would involve "a bitter fight" and that "the success of this plan means the utter annihilation of the union so far as our mines are concerned . . . ."

Recent occurrences in Colorado, known as the Ludlow Massacre, made clear how bitter the fight might become. But Bache and Denman decided upon the course proposed and made appropriate preparations. It was arranged to begin with one mine. No. 4 was selected. That mine was owned by an Arkansas corporation. It had made a contract with the union to employ only union labor; and the contract had some months to run. To avoid that contract the mine was leased to a new corporation. The lessee corporation was organized under the laws of West Virginia so that, in case of need, the Federal Court might be applied to for an injunction. Then the mine was shut down and all employees were discharged. Soon guards arrived, men furnished by a private detective agency, experienced and well supplied with rifles and ammunition. All removable inflammable material around the mine was taken away. A wire rope was stretched around the enclosure. Notices were posted warning all but employees off the premises. Electric lights were placed at intervals with reflectors throwing the light outside of the enclosure. As soon as the entrenchment had been completed, non-union men, from neighboring States, were brought in at intervals, in small numbers. On Saturday, April 4, 1914, operations at the mine were resumed but as an "open shop."

On the Monday following came what the defendants call a demonstration and the plaintiffs a riot. Union miners and other citizens from all the surrounding villages gathered at a schoolhouse near No. 4. The band played. Speeches of protest were made. The excited crowd pressed forward, attacked the guards and the non-union employees and beat them up badly. Unconditional surrender followed; and on the tipple was hoisted a banner with the legend: "This is a union man's country." Two days later an injunction was secured. Additional guards furnished by the detective agency arrived — increasing the number to sixty or seventy — all armed with long-distance rifles and supplied with many thousand rounds of ammunition. Throughout the next three months conditions grew ever more menacing. There were evictions from company houses to provide shelter for the new employees, and the dispossessed families settled in tent colonies near by. Finally on July 17 came what is called "the battle." Armed men, undoubtedly unionists, surrounded Mine No. 4 and opened fire upon the guards and the employees. These soon beat a hasty retreat. Some of them were caught and brutally shot. Fire was set to the tipple and other buildings and was fed by all procurable furniture, furnishings and supplies belonging to the company. Then the process of wanton destruction, in part by dynamiting, was extended to other Bache-Denman mines. One of these mines had not been run at all for more than two years. And at others there had not yet even been an attempt to operate on the open-shop basis.

Throughout these trying months the operators acted strictly within their legal rights. The unionists, on the other hand, had been lawless aggressors, violating grievously the laws of Arkansas and also in many respects the injunction issued by the Federal Court. No fact urged by them in extenuation would, if established,

afford legal justification for any of the injury inflicted. The unionists say that the Bache-Denman interests were bound by contract
to continue to operate their mines on the union shop basis until
after July 31 and, in order to evade their contract, shut down Mine
No. 4 and leased it to a foreign corporation. But the lease was a
valid instrument, and the fact that the motive for making it to a
foreign corporation was to enable the lessee to seek an injunction
in the Federal Court, did not invalidate the lease or defeat the
jurisdiction of that court. *McDonald v. Smalley*, 1 Pet. 620, 624
[1828]. The unionists say further that the operators were determined to lower their standard of living by destroying their union
and forcing a reduction of wages, longer hours of work and more
burdensome working conditions; and that the guards had insulted
women and children, had procured illegal arrest of unionists and
had generally terrorized the community. Obviously such acts, no
matter how aggravated, would afford no excuse in law for malicious destruction of plaintiffs' business and mining properties.
Nor is there any basis for a claim that the destruction was wrought
in the exercise of any right of self-defense recognized by the law.

To destroy a business is illegal. It is not illegal to lower the
standard of working men's living or to destroy the union which
aims to raise or maintain such a standard. A business is property;
the law protects it; and a statute which denies to its owner the
right to protection by injunction against striking employees violates the Fourteenth Amendment, although there is no threat of
violence or of injury to tangible property. *Truax v. Corrigan*, decided December 19, 1921 [257 U.S. 312]. A man's standard of living is not property; and the law does not protect by injunction or
otherwise. Statutes designed to maintain or raise the workingman's standard of living, by affording labor unions protection
against employers discriminating against union members, are unconstitutional. *Adair v. United States*, 208 U.S. 161 [1908]; *Coppage v. Kansas*, 236 U.S. 1 [1915]. Even the right to self-help by
means of a strike against such discrimination has been denied to
the unions in some jurisdictions. And, although the employment
be at will, persons may not be solicited to join the union while so
employed, if they have agreed as a condition of employment not
to join the union. *Hitchman Coal & Coke Co. v. Mitchell, supra.* Nor may a union protect itself by a refusal of its members

to work upon the product of an employer who is attacking the union, if the necessary effect of such refusal is to injure a third person. *Duplex Printing Co. v. Deering*, 254 U.S. 443 [1921]. Such being the law every citizen should obey it; and the court must enforce it. It may be morally wrong to use legal processes, great financial resources and a high intelligence to lower miners' standards of living; but so long as the law sanctions it, economic force may not be repelled by physical force. If union members deem the law unwise or unjust, they may, like other American citizens, exercise their political right to change it by new legislation, and, if need be, by constitutional amendment. But no government may tolerate willful disobedience to its laws.

The cause of action here sued on, however, is not for malicious trespass upon property or persons. The suit is brought under Section 7 of the Anti-trust Law for injury done to the plaintiffs' business and property by reason of a combination or conspiracy to restrain interstate commerce. Of the four essential elements in the cause of action alleged, three only are supported by evidence. There are shown injury to plaintiffs, combination by defendants, and unreasonable restraint of trade; but the restraint proved is of intrastate trade. The only direct restraint here applied was upon the employment and treatment of labor engaged in the production of coal. This is shown by the declarations testified to: "We are going to clean those scabs out of work here . . . . We are not going to let them dig coal." The miner injured in mining coal even for interstate transportation is not entitled to the compensation provided by the federal law for those injured in interstate commerce. *Delaware, Lackawanna & Western R.R. Co. v. Yurkonis*, 238 U.S. 439, 444–45 [1915]. The child may not be protected by Congress from being employed in manufacturing articles intended for sale in interstate commerce. *Hammer v. Dagenhart*, *supra*, cited with approval in *Bailey v. Drexel Furniture Co.*, decided May 15, 1922 [*Child Labor Tax Case*, 259 U.S. 20]. And the reason for the decision both of the *Employers' Liability* case and of the *Child Labor* case is that production of an article has only an indirect relation to interstate commerce, even if intended for interstate shipment when produced. Compare *Blumenstock Bros. v. Curtis Publishing Co.*, 252 U.S. 436, 443 [1920]. In the *Dagenhart* case Congress attempted, in effect, to force employers to accede to certain standards in working conditions and employment — just as this union of coal miners did. It was argued there that such action was within the power of Congress, because child-made goods competed in interstate commerce with the products of other States made under better conditions. But this Court held that the connection between restraining these employers from using child labor and interstate commerce in the goods was too remote to bring the law within the power of Congress. Here it is argued that this conspiracy to prevent the use of non-union labor in mining coal and to tie up mines which did use it, was for the direct purpose of lessening the competition in interstate markets with coal mined by union men. But the purpose and effect alleged are as indirect here as in the *Dagenhart* case. Its purpose and its natural and reasonable effect were solely to prevent coal mining with non-union labor. Its relation to interstate commerce lacked that direct connection which this Court has held to be necessary to bring the transaction within the scope of federal concern.[1] Compare *Crescent Cotton Oil Co. v. Mississippi*, decided November 14, 1921 [257 U.S. 129]; *Federal Baseball Club v. National League*, decided May 29, 1922 [259 U.S. 200].

The contention of the mine owners is not advanced by showing that the destruction of their mines was pursuant to a general policy of the United Mine Workers of America to organize all the coal miners in the United States and to this end to prevent the operation of any mine by non-union labor. The activities of the union, even if extended into each of the twenty-eight States in which coal is mined and if successful in each, would, although the method continued to be illegal, still be only a restraint of intrastate trade

---

[1] As evidence of the fact that the combination was directed against the interstate shipment of the coal rather than the mere mining of it, the plaintiffs point to the fact that on some occasions disorder followed not the opening of the mine but the hoisting of the coal and that some coal in cars was destroyed. It may be answered that for one on the outside the hoisting is the conclusive evidence, and about the only evidence, that mining is going forward rather than mere repair, maintenance or preparation. In regard to the cars destroyed, since they were at the tipple, it is obvious that they were destroyed when that was burned and that no peculiar significance is to be attached to that particular bit of destruction more than to any other. The Mammouth Vein Mine No. 1, the buildings of which were burned July 17, 1914, had not been operated since March 28. The Dallas mine, to which fire was set July 19, 1914, had not been operated for two years. The Coronado mine, the buildings of which were destroyed July 20, 1914, had not been operated since April 18, 1914.

in mining labor. For the intent and effect of the combination is solely to secure control of the working conditions in the purely intrastate operation of mining coal. The restraint could become one of interstate trade only if the purpose and effect were to monopolize or control the production, distribution or price of the article which moves in interstate commerce or to prevent its sale; and of such a purpose or effect there is not even a suggestion in this case. The extent of the activities of the United Mine Workers is legally immaterial, because the sole purpose and only direct effect of the combination, whether confined to one State or extended to many, is merely to regulate the conditions under which, in the several States, the employment of labor in the mining of coal shall proceed.

This case is wholly unlike *United States v. Workingmen's Amalgamated Council of New Orleans*, 54 Fed. 994 [1893]; 57 Fed. 85 [1893]; and *In re Debs*, 158 U.S. 564, [1895], where the conspiracies were to restrain the actual movement of goods already in interstate commerce. It differs from *Loewe v. Lawlor*, 208 U.S. 274 [1908], where the immediate intention and effect of the conspiracy was to prevent the buying and selling of goods in interstate commerce and where its effect upon conditions of employment was a secondary purpose and indirect effect. It resembles, in the matter here under consideration, *Hopkins v. United States*, 171 U.S. 578 [1898], where the rules which should govern this case are fully discussed and clearly stated. The indirect burden which this conspiracy could conceivably impose upon interstate commerce is comparable rather to that which results from the taxes imposed by States upon instruments of interstate commerce within their border, *Atlantic & Pacific Telegraph Co. v. Philadelphia*, 190 U.S. 160 [1903]; *St. Louis Southwestern Ry. Co. v. Arkansas*, 235 U.S. 350 [1914]; or taxes upon occupations which have only an indirect relation to interstate commerce, *Ficklen v. Shelby County*, 145 U.S. 1 [1892]; *Williams v. Fears*, 179 U.S. 270 [1900]; *Ware & Leland v. Mobile County*, 209 U.S. 405 [1908]. The sole purpose and the proximate result of the conspiracy here under review was to prevent employment of non-union men and incidentally production. It was not to interfere with commerce. Under the decisions of this Court it is such purpose or proximate result which determines the scope of congressional action.

The mere extent of the activities of the United Mine Workers of America is legally immaterial. Suppose manufacturers in the States which prohibit child labor should, through the National Child Labor Committee or the Federal Council of the Churches of Christ of America, combine with citizens of the States which permit child labor, to prevent in the latter States the manufacture with child labor of goods intended for sale in interstate commerce, would anyone contend that such a combination would be in restraint of interstate trade within the meaning of the Sherman Law? The fact that the means adopted in preventing coal mining with non-union men were, in this case, illegal and criminal under the law of Arkansas, does not differentiate the case from the one suggested. That fact shows that the restraint was unreasonable, that is, was not permissible interference with the plaintiffs' business; but it has no tendency to show that it was a restraint of interstate trade. The specific conspiracy shown was one to violate the laws of Arkansas; and for that and that alone the conspirators were, under the laws of the State, punishable criminally and liable civilly in its courts.

I am, therefore, unable to find in this record any legal evidence to sustain a finding of restraint of interstate commerce. I cannot believe that the jury would have found any, had it not been coerced by the instruction of the presiding judge. The instruction complained of was in effect a direction to bring in a verdict for the plaintiffs. The character of this instruction would alone entitle defendants to a reversal as is shown by Circuit Judge Hook in his dissenting opinion, 258 Fed. 829, 847 [1919].

Preparation of this opinion was started in the Brandeis office as soon as a decision had been reached at conference and before any majority opinion was circulated. Brandeis' law clerk at this time was Dean Acheson, and his memory of the case is vivid. "It is my very clear recollection," Mr. Acheson has written, "that no majority opinion was circulated during the 1920 term, but it is my recollection that the case was decided for affirmance and that we went to work immediately upon knowing this."[35] There is preserved in the file an incomplete law clerk's memorandum prepared in the form of a dissent and dated January 1921. (The lapse of time from the date of the argument is doubt-

less explained by the fact that work on the *Coronado* case had to be
interrupted by both the law clerk and the Justice in order to finish
Brandeis' dissent in *Duplex Printing Press Co. v. Deering*. That case
had been argued at the previous term and was decided on January 3,
1921.) Mr. Acheson has explained the origin of this memorandum:

> Generally I came down to the Justice's office on Sunday morning after a
> conference. [Saturday was the Court's conference day.] The Chief Justice's
> messenger brought around the assignment slips fairly early. These were
> printed slips bearing the names of the Justices with blank spaces to the right
> of them, into which the Chief Justice wrote the numbers of the cases which
> he had assigned to Justice Brandeis for opinion. The same was done with each
> of the Justices. Brandeis would instruct me to begin work on certain of the
> numbered cases and would say that others he would start on. At this time we
> rarely had much discussion about the cases or the opinion, although he would
> answer any questions or discuss any point which I wished to discuss with him.
> Usually, however, I knew very little about the case, except that it was to be
> affirmed, reversed or dismissed, and I would go to work on the record and
> briefs to find out about it. He did not look with much favor on his law clerks
> spending time in the court room listening to arguments, although on a case of
> outstanding interest he was broadminded on this.
>
> My work usually was cast in the form of a draft opinion, since he found this
> the most helpful way to get it. When he finished his preliminary work on
> opinions which he took, he would give me the material to check, criticize, or
> rewrite, as I thought best. In those days he wanted a good deal more rigorous
> criticism from his law clerk than I think he regarded as necessary later in his
> judicial career. When I finished my work on a draft which had been assigned
> to me or got as far as I could, I gave it to him. As you know from the files, he
> tore it to pieces, sometimes using a little, sometimes none.

. . . .

> My recollection is pretty clear that, immediately upon the decision of the
> [*Coronado*] case in conference, the Justice informed me that he would dissent
> and told me to get to work on a draft. I believe that the draft that you enclose
> was done without much consultation with the Justice. It does not surprise me
> that it is uncompleted. He quite often took from me a case on which I was
> working when he had completed work which he was doing and wanted me
> to concentrate on that. He would then go ahead in his own way on the papers
> which he had taken from me. This may well have been the reason here, and
> I am inclined to think that it probably was, because, as you point out, some
> of the phrases from my work appear in his drafts.[36]

Like Brandeis' unpublished opinion, the Acheson memorandum in
the form of a draft dissent in *Coronado* dwells on the violent drama of
the facts. But the rhythm of the young Acheson's statement differs
markedly from that of Brandeis'. Acheson tended to characterize the
situation swiftly and sharply. "The facts," he said, "present a picture of
a primitive struggle clothed in the forms of industry." The management
having decided to discontinue relations with the union, "There was no

conference with the men, nor was there any process of law to determine the justice of this proposal to sacrifice standards of work and living in order that operation might continue at a profit . . . . There is a refreshing absence of hypocrisy about this matter; both sides understood clearly that the conflict between cheap labor and union standards was to be settled on the basis of power — physical, economic and legal — with no interference from principle. Both sides armed . . . ." Then: "Conditions became like those in a country occupied by a small invading force. . . . Engagements took place between small parties of the invading force and the inhabitants. The enemy was boycotted in the towns; it was accused of assaulting women." Mr. Acheson recalls that at the home of William Hard, now an editor of *Reader's Digest*, then a journalist living in Washington, he had heard groups of miners from Harlan County and from Pennsylvania refer to the State Police as "Cossacks." [37] The allusion may be read between the lines of the memorandum.

These incisive formulations contrast with Brandeis' marshaling of details in a tense but deliberate procession to the climax of "unconditional surrender," of the banner on the tipple with the legend, "This is a union man's country," and of "the battle" of July 17. Brandeis no doubt needed the detail to drive home the implication that here was the bitter fruit of the Court's unwise stewardship in labor matters; here were the consequences of stripping the laboring man, in case after case, of the right peaceably to apply economic pressure. Brandeis wanted a picture in full color. But it is also true that he generally mistrusted the effort to convey facts by summary characterization, and that the naturalistic factual narrative, shunning the appearance of artistry, was an enduring feature of his judicial style. Scrupulously respecting the integrity of each fact and extending to each the equal protection of full statement, Brandeis' style could lead to an occasional cluttered opinion.[38] But it could also, as here and in other instances, result in its own kind of powerful impact.[39]

The grounds upon which the Acheson memorandum would have placed a decision in favor of the union differed substantially from those ultimately adopted by Brandeis in his opinion. Acheson conceded that the object of the union's action was to "prevent competition in the standards of living" of the employees of coal mine operators throughout the nation. He distinguished this purpose from one "to limit competition in the price and quality of coal" sold by such operators. To insist upon minimum wage standards was simply to deprive some operators of a subsidy and to shift competition from "wages to quality," thus allowing free play to "a genuine Selection of the Fittest, unhandicapped by any bounty" (quoting from Sidney and Beatrice Webb, *Industrial Democracy* [1902], p. 790). The Sherman Act forbade restraints on trade in the articles of commerce, and when the union by a boycott imposed such a restraint, as in *Loewe v. Lawlor*, the Act applied. "But the conditions of life and the labor of a human being are not articles of commerce. This is not a matter of law or of fact, but of the culture of a people. It seems to me to be one of the fundamental conceptions of our political philosophy and not to rest for its truth either on the Civil War or the Clayton Act."

In his first complete draft of a dissent, Brandeis made an argument similar in many respects to the one his law clerk had presented. This draft, done in March 1921, ended with the following paragraphs:

Circumstances are, of course, conceivable under which trade might be restrained by forcibly preventing production; just as it might be restrained by an agreement to limit production. But unless the circumstances are such that an agreement not to operate the mines except by union labor, or not to operate them at all, would be, in legal contemplation, a restraint of interstate commerce, the prevention of such operation by force, however otherwise unlawful, would not be such a restraint. Obviously an agreement to unionize or shut down one or all of these little mines would not have been a restraint of interstate commerce. The production of coal in the United States in that year [Brandeis' figures are for 1913] was 569,960,219 tons, of which 478,435,297 tons were, like the plaintiffs' product, bituminous. This production of bituminous coal was distributed over twenty-nine States,° and only 2,234,107 tons — less than one-half of one per cent. — were mined in Arkansas.† Not only was the total Arkansas production thus a very small factor in the coal sold in interstate commerce, but the plaintiff mines produced only a small fraction of that mined within the State. There was no attempt to show that shutting off the supply of coal from plaintiffs did or by any possibility could appreciably affect the supply in any interstate market. Obviously there was not such a lessening of competition in interstate commerce as the Anti-trust Law condemns. *United States v. United States Steel Corporation*, 251 U.S. 417 [1920]; *United States v. United Shoe Machinery Co.*, 247 U.S. 32 [1918].

Plaintiffs' claim is rested, however, upon a much broader basis. It is said that the destruction wrought here was pursuant to a general plan of the United Mine Workers of America to protect union-mined coal from the competition of non-union mined coal. These facts, if established by competent evidence, would not constitute a restraint of interstate commerce. A coal mine is not an instrument of commerce; nor is coal. To forcibly prevent its production; to wantonly destroy it when produced, is an illegal interference with property; but it is not a restraint of commerce forbidden by the Anti-trust

° United States Geological Survey, Mineral Resources of the U.S. Part II, Coal, 1917. Part A, p. 601. The bill enumerates only 23 States.

† The production in States nearby was much larger. Kansas, 7,202,210; Missouri, 4,318,125; Oklahoma, 4,165,770; Colorado, 9,232,510; Illinois, 61,618,744; Texas, 2,429,144; New Mexico, 3,708,806. The production of Pennsylvania was 173,781,217 tons; of West Virginia, 71,254,136; of Ohio, 36,200,527.

Law. For it affects commerce only indirectly; and it is direct restraints alone which the Anti-trust Law forbids. In ordinary times when supply readily overtakes demand, and sales are made on small profits, mine owners operating at high costs could not hold their trade long in competitive markets as against others who have a low operating cost. There is a Gresham law in industry as well as in finance. Unions, like employers, must reckon with it. When unions undertake to secure higher wages, shorter hours and better working conditions — which under most circumstances involve higher operating costs — they necessarily assume the burden of reasonably equalizing operating costs in the several fields. To deny to unions the right to effect such equalization is to deny them the right to exist. Union leaders contend that in many industries — and specifically in coal mining — such equalization can be effected only by unionizing the competing plants. To this end the national (or so-called international) unions send their organizers into the non-union territory. There they seek to convert the non-unionists and induce them to join the union. Having done so the national unions cause employees to make demands for higher wages, and other union conditions; and induce, if need be, strikes to enforce compliance with such demands. Thus the national unions customarily strive to prevent low paid non-union labor from competing with highly paid union labor; and in so doing prevent the production of non-union made goods from competing with union-made goods. And the competition thus affected involves in most cases to some extent interstate commerce. Union leaders say that this course is indispensable to the life or growth of a union; so long as the incidents of the relation of employer and employee are determined by a struggle of contending parties, while employers are free to make wages low, and to oppose organization and collective bargaining. The court must know judicially that this is true. Does the Anti-trust Law deny to labor unions these means of maintaining higher standards of living achieved in certain localities and of extending the area in which they shall prevail? Such process of organization and strikes may, of course, although conducted peaceably, violate some law. That is illustrated by *Hitchman Coal & Coke Co. v. Mitchell*, 245 U.S. 229. But the question here is whether the process violates the Anti-trust Law. On the decision of that question the circumstance that defendant has in the course of suppressing the competition violated other laws has no legal bearing.

Brandeis made a few formal revisions in this draft, and received a clean print of it on March 12. Another revision followed, and this time it was one of substance. Brandeis now pitched his argument strictly on the ground that mining was not interstate commerce, and that mining alone was what the union had restrained. Though he now rejected its line of reasoning, Brandeis did draw, for a striking passage of his own appearing in the finished opinion, on this language from the Acheson memorandum: "There is no legal right to live, much less to a standard of living. There is a legal right to use or disuse one's property as one chooses, to employ whom one likes at whatever wages offer a more attractive alternative to starvation, and to protect one's property by repelling force with force."

Of course, Acheson's analysis and Brandeis' own in the early draft just quoted are the realistic and satisfying ones, and carry a conviction that is lacking in Brandeis' ultimate opinion. It was this sort of analysis that was destined in the end to prevail, both with Congress and with the Court of a later day. And there cannot be much doubt that Brandeis, like his eloquent law clerk, believed it both unwise and offensive to deal with man's labor as a commodity of commerce in terms of the Sherman Act. Brandeis thought that manufacturing and mining *were* interstate commerce in the sense of being subject to appropriate federal regulation, and he knew, surely, that only as a verbal exercise could the purpose and effect of the battle in *Coronado* be distinguished from the purpose and effect of the boycott in *Loewe v. Lawlor.* The tenor of Brandeis' dissents in *Duplex Printing Press Co. v. Deering, Truax v. Corrigan,* and *Bedford Cut Stone Co. v. Stonecutter's Association* confirms this.

Brandeis believed that some control needed to be exercised over labor's methods of economic warfare. But the heart of the matter for him was that the problem was properly a legislative one. The Sherman Act provided no policy guidance; certainly none directed at labor relations. If applied, it could be used only as a carte-blanche mandate for judicial action. Yet labor problems dramatically emphasized the limitations of the judicial process as an instrument for the formulation of social policy. To these limitations Brandeis was always, and in many different contexts, very much alive.[40] Judge-made law is episodic; it is remedial and seldom prophylactic; and it can forbid, but is seldom able to permit and regulate. Brandeis expressed his viewpoint in the celebrated passage, also drafted with the aid of Dean Acheson, with which his dissent in *Duplex Printing Press Co. v. Deering* ends. It is as follows:

Because I have come to the conclusion that both the common law of a State and a statute of the United States [the Clayton Act] declare the right of industrial combatants to push their struggle to the limits of the justification of self-interest, I do not wish to be understood as attaching any constitutional or moral sanction to that right. All rights are derived from the purposes of the society in which they exist; above all rights rises duty to the community. The conditions developed in industry may be such that those engaged in it cannot continue their struggle without danger to the community. But it is not for judges to determine whether such conditions exist, nor is it their function to set the limits of permissible contest and to declare the duties which the new situation demands. This is the function of the legislature which, while limiting individual and group rights of aggression and defense, may substitute processes of justice for the more primitive method of trial by combat.[41]

The reason why Brandeis did not set forth, in his opinion in the *First Coronado* case, what were for him the decisive considerations seems plain. Brandeis must have seen a possibility of yet carrying a majority. It was in this case most important to do so. To hold the union liable was to give federal courts jurisdiction under the Sherman Act in a wider area than ever; it was to make it possible for federal courts to enjoin almost every local strike against a concern which sold its goods in interstate commerce. The courts, operating in their episodic fashion, had hurt, but had not as yet stifled, the labor movement. A decision against the union in *First Coronado* might have enabled them to do so. If such a decision was to be averted, it was exceedingly doubtful that the brethren would be moved by Sidney Webb's particular brand of Social Darwinism. Most of them were of another persuasion.[42] The only chance lay in the line of argument which Brandeis did adopt. Brandeis did not think this argument sound, but he did not — nor did he need to — pretend otherwise. He said to the Court only: This is your law, as you have laid it down elsewhere. Consistently with it you can do but one thing, and that is to hold the union not liable.

Having completed his dissent to his satisfaction, Brandeis stopped work on it at the end of March 1921. On May 19, 1921, Chief Justice White died. Perhaps because the assignment of the majority opinion had been taken by the Chief, perhaps because the Court was now evenly divided, perhaps for both reasons, the case was put over. In January of the following year, some three months after Taft, the new Chief Justice, had taken his seat, the case was restored to the docket, and it was reargued in March 1922. Then, as Brandeis recalled, it was passed from week to week at conference. At one point Taft presented his conclusions. They were that the union, though an unincorporated association, was suable; that the evidence showed an intent to restrain interstate commerce in violation of the Sherman Act; that the Act as so construed was constitutional; and that, consequently, the union was liable. At this juncture Taft had not set anything down in writing. Brandeis made known the views expressed in his dissent, although it is not clear whether he circulated the opinion.[43]

Toward the end of May 1922 Brandeis put a few finishing stylistic touches on his dissent. Evidently he expected to deliver it. But Taft, as he tried to write out the conclusions he had voiced, changed his mind. The end of the term was now approaching — the June days, which, Brandeis once said before passage of the Twentieth Amendment, "are like March 3rd in Congress."[44] Taft's opinion, holding the union not liable, was handed down on June 5, 1922, the last day of the term. It spoke for a unanimous Court. "They will take it from Taft but wouldn't take it from me," Brandeis commented later. "If it is good enough for Taft, it is good enough for us, they say — and a natural sentiment."[45]

Taft dealt at great length with the question whether the union, though an unincorporated association, was a suable entity. There was no need to do so, since the suit was to be dismissed anyway. But it is easy to see why Taft felt it politic just the same to hold that unions could be sued. Taft distrusted the unions. He felt that they were "distinctly arrayed against the Court." So he said in a letter to his brother Horace, written May 7, 1922, while he was working on the *Coronado* case, and apparently before he had changed his mind about the result. He added that "we have to hit [the unions] every little while, because they are continually violating the law and depending on threats and violence to accomplish their purpose." [46] Having changed his mind, Taft felt it necessary to do some "hitting" in an opinion which otherwise encouraged union activity.

For the rest, Taft followed the reasoning of Brandeis' dissent, holding that no intention to restrain interstate commerce had been shown, and citing *Hammer v. Dagenhart*, for the proposition that coal mining was not interstate commerce and not within the power of Congress to regulate. But, very wisely and fortunately, Taft added that possibly "certain recurring practices," though not really part of interstate commerce, but likely to obstruct, restrain or burden it, might be within the power of Congress to regulate. None, he said, were shown in this case.[47]

The decision in *First Coronado* drew a great deal of public attention. Much of the comment centered on the holding that unions were suable entities, and Taft's opinion was widely reckoned a great setback for labor. Unaware, when the Clayton Act was passed, of its defeat, labor on the whole did not now grasp the fact of its victory. There was no substantial reason to object to the imposition of social responsibility on unions by the gesture of making them subject to suit. To be sure, some minor harrassments might ensue. And some problems of the law of agency would arise.[48] But the main issue was not whether unions could be sued, but what they could be sued for.[49] Brandeis, of course, had seen this as the heart of the case, and there were those on the outside who did also.[50]

Though the *First Coronado* case had a sequel, its career was not as eventful as it would have been if the decision had gone the other way. To begin with, the holding was strictly applied to free another union from Sherman Act liability for striking a manufacturer who shipped his product in interstate commerce.[51] McKenna, Van Devanter, and Butler dissented, and this case illustrates what might have been going on had there been a different *First Coronado* decision. The *Coronado* case itself came up for the second time in 1925. A new trial was had following the first decision. At its conclusion, the District Court directed a verdict for the union on the authority of the *First Coronado* case, and the Circuit Court of Appeals affirmed. But some new evidence had been adduced. A dissident union official had testified to what everyone had known all along: namely, that the union's policy was to prevent non-union mines from underselling the product of union labor, and that one purpose of the union's fight against the Coronado Company's lockout and nonunion operation had been to carry out this policy.

Everyone had known this all along, but the evidence now showed that union officials had said it. Thus, as Taft held in another opin-ion for the Court, the union's intent "was shown to be to restrain or con-trol the supply . . . or the price" of goods moving in interstate com-merce. Hence the Sherman Act was shown to have been violated. Once more a new trial was in order.[52] Brandeis did not dissent. After all, none of the essential facts had changed. The protection of the *First Coronado* decision remained available to unions whose leaders either had no fall-ing-out among themselves, or kept their mouths shut. Moreover, acqui-escence in this decision was the price of victory in the first case, for, in terms of Taft's reasoning there, which Brandeis had himself suggested, intent did make a difference, and the holding in *Second Coronado* fol-lowed logically enough.

Actually, *Second Coronado* had more favorable than ill effects from Brandeis' point of view. It never formed the basis for any antilabor de-cisions the Court would not have reached anyway, on ample other pre-cedent. In the immediate aspect, it cost the union just $27,500, as com-pared with an earlier verdict against it of $625,000. The smaller sum is what the Coronado Company settled for rather than undergo a third trial.[53] Most important, *Second Coronado* eased the effect of the first decision as a precedent restricting the federal power to regulate com-merce, although that effect was in any event qualified, and only cumu-lative.[54]

VI

The Original Package —
A Commerce Clause Mystery

Ever since 1824, when John Marshall handed down his momentous judgment in *Gibbons v. Ogden*,[1] the Supreme Court has acted as
the guardian of a free national market. As has often been remarked, it
was essential that some central authority exercise such a guardianship.
The Court assumed it by drawing from the Commerce Clause of the
Constitution, which empowers the Congress to regulate interstate and
foreign commerce, the sweeping negative inference that the states
must keep hands off, even though Congress may not have seen fit to
legislate. But the doctrine could not be maintained as sweepingly and
as rigidly as that. It was never intended, by encouraging the free flow of
commerce, to impair the existence of the states as viable units of government. Yet that would have been the result of the successful operation of the Commerce Clause, if in promoting the rise of a national
economy it had been permitted to withdraw more and more and finally
nearly all wealth-producing activity from the regulatory and taxing
jurisdiction of the several states. The problem has been to balance the
needs of a state as against those of the nation, and not to force the sacrifice of what is vital to the one for the sake of what is trivial to the other.

Realistically, the Court is required, in case after case, to project and
judge the effect of myriad state regulations and taxes over time and
space.[2] The task is staggering in its complexity and presents a peculiar
challenge to the accustomed judicial process. The source of the challenge is the particular unsuitability in Commerce Clause cases of all
forms of shorthand, of labels and formulas, and indeed, of most generalizations. These are ever-dangerous tools for judgment. But the more
so in Commerce Clause cases, where the need is, above all, for a flexible
pragmatism, of the sort that will soon tear any formula asunder.[3] The
result of the Court's struggle to meet this challenge has been that not
only does the judicial history of the Commerce Clause show cyclical
fluctuations, such as the long look will generally reveal in the Court's
work, but that, in the shorter view, there is more confusion than in other
areas. Lines of cases emerge, have their progeny and come to arid ends;

and rules, formulas, and labels, to whose comfortable coherence judges unceasingly try to escape from the distress of disconnected judgments, have short lives, and if not abandoned, are soon gutted of meaning.

Sonneborn Bros. v. Cureton,[4] the occasion for the unpublished opinion here printed, is an instance — not the first or the last — of the Court's emergence from a conceptual corner into which it had painted itself in dealing with state fiscal measures under the Commerce Clause. Brandeis played a major role in bringing about the decision. The history of the case illustrates, as do the events relating to *Strathearn S.S. Co. v. Dillon*, the *Arizona Employers' Liability Cases*, and *United Mine Workers v. Coronado Co.*, his effectiveness as an advocate within the Court. Moreover, it was in connection with *Sonneborn* that Brandeis undertook his first comprehensive study of the problem of state taxation affecting interstate commerce. The conclusions he reached at this time appear to have dominated his future course in this field.

The specific issue of *Sonneborn Bros. v. Cureton* was bequeathed to the Court by John Marshall himself. A few years after *Gibbons v. Ogden*, the matrix Commerce Clause case, Marshall decided *Brown v. Maryland*.[5] The license tax which the Court struck down in that case fell on an import from a foreign country, and Marshall held that a Constitutional immunity from state taxation attached to such an import so long as it remained in its original package. This rule of thumb carried out the undoubted purpose of the Framers to prevent the seaboard states from enriching themselves at the expense of inland states by virtue of their position astride foreign trade routes. Marshall, however, seized the opportunity to say *obiter* that he supposed a like immunity from state taxation would apply to imports from a sister state, so long as they remained in their original, unbroken packages. "In his eagerness to save national commerce from the particularism of the states, Marshall would have unduly contracted the available resources of the states' taxing power. He overreached himself. His doctrine was formally rejected in *Woodruff v. Parham*,[6] and that, too, at a time, in 1868, when the dominant mood of the Court was nationalistic." [7] In the case last mentioned, the Court upheld a city sales tax imposed on goods brought in from another state and sold in their original packages.

Not long after Brandeis' accession, the Court, at three successive terms, again took up the original-package formula. It invoked it to strike down state taxes in *Standard Oil Co. v. Graves*,[8] a unanimous decision written by Day and handed down in April 1919; *Askren v. Continental Oil Co.*,[9] in which Day again spoke for a unanimous Court exactly a year later; and *Bowman v. Continental Oil Co.*,[10] decided in 1921 by another unanimous Court, this time speaking through Pitney. But the return trip to the original-package doctrine negotiated in these cases was interrupted by an apparent detour. In *Wagner v. City of Covington*,[11] decided by Pitney in December 1919, after *Graves* but before *Askren*, the taxpayer operated a soft-drink bottling plant in Cincinnati, across the Ohio River from the city of Covington, Kentucky. Every so often, evidently on a regular basis, he sent his trucks into Covington, where he furnished his bottled drinks — original packages, so-called — to retail merchants. For this activity, the city exacted from him a license tax as a dealer in soft drinks. The sales in question, Pitney found, took place in Covington, simultaneously with the delivery of the goods. The tax was, therefore, a valid peddler's license tax of the kind which had frequently been upheld in cases following *Woodruff v. Parham*, whether or not the sales were of original packages.[12] Aside from the hardly decisive fact that no peddlers were involved in *Graves*, *Askren*, and *Bowman*, it is difficult to see why the original-package doctrine should have failed to dictate in *Wagner v. City of Covington* the same result as in the other three cases.

Thus, enmeshed in tangled lines of cases, the law stood when *Sonneborn Bros. v. Cureton* was first argued in March 1922. Within a month, another strand was added to the tangle. This was *Texas Co. v. Brown*,[13] which had been argued some time before *Sonneborn* and came down on April 17, 1922. Pitney here, as in the *Wagner* case, declined to apply the original-package formula to a tax which fell on sales executed after the goods had been shipped into the state.

Although the decision in *Texas Co. v. Brown* was announced nearly a month after the first argument of *Sonneborn*, the result must have been agreed to and the opinion assigned to Pitney earlier, since the case had been argued a few months before, at the beginning of the term. Nevertheless, in *Sonneborn*, a majority decided to rely on the original-package doctrine in order to strike down a state tax hardly distinguishable in its consequences from the one involved in the *Brown* case. *Graves*, *Askren*, and *Bowman* were to be reaffirmed, and the writing of the Court's opinion was assigned to McReynolds. Brandeis, though he had gone along with the Court in the earlier cases, was in dissent here. He promptly went to work on the opinion which is printed below.

This tax, Brandeis said, fell impartially on intrastate as well as interstate commerce; to declare it invalid was to require the state to discriminate against its own commerce. The Court was doing so for no reason other than that the tax was deemed to violate a formal rule. If that was true, then the rule was wrong. But precedent as well as reason argued against the Court's result. *Brown v. Maryland* was inapplicable. *Woodruff v. Parham* was the governing case, and it had never been overruled; indeed, the Court had consistently approved it in subsequent cases, including *Texas Co. v. Brown*, and another, otherwise unrelated case just decided. Under *Woodruff v. Parham*, the original-package formula was irrelevant; what mattered was whether the goods had come to rest in the taxing state. Here they had done so, having been in storage before being sold. And by no test stated in any other case could this tax be held bad. To be unconstitutional it would have had to burden, obstruct, or discriminate against interstate commerce, none of which it did. Only the *Graves*, *Askren*, and *Bowman* cases might be thought to intimate a contrary result. But in those cases it was not clear whether in fact the goods had come to rest in the taxing state. *Graves*, in particular, was distinguishable on another ground as well.

SUPREME COURT OF THE UNITED STATES

No. 191. — October Term, 1921.

Sonneborn Brothers, etc., Appellants, vs. Walter A. Keeling, Attorney General, et al.*	Appeal from the District Court of the United States for the Western District of Texas.

[May 15, 1922]

Mr. Justice BRANDEIS, dissenting.

The production and refining of oils is an industry which has for many years been extensively carried on in Texas; and from taxes imposed on that industry the State derives large revenues. By Act of May 16, 1907, c. 18, sec. 9, p. 484 (now Revised Civil Statutes, Art. 7377 [1911]), it imposes upon wholesale dealers in oil refined from petroleum an occupation tax equal to two per cent. of the gross amount collected and uncollected from any and all sales made within the State. The statute, as construed and applied by the state authorities, includes as sales on which the tax is to be figured only those where the sale was made in Texas, by a dealer having an established place of business in Texas, of oil which was stored

---

* This was the name of the case when it was first argued. Subsequently, owing to a change of incumbents in the office of Texas Attorney General, Cureton was substituted as party defendant for Keeling, his predecessor. — A.M.B.

by him in Texas at the time of sale and for which no order had
been received before the oil was so stored, and which, when sold,
was delivered in Texas to the purchaser out of the dealer's store-
room. Where all the above conditions exist, the statute is construed and applied so as to include in the computation of the tax,
sales of oils refined in another State although the dealers are citizens of another State and the oil when sold and delivered was still
in the original package in which it was received from the other
State. It is, thus, a two per cent. tax on intrastate sales.

To enjoin collection of this tax Sonneborn Brothers of Maryland
and New York brought this suit in the federal court for western Texas. They are wholesale dealers in refined oils, who established a
place of business at Dallas, Texas, in 1910, and since then have
had there an office and warerooms and have also rented at San Antonio space in a public warehouse. At these places they have conducted their business, bringing into the State oils refined in some
other State and making sales of such oils, part in intrastate, part in
interstate commerce, part in original packages, part in broken
packages. The sole question presented is whether the statute imposing this occupation tax is void under the Commerce Clause in
so far as it measures the tax by intrastate sales so made in original
packages. The District Court sustained the tax. This Court holds
the statute so applied to be void as being a burden on interstate
commerce. It is held to be a burden solely because it is found to be
obnoxious to a test or rule heretofore applied. This proves, to my
mind, either that the tentative test is here wrongly applied or that
the test requires reformulation. For the facts demonstrate that the
Texas law as construed and applied is not a direct tax upon interstate commerce and that it neither obstructs, nor discriminates
against, interstate commerce. To strike down the tax will necessarily result in discrimination against intrastate commerce. Surely
the makers of the Constitution did not intend to require that.

Goods imported from foreign countries are immune from taxation
in any form as long as they remain in the original package and in
the possession and ownership of the importer. This is true not only
of a license tax upon the occupation of the importer, *Brown v.
Maryland*, 12 Wheat. 419 [1827]; but also of a tax upon the occupation of him who, like an auctioneer, aids the importer, in so far

as the tax upon him is measured by sales of the imported goods, *Cook v. Pennsylvania*, 97 U.S. 566 [1878]; and of a tax upon the goods themselves, although imposed merely by including them among the property subject to the general property tax, *Low v. Austin*, 13 Wall. 29 [1872]. The reason for this broad immunity granted to imports, as has since been made clear, is not that state taxation is repugnant to the power vested in Congress to regulate foreign and interstate commerce. It is that such taxation violates Article 1, section 10, clause 2, which prohibits States from levying any impost or duty on imports. But the introduction of goods from one State into another is not importation within the meaning of this clause of the Constitution; and the rule of *Brown v. Maryland* has no application to goods brought into one State from another. Such goods may be taxed as freely while they remain in the original package, as they may after the package is broken. The taxation must, of course, conform in either case to the Commerce Clause and to other applicable provisions of the Constitution.

In *Woodruff v. Parham*, 8 Wall. 123 [1869], the distinction between the rule governing imports from foreign countries and that governing goods from other States was first set forth. And in that case it was also first held that the taxation of goods introduced from other States, although they remain in the original package, does not violate the Commerce Clause. The form of taxes there sustained was an intrastate sales tax; and both the provisions of the tax law and the conditions under which the tax was imposed, were (as appears from the record) in essence the same as those here presented. Mobile had laid by ordinance a tax for municipal purposes of fifty cents on every $100 of gross sales of merchandise made within the city. Woodruff & Parker were commission merchants and auctioneers with a place of business there. Prior to the suit they had received goods from States other than Alabama of the value of $300,000 and had sold the goods in the original and unbroken packages to consumers and other purchasers in Mobile. The tax assessed on account of the sales was $1,500. The merchants contended, among other things, that the sales tax as applied to the goods in original packages was invalid because the tax violated the Commerce Clause. The question of the effect, if any, of the goods remaining in original packages was, thus, pointedly presented;

and, likewise, the economic effect both of recognizing and of denying to the States power to lay an intrastate sales tax applicable to
products of other States.

Counsel for Woodruff & Parker, referring to New York as the
great commercial city, said: "Is it competent to New York to demand a tax upon each and all these articles in the hands of the
merchants receiving them, for sale, in their original form, from the
States of their growth and production? Or to demand a tax upon
the gross proceeds of their sale, after the sale has been made?"
Counsel for Mobile answered: "If the exemption now contended
for were sustained, goods manufactured in the State would be subject to the tax, while goods of the same character manufactured in
another State would go free. The Constitution cannot be construed
to present such a result. When it declared that 'citizens of each
State shall be entitled to all the privileges and immunities of citizens in the several States,' it provided for harmony by securing
equality. While it might be admitted that a State cannot lay a *discriminating* tax, for the purpose of aiding its domestic manufac-
tures, it would be strange, if its taxing power was so restricted, as
to work a discrimination against its own manufacturers" [8 Wall.
at 127–28]. And the Court concluded: "The case before us is a
simple tax on sales of merchandise, imposed alike upon all sales
made in Mobile, whether the sales be made by a citizen of Alabama
or of another State, and whether the goods sold are the produce
of that State or some other. There is no attempt to discriminate in-
juriously against the products of other States or the rights of their
citizens, and the case is not, therefore, an attempt to fetter commerce among the States, or to deprive the citizens of other States
of any privilege or immunity possessed by citizens of Alabama"
[8 Wall. at 140].

It is more than half a century since *Woodruff v. Parham* was
decided. We have never questioned in any way the soundness of
the decision or of its reasoning. And we have cited the case very
often as a precedent; twice at this term of the Court. *The Texas
Company v. Brown*, decided April 17, 1922 [258 U.S. 466, 476];
Stafford v. Wallace, decided May 1, 1922 [258 U.S. 495, 526]. Re-
lying upon it, we held in *Brown v. Houston*, 114 U.S. 622 [1885],
that goods, the product of another State, may, although remaining
in the original package, be taxed under a general *ad valorem* tax;

in *Pittsburg Coal Co. v. Bates*, 156 U.S. 577 [1895], that they may
be taxed as part, or the whole, of a merchant's stock in trade; in
American Steel & Wire Co. v. Speed, 192 U.S. 500, 509, 519 [1904],
that they may be subjected to a merchants' tax computed upon the
average capital invested in the business; in *Wagner v. City of Covington*, 251 U.S. 95 [1919], that they may be subjected to an occupation tax of fixed amount. And in *Bacon v. Illinois*, 227 U.S. 504,
516 [1913], we said: "Thus, goods within the State may be made
the subject of a nondiscriminatory tax though brought from another State and held by the consignee in the original packages."
The right to tax such goods remaining in the original packages,
and to tax the business of selling them, has, thus, been sustained
under precisely the same conditions under which taxation of such
goods when no longer in the original package is sustained; that is,
where there is no discrimination against the goods or the citizens
of another State and the tax does not obstruct commerce. Because
the tax was free from these vices, the Court upheld in *Machine Co.
v. Gage*, 100 U.S. 676 [1880], and *Emert v. Missouri*, 156 U.S. 296
[1895], peddler occupation taxes, and in *Kehrer v. Stewart*, 197
U.S. 60 [1905]; *Armour Packing Co. v. Lacy*, 200 U.S. 226 [1906];
and *Singer Sewing Machine Co. v. Brickell*, 233 U.S. 304 [1914],
taxes upon the local distributing agents who had established places
of business. Because taxes under review were found to be discriminatory, they were declared void in *Welton v. Missouri*, 91 U.S.
275 [1876]; *Guy v. Baltimore*, 100 U.S. 434 [1880]; *Webber v. Virginia*, 103 U.S. 344 [1881]; *Walling v. Michigan*, 116 U.S. 446
[1886]; *I.M. Darnell & Son Co. v. City of Memphis*, 208 U.S. 113
[1908]; and *Chalker v. Birmingham & Northwestern Railway Co.*,
249 U.S. 522 [1919]. The taxes held void in *Looney v. Crane Co.*,
245 U.S. 178 [1917], and many like cases were so large as to obstruct interstate commerce.

The fact that a tax does not discriminate against interstate commerce and is not so large as to obstruct such commerce, will not, of
course, save it, if the tax imposes a direct burden upon interstate
commerce. Such a direct burden is imposed, and hence the tax is
void, in all cases where, like the general property tax in *Coe v. Er-
rol*, 116 U.S. 517 [1886], it is assessed upon goods moving in interstate commerce, or where it is imposed upon persons moving in
connection with, or who act in inaugurating or completing the

transactions in interstate commerce. Such were the taxes held void in *Robbins v. Shelby County Taxing District*, 120 U.S. 489 [1887]; *Brennan v. Titusville*, 153 U.S. 289 [1894]; *Stockard v. Morgan*, 185 U.S. 27 [1902]; *Caldwell v. North Carolina*, 187 U.S. 622 [1903]; *Norfolk and Western Railway Co. v. Sims*, 191 U.S. 441 [1903]; *Rearick v. Pennsylvania*, 203 U.S. 507 [1906]; *Dozier v. Alabama*, 218 U.S. 124 [1910]; *Crenshaw v. Arkansas*, 227 U.S. 389 [1913]; *Stewart v. Michigan*, 232 U.S. 665 [1914]; and *Browning v. City of Waycross*, 233 U.S. 16 [1917]. And because it was found that taxes on the gross receipts of interstate commerce impose a direct burden upon it, such taxes were held void in *Case of State Freight Tax*, 15 Wall. 232 [1873; carrier tonnage tax]; *Philadelphia Steamship Co. v. Pennsylvania*, 122 U.S. 326 [1887]; and *Galveston, Harrisburg & San Antonio Ry. Co. v. Texas*, 210 U.S. 217 [1908]; and because it was found that such taxes imposed a direct burden on foreign commerce, they were held void in *Crew Levick Co. v. Pennsylvania*, 245 U.S. 292, 296 [1917].

The circumstance that goods shipped into one State from another remain in the original package may be evidence bearing on the question of fact whether the movement in interstate commerce had ended before the tax was imposed; but clearly it does not establish as a matter of law that movement in interstate commerce was continuing. A sale may be wholly intrastate, although the subject-matter of the sale happens to remain in the original package. For goods shipped in interstate commerce may come to rest, although they are still in the original package; as they may still be moving in interstate commerce, although the package has been broken. The goods of Sonneborn Brothers had come to rest in Texas before the first step was taken in the transactions which resulted in the intrastate sale. There was neither an order for the goods, nor even solicitation for such an order, until after the receipt of the goods in the warerooms. When goods received in the Texas warerooms of Sonneborn Brothers under these conditions were thereafter sold and delivered within the State, the transaction was a wholly intrastate one. The fact that the goods had come to the warerooms by an interstate movement was merely a matter of history. And as the tax was assessed only on those sales for which orders were taken after the oil was received in Sonneborn Brothers' Texas warerooms and on which delivery was made from such warerooms, the burden

which a possible intrastate sales tax casts upon the interstate movement which preceded it, was clearly indirect and remote.

Every tax imposed by a State burdens to some extent all commerce within it or with it, because every tax necessarily increases,
in some degree, the expenses incident to business and lessens, in
some degree, the ability of purchasers to buy. But there is a marked
difference between the direct burden imposed upon intrastate
commerce by an intrastate sales tax and the indirect burden cast
upon the preceding interstate function of bringing into the State
goods which may thereafter become the subject of intrastate commerce. The burden which an intrastate sales tax imposes upon intrastate commerce is not only direct, and immediate, but it is inevitable. On the other hand the intrastate sales tax can affect the
preceding interstate movement of bringing the goods into the State
only indirectly and remotely. It may prove that the taxing statute
casts no burden at all upon the movement. This is true of the Texas law; for the sales tax does not affect any of the oil sold in interstate commerce, even if the sale and delivery are both in Texas;
and a sale is deemed one in interstate commerce, if the oil is delivered to the purchaser pursuant to an order taken before the oil
was physically in the warerooms or storehouse within the State. All
the oil brought in may be sold pursuant to such orders. That this
is not a fanciful suggestion is shown by the fact that three-fourths
of all oil brought in by Sonneborn Brothers during the ten-year
period was deemed interstate commerce and hence not affected
by the tax.

It is contended that *Askren v. Continental Oil Co.*, 252 U.S. 444
[1920], and *Bowman v. Continental Oil Co.*, 256 U.S. 642 [1921],
show that the Texas sales tax is void so far as applied to sales in
original packages. There are expressions in the opinions which, if
read without reference to the special facts and the contentions of
the parties, might seem to lend support to that contention. But, if
the facts involved in those cases and the contentions are borne in
mind, as they should be, it will be found that both decisions are
consistent with the view expressed above. The excise tax there
under consideration was held to be void in so far as it was assessed
upon sales in interstate commerce; and it was shown that about 5
per cent. of the sales had been made in tank cars, drums and other
original packages. All these sales in original packages may have

been sales in interstate commerce. Every one of them may have been a transaction in which an order taken before the oil reached New Mexico was filled by delivery thereafter. Under such circumstances, as was shown in *Western Oil Refining Co. v. Lipscomb*, 244 U.S. 346 [1917], sales are transactions in interstate commerce, exempt from state taxation in any form, whether the goods remain in the original packages or are delivered in broken packages.

The sole issue presented below in the *Bowman* case was whether the taxes assessed must be held wholly void, because they were void in part. This Court held that in respect to a tax measured by sales, the rule of *Ratterman v. Western Union Telegraph Co.*, 127 U.S. 411 [1888], applied; and we held the tax valid as to all intrastate sales. We held, however, as to the $50 license tax, that no such separation or division could be made, and, therefore, declared the license tax void. In the *Askren* case, the Court did say, p. 449, that as to gasoline brought into the State in tank cars, it was unable to discover any difference in plan of importation and sale between that case and *Standard Oil Co. v. Graves*, 249 U.S. 389 [1919], where the statute held void, while ostensibly an inspection act, levied fees so high as to yield a large revenue. The statute involved in the *Graves* case differs widely from the Texas law. Under the Washington statute no oil brought into the State could legally be sold until it had been inspected; and inspection could not be had without paying charges illegal because of their amount. The fee there exacted was not in any sense a sales tax. It was void, not because it imposed an intrastate sales tax on goods in original packages, but because it raised an obstruction to interstate commerce. The distinction between oil delivered on orders taken before its arrival in the State and sales on orders taken thereafter was not discussed in the *Askren* case, the *Graves* case or the *Bowman* case; and the facts in this respect do not appear. In the *Askren* case the company's contention rested wholly on the doctrine of *Leisy v. Hardin*, 135 U.S. 100 [1890]; and it had been shown in *American Steel & Wire Co. v. Speed*, 192 U.S. 500, 520–21 [1904] (as *Emert v. Missouri*, 156 U.S. 296 [1895]; and *Pittsburg Coal Co. v. Bates*, 156 U.S. 577 [1895], had established), that the rule of *Leisy v. Hardin* is not applicable to tax cases. That we did not intend to depart from this view in the *Askren* case, may be inferred from the fact that our decision was rested (p. 450) on *Wagner v. City of*

Covington, supra. The opinion in *Texas v. Brown, supra,* decided April 17, 1922, makes clear the scope and effect of the *Bowman, Askren* and *Graves* cases and shows that there was no intention to overrule *Woodruff v. Parham.*

Because the Texas intrastate sales tax as construed and applied is not a direct burden upon interstate commerce, does not in any way discriminate against interstate commerce, and is not so large as to obstruct interstate commerce, I am of opinion that it is valid even when imposed on goods in the original packages.

Brandeis sent a nearly finished draft of this opinion, lacking only a few minor revisions, among them insertion of the reference to the opinion in *Texas Co. v. Brown,* to Pitney with the following notation: "This is not for circulation. I am sending it to you in amplification of my letter of today re your opinion in 126." Brandeis' letter is unfortunately not available. No. 126 was *Texas Co. v. Brown.* Pitney returned this draft without comment. A few days later, the *Brown* case came down. We don't know whose influence prevailed with whom, but Pitney's opinion in *Brown* had two things in common with Brandeis' in *Sonneborn.* One was the emphasis on the fact that the goods had come to rest in the taxing state. The other was a strained attempt to distinguish the *Graves* case. Like Brandeis, Pitney pointed out that the tax in that case was an inspection fee. If it does no more than cover the reasonable cost of inspection, such a fee is not considered a tax, but is treated as a valid exercise of state regulatory power. The fee in *Graves,* Pitney said, was held excessive, and for that reason it was bad.[14] But the amount by which the fee exceeded the cost of inspection could be regarded as a tax and dealt with as such. This was precisely what Pitney was doing in the *Brown* case itself, which also involved an excessive inspection fee. He held the excess valid as a tax, although it fell on original packages. The Court in *Graves* had held the excess invalid as a tax.

Shortly after Brandeis sent a draft of his dissent to Pitney, McReynolds circulated a majority opinion. It was brief and perfunctory; a mere flick of the wrist. After setting out the facts, McReynolds said: "This subject was recently before us in *Askren v. Continental Oil Co.,*" from which he went on to quote. Then:

In *Crew Levick Co. v. Commonwealth of Pennsylvania,* 245 U.S. 292, 295, we held that a state tax imposed upon the business of selling goods in foreign commerce, in so far as it is measured by the gross receipts from merchandise shipped to foreign countries, is in effect a regulation of foreign commerce and an impost upon exports.

The principles approved by the two cited cases seem conclusive of the question now presented. The tax cannot be upheld. . . .

McReynolds did not explain how he derived support from the *Crew Levick* case, which really had nothing to do with the original-package doctrine as applied in *Sonneborn*.

McReynolds' opinion was dated for delivery on May 15, 1922. The final draft of Brandeis' own opinion bore the same date. But the case was not decided on that day. Before the end of the term, Brandeis got two returns. Clarke said: "I cordially agree. Well done." On May 22, Pitney sent a note: "Dear Judge, I am going with you in No. 191 [*Sonneborn*]; but have mislaid your opinion. Have ordered some discarded drafts burned [fortunately this was a practice not followed at this time in the Brandeis office], and fear this may thus undeservedly have been cremated. Can you send me another copy on which I may suggest verbal comments?" A notation by Brandeis indicates that he did send another copy. But there was no further return from Pitney or anyone else.

Sonneborn was set down for reargument, and was heard again at the beginning of the following term, on October 5, 1922. By that time Clarke had resigned, and Sutherland had been appointed to his place, taking his seat on October 2, the first day of the new term. On November 13, 1922, Day retired and was replaced by Butler on January 2, 1923. On December 31, 1922, Pitney, like Clarke a prospective fellow dissenter of Brandeis in this case, also retired. Sanford, his successor, was seated on February 19, 1923. On the last day of the term, June 11, 1923, *Sonneborn* came down with an opinion by Taft discarding the original-package doctrine and upholding the tax. The decision was unanimous, but, though no notation appears to this effect, it was presumably made by a seven-man Court, since Butler and Sanford, having heard neither the reargument nor the first argument, should, if custom was followed, have taken no part.

Taft's opinion shows plainly the influence of Brandeis. Like Brandeis, Taft relied on *Woodruff v. Parham* and on the fact that it had never been overruled. Similarly, he held that the critical question was whether the goods had come to rest in the taxing state before their sale. But Taft took a somewhat bolder, though still not the most direct, course in dealing with the recent *Graves*, *Askren*, and *Bowman* cases. Counsel in those cases, he said, had not argued the question whether the goods had come to rest in the taxing state, and the Court had not dealt with it, though it now turned out to be decisive. If in fact the goods on which the tax fell in those cases had not come to rest, then the cases were correctly decided. To the extent, however, that the Court had relied on the original-package doctrine, the cases were, Taft added, hereby "qualified." And this included the *Graves* case, which Taft did not deign to distinguish along the line taken by Brandeis and Pitney.

There were, as mentioned, no dissents from Taft's holding. McReynolds, standing alone, concurred, merely adding that Taft's opinion seemed out of harmony with the theory of the other recent cases. Nevertheless, McReynolds said, there had been great confusion, and it was perhaps just as well to declare a flat and certain rule. Logically the doctrine of *Brown v. Maryland* should apply. But — with a heavy sigh — "Logic and taxation are not always the best of friends." [15]

Speaking confidentially the summer after the *Sonneborn* decision, Brandeis was jubilant in referring to it: "That's my opinion," he said. "Taft wrote it on the basis of a memo in which I analyzed all the cases. In the earlier ones I followed Pitney and Day when I knew nothing and assumed they did. But upon study I found that the Court had gone off, largely through Day's strong, passionate talk and loose language. I don't know whether we could have got the *Sonneborn* decision if Day had been on the Court. He felt so fiercely about it." And somewhat later, Brandeis remarked: "I went along with Day's opinion [in the *Graves* and *Askren* cases] because I didn't know anything about the subject — I thought there was some mystery about it. Then I began to study it and felt we must retrace our steps. Day was furious — he would change himself, but no one could change him." Later still, and in another connection, Brandeis once said: "It takes three or four years to find oneself easily in the movements of the Court." [16]

It would seem, in light of these remarks, that Day was able to introduce his pet idea, the original-package doctrine, when three new Justices were still not quite at ease in the movements of the Court: McReynolds, Brandeis, and Clarke. By the time *Sonneborn* came along, Brandeis had fully found himself, and soon thereafter the champion of the idea departed. Sutherland was new and uncommitted. So was Taft, who took his seat on June 30, 1921, and had thus not participated in *Graves, Askren*, or *Bowman*. Butler and Sanford probably took no part in *Sonneborn*. Pitney, the writer of *Bowman*, had become converted before his retirement, and that must have had its effect on the others. In these circumstances, the fact that Brandeis' opinion carried conviction for Taft tipped the scales.

It is not surprising that the opinion of the Court announcing the new rule should have been written by Taft, rather than assigned by him to Brandeis, who, after all, had been the first to put forward the view it represented. Much the same thing happened in *United Mine Workers v. Coronado*, after which Brandeis, as we have seen, remarked that "they will take it from Taft but wouldn't take it from me." In *Sonneborn* Taft did one thing that made the result even easier to take, and it was a thing Brandeis would not have done. Taft went to some lengths to draw a distinction — Brandeis in his opinion had dismissed it with a brief allusion — between regulatory and fiscal measures. Stringent rules, Taft suggested, including the original-package formula, would continue to apply to state regulatory statutes, though they were being relaxed with respect to fiscal ones. The distinction was to some extent supported by the precedents.[17] As will appear in a subsequent chapter, it had serious consequences. Brandeis let it pass here, but he couldn't have disagreed more.

The *Sonneborn* decision was well received. It made sense and it dispelled confusion.[18] Although in dealing with the inconsistent *Graves*, *Askren*, and *Bowman* cases, Taft was more straight-forward than Brandeis had been in his opinion, he was still sufficiently evasive to bring down upon his head the wit of Thomas Reed Powell. Powell commented pleasantly on Taft's "characteristic urbanity"; then he pounced: "It is surprising that the Court should find more comfort in the thought that it did not know what it was deciding or what it was talking about [in the earlier cases] than in the thought that it knew both but overlooked the precedents and considerations which would have induced it to decide differently." [19]

The original-package doctrine retained its authority as applied to imports from foreign countries, as well as some influence in cases involving state regulatory statutes.[20] In its own context, however, the burial which Brandeis and Taft performed has stood the test of time. *Sonneborn* was thus an important decision. The coming-to-rest rule, which *Sonneborn* substituted for the original-package formula, has itself been relaxed. Without insisting on rigid adherence to its formal requirements as enunciated in *Sonneborn*, the Court has sought to effectuate the rule's underlying purpose. It has generally allowed taxation in the state of sale when there was no danger of a duplicating tax elsewhere.[21] Otherwise, however, as is typical in this field, the effect of *Sonneborn* was negligible. Taft's and Brandeis' tidy and assured collections of cases under the headings of "burden on commerce" and "obstruction of commerce" did not, as they could scarcely have been expected to do, solve the Court's difficulties in operating with those terms. The untidy course of Commerce Clause adjustments has continued as before.[22]

In March 1922, when he started to work on his *Sonneborn* dissent, Brandeis had written in only one Commerce Clause tax case. This was *Underwood Typewriter Co. v. Chamberlain*,[23] in which a tax on the net

profits earned within the state by a foreign corporation was attacked
mainly on Due Process, but also on Commerce Clause, grounds. The
case is important, but it caused no great difficulty. Brandeis, speaking
for a unanimous Court, disposed of the Commerce Clause point in one
brief paragraph. And his file in the case shows that no extensive research
underlay this summary treatment. When *Sonneborn* came along, it was
therefore, as Brandeis said, a mystery. But he assaulted it with a will,
frontally and from the flanks. He took on the whole subject, not simply
the limited question whether the Court had gone off in applying a particular formula. Reading five or six cases would have given him the
answer to that. What Brandeis learned and what he thought in connection with *Sonneborn* affected, indeed, one may say, determined his
views on a large segment of Commerce Clause issues for the rest of his
career. His file in the case is, therefore, of more than usual interest.

Three pages of notes in Brandeis' hand bear witness to his first readings. From Pitney's opinion in *Crew Levick Co. v. Pennsylvania*, the
case McReynolds was to rely on, Brandeis copied a passage indicating
why the holding there, dealing with a gross receipts tax, would be irrelevant in *Sonneborn*.[24] He also wrote down this definition of a "direct
burden on commerce," to which he had frequent occasion to revert in
future cases: "That portion of the [gross receipts] tax which is measured by the receipts from foreign commerce necessarily varies in proportion to the volume of that commerce, and hence is a direct burden
upon it." [25] Brandeis noted as well some additional cases involving
gross and net receipts, and excise and license taxes.[26] All this did not
touch the tax in *Sonneborn*. Nor did a further set of cases having to do
with taxes on exports.[27] Brandeis was surrounding the subject. He came
nearer his immediate issue with an exhaustive series of eight articles by
Thomas Reed Powell entitled, "Indirect Encroachment on Federal Authority by the Taxing Powers of the States." [28] Powell allowed that on
the whole the Court had succeeded in maintaining a reasonable balance
between the interests of the states and of the nation, but he did wish
the Court would pay less heed to the formulas it kept inventing and
would face up more candidly to the practical nature of its task.

On the basis of the cases he had noted, and a number of additional
ones, Brandeis in his first, short draft stated what the tax in *Sonneborn*
was not; in a phrase, it was not a "burden on commerce." That being so,
he went on, showing perhaps the influence of the Powell articles, no
other formula was relevant. The concluding sentences of this draft were:
"To goods brought in from one State to another that clause [Article I,
Section 10, dealing with foreign imports, on which *Brown v. Maryland*
had, properly speaking, turned] does not apply. These goods have only

such protection as is afforded by the grant to Congress of the power to regulate interstate commerce. That means, so far as here relevant, the State may not discriminate against interstate commerce."

Brandeis now continued his readings, and as he did so the problem became more and more complicated. The extent of his labors is indicated by several hundred small memorandum slips, each covered with a one-phrase or one-sentence summary in Brandeis' hand of one or two cases. This multitude of slips has been preserved in the file for *Shafer v. Farmers Grain Co.*, a different kind of Commerce Clause case, discussed in a later chapter, in which Brandeis also wrote an unpublished opinion. Some of the notations were made after *Sonneborn*, in connection with *Shafer*. But it seems almost certain that the largest number of them represent work done in preparing the *Sonneborn* opinion. *Shafer* was first argued in May 1923, shortly before *Sonneborn* finally came down. It is not unnatural that, as one file was being closed and another one opened, references collected in *Sonneborn* which might prove useful in *Shafer* should have been kept available, and should then have found their way into the *Shafer* folder.

As he accumulated cases, Brandeis continually revised his draft. He retained the discrimination criterion, but elaborated the burden-on-commerce notion, subdividing it into direct and indirect burdens; and he added another, not very distinct test: does the tax obstruct commerce? Brandeis classified the mounting number of cases under these headings. The opinion was now a concise survey of a broad field. And it no longer ended simply with the conclusion that "so far as here relevant" the fact that the state did not discriminate against interstate commerce was sufficient to dispose of the issue. When the draft was in this advanced form, Brandeis for the first time stopped to take account of the *Askren*, *Graves*, and *Bowman* cases. Then he sent it to Pitney. He had obviously considered his problem *de novo*, and made up his mind on that basis, before reaching the difficulty of the recent inconsistent cases.

Up to this point Brandeis appears to have made no use of the services of his law clerk. This draft — the one in which *Askren*, *Bowman*, and *Graves* were first dealt with — Brandeis gave to his law clerk, William G. Rice, now and for many years professor of law at the Wisconsin University Law School, for comment. Rice joined issue radically. He was for discarding all other tests and all other formulas as completely unserviceable and keeping only one; namely, whether the state tax discriminated against interstate commerce. If it did not, it should be declared valid. At the first appearance of the phrase, a tax "not large enough to obstruct" interstate commerce, Rice asked: "What does this mean?" On the coming-to-rest concept, which Brandeis was substituting for the original-package doctrine, Rice commented: "This test is just as fallacious as the original-package rule, in my opinion."

From marginalia, Rice erupted onto three typewritten pages:

It seems to me that the whole conception of invalidity of direct burdens on interstate commerce is wrong and should be repudiated despite the wealth of authority supporting it. . . . The talk of a direct burden on interstate commerce leads to the ridiculous original-package and coming to rest language and really preserves commerce from improper interference in no wise. Complete free trade between the states was the object of the constitution, and it is in no way accomplished by drawing a physical line between what is and what is not interstate commerce. That such a line can be drawn with advantage, seems to me a very primitive conception, the invalidity of which the Court recognized in *Woodruff v. Parham* and ought to have kept in mind ever after. . . . Would it not then be possible to approach all these direct burden cases with a healthy skepticism and deal with them a little derisively rather than endorse and try to distinguish them? They are a pretty solid wall, it is true. But surely it is a little ridiculous, for instance, to have a series of cases holding that it is lawful to tax peddlers selling goods from abroad, but unlawful to tax drummers getting orders for such goods. Likewise what economic difference is there in the present case, whether the oil is in New Jersey, en route, or "at rest" in Texas when the contract to sell is made? The two methods of soliciting sales are economically identical. A tax on one method has exactly the same effect as a tax on the other. Each is equally an impediment to interstate commerce in its economic sense; and neither is any impediment to interstate commerce as compared with intrastate commerce, if the tax does not discriminate between them.

Brandeis' first draft had embodied something like Rice's attitude. It was not quite as radical. Brandeis at no time repudiated the burden-on-commerce formula; but he did, at first, put it to one side. Was he forced back to it and to similar formulas by the accumulation of cases? It was impossible to rethink each of the dozens of Commerce Clause adjustments, and there was no other intelligible way, at this late date, to organize them. So Brandeis may have come to feel as he was revising his first draft. The discrimination criterion had an engagingly simple and practical appearance. But could it be hoped that any single formula would prove serviceable in all the incredible variety of Commerce Clause tax cases? There was, in any event, no sense in trying to make a clean sweep in order to get rid of one palpably unreasonable formula; especially since such a moving of mountains was not likely to persuade the brethren to accept Brandeis' result in *Sonneborn*. All that could come of such an effort was a very pretentious dissent.

We do not know, of course, whether what has been said accurately reconstructs Brandeis' reasoning. We do know that, before he asked for his law clerk's comments, he had considered more or less the line of argument Rice urged. And we know that he made no concessions to it — at this time, or in the future. As is evident from a number of opinions, including the unpublished ones in *Stratton v. St. Louis Southwestern Ry.* and *Shafer v. Farmers Grain Co.*, two types of Commerce Clause cases belonged for Brandeis in a class by themselves, and the views he developed in *Sonneborn* had no relevance to them. These were cases involving state social and economic regulations and state taxation, regulatory rather than wholly fiscal in nature, of foreign corporations. In both kinds of cases, as has been remarked, the majority of the Court of the twenties and thirties tended to apply through the Commerce Clause the laissez-faire philosophy to which it normally gave effect by way of the Due Process Clause. Brandeis, in turn, brought to these cases the realistic analysis of social and economic conditions and the hospitality to legislative policy which guided him in applying the Due Process Clause. But his Commerce Clause opinions on fiscal matters after *Sonneborn* stand out from the body of his work. They are, for Brandeis, strangely formal, and they adhere unfalteringly to the concept of direct and indirect burdens, which he adopted once and for all in *Sonneborn*.[29] He freshened, he renewed many areas of the law with a sense of the actualities on which the Court necessarily imposes its order when it decides the great issues that come before it. His opinions were life-size. He was the Court's window to the world of affairs, of facts and actions, which must be sensed before it can be rationalized, and which is so easily lost sight of in the marble temple. But not so in these cases; another Brandeis seems to speak in them.

Brandeis conceded no more to his law clerk with respect to his manner of distinguishing the *Graves, Askren,* and *Bowman* cases than he did on the issue of his basic approach. But not because Rice was timid to argue his objections. For example, Rice noted: "I think your analysis of the *Askren* case is not fair. It can't be explained away. It is just *wrong* . . . ." Brandeis was unshaken. But his method of dealing with cases that blocked the way to results he desired evolved further over the years. He never ceased to exercise, and perhaps delight in, a ruthless technical ingenuity in the contrivance of distinctions. But he came also, at times, to press the Court frankly to overrule precedents he deemed wrongly decided. And more than once he was to point with pride (and not without some hidden irony) to the example of Taft's relative forthrightness in "qualifying" the *Graves, Askren,* and *Bowman* cases.[30]

Opening page of the abandoned first draft of Brandeis' opinion in *Atherton Mills v. Johnston*, showing that, despite his eventual concurrence in the opposite result, Brandeis believed that the Child Labor Tax Act of 1919 should be held constitutional. The figure 406 at the upper right is the docket number of the case.

Return by Van Devanter on the back of Brandeis' opinion in *St. Louis, Iron Mountain & Southern Ry. v. Starbird.* (The case was decided at October Term 1916 and had two docket numbers, 275 and 796.) The words "good suggestion" are in Brandeis' hand (the address is not) and refer to Van Devanter's com-

---

This opinion was prepared at a time

when it appeared that the decision

might have gone against the interpre-

tation of the act which is here ad-

vocated. The Chief Justice was wavering

Pitney, Van Devanter, Day and McKenna

were contra. I don't remember whether

a copy was sent to the Chief or not.

But eventually it was decided according

to this view and Judge Day wrote a poor

opinion.

This took the Justice two weeks of
hard work while court was sitting.

A memorandum by Dean Acheson, Brandeis' law clerk in 1919–21, which was filed with a copy of Brandeis' unpublished opinion in *Strathearn S. S. Co. v. Dillon.* Mr. Acheson's judgment of Day's opinion passes the test of time.

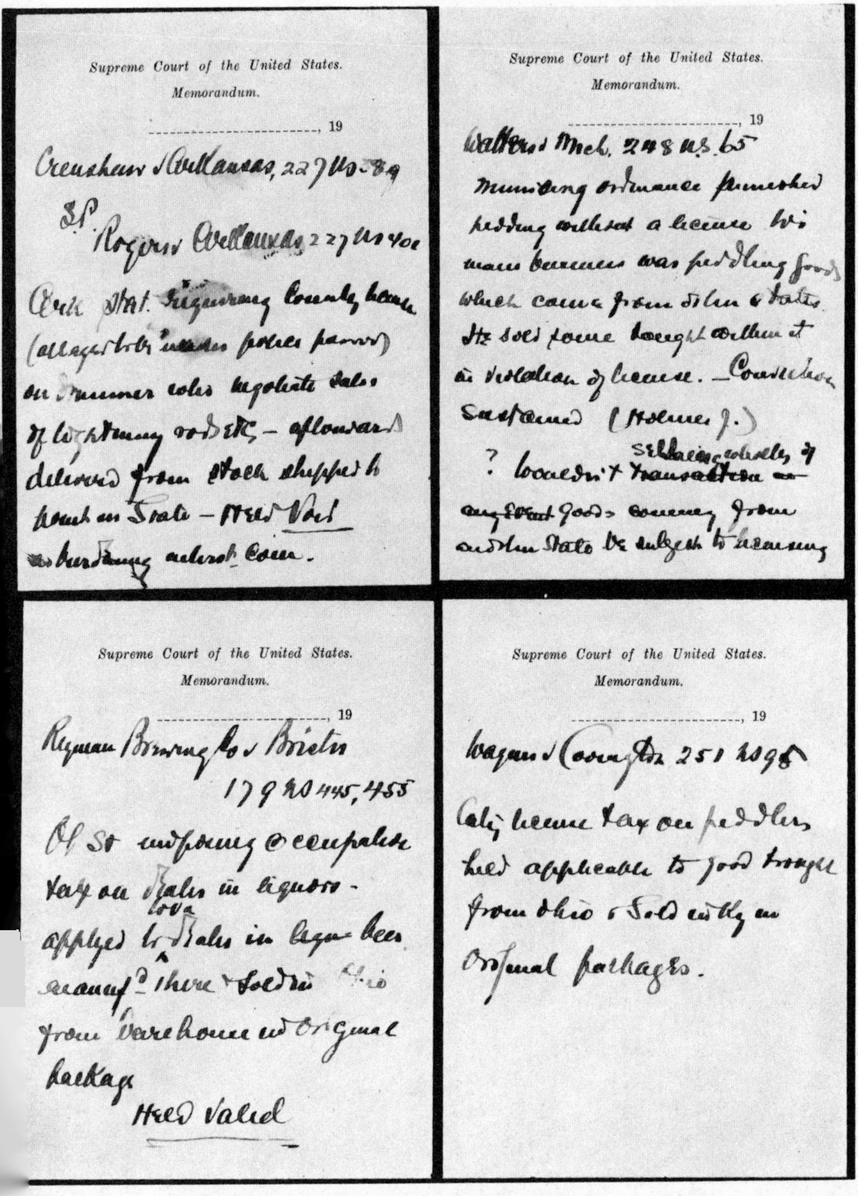
Supreme Court of the United States.
Memorandum.
19
Crenshaw v Arkansas, 227 US 389
S.P. Rogers v Arkansas 227 US 401
Ark Stat. requiring County license (alleged to be under police power) on drummers who negotiate sales of lightning rods etc. — afterwards delivered from stock shipped to them in State — Held Void as burdening interst. Com.
Supreme Court of the United States.
Memorandum.
19
Walters v Mich. 248 U.S. 65
Municipal ordinance punished peddling without a license. W.'s manufacturer was peddling goods which came from other States. He sold some bought within it in violation of license. — Conviction sustained (Holmes J.)
? wouldn't selling wholly of any sort goods coming from another State be subject to licensing
Supreme Court of the United States.
Memorandum.
19
Reymann Brewing Co v Brister
179 US 445, 455
O. St. imposing a compulsive tax on sales in liquors — applied to sales in lager beer manuf^d there & sold in Ohio from warehouse in original packages
Held valid
Supreme Court of the United States.
Memorandum.
19
Wagner v Covington 251 US 95
City license tax on peddlers held applicable to goods brought from Ohio & sold only in original packages.

our of some hundreds of similar slips bearing witness to the extensive investigation cases Brandeis personally undertook in connection with *Sonneborn Bros. v. Cureton.* is opinions often represented only the smallest part of his labors. These slips con-n brief summaries of cases; on one Brandeis noted a query, as well as the fact that e case briefed had been written by Holmes.

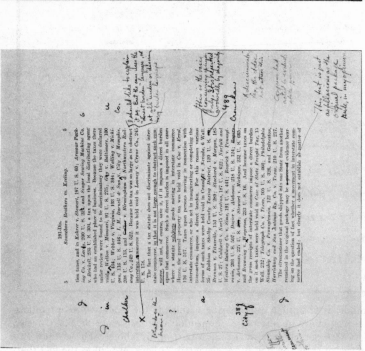

A page from a late version of Brandeis' opinion in *Sonneborn Bros. v. Cureton* (Keeling was the original party defendant), which the Justice gave to his law clerk of the year 1921–22 for comment. The clerk, William G. Rice, tried inter radically, showing how far Brandeis' law

A note to Brandeis from Pitney, asking for another copy of the *Sonneborn* opinion (docket no. 191). The notation, "New copy sent by LDB May 23," was made by Brandeis.

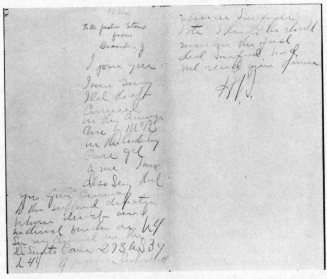

A note from Brandeis to his law clerk for 1929–30, the late Harry Shulman, penciled on an early draft of Brandeis' opinion in *Stratton v. St. Louis Southwestern Ry.*, to guide Shulman in pursuing further researches.

Stone's return on the back of Brandeis' dissent in the *Stratton* case (docket no. 98). References are to an opinion in an earlier case by McReynolds, in which Stone had joined; to a passage on page 4 of Brandeis' *Stratton* opinion; and to the apparent intention of Sutherland, writing for the Court in *Stratton*, to note concurrence with the majority on the part of Sanford, who had participated in the decision of the case at conference, but had died before circulation of Brandeis' dissent.

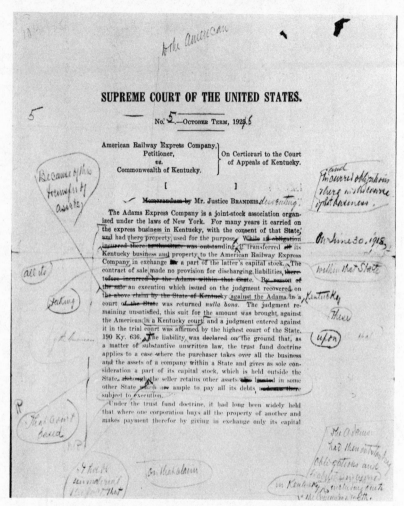

First page of a late print of Brandeis' opinion in the *American Railway Express* case, bearing the Justice's final revisions. The print had been received from the printer at the previous term of court, when the case had been reargued and Brandeis had done his main work on it. The empty brackets in the heading would normally contain the date set for the opinion's delivery; none had yet been scheduled for this case. The phrase, "of the American," in the left margin is in the hand of Brandeis' law clerk for 1926–27, Robert Page.

Brandeis' return to Holmes' first circulation of an opinion in *Bullock v. Florida* (docket no. 262). The "saving clause in the last paragraph" was one of the few things in this opinion that Brandeis did like.

Page 3 of Holmes' early opinion in *Bullock v. Florida*, bearing the comments of Brandeis, who roundly disagreed with Holmes' result. The phrase "or express contract" in the right margin is in Holmes' hand, as is the cancelation of two lines toward the bottom.

------------ *June 4* ------------, 192 0

The changes are few but I hoped would cut down the decision to a denial of the duty to go on — but the truth is that I feel a little confused by they of a way to avoid throwing the case on to someone else and don't feel satisfied and yet hardly know what more to say or do.

O W H

A note from Holmes to Brandeis accompanying a revised opinion in the *Bullock* case, this time adopting the result Brandeis favored. "The changes are few," Holmes writes, "but I hoped would cut down the decision to a denial of the duty to go on" — on the part, that is, of the railroad which was a party in the case and was claiming that the state of Florida forced it to continue operations at a loss. Holmes then expresses concern that the changed opinion might not satisfy his former majority and might cause the case to be assigned to someone else. This did not happen.

VII

The Curse of Bigness

If there is a single idea emerging from Brandeis' lifework with which, more than with any other, his name was linked in his own day and on which it remains most boldly imprinted, it is this: The giantism of our time, discernible in almost all spheres of life, is a deeply disturbing, though a controllable, phenomenon. And it is not unjust that his insistent concern with bigness should generally be considered the dominant theme in Brandeis' social philosophy. For it is the theme that represents the most thoroughly harmonious confluence of the impulses of Brandeis' temperament, the morality and aspirations with which he came to manhood, the vast experience of affairs he accumulated in his middle years, and the lessons he derived from experience by hard, rational analysis.

The curse of industrial bigness, as Brandeis saw it, was not only, and not even chiefly, economic. "By their by-products," he told the Senate Committee on Interstate Commerce in 1911, "shall you know the trusts." The trusts had to be studied, he said, "through the spectacles of people's rights and people's interests; [you] must consider the effect upon the development of the American democracy. When you do that you will realize the extraordinary perils to our institutions which attend the trusts . . . ." A corporation could become too large to be the most efficient instrument of production and distribution, but, more importantly, "whether it has exceeded the point of greatest economic efficiency or not, it may be too large to be tolerated among the people who desire to be free." [1]

Nor was the evil of undue size one peculiar to industrial organizations. In a letter to Paul U. Kellogg, editor of the magazine *The Survey*, Brandeis, commenting on a study of the effects of prohibition in a so-called typical town, seized upon an incidental statement to the effect that a typical American city was not necessarily undistinguished by characteristics peculiarly its own. "The great America for which we long," Brandeis wrote, "is unattainable unless that individuality of communities becomes far more highly developed and becomes a common American phenomenon. For a century our growth has come through national expansion and the increase of the functions of the Federal

Government. The growth of the future — at least of the immediate future — must be in quality and spiritual value. And that can come only through the concentrated, intensified striving of smaller groups. The field for special effort shall now be the State, the city, the village — and each should be led to seek to excel in something peculiar to it. If ideals are developed locally — the national ones will come pretty near to taking care of themselves." [2] The same exhortation may be found in the fascinating correspondence, published by Bernard Flexner, dealing with Brandeis' efforts to build up the University of Louisville. Brandeis encouraged no visions of a major national seat of learning. "Our University can become great . . . ," he wrote, "only if it is essentially Kentuckian — an institution for Kentuckians developed by Kentuckians." He wanted the library to be a generally serviceable one, but he urged that it concentrate on Kentuckiana and started it along this path not only with advice but also with modest and carefully planned gifts of money and books. Setting the suitable example for one who believed in the virtue of responsible, small-scale initiative, he was not uninterested in assuring himself that "the work is being done economically and efficiently; and that our money is doing 'duty,' as they say of water in the arid states." [3]

On the occasion of Brandeis' seventy-fifth birthday, in 1931, Ray Stannard Baker wrote him: "I am comforted by one of the things I have felt that you have taught, which I have come in recent years deeply to believe: that progress does not come by wholesale, by mass emotion, by flags and oratory. It comes by the effort on the part of each man, in his own place, learning what he is good for, and doing his own job to the uttermost." [4] Expressing the same thought, Brandeis himself, a decade earlier, had written to Harold J. Laski: "I hope you will develop further the cult of the unit of greatest efficiency and spread further the truth that progress must proceed from the aggregate of the performances of individual men — and that each is a wee thing, despite the aids and habiliments with which science, invention and organization have surrounded him. When once these truths are widely recognized we shall, I believe, have vision, wisdom and ingenuity enough to adjust our institutions to the wee size of man and thus render possible his growth and development." [5]

All this, however — the danger of political and social power being wielded from the overly impregnable bastion of economic concentration, the loss of a healthy diversification of attention and achievement in a country as large and as heterogeneous as ours, the sheer diminishing of returns bred by all indiscriminate mass efforts — all this was not the heart of the matter. "The twentieth century," Paul A. Freund has said, "is an era of mass movements; of the separation of ownership from control; of impersonal and anonymous corporate arts, obscuring responsibility and shielding individuals from the consequences of their failings . . . . To him [Brandeis] the rise of giantism and the moral dilemmas it has posed — the curse of bigness, as he was not ashamed to describe it — was lamentable, corrupting man's character . . . ."[6]

Brandeis was not ashamed to speak of the "curse" of bigness. He might not have been ashamed either to define man's goal on earth as being "to strive, to seek, to find, and not to yield." The curse of bigness was that it crushed the will to strive and to seek, because it made it exceedingly difficult for the individual to find and to know that he has found; and it made it often impossible not to yield. Bigness crushed the human spirit. It was, of course, not the only feature of our society which could tend to do so. Certain restrictions on freedom of speech and thought had the same effect and were to be resisted for precisely the same reason. It was in a free-speech case that Brandeis wrote: "Those who won our independence believed that the final end of the state was to make men free to develop their faculties."[7] And the same danger arose from invasions of privacy. "The makers of our Constitution," Brandeis said in asserting a constitutional right against wire-tapping, "undertook to secure conditions favorable to the pursuit of happiness. They recognized the significance of man's spiritual nature, of his feelings and of his intellect. They knew that only a part of the pain, pleasure and satisfactions of life are to be found in material things."[8] But giantism epitomized the problem for Brandeis because it revealed it in its acutest and most pervasive form; and perhaps because it invited from him an attack in which he was able to use every weapon in his arsenal. For a moralist who was a lawyer and economist in command of unsurpassed resources of information and analytic power, this was the fitting target.

There went along, to be sure, with Brandeis' unremitting distrust of the burgeoning growth of his own day, a loving regard for things and men as they had once been. In this, no doubt, there was a romantic strain. Brandeis' enthusiasm, for example, for the enterprise and self-reliance of early New England seamen, of which he read in Samuel Eliot Morison's *Maritime History of Massachusetts*, was touched with nostalgia and surely some idealization. He admired, as Frank W. Buxton, editor of the Boston *Herald*, wrote to Felix Frankfurter after an interview with Brandeis in August 1938, "achievements by men who had not only an opportunity to exert themselves but the irresistible will to do so." It was, at least in part, of a like admiration that his Zionism had been born. There is the touch of idealization also in

Brandeis' descriptions in judicial opinions of early American industrial development, which he contrasts with modern bigness in terms of a loss of virtue. But the idealizing backward glance of the romantic was only an occasional indulgence with Brandeis. He had no illusions about the hazards, the cruelties, the failures which could visit the efforts of the brave and self-reliant. Indeed, the hazards and the failures formed the backdrop against which the effort attained nobility. One ventures to surmise that Brandeis thought them necessary. If there is no such thing as personal failure and disaster, there is no such thing as personal success, and if mistakes do not entail hard consequences, can men fully savor the deep and just satisfaction which should attend achievement? Life was an adventure and the world a fierce place, and it was profoundly immoral to obliterate the distinction between success and failure, because to do so was to sin against the worthiest aspirations of the human spirit. Certainly Brandeis had compassion, and he was grieved by, and would try mightily to remedy, wanton man-made cruelty. But hardship as such did not necessarily appall him. Helplessness, dependence, irresponsibility did.

Throughout his mature professional life, Brandeis gave frequent public expression — often, of course, necessarily fragmentary — to his views about giantism. He addressed himself to the problem in many and varied contexts. His testimony to a Congressional committee in 1911 has been alluded to. He testified at other times in much the same vein. A series of articles in *Harper's Weekly*, published in book form in 1914 and again in 1932 under the title, *Other People's Money*, dealt with the results of the concentration of financial and industrial power in a few Eastern banking houses. Another collection of papers dating from the years before his accession to the Bench was published in 1934, under the title, chosen by Brandeis himself from a number of suggestions, *The Curse of Bigness*.[9] In Brandeis' judicial writings, various aspects of the problem are touched upon again and again. His most comprehensive and eloquent pronouncements came in two famous dissents of the depression years, *New State Ice Co. v. Liebmann*[10] and *Liggett Co. v. Lee*.[11]

In the first of these dissents, Brandeis defended the right of a state to employ drastic and novel measures in meeting the economic crisis. The measure in question, involving close governmental control and planning of production, probably did not have his sympathy. The task government was setting itself struck him as entailing judgments and prophesies too formidable to be efficiently and honestly made on a continuing basis. The task was too *big*. "Man," he remarked, "is weak and his judgment is at best fallible." But the crisis was too big also, and in dealing with it, diversified local efforts were to be encouraged. "It is one of the happy incidents of the federal system," he wrote, "that a single courageous State may, if its citizens choose, serve as a laboratory; and try novel social and economic experiments without risk to the rest of the country." [12]

The second of these cases concerned the power of the state of Florida to impose a discriminatorily heavy tax on chain stores. In supporting the tax, Brandeis spoke of the justifiable "sense of some insidious menace inherent in large aggregations of capital, particularly when held by corporations." He referred to the "social significance" of "size alone." "So-called private corporations," he said, were sometimes able to dominate a state. "Such is the Frankenstein monster which States have created by their corporation laws." Florida was free to believe that the chain store was "thwarting American ideals," that it was "converting independent tradesmen into clerks," and that it was "sapping the resources, the vigor and the hope of the smaller cities and towns." There was, indeed, a widespread belief that, because of "giant corporations," "individual initiative and effort are being paralyzed, creative power impaired and human happiness lessened." If the people of a state shared that belief, Brandeis concluded, there was nothing in the Constitution to prevent them from trying by taxation to cripple or destroy the Frankenstein. "To that extent, the citizens of each State are still masters of their destiny." [13]

The long and arduous battle that Brandeis waged against institutional elephantiasis was, of course, far from uniformly successful. Yet no setback ever deterred him from pressing the fight. He believed that the trend to bigness was not irreversible, and that it could be arrested, slowly but effectively, by education and by the steady application of admittedly peripheral corrective measures. The romantic strain again, the gallant quixotic stance? Perhaps. But this belief sprang from the same source as Brandeis' distrust of bigness itself, and it was just as central to his thought. Man is a wee thing, Brandeis wrote Laski. "Man," he said in *New State Ice Co. v. Liebmann*, "is weak and his judgment is at best fallible." But he held also that man's judgment, properly informed, has an immense potential, and that it should enable him to command circumstances and to shape the conditions of his life to a rational and satisfactory pattern. Man's single fatal limitation was his reluctance to understand his own limitations and to pace himself and his efforts accordingly. But this reluctance could be, and it had to be, overcome. The paradox of limited man and his practically limitless potential was thus at the core of Brandeis' faith, and it gave him his unique combination of passion and patience — the

controlled passion and the militant patience which are indispensable to
the effective pursuit of any social goal.

Brandeis' hitherto unpublished opinion in *Stratton v. St. Louis Southwestern Ry.* is, like *Liggett Co. v. Lee,* a fully developed, head-on judicial attack on industrial bigness, and it takes its place alongside that
great dissent. Brandeis drew on his *Stratton* file in preparing the *Liggett* dissent, which came a few years later, and he drew also on some
of the language he had used in this opinion. The *Stratton* case is significant as well for a rather more technical Commerce Clause discussion, and for its concluding remarks on the weight to be accorded to
precedent in constitutional litigation. Taken as a whole, the opinion is,
like the *New State Ice* case and *Liggett Co. v. Lee,* another monument
to Brandeis' power in adducing massive information to the support of
an appeal to first principles. It stands high among the finest examples
of his judicial work.

The issue in the *Stratton* case was this: Might a state condition the
grant to a foreign (the word is used to denote incorporation in another
state) corporation of the privilege to do intrastate business upon payment of a tax measured, in part but without apportionment, by the extent of the corporation's extraterritorial holdings; that is to say, in effect, measured by its size? A tax graduated in accordance with the corporation's capital stock is so measured. Briefly stated, the principal arguments against such a tax are that it represents an attempt by the state
to reach assets beyond its jurisdiction and thus violates the Due Process
Clause; and that, though disguised as an exercise of the power to regulate and tax intrastate commerce, it in fact falls also or mainly on interstate business, thus violating the Commerce Clause. The answering contention in support of the tax is that it is not laid on property beyond the
jurisdiction, but rather simply uses such property to measure the price
of a privilege which the state is free to withhold. To the Commerce
Clause objection the reply is made that almost any tax payable by a
person or corporation engaged in interstate as well as intrastate commerce must fall in some degree on the former, and that many varieties
of taxes, not essentially unlike unapportioned capital stock taxes in
their practical consequences, have been allowed to do so.

On both sides of this dispute, it is assumed that a state retains under
the Constitution at least some authority to exclude foreign corporations from its territory, or at any rate to refuse them entry. In the early
days of our federal experience, which were also the early days of our
experience with corporate business, it was thought that a state had such
a power, and that it was absolute. Having this absolute power, a state

was also thought to possess the concomitant right to set any monetary or other conditions it chose upon the entry of foreign corporations.[14] However, inroads were soon made upon this edifyingly logical doctrine,[15] and with the growth of an integrated national economy it was not long before there was more to the inroads than to the original doctrine. Before the turn of the century it had been held that a state could not exclude a foreign corporation seeking to engage in interstate commerce within its borders.[16] States presumably retained a right to exclude foreign corporations from doing intrastate business. But even this authority was soon limited. In 1910, a divided Court held that unapportioned capital stock taxes, imposed on foreign railroad and telegraph companies doing both interstate and intrastate business, were unconstitutional, although they were levied as a condition upon the grant only of the privilege to do intrastate business.[17] This holding was a bold, fresh departure, of the sort which our law is not prone to assimilate suddenly in all its implications. The following years, therefore, saw some backing and filling.

An unapportioned capital stock tax on the privilege to do intrastate business came before the Court again in 1913. It was imposed on a foreign company engaged in manufacturing rather than transportation or communication, and the Court this time — the case was *Baltic Mining Co. v. Massachusetts* [18] — explained the earlier holding by pointing out that for railroad and telegraph companies, intra- and interstate business were, as a matter of economic fact, inseparable. In these circumstances, the state could not withdraw permission to engage in intrastate business, for it would then, by the same act, also prohibit the doing of interstate. There was no power to exclude from interstate commerce, and the state could exact no price for a privilege it could not deny. But this was not necessarily true of concerns engaged in manufacturing and in buying and selling, whose intra- and interstate activities were separable. So reasoning, the Court upheld the tax in the *Baltic* case, remarking also that, unlike the taxes in the earlier cases, this one was subject to a ceiling of $2,000, and thus would in any event entail only a slight burden on interstate commerce, even if it were held to cause one at all.

In the decade following the *Baltic Mining Co.* decision, it appeared that the law, in one of its typical processes, was being settled along the lines of a comfortable compromise. Taxes imposed on foreign corporations for the privilege of doing intrastate business would be upheld, regardless of the activity the corporation was engaged in, whether railroading or manufacturing, provided that, as in the *Baltic* case, there was a maximum beyond which the tax would not rise, and that the maximum was within reason. Where there was no maximum, the tax would fall, again regardless of the nature of the business taxed.[19]

This was a good practical adjustment. But it struck some of the brethren as suffering from a mortal logical flaw. For to make the validity of a tax depend on its amount was apparently to admit that after a certain point it would, as the phrase went, burden commerce. Yet the Constitution had been held to forbid burdens on interstate commerce, whether small or large. There could be no such thing as a tax which was only a little bit unconstitutional, and hence valid. There was also another, more substantial, though by no means unanswerable, objection; namely, that the rule of the *Baltic* case required the Court to apply too fluid, too uncertain a standard; one which offered no safe guidelines to the parties concerned; a breeder of litigation. And so, in 1929, some sixteen years after the decision in *Baltic*, the Court turned about and declared that unapportioned capital stock taxes exacted from foreign corporations for the privilege of doing intrastate business were unconstitutional, whether or not a reasonable maximum was provided for. Only one feature of the compromise worked out in the years after the *Baltic* decision was preserved. That was the obliteration of the distinction between transportation and communication businesses on the one hand and manufacturing concerns on the other. The prevailing doctrine was now clear, simple, and absolute. The case in which it was announced was *Cudahy Packing Co. v. Hinkle*.[20]

There had for a few years been hints that a doctrine such as the *Cudahy* case laid down was in the offing. It was not till *Cudahy*, to be sure, that the Court had a go at the old *Baltic Mining Co.* case in straightaway fashion. But there had been some earlier sniping from the cover of fortified positions on the flanks. In 1925, in *Alpha Portland Cement Co. v. Massachusetts*,[21] McReynolds, who was to write for the Court in *Cudahy*, struck down an apportioned privilege tax measured by so much of the net income and capital stock of a foreign corporation as was attributable to transactions occurring in the taxing state. The company in question was engaged solely in interstate business, and McReynolds held that it could therefore not be taxed even in this apportioned fashion, anymore than it could be excluded. This was and is debatable doctrine, though there was precedent for it.[22] But McReynolds did not stop there. He seized the occasion for the gratuitous remark that a tax which was levied on, or burdened, interstate commerce was unconstitutional, regardless of its amount, small or large. So far as the *Baltic* case reflected a different view, he said, it was now "definitely disapproved." [23] A year earlier, the Court, without mention of the *Baltic* case, had held, in *Air-Way Electric Appliance Corp. v. Day*,[24] that an apportioned foreign corporation tax, although it would plainly have been valid if measured by issued capital stock, violated both the Commerce and Equal Protection Clauses, because it was measured by total authorized capital stock. In this form, the Court said, the tax bore no relation to the corporation's real assets or to the value of the privilege to do intrastate business for which it was the supposed payment. This holding cut some ground from under the *Baltic* case and its progeny, for in those cases the Court had not taken the distinction between authorized and issued capital stock, and in some of the cases, including *Baltic*, in which the tax was upheld, it was measured by authorized stock.[25] When he came to write *Cudahy*, McReynolds noted that the tax there was vulnerable to attack because it was also measured by authorized stock; and he cited the *Air-Way Electric* case. But he found it unnecessary to reach this issue, since his holding rested on a broader principle applicable equally to taxes measured by authorized or issued stock.[26]

Stratton v. St. Louis Southwestern Ry. was argued in January 1930, a little less than a year after the *Cudahy* decision had been handed down. The tax challenged in *Stratton* was imposed by Illinois on both foreign and domestic corporations for the privilege of doing intrastate business. As here applied, it was measured by issued capital stock, without apportionment, and rose to a maximum of $1,000. As might have been expected, the decision at conference went against the tax, despite the maximum and despite the absence of any authorized capital stock question. The writing of the opinion was assigned to Sutherland. Within a month, the latter circulated an opinion of the Court. It was dated for delivery on February 24, 1930. There was no doubt, Sutherland said, that a state could impose a tax for the privilege of doing intrastate business. But the issue was the measure of the tax, and on that *Cudahy Co. v. Hinkle* was decisive. To be sure, the maximum amount of the Illinois tax — $1,000 — was not large. But, since *Cudahy*, the amount was unimportant. "To sustain the comparatively moderate tax here assailed," Sutherland added, "is to open the door at once to the state to increase the amount to an oppressive extent, for, as this court has frequently said, the power to tax is the power to destroy."

Brandeis was not on the Court in 1910, when the precursor of the *Cudahy* rule was first put forward, nor in 1913 when it was modified in the *Baltic Mining Co.* case. But he acquiesced in the compromise which evolved after the *Baltic* decision. He went along in upholding taxes with a maximum, and striking down unapportioned taxes without one. He was silent in the *Air-Way Electric* case, which threatened part of the compromise derived from *Baltic*. But he was in dissent against the other holdings from which a flanking movement was in progress. Thus he noted his disagreement in *Alpha Portland Cement*, having earlier written in a similar case.[27] In *Cudahy*, Brandeis dissented, invoking *Baltic* and its doctrine. Such being his position, Brandeis opposed the conference decision in the *Stratton* case, and he undertook to set forth his views. He had reached the drafting stage by the time Sutherland's opinion of February 24 was circulated, but it took him another month to complete, with full documentation, the opinion which is printed below. Brandeis' dissent in *Cudahy* had been brief. This time he mounted a full-scale assault against the majority.

The Court's holding, Brandeis wrote, was unsound legally as well as economically, and he proceeded to deal with it under both heads. The Commerce Clause, he said, using the traditional idiom he had adopted after his first full study of it in connection with *Sonneborn Bros. v. Cureton* more than a decade earlier, invalidated only direct burdens on interstate commerce. Indirect ones were unaffected. Thus it was not denied that property used in interstate commerce could be taxed by the state in which it was found. This was an indirect burden. By the same token this very tax, if laid upon a domestic corporation engaged in interstate commerce, would be valid. If it was an indirect burden as applied to a domestic corporation, it was an indirect one as applied to a foreign corporation. Nor could this tax be deemed a direct burden, when apportioned capital stock and net income taxes, rising to considerably higher amounts and, as a practical matter, having the same effect, were held not to be. Declaring such taxes constitutional and yet striking down the tax in this case was an utterly mechanical and unrealistic exercise. It was said — this was a reference to Sutherland's opinion — that to uphold this small tax was to open the door to larger ones, since the power to tax was the power to destroy. A short answer was that the power to tax was not the power to destroy so long as the Court had authority to pass on state action. This tax, far from being arbitrary or capricious, was supported by well-established precedent and rested upon economic truths. Throughout the better part of our history, the states had imposed severe restrictions, grounded in recognition of the evils of bigness, upon corporate size and activity. These restrictions were originally applied by the state of incorporation, and they were rendered largely futile when a few states, for the sake of filing fees and other income, began to provide a haven for incorporation not subject to such restraints. Taxes on foreign corporations, like the one in this case, represented an effort to redress the balance. Despite the *Cudahy* decision, and whether that case was distinguished because the measure of the tax here was issued rather than authorized stock, or simply overruled, this tax should be upheld, and the authority of the *Baltic* case restored.

"Life implies growth. Only change is abiding . . . . Formulas block the paths to truth and wisdom . . . . For we may not close the mind to the lessons of experience and abdicate the sway of reason."

SUPREME COURT OF THE UNITED STATES *

No. 98. — October Term, 1929.

William J. Stratton, Secretary of State, Appellant, vs. St. Louis Southwestern Railway Company.	Appeal from the United States Circuit Court of Appeals for the Seventh Circuit.

[April 14, 1930]

Opinion of Mr. Justice BRANDEIS.

The State of Illinois adopted a uniform policy for the taxation of the privilege it confers upon domestic and foreign corporations to hold property and do intra-state business in Illinois. It imposed an annual franchise tax of 5 cents per $100 of the proportion of the issued capital stock of such corporations represented by business transacted and property located in Illinois, fixing a minimum for such tax graduated according to the issued capital stock. The minimum ranges from $10 for a corporation with $50,000 or less of issued capital stock to $1,000 for a corporation with issued stock of $20,000,000, or more. This minimum is payable for the privilege, even if in the tax year the corporation has no property within the State and does no business there. The question for decision is

---

* Footnote 6 of this opinion, as Brandeis circulated it to the Court, embodied what Stone, in his letter of April 11, 1930, which is quoted further on in this chapter, referred to as a "slip." "I understand," Stone wrote, "that you have caught the slip in the note on page 6, where obviously you meant to make the denominator of your fraction to include all business and property both within and without the state." Brandeis did catch it. Although the opinions printed in this book are given verbatim, except for the correction of obvious mechanical errors, and although what occurred in this instance was perhaps not properly such an error, this footnote and the sentence to which it relates are given as corrected to eliminate the "slip" mentioned by Stone. — A.M.B.

whether this minimum provision, as here applied, violates the Federal Constitution.

The St. Louis Southwestern Railway, a Missouri corporation, secured from Illinois the privilege which is the subject of this tax. In 1926, the Railway's issued capital stock was $36,249,750. Its total property was valued at $76,793,697.79. That located in Illinois was valued at $786,196. Its total business during the year was $18,-201,955.32. That transacted wholly in Illinois was $2,868.36. If assessed at the rate of 5 cents per $100 of the proportion of its issued capital stock represented by property and business in the State, the tax would be only $135.21. It was assessed $1,000, the minimum tax applicable to a corporation of its size. The Railway claims that, as applied to it, the $1,000 minimum tax unduly burdens interstate commerce; deprives it of property without due process of law, because the tax is laid on property outside of the State; deprives it of the equal protection of the laws; and is generally arbitrary and capricious because it bears no relation to the benefit conferred. The District Court held that the tax was valid. 27 F. (2d) 1005 [1928]. The Circuit Court of Appeals held it void. 30 F. (2d) 322 [1929]. In my opinion, the tax violates no provision of the Federal Constitution.[1]

The Railway's contentions seem to me unsound, economically as well as legally. There is here no attempt to exclude or to expel a foreign corporation, *Western Union Tel. Co. v. Kansas*, 216 U.S. 1 [1910]; no denial to a foreign corporation already in the State of a privilege enjoyed by domestic ones; and no imposition upon a foreign corporation of a burden from which domestic ones are free, *Southern Ry. Co. v. Greene*, 216 U.S. 400 [1910]; *Hanover Fire Ins. Co. v. Harding*, 272 U.S. 494 [1926]. In the exercise of its power to determine its fiscal and social policy, the State has placed all corporations, foreign and domestic, upon an equality.[2] It has imposed a tax of a familiar type. As applied to domestic corporations,

[1] Much that I said in Cudahy Packing Co. v. Hinkle, 278 U.S. 460, 467 [1929]; Louisville Gas & Electric Co. v. Coleman, 277 U.S. 32, 42 [1928]; Quaker City Cab Co. v. Pennsylvania, 277 U.S. 389, 403 [1928]; Ozark Pipe Line Corp. v. Monier, 266 U.S. 555, 567 [1925]; and Texas Transport & Terminal Co. v. New Orleans, 264 U.S. 150, 155 [1924], when discussing other taxes on foreign corporations, is applicable here.

[2] See the illuminating discussion by the late Gerard C. Henderson, The Position of Foreign Corporations in American Constitutional Law (1918), especially pp. 118, *et seq*.

the constitutionality of this kind of tax is conceded. To hold it invalid as applied to foreign corporations would discriminate in their favor and against domestic corporations.[3]

First. The proper approach in determining the constitutional validity of a state tax has long become established constitutional doctrine. Taxation and commerce are practical rather than theoretical conceptions. *Galveston, Harrisburg & San Antonio Ry. Co. v. Texas*, 210 U.S. 217, 225 [1908]; *Farmers Loan & Trust Co. v. Minnesota*, 280 U.S. 204, 212 [1930]; *United Rys. & Electric Co. v. West*, 280 U.S. 234, 280 [1930]. Every case involving the validity of a tax under the Commerce Clause or the Fourteenth Amendment must be decided largely on its own facts. *Baltic Mining Co. v. Massachusetts*, 231 U.S. 68, 85 [1913]; *Kansas City, Fort Scott & Memphis Ry. Co. v. Botkin*, 240 U.S. 227, 233 [1916]; *Hump Hairpin Mfg. Co. v. Emmerson*, 258 U.S. 290, 295 [1922]. A corporation, whether domestic or foreign, enjoys the privilege of holding property and doing a local business within a State only by permission of the State. *Bank of Augusta v. Earle*, 13 Pet. 519 [1839]; *Home Ins. Co. v. New York*, 134 U.S. 594, 600 [1890]; *Hammond Packing Co. v. Arkansas*, 212 U.S. 322, 343 [1909]; *Hanover Fire Ins. Co. v. Harding*, 272 U.S. 494, 507 [1926]; *Bothwell v. Buckbee, Mears Co.*, 275 U.S. 274 [1927]. The price charged for this privilege lies ordinarily in the discretion of the State. *Ashley v. Ryan*, 153 U.S. 436, 441 [1894]; compare *Crescent Oil Co. v. Mississippi*, 257 U.S. 129, 137 [1921]. Its tax is not to be invalidated for theoretical reasons or by the application of formulas, but only if in practical operation and effect it constitutes an unlawful exaction. *U.S. Express Co. v. Minnesota*, 223 U.S. 335, 345 [1912]; *Kansas City, Fort Scott & Memphis Ry. Co. v. Botkin, supra,* at 231, 233. We should be concerned, therefore, not with the mode adopted by the State for computing the tax, but with its practical effect and operation. For, the "validity of the tax can in no way be dependent upon the mode which the State may deem fit to adopt in fixing the amount for any year which it will exact for the fran-

[3] Compare *Horn Silver Mining Co. v. New York,* 143 U.S. 305, 315 [1892]: "It does not lie in any foreign corporation to complain that it is subjected to the same law with the domestic corporation." And *New York v. Latrobe,* 279 U.S. 421, 427 [1929]: "A state which has adopted a permissible scheme of franchise tax for domestic corporations . . . has a legitimate interest in imposing a like burden on foreign corporations which it permits to carry on business there. . . ."

chise." *Home Insurance Co. v. New York, supra,* at 600. "The selected measure may appear to be simply a matter of convenience in computation . . . and if the tax purports to be laid upon a subject within the taxing power of the State, it is not to be condemned by the application of any artificial rule . . ." *Kansas City, Fort Scott & Memphis Ry. Co. v. Botkin, supra,* at 233; *Ray Consolidated Copper Co. v. United States,* 268 U.S. 373, 376 [1925]; *New York v. Latrobe,* 279 U.S. 421, 427 [1929]. Tested by these rules, the minimum tax must be deemed valid, unless "the conclusion is required that its necessary operation and effect is to make it a prohibited exaction," *Kansas City, Fort Scott & Memphis Ry. Co. v. Botkin, supra,* at 233, in violation of the Commerce Clause, or the Due Process Clause, or the Equal Protection Clause of the Federal Constitution.

Second. The minimum tax does not violate the Commerce Clause. Every tax, wherever laid and whatever its nature, burdens the taxpayer. If it is laid upon a concern engaged in interstate commerce, it necessarily burdens such commerce. Compare *U.S. Glue Co. v. Oak Creek,* 247 U.S. 321, 327 [1918]. But only direct burdens are prohibited. Taxes which are deemed indirect burdens upon interstate commerce are valid even if the resulting burden is heavy, like that of the state tax commonly laid upon the railroad plant of an interstate carrier within its borders. Property within the State may be taxed even if it is used exclusively in interstate commerce, *Atlantic & Pacific Tel. Co. v. Philadelphia,* 190 U.S. 160, 163 [1903]; *Wells, Fargo & Co. v. Nevada,* 248 U.S. 165, 167 [1918]; *Union Tank Line Co. v. Wright,* 249 U.S. 275, 282 [1919]; and, in valuing such property, any additional increment of value which may be derived from its use in interstate commerce may be considered. *Galveston, Harrisburg & San Antonio Ry. Co. v. Texas, supra,* at 225; *Cudahy Packing Co. v. Minnestoa,* 246 U.S. 450, 456 [1918]; *Pullman Co. v. Richardson,* 261 U.S. 330, 338 [1923].

The subject of the tax here in question is a privilege admittedly within the taxing power of the State. Objection to it is made solely on the ground that it is measured by the total issued stock. Its validity as respects domestic corporations is not questioned. I know of no good reason for the differentiation. This license fee charged a foreign corporation for the privilege of holding property or doing business within the State seems to me, in all essentials, comparable to the franchise tax laid upon a domestic corporation.[4] Both burden the taxpayer, and hence commerce; but both burdens upon the commerce are indirect. The Illinois minimum tax upon this Missouri corporation does not differ legally from the tax which Missouri does or could lay upon it as a domestic corporation for the corporate privilege conferred.

The minimum tax meets all the tests commonly applied in determining whether a tax is obnoxious to the Commerce Clause. It is not levied for the privilege or act of engaging in interstate commerce. Compare *McCall v. California*, 136 U.S. 104 [1890]; *Atlantic & Pacific Tel. Co. v. Philadelphia*, 190 U.S. 160, 162 [1903]; *Texas Transport & Terminal Co. v. New Orleans*, 264 U.S. 150 [1924]; *Di Santo v. Pennsylvania*, 273 U.S. 34 [1927]. Its payment is not a condition precedent to carrying on commerce including interstate. Compare *Western Union Tel. Co. v. Massachusetts*, 125 U.S. 530, 553–4 [1888]; and see *Postal Telegraph Cable Co. v. Adams*, 155 U.S. 688, 696 [1895]; *Underwood Typewriter Co. v. Chamberlain*, 254 U.S. 113, 119 [1920]. It is not levied on interstate commerce. Compare *Passenger Cases*, 7 How. 283 [1849]; *State Freight Tax*, 15 Wall. 232 [1873]; *Telegraph Co. v. Texas*, 105 U.S. 460 [1882]; *Alpha Portland Cement Co. v. Massachusetts*, 268 U.S. 203 [1925]. It does not grow, or shrink, according to the volume of such commerce. Compare *Ratterman v. Western Union Tel. Co.*, 127 U.S. 411 [1888]; *Crew Levick Co. v. Pennsylvania*, 245 U.S. 292 [1917]. It does not fluctuate according to the amount, or proportion, of the capital or property employed in that commerce. Compare *Gloucester Ferry Co. v. Pennsylvania*, 114 U.S. 196 [1885]; *Fargo v. Hart*, 193 U.S. 490 [1904]; *Galveston, Harrisburg & San Antonio Ry. Co. v. Texas, supra; Union Tank Line Co. v. Wright, supra; Wallace v. Hines*, 253 U.S. 66 [1920]. It is not furtively directed against interstate commerce. Compare *Looney v. Crane Co.*, 245 U.S. 178, 191 [1917]; *Ohio Tax Cases*, 232 U.S. 576, 593 [1914]; *Hump Hairpin Mfg. Co. v. Emmerson, supra*, at 295. It is not excessive in amount so as to obstruct interstate commerce. See *Kansas City, Memphis & Birmingham R.R. Co. v. Stiles*,

[4] Compare Southern R.R. v. Greene, 216 U.S. 400, 417–18 [1910]: "It would be a fanciful distinction to say that there is any real difference in the burden imposed because the one is taxed for the privilege of the foreign corporation to do business in the State and the other for the right to be a corporation." And see note 8, *infra*.

242 U.S. 111, 119 [1916]; *Wells, Fargo & Co. v. Nevada*, 248 U.S. 165, 168–9 [1918]; *Southern Ry. Co. v. Watts*, 260 U.S. 519, 530 [1923]. It is not contended that this minimum tax, together with all other taxes levied by Illinois, exceeds the amount which could be properly levied on the $784,000 worth of property located in Illinois. Compare *St. Louis, Southwestern Ry. Co. v. Arkansas*, 235 U.S. 350, 366, 367 [1914]; *Pullman Co. v. Richardson, supra*, at 339. Nor is there any evidence that the net income from business transacted entirely within the State is not sufficient to pay the tax. Compare *Pullman Co. v. Adams*, 189 U.S. 420, 421 [1903]; *Bass, Ratcliff & Gretton Ltd. v. State Tax Comm.*, 266 U.S. 271, 280, 283, 284 [1924].

The error of adopting an artificial or mechanical formula as to the validity of a specific measure of a franchise tax, instead of looking solely to the subject and practical effect of the tax, is well illustrated by the facts of this case. The Court holds that insofar as the tax is measured by the proportion of the total issued stock represented by property and business within the State, it is constitutionally unobjectionable; while insofar as the minimum is measured by the total issued stock it is unconstitutional. Yet, in fact, the measure in both cases is the total issued stock. Even on the proportion basis, the amount of the tax varies directly with the total issued stock, regardless of identity in the amount of property and business in Illinois and elsewhere.[5] Moreover, a tax based upon the proportion of the property and business within the State to the whole — which is confessedly valid — bears a close, and possibly unjust, relation to the amount of interstate commerce and property outside of the State, at any given capitalization. On the

[5] A constant fraction (the proportion of property and business within the State to the whole) applied to a varying base (the issued stock) will, of course, produce an amount which will vary in direct proportion to the size of that base. Thus a corporation having the same amount of property and business in Illinois and elsewhere as the Railway, but having an issued capitalization of only $10,000,000 would pay, on the proportion basis, a tax of $37.30; while the Railway would pay $135.21. Under the same circumstances, a corporation having issued capital of $90,000,000 would pay a tax of $335.70. For, the ratio of the Railway's property and business in Illinois to its total property and business is .00746. Five cents on each hundred dollars of (.00746 × $10,000,000) is $37.30. The same for (.00746 × $90,000,000) equals $335.70. Under these circumstances, it may well be concluded that the use of the total, rather than a portion of the issued stock, does not alter the basis of the tax. As stated in International Shoe Co. v. Shartel, 279 U.S. 429, 433 [1929], it only increases the rate of the tax. And since the tax thus computed is not excessive, this mode of computation does not invalidate it.

other hand, the minimum tax bears none. The latter is constant for given capitalizations regardless of the amount of interstate commerce and property out of the State. The former, for given capitalizations and local property and business, varies inversely with the total amount of property and business.[6]

Third. The tax is not levied on property beyond the jurisdiction of the State in violation of the Due Process Clause. It is levied on a privilege admittedly within the State's taxing power. There is no suggestion that the State is covertly attempting to tax a forbidden subject under the guise of a tax on a permissible one. The tax manifests a laudable policy to approximate justice in taxation, applying equally to all corporations, domestic or foreign. No reason is given for disregarding the avowed lawful purpose of the tax and attributing to it an ulterior and forbidden one. The formula that a franchise tax on a foreign corporation, measured by its issued capital stock, necessarily depends upon the existence of capital stock representing property outside the State and is therefore a tax upon such property, seems to me unfounded assumption and a regrettable departure from our established rule to look at the substance rather than the shadow. There is no pretense even that the minimum tax, together with all other Illinois taxes, exceeds the amount validly taxable against the property located in Illinois; and no reason to suppose that the tax must be paid out of property beyond the jurisdiction of the State.

Moreover, the mere fact that a tax must be paid out of the earnings of physical property located beyond the State is not sufficient to invalidate it under the Due Process Clause. The franchise tax

[6] If to a constant base (the issued stock) is applied a fraction with a constant numerator (property and business within the State) but a changing denominator (total property and business), the product will, of course, vary in inverse proportion to the size of that denominator. Thus assuming the same amount of property and business in Illinois (approximately $790,000), and the same amount of stock (approximately $36,000,000), if the Railway's total business and property amounted to only $40,000,000 its tax on the proportion basis would be $355.50, instead of the $135.21. And if its total business and property amounted to $180,000,000, under the same circumstances, its tax would be only $79.00. There is little reason for reducing the tax on taxable property merely because of the taxpayer's ownership of other property which is not taxable. The minimum tax bears no relation in practical operation and effect to the amount of interstate commerce and does not burden that commerce, unless it can be proved that the amount is so excessive, when compared with the privilege enjoyed, as to constitute a burden on that commerce, which cannot be avoided by renouncing the privilege. Compare Western Union Tel. Co. v. Kansas, *supra.* This is obviously not the case.

on a domestic corporation, enjoying the same privilege as the Railway, may be measured by its authorized or issued stock, even though only a part or none of its business and property is located within the State, *Kansas City, Memphis & Birmingham R.R. Co. v. Stiles, supra; Cream of Wheat Co. v. Grand Forks,* 253 U.S. 325 [1920]. As stated in *Kansas City, Fort Scott & Memphis Railway Co. v. Botkin, supra,* at 232–3: "The authority of the State to tax this privilege, or franchise, has always been recognized and it is well settled that a tax of this sort is not necessarily rendered invalid because it is measured by capital stock which in part may represent property not subject to the State's taxing power . . . . And, agreeably to the principle above mentioned, it has never been, and cannot be, maintained that an annual tax upon this privilege is in itself, and in all cases, repugnant to the Federal power merely because it is measured by authorized or paid-up capital stock. The selected measure may appear to be simply a matter of convenience in computation and may furnish no basis whatever for the conclusion that the effort is made to reach subjects withdrawn from the taxing authority."

No one would suggest that the Delaware franchise tax on domestic corporations, measured by authorized stock, is void as to the many Delaware corporations which have no property and do no business in Delaware.[7] But if such a tax is not subject to the objection that it taxes property outside the State, why should a similar tax laid upon a foreign corporation for the similar privilege of holding property and doing business within the State be open to it?[8] In *Pembina Mining Co. v. Pennsylvania,* 125 U.S. 181 [1888] — a case recently cited with approval in *Investors Syndicate v. McMullen,* 274 U.S. 717 [1927] — it was held that such a privilege tax upon a foreign corporation may be imposed, even though it must be paid out of property beyond the jurisdiction of the State. There, this Court upheld a Pennsylvania statute which imposed a tax of "one-fourth of a mill on each dollar of capital

---

[7] See note 48, *infra.*

[8] It has never been questioned that the power to do intrastate business and hold property in a given State, as a corporation, depends, for foreign and domestic corporations alike, on the will of that State. Unless that State grants the privilege to a corporation seeking it, the mere incorporation in Delaware or elsewhere is valueless. The privilege thus granted to a foreign corporation may, indeed, be much more valuable than the privilege to be a corporation granted by the State of incorporation.

stock . . . authorized" (p. 182) on all foreign corporations which did not invest or employ any capital in the State, but had offices there for the use of officers, stockholders or agents; saying (p. 186): "We do not perceive the pertinency of the position advanced by counsel that the tax in question is void as an attempt by the State to tax a franchise not granted by her, and property or business not within her jurisdiction. The fact is otherwise. No tax upon the franchise of the foreign corporation is levied, nor upon its business or property without the State. A license tax only is exacted as a condition of its keeping an office within the State for the use of its officers, stockholders, agents and employés; nothing more and nothing less . . . ." Similar taxes were upheld in *Cheney Bros. Co. v. Massachusetts*, 246 U.S. 147, 155 [1918], with respect to two corporations there involved.

The minimum tax is measured entirely by the issued stock and not at all by property, whether within or without the State. It is a step tax; but it does not vary in direct proportion with the issued stock and a maximum is fixed. *General Railway Signal Co. v. Virginia*, 246 U.S. 500, 511 [1918]. The validity of this measure should no more be subject to question than the validity of a tax at a flat rate for all no-par shares of foreign corporations, regardless of their actual value; or of a tax statute which fixes a value for all no-par shares of foreign corporations regardless of their actual value. *New York v. Latrobe, supra; International Shoe Co. v. Shartel*, 279 U.S. 429 [1929]. While the Illinois tax, measured by the valid proportion method, fluctuates with the amount of property and business without the State,[9] the minimum tax bears no relation whatever to the amount of property or business either within or without the State. The Railway's property and business outside the State is over $76,000,000. The minimum tax would be the same for the corporation if that property and business were anywhere above or below that figure, so long as its issued capital was at least $20,000,000.

It is said that to sustain this moderate tax is to open the door to oppressive burdens and to oblige every carrier to hold its property subject to the exertion of the taxing power of every State in which it does business, since "the power to tax is the power to destroy." A short answer is that power to tax is not power to destroy so long as this Court possesses the authority to pass on the constitution-

[9] See note 6, *supra*.

ality of State action. Permitting a little does not, of itself, necessitate also the granting of too much. If the tax should indeed be one that is oppressive and prohibited, the taxpayer will not be without redress. Compare *Western Union Tel. Co. v. Kansas, supra; Pullman Co. v. Kansas*, 216 U.S. 56 [1910]; *Looney v. Crane Co., supra; Wallace v. Hines, supra; Dane v. Jackson*, 256 U.S. 589, 599 [1921]. Moreover, here, unlike *M'Culloch v. Maryland*, 4 Wheat. 316, 431 [1819], the subject matter of the tax is lawfully taxable by this State. The sole ground upon which the tax is invalidated is that an unlawful measure is employed. The unlawfulness of this measure is not proved by assuming that the subject is prohibited. "The principle [that the power to tax involves the power to destroy], of course, is important only where the tax is sought to be imposed upon a non-taxable subject . . . ." *Macallen Co. v. Massachusetts*, 279 U.S. 620, 628 [1929]. Assuredly, the State could lawfully impose upon the Railway the same tax or even a greater one by employing a higher rate or a measure deemed unobjectionable.[10] The Constitution does not confer upon corporations, even if engaged in interstate commerce, a right to enjoy the privilege of doing intrastate business. *Bank of Augusta v. Earle, supra; Paul v. Virginia*, 8 Wall. 168 [1869]; *Pembina Mining Co. v. Pennsylvania, supra; Investors Syndicate v. McMullen*, 274 U.S. 717 [1927], affirming, *per curiam*, 113 Neb. 816 [1925].

Fourth. The minimum tax does not deny the Railway equal protection of the law. No claim is made of purposeful discrimination either between domestic and foreign corporations or among foreign corporations. Compare *Southern Ry. Co. v. Greene, supra; Hanover Ins. Co. v. Harding, supra.* The argument is that in operation the minimum tax produces an inequality. It is said that the statute is discriminatory on its face, in that it provides two bases for the tax; for some corporations, the proportion of capital stock represented by property and business within the State, for others, the total issued stock. The statement is not accurate. The statute provides for all corporations a single tax measured by the propor-

[10] It may be said here, as in Maine v. Grand Trunk Ry. Co., 142 U.S. 217, 229 [1891]: "If the amount ascertained were specifically imposed as the tax, no objection to its validity would be pretended." And as in Hump Hairpin Mfg. Co. v. Emmerson, *supra*, at 296: "If this same amount of tax had been imposed . . . without reference being made to the basis of its computation, very certainly no objection to its validity would have been thought of."

tion of the issued capital stock which the property and business within the State bears to the total property and business everywhere; but adds the proviso that the tax payable shall in no event be less than a certain amount, the minimum being fixed according to the total issued stock. The presence of a minimum in a taxing statute does not, of course, produce such inequality as the equal protection clause prohibits.[11] The question is, therefore, only whether the measure of the minimum tax produces such inequality.

The Railway complains that other corporations with smaller capitalizations would pay smaller taxes even though they had as much, and possibly more, property and business in Illinois. But when a tax is measured by the par value of stock, *St. Louis Southwestern Ry. Co. v. Arkansas, supra; Hump Hairpin Mfg. Co. v. Emmerson, supra;* or at a flat rate on all no-par shares, *New York v. Latrobe, supra;* or at a rate on an assumed value which is the same for all no-par shares, *Margay Oil Corp. v. Applegate,* 273 U.S. 666 [1927]; *International Shoe Co. v. Shartel, supra,* similar inequality between corporations having the same amount of property within the State but different capitalizations is bound to result, whether the base is the total issued stock or only the proportion represented by property and business in the State. The amount produced by either measure fluctuates, as has been shown, with the total issued stock irrespective of identity in the amount of property or business. The resulting inequality complained of is inevitable with any measure which includes capital stock. For the issued stock and the amount of property and business are things which bear no necessary relation to each other. Compare *Ray Consolidated Copper Co. v. United States, supra,* at 377; *New York v. Latrobe, supra,* at 426.

It is thus settled that such inequality does not violate the Equal Protection Clause. The Constitution does not require a franchise tax to be measured by the amount of property or business or by any other specific means. Nor does it require a State "to adopt the best possible system of taxation." *New York v. Latrobe, supra,* at 427. Within the limits of the Commerce Clause and the Fourteenth Amendment, the State is free to adopt any convenient measure. As was said at last term in *New York v. Latrobe, supra,* at 427: "A state which has adopted a permissible scheme of franchise tax for

[11] All the tax statutes cited in notes 48 and 50, *infra,* provide minima.

domestic corporations, based on capital stock, . . . has a legitimate interest in imposing a like burden on foreign corporations which it permits to carry on business there, and we can perceive no constitutional objection to its protecting that interest by such a tax where, as here, it is limited to shares actually issued, is not assailed as confiscatory, does not reach either directly or indirectly property beyond the state and does not discriminate between foreign and domestic corporations, or between foreign corporations of like organization and property." Compare *Quaker City Cab Co. v. Pennsylvania,* 277 U.S. 389, 405 [1928]; and *Stebbins v. Riley,* 268 U.S. 137, 141 [1925]; *Louisville Gas & Electric Co. v. Coleman,* 277 U.S. 32, 42–9 [1928]. The kind and number of shares with which a corporation is permitted to enter the State is a part of the privilege conferred; and it is not inappropriate to consider them in taxing it. This is, in effect, conceded when the validity of the Illinois tax, insofar as it is proportioned to property and business within the State, is admitted. For that measure, as has been shown, is ultimately dependent upon the total issued stock.[12]

Fifth. The minimum tax is not arbitrary or capricious. It has well established precedent; rests upon economic truths; and bears a close relation to the benefit conferred.

Whatever may be the situation with respect to interstate commerce, it is unquestioned that, as respects intrastate commerce, the power to determine whether and under what conditions business shall be conducted by corporations rests exclusively with the several States.[13] These have differed much in their policies as to incorporation; and the policy of each has changed from time to time. But throughout the greater part of our history, the States guarded jealously their control over grants of the corporate privilege; and they have made it a source of revenue. Severe restrictions on corporate size and activity long prevailed. These restrictions originated in fear. First, there was the fear of monopoly. Then, the fear

[12] In Cudahy Packing Co. v. Hinkle, 278 U.S. 460, 467 [1929], it was said: "Whether, because reckoned upon authorized and not upon actual capital stock, the challenged legislation fails to require like fees for equal privileges within the doctrine of *Air-Way Electric Appliance Corp. v. Day,* 266 U.S. 71 [1924], we need not now consider."

[13] Except as limited by the doctrine of unconstitutional conditions and the application of the Fourteenth Amendment to corporations already in the State. See Hanover Fire Ins. Co. v. Harding, *supra,* at 507; Henderson, note 2, *supra,* ch. 6–9 inc.

of a domination more general. Fear of encroachment upon the liberties and opportunities of the individual. Fear of the subjection of labor to capital. Fear that the absorption of capital by corporations, and their perpetual life, might bring evils similar to those which attended mortmain.[14] There was a sense of some insidious menace inherent in large aggregations of capital. Incorporation for business purposes was long denied after it had been freely granted for religious, educational and charitable purposes.[15] And when finally granted for business purposes, fees graduated according to the capital stock were commonly exacted as compensation for the privilege.

The earliest statute permitting incorporation for a business purpose under a general law was that enacted in New York in 1811.[16] It was not until 1850 that incorporation under a general law for limited business purposes was commonly permitted.[17] The extension of the privilege to every lawful business did not become common until after 1875.[18] The enactment of these general incorpora-

---

[14] It was doubtless because of this, that the earlier statutes limited the life of corporations to fixed terms of 20, 30 or 50 years. See the statutes cited in subsequent notes.

[15] The power of legislatures to grant special charters was sometimes strictly limited, even before the adoption of constitutional amendments withdrawing that power entirely. Thus the New York Constitution adopted in convention in November, 1821, and by popular vote in January, 1822, required the assent of two-thirds of each house for any act "creating, continuing, altering or renewing any body politic or corporate" — Art. 7, § 9; L. 1822–24, p. x [N.Y. Sess. Laws 1823, p. x]. A similar provision was added to the Constitution of Delaware in 1852 — Art. 2, § 17; Rev. Code 1852, p. xxvi. The Constitution of Illinois, adopted in 1848, provided that no act authorizing the formation of a corporation with banking powers should be effective unless ratified by popular vote — Art. X, § 5; Stat. 1857, p. 71 [1858].

[16] Act of March 22, 1811, c. 67, 1 Rev. L. (1813), p. 245 [N.Y. Sess. Laws 1811, p. 111]. The purposes for which corporations might be formed under that law were limited to manufacturing woolen, cotton or linen goods; making glass; making, from ore, bar-iron, anchors, mill-irons, steel, nail rods, hoop iron, ironmongery, [sheet copper,] sheet lead, shot, white lead and red lead. Corporate life was limited to 20 years. The capital stock was limited to $100,000, §§ 1, 2, and 5.

[17] The first general act in New Jersey was that of February 25, 1846, L. 1846, p. 64. In Michigan — May 18, 1846, Act 148, L. 1846, p. 265. In Illinois — February 10, 1849, L. 1849, p. 87. In Pennsylvania — April 7, 1849, No. 368, L. 1849, p. 563. In Massachusetts — May 15, 1851, c. 133, Gen. Stat. 1860 (2 ed.), p. 341 [Mass. Acts and Res. 1849–51, p. 633]. In Maine — March 19, 1862, c. 152, L. 1862, p. 118. In Delaware — March 21, 1871, c. 152, 14 Del. L. 229. In general, the objects of incorporation under these acts were limited to mining, manufacturing, mechanical or chemical business; and a limited life was conferred.

[18] New York — L. 1866, c. 838, p. 1896; L. 1875, c. 611, p. 755. Illinois — July 1, 1872, L. 1872, p. 296 [Ill. Sess. Laws 1871–72, p. 571]. Massachusetts — Act of April 14, 1874, c. 165, § 1 [Mass. Acts and Res. 1874–75, p. 109]. Pennsylvania —

tion laws did not imply that the apprehension of corporate domination had been wholly overcome. The legislation was partly an expression of the longing for equality; a protest against the special
privilege incident to special incorporation acts.[19] Hence, while the
right to incorporate was freely granted, nearly every State limited,
until recently, the amount of the authorized capital. In New York
the maximum was at first $100,000 for some businesses and as little
as $50,000 for others.[20] Massachusetts imposed a maximum limita-
tion until 1903; and the maximum was apparently dependent upon
the supposed requirement of the efficient unit. Thus, in some kinds
of business it was $500,000; in others, $1,000,000; in still others,
$100,000; and in some as low as $5,000.[21] Pennsylvania's first gen-

---

April 29, 1874, L. 1874, p. 73. Maine — February 3, 1876, c. 65, L. 1876, p. 51.
Michigan — September 19, 1885, Act 232, L. 1885, p. 343. Delaware — April 11,
1893, c. 702, 19 Del. L. 899 [? see Act of March 14, 1883, 17 Del. Laws, c. 147,
§ 10, p. 217, and Act of March 10, 1899, 21 Del. Laws, c. 273, § 1, p. 445].

[19] That the longing for equality and the dread of special privilege were largely
responsible for the general incorporation laws is indicated by the unanimity with
which the States amended their Constitutions so as to prohibit the grant of special
charters. The first constitutional provision requiring incorporation under general
laws seems to be that in the New York Constitution of 1846 — Art. 8, § 1, Rev. Stat.
1846 (3 ed. 1848), p. 423 [vol. 3]. The other States followed in later years. See, e.g.,
Illinois — 1848, Art. X, § 1, Stat. 1857, p. 70; Michigan — 1850, Art. 15, § 1, Comp.
L. 1857, p. 70; Pennsylvania — 1874, Art. 3, § 7 [Pa. Laws 1874, p. 8]; Maine —
1875, Art. H, Part Third, § 14, L. 1876, p. 17; New Jersey — 1875, Art. 4, §7, ¶ 11,
1 Gen. Stat. 1709–1895, p. liv.

[20] See note 16, *supra*. The Act of 1811 was extended to cover the manufacture
of morocco and other leather; but for such objects the capital stock was not to
exceed $60,000; April 14, 1817, c. 223, L. 1817, p. 265. Further objects were added
from time to time, with the general limitation of $100,000 or lower limitations; as,
for example, $50,000 for corporations manufacturing salt. L. 1821, c. 231, § 19,
p. 234; 1 Rev. Stat. 1829, c. 9, § 90, p. 266.

[21] The first general act, note 17, *supra*, permitted incorporation for "any kind of
manufacturing, mechanical, mining or quarrying business." It limited the maximum
to $200,000. Act of March 19, 1855, c. 68, § 1 [Mass. Acts and Res. 1854–55,
p. 534], increased the maximum to $500,000. The Act of May 9, 1870, c. 224 (Acts
& Res. 1870, p. 154) repealed previous acts (§ 68) and made more comprehensive
provisions: cutting, storing and selling ice, or carrying on any agricultural, horti-
cultural, mechanical, mining, quarrying or manufacturing business, printing and
publishing — a maximum of $500,000 (§ 2); cooperation in any of the above busi-
nesses and cooperative trade — $50,000 (§ 3); opening outlets, canals or ditches,
propagation of herrings and alewives — $5,000 (§ 4); making and selling gas for
light in cities or towns — $500,000 (§ 5); common carriage of goods — $1,000,000
(§ 6). Later acts provided for the manufacture and distribution of gas for steam,
heat, power and cooking; and for the furnishing of hydrostatic and pneumatic pressure. A maximum of $500,000 was prescribed. Acts of April 9, 1879, c. 202 [Mass.
Acts and Res. 1879, p. 541]; May 15, 1885, c. 240 [Mass. Acts and Res. 1885,
p. 684]; April 11, 1891, c. 189 [Mass. Acts and Res. 1891, p. 776]; May 27, 1893,
c. 397 [Mass. Acts and Res. 1893, p. 1126]. The same limit was prescribed for
corporations to erect and maintain hotels, public halls, and buildings for manufac-

eral act contained no maximum limit. Later, a limit of $500,000 was imposed.[22] Then it was raised for some businesses, and later for all, to $1,000,000; [23] with the permission to increase to $5,000,-000 upon satisfying the Attorney General of the reasonableness of so large a capitalization.[24] The limit was not removed until 1905.[25] The maximum in Vermont was $1,000,000, until 1911.[26] And the capitalization could exceed $10,000,000, until 1915, only if in the opinion of a judge of the supreme court such a capitalization would not tend "to create a monopoly or result in restraining competition in trade." [27] Mining corporations in Maryland were not permitted, until 1918, to hold more than 500 acres of land (except in Allegheny County, where 1,000 acres was allowed); or have more than $3,000,000 of capital stock.[28] In New Hampshire, the maximum

---

turing purposes. Acts of April 24, 1872, c. 244 [Mass. Acts and Res. 1872, p. 178]; March 9, 1888, c. 116 [Mass. Acts and Res. 1888, p. 86]. The maximum limit was raised to $1,000,000 for manufacturing and mechanical business by Act of March 22, 1871, c. 110, § 1 [Mass. Acts and Res. 1871, p. 499]; and for mining corporations by Act of May 3, 1875, c. 177, § 3 [Mass. Acts and Res. 1875, p. 770]; and to $100,000 for cooperative trade by Act of April 11, 1879, c. 210 [Mass. Acts and Res. 1879, p. 548]. By Act of April 14, 1873, c. 179 [Mass. Acts and Res. 1873, p. 600], the general act was extended to the common carriage of persons — except by railroad — and a limit of $1,000,000 was imposed. The Act of April 14, 1874, c. 165 [Mass. Acts and Res. 1874, p. 109], authorized incorporation for "any lawful business," not specifically provided for, and limited the amount of stock to $1,000,000. The maximum limit for manufacturing and mechanical corporations was removed by Act of March 28, 1899, c. 199 [Mass. Acts and Res. 1899, p. 161]. For all the other corporate purposes, the limitations above-named remained until the passage of the Business Corporation Law, June 17, 1903, c. 437 [Mass. Acts and Res. 1903, p. 418]. By that time commissions with power to supervise the issues of public service corporations had long been established. Act of June 11, 1885, c. 314 [Mass. Acts and Res. 1885, p. 769]; Act of June 5, 1894, c. 450; Act of June 5, 1894, c. 452; Act of June 9, 1894, c. 462 [Mass. Acts and Res. 1894, pp. 513, 514, 537].

[22] The first Act passed in 1849, note 17, *supra*, contained no limit. But a limit of $500,000 was imposed by Act of July 18, 1863, No. 949, L. 1864, p. 1102 [§ 29, p. 1106].

[23] The limit was raised to $1,000,000 for iron and steel corporations by Act of March 21, 1873, No. 4, L. 1873, p. 28, and it was extended to other corporations by Act of April 29, 1874, L. 1874, p. 73, which also increased the limit for the former to $5,000,000 [§§ 11, 38, pp. 79, 99].

[24] Act of April 18, 1873, No. 54, L. 1873, p. 76.

[25] Act of April 22, 1905, No. 190, amending Act of February 9, 1901, No. 1; 5 Purdon's Digest, 1905–09 Supp. (13th ed.), p. 5340.

[26] Pub Stat. (1906), Tit. 25, c. 187, § 4311, p. 830. The Act of January 28, 1911, No. 143 (L. 1910, pp. 140, 141–2) fixed the limit at $10,000,000, with the proviso quoted in the text.

[27] This provision was repealed by General Corporation Act, April 1, 1915, No. 141, L. 1915, p. 222.

[28] Bagby's Code (1911), Art. 23, § 245, p. 648; repealed by Act of April 10, 1918, c. 417, L. 1918, p. 884.

was $1,000,000 until 1907;[29] then increased to $5,000,000;[30] and not removed until 1919.[31] In Michigan the maximum was at first $100,000;[32] was gradually increased until it reached $25,000,000 for some corporations and $10,000,000 for others in 1903;[33] and it stood there until 1917,[34] when it was increased to $50,000,000.[35] This limit was not removed until 1921.[36] Indiana did not permit petroleum and natural gas corporations to have more than $2,000,-000 of capital stock until 1921.[37] Missouri imposed a maximum limit upon the capital stock of all business corporations until 1927.[38] And Texas still has such a limit for certain corporations.[39] The history in other States was much the same.[40]

[29] Pub. Stat. (1901), c. 147, § 6, p. 470.

[30] Act of April 5, 1907, c. 129, L. 1907, p. 131.

[31] Business Corporation Law, March 28, 1919, c. 92, L. 1919, p. 113.

[32] Act 148, May 18, 1846, § 6, L. 1846, pp. 265, 267 — corporations for mining or manufacturing iron, copper, etc.

[33] Act 232, June 18, 1903, 3 Howell's Mich. Stat. (1913), § 9533, p. 3815. The $25,000,000 maximum was for mercantile and manufacturing corporations. It had previously been raised to $5,000,000 by Act 232, September 19, 1885, § 2, L. 1885, p. 343. For mining corporations, a different maximum was fixed: $500,000 by Act 41, February 5, 1853, L. 1853, p. 53; $2,500,000 by Act 113, May 11, 1877, § 4, L. 1877, p. 87; and $10,000,000 by Act 233, September 17, 1903, Howell's, *supra*, § 7783, p. 3158, § 7804, p. 3165.

[34] See Dodge v. Ford Motor Co., 204 Mich. 459, 494 [1919].

[35] Act 254, May 10, 1917, § 2, L. 1917, pp. 529, 530.

[36] General Corporation Act, No. 84, April 26, 1921, L. 1921, p. 125, contains no limit on the amount of stock. Corporate life is limited to 30 years [Part 1, c. 2], § 5(b).

[37] Until 1921, corporations for various objects were formed under various acts. For mining corporations, a limit of $2,000,000 was prescribed. 2 Burns' Ind. Stat. (1914), § 5137; 2 *id.* (1926), § 5547. In 1921, a general act, applicable to corporations for any lawful business, was passed, without limitation on the amount of stock. Act of February 28, 1921, c. 35, L. 1921, p. 93.

[38] By Act of March 30, 1907, L. 1907, p. 166, the maximum was increased to $50,000,000 from the $10,000,000 limit previously in force; Rev. Stat. 1899, c. 12, Art. 9, § 1320, p. 429; Rev. Stat. 1919, c. 90, Art. 7, § 10152. The act was repealed and no maximum provided in Act of April 8, 1927, L. 1927, p. 395; 1927 Supp. to Rev. Stat., § 10152.

[39] 1 Rev. Civ. Stat. (1925), Tit. 32, Art. 1302, ¶¶ 15, 16, 27. See Act of March 9, 1925, c. 51, L. 1925, p. 188. [These provisions continued in force until 1955. See Texas Bus. Corp. Act of April 15, 1955, Tex. Sess. Laws 1955, c. 64, p. 239].

[40] *Alabama* — until 1876, the limit was $200,000. Rev. Code 1867 (Walker), part 2, Title 2, c. 3, § 1759; Act No. 282, March 3, 1870, § 3, L. 1869, p. 320. Under the Code of 1876 (Wood & Roquemore), § 1811, p. 509, (Act of February 28, 1876, § 9, L. 1875–6, p. 244), the limit was $1,000,000. Under the Code of 1897 (Civil, c. 28, § 1259, p. 429), it was $10,000,000. *Arizona* — Comp. L. 1864–71, c. 51, § 19, p. 486 — $5,000,000. *Illinois* — $300,000, Act of June 22, 1852, L., p. 135; $1,000,000, Act of February 17, 1857, L., p. 110; $500,000, Act of February 18, 1857, L., p. 161. *Maine* — $50,000, Act of March 19, 1862, c. 152, § 3 [Me. Acts and Res. 1862, p. 119]; $200,000, Act of February 28, 1867, c. 125, § 7 [Me.

The jealous care with which the size of capitalizations was limited,[41] the guarded steps with which corporations were permitted to increase their size, show the temper of public opinion toward large aggregations of capital and power. But restrictions on incorporation are futile and, indeed, injurious to the public revenue if they can be circumvented by foreign incorporation.[42] The gradual removal of these limitations by the States in recent years has been doubtless due, in large part, to the immense strides of foreign incorporation impelled by the heedless liberality of the incorporation laws of a few States patently eager for the revenue derived from filing fees and franchise taxes [43] — which are commonly meas-

Acts and Res. 1867, p. 73]; February 26, 1870, c. 93, § 1 [Me. Acts and Res. 1870, p. 70]; $500,000, Act of February 3, 1876, c. 65, § 2 [Me. Acts and Res. 1876, p. 51]; $2,000,000, Act of February 14, 1883, c. 116, § 1 [Me. Acts and Res. 1883, p. 95]; $10,000,000, Act of March 25, 1891, c. 99, § 1[Me. Acts and Res. 1891, p. 88]. The Act of March 21, 1901, c. 229 [Me. Acts and Res. 1901, p. 240; see § 8, p. 242], was the first to prescribe no limit. *Wisconsin* — Until 1879, $250,000, Rev. Stat. 1878, c. 86, § 1771, p. 515 [the $250,000 limit is set out in § 1772(3), p. 516]; Act of February 7, 1879, c. 7, L. 1879, p. 10. Limits were imposed in some cases even by *Delaware* (March 21, 1871, c. 152, 14 Del. L. 229) and *New Jersey* (March 30, 1865, c. 379, L. 1865, p. 707; March 31, 1869, c. 374, L. 1869, p. 1001).

[41] In addition to limitations on capital stock, severe restrictions on the amount of corporate indebtedness, bonded or otherwise, were very common. See, e.g., N.Y. Laws 1825, p. 449, § 3, 1 Rev. Stat. (1852), c. 18, Tit. 4, § 3, p. 1175; Ill. Laws 1849, p. 87, § 22, p. 92; Ill. Laws 1872, p. 296 [Ill. Sess. Laws 1871–72, p. 575] § 16, p. 300; Pa. Laws 1874, p. 73, § 13, p. 80; Maine Laws 1867, p. 72, § 24, p. 75; N.J. Laws 1846, p. 64, § 28, p. 69; N.J. Laws 1874, p. 124, § 16, p. 129.

[42] "It is often asked why men procure a charter from a state in which, perhaps, no part of the actual business is carried on. The answer is that under existing laws it is often possible for foreign corporations to do business in certain states on better terms than domestic corporations." John S. Parker, Where and How — A Corporation Handbook (2 ed. 1906), p. 3. The device was much used. "The *Evening Post* has frequently pointed out that New York capital is driven to shelter in New Jersey by reason of the more liberal laws of that State governing the incorporation of companies as compared with the laws of New York. Nearly all large corporations doing business in this city and State are incorporated under the laws of New Jersey or some other State, where more liberal laws prevail and in which inducements are thereby held out to attract capital thither and make it their legal home." — N.Y. Evening Post, March 23, 1896, quoted in Business Corporations Under the Laws of New Jersey (1896), p. 47, published by the N.J. Corporation Guarantee and Trust Co.

[43] "Many years ago the corporation laws of New Jersey were so framed as to invite the incorporation of companies by persons residing in other states and countries. The liberality and facility with which corporations could there be formed were extensively advertised, and a great volume of incorporation swept into that state. . . .

"The policy of New Jersey proved profitable to the state, and soon legislatures of other states began active competition. . . .

"Delaware and Maine also revised their laws, taking the New Jersey Act as a model, but with lower organization fees and annual taxes. Arizona and South Dakota

ured by the authorized or issued stock.[44] Even with the recognition
of the superiority of the corporation as an instrument of business
and the desire for boundless industrial and commercial development, the apprehension of corporations with huge capital was not
allayed until after the introduction of two governmental devices
designed to protect the rights and opportunities of the individual.
Commissions to regulate public utilities — to curb the exactions of
sanctioned monopolies.[45] Anti-trust laws — to prevent monopolies
in industry and commerce.[46]

If, with doubts as to the efficacy of these measures, apprehen-

---

also adopted liberal corporation laws, and contenting themselves with the incorporation fees, require no annual state taxes whatever.

"West Virginia for many years has been popular with incorporators, but in 1901,
in the face of the growing competition of other states, the legislature increased the
rate of annual taxes." John S. Parker, *supra*, note 42, p. 4. And West Virginia thus
lost her popularity. On the other hand, too drastic price cutting was also unprofitable. The bargain prices in Arizona and South Dakota attracted wild-cat corporations. Investors became wary of corporations organized under the laws of Arizona
or South Dakota and both States fell in disrepute among them and consequently
among incorporators. See Connyngton on Corporate Organization (1913), ch. 5.

Companies were early formed to secure charters for corporations at the least
cost and under the most favorable laws. These companies advertised their service
extensively; and also the liberality of the laws of certain States. Thus in its pamphlet,
"Business Corporations Under the Laws of Maine" (1903), the Corporation Trust
Co. enumerated among the advantages of the Maine laws: the comparatively low
organization fees and annual taxes; the absence of restrictions upon capital stock or
corporate indebtedness; the authority to issue stock for services as well as property,
with the judgment of the directors as to their value conclusive; and, significantly
enough, "the method of taxation, which bases the annual tax upon the stock issued,
does not necessitate inquiry into or report upon the intimate affairs of the corporation." See also its pamphlet "Business Corporations Under the Laws of Delaware"
(1907).

The States themselves advertised their wares. Thus, in an official pamphlet containing the corporation laws of Delaware (1901), the Secretary of State wrote in the
preface: "It is believed that no state has on its statute books more complete and
liberal laws than these"; and the outstanding advantages were then enumerated.
See also a pamphlet, "Organization of Corporations," issued by the Secretary of
State of Maine in 1904.

[44] See Report of the Massachusetts Committee on Corporation Laws (1903),
pp. 265–288; House Committee on the District of Columbia, Report of Hearings of
January 16, 1905, on H.R. 11811 and 12303 (Gov't Ptg. Office 1905). And see
note 50, *infra*.

[45] When the Act to Regulate Commerce was passed in 1887, there were commissions in 25 States. Vanderblue and Burgess, Railroads (1923), p. 15. See M. H.
Hunter, "The Early Regulation of Public Service Corporations," 7 Am. Ec. Rev.
569 (1917), reprinted in Dorau, Materials for the Study of Public Utility Economics (1930), pp. 283–294. And see note 21, *supra*.

[46] See Laws on Trusts and Monopolies, compiled by Nathan B. Williams for the
House Committee on the Judiciary, 1913 (revised ed. 1914), Gov't Ptg. Office; U.S.
Bureau of Corporations, Trust Laws and Unfair Competition (1915).

sion should recur, States may look to other means. Compare *Jones v. City of Portland,* 245 U.S. 217 [1917]; *Green v. Frazier,* 253 U.S. 233 [1920]; *Standard Oil Co. v. City of Lincoln,* 275 U.S. 504 [1927]. They may resort to the drastic limitations on capitalization of not only domestic corporations, but also of foreign corporations permitted to enter. Or, they may seek, through an exercise of the taxing power, to counterbalance the alleged undue advantages enjoyed by large corporations. If a progressive privilege tax graduated for this purpose according to the size of the licensee, itself or as a member of a larger unit, should be resorted to, it would seem to fall within the sanctioned use of the taxing power in aid of social and economic policy. *American Sugar Refining Co. v. Louisiana,* 179 U.S. 89, 95 [1900]; *Williams v. Fears,* 179 U.S. 270, 275 [1900]; *Armour Packing Co. v. Lacy,* 200 U.S. 226, 235 [1906]; *Southwestern Oil Co. v. Texas,* 217 U.S. 114, 126 [1910]; *Quong Wing v. Kirkendall,* 223 U.S. 59, 63 [1912]; *Fort Smith Lumber Co. v. Arkansas,* 251 U.S. 532, 534 [1920]. There is more reason for permitting them to use the progressive privilege tax for purely revenue purposes, as Illinois appears to have done in its minimum tax. To make the price of the corporate privilege rise in proportion to the amount of the company's issued capital is, at least, consistent with reason and unquestionably valid for domestic corporations. No provision of the Constitution in terms prohibits such legislation concerning foreign corporations. I find nothing between the lines of the Commerce Clause, the Due Process Clause or the Equal Protection Clause denying the State the power to do so in this case.

The minimum tax is not imposed for the exercise of the privilege to do business in the State. Like the consideration demanded for an option, it is the price charged for the opportunity conferred. It must be paid even if, during the tax year, no property is located and no business is done in the State. The value of the opportunity depends largely on the financial resources of the corporation which enjoys it. Obviously, the power inherent in the possession of large financial resources is not dependent upon or confined to the place where the assets are located. Great power may be exerted by a corporation in Illinois although it has little property located there. And the value to it of the privilege to exert the power is not necessarily measured by the amount of the property located there or the volume of local business done within its borders. Moreover, it is a matter of indifference, insofar as the minimum tax is concerned, whether the opportunity is availed of or not. The State has granted a large privilege. It may demand a corresponding price.[47]

This Court recognized early, and affirmed recently, that a franchise tax need not be measured by the extent of the exercise of the privilege conferred; and may be measured by the extent of the opportunity afforded. In upholding the tax involved in *Provident Institution v. Massachusetts*, 6 Wall. 611 [1868], the Court said (p. 630): "The amount of the tax does not depend on the amount of the property held by the institution, but it depends upon the capacity of the institution to exercise the privileges conferred by the charter." At the last term, we said in *New York v. Latrobe, supra*, at 426–7: "The kind and number of shares with which a foreign corporation is permitted to carry on its business within the state is a part of the privilege which the state extends to it and is a proper element to be taken into account in fixing a tax on the privilege . . . . Although permissible, a franchise tax need not be based solely on the amount of business done or property owned within the state." Compare *Ray Consolidated Copper Co. v. United States, supra*, at 376. A franchise tax measured by the total issued stock is concededly reasonable and proper for domestic corporations. *Kansas City, Memphis & Birmingham R.R. Co. v. Stiles, supra; Roberts & Schaefer Co. v. Emmerson, supra*. Such is the measure now used in many States.[48] And, until ob-

[47] Clearly, the privilege conferred is taxable, if its retention is desired, even though it is not exercised. Under such circumstances, the issued capital stock affords an eminently reasonable measure, since it approximates the potential extent to which the privilege may be availed of. It is also plainly reasonable to adopt for the minimum tax the same measure that is used when the privilege is not exercised at all.

[48] See e.g., *Alabama*, Gen. Acts 1927, Act No. 163, §§ 43, 53, pp. 172, 176; *Colorado*, Comp. L. 1921, § 7270; *Delaware*, L. 1929, vol. 36, c. 6, § 3, p. 21; *Georgia*, L. 1927, Part I, Tit. II, § 2, ¶ 44, p. 69; *Idaho*, 2 Comp. Stat. 1919, c. 188, § 4782; *Kansas*, Rev. Stat. 1923, § 17–701; *Maine*, Rev. Stat. 1916, c. 9, § 18, p. 209; *Maryland*, Bagby Code 1924, Art. 23, 109, p. 701; *Michigan*, Pub. Acts 1921, Act 85, § 4, p. 190, but see Public Acts 1929, Act 175, p. 484; *Nebraska*, Comp. Stat. 1922, § 681, p. 323; *Oklahoma*, Harlow's Supp. 1929, § 9947, p. 833; *Oregon*, 2 Olson's L. 1920, § 6883, p. 2748; *Texas*, 2 Rev. Civ. Stat. 1925, Art. 7084; *Washington*, L. 1929, c. 227, § 4. In some of these the measure is authorized capital stock; in some, paid-up stock; in some, issued and outstanding stock. If the first is valid, the latter are, *a fortiori*. For early measures of the same kind, see note 44, *supra*.

stacles were interposed by recent decisions of this Court,[49] the same measure had long been used in taxing the privileges of foreign corporations to hold property and transact local business within the State.[50] In view of this long practice, the social and economic truths upon which the tax rests, and the permissible policy of States to treat domestic and foreign corporations on a parity, *New York v. Latrobe, supra*, at 427, the Illinois tax cannot be held arbitrary and capricious.

Sixth. It is urged that recent decisions require us to hold the tax void. I do not recall any decision of this Court which has held that a relatively small tax, charged a foreign corporation annually for the privilege of holding property within a State and of transacting there intrastate as well as interstate business, violates the Federal Constitution because it is measured by the issued capital. Of the decisions most nearly in point, two would seem to require that this minimum tax be held valid. In *General Railway Signal Co. v. Virginia, supra*, a filing fee of $1,000 imposed upon a foreign corporation with an authorized capitalization of $5,000,000, and measured by the authorized capital — the last step being $5,000 — was sustained by a unanimous Court. In *Cheney Bros. Co. v. Massachusetts, supra*, an annual license tax fixed by the amount of the authorized capital but limited to $2,000 was likewise sustained by a unanimous Court. These decisions are so recent that four of the Justices who participated in them are still members of the Court. Those two cases applied the rule which had been declared

[49] International Paper Co. v. Massachusetts, 246 U.S. 135 [1918]; Air-Way Electric Appliance Co. v. Day, 266 U.S. 71 [1924]; Alpha Portland Cement Co. v. Massachusetts, *supra*; Cudahy Packing Co. v. Hinkle, 278 U.S. 460 [1929].

[50] See in addition to the statutes involved in the cases cited in note 49, *supra*: *Arkansas*, Acts 1909, Act 260, p. 780; *California*, L. 1906–07, c. 347, p. 664 (see Albert Pick & Co. v. Jordan, 169 Cal. 1 [1914], aff'd 244 U.S. 647; and compare Mulford Co. v. Curry, 163 Cal. 276 [1912]); *Colorado*, Sess. L. 1907, c. 211, p. 548 (but see Atchison, T. & S. F. R. R. Co. v. O'Connor, 223 U.S. 280 [1912]); *Georgia*, L. 1907, pp. 33, 34; *Nebraska*, L. 1909, c. 25, §§ 1, 2, p. 198; *North Carolina*, Pub. L. 1909, c. 438, § 83, p. 683; *Oregon*, Gen. L. 1903, p. 43, § 5 (but see Hirschfeld v. McCullagh, 64 Oreg. 502, 516 [1913]; and 2 Olson's Oreg. L. 1920, §§ 6883, 6884, p. 2748); *Tennessee*, Acts 1907, c. 434, p. 1477–8; *Texas*, Gen. L. 1907, pp. 502–8; *Utah*, L. 1907, c. 107, p. 126; *Vermont*, Pub. Stat. 1906, §§ 752–4. See also Chicago, M. & St. P. Ry. Co. v. Swindlehurst, 47 Mont. 119 [1913]; Northern Pacific Ry. Co. v. Gifford, 25 Idaho 196 [1913]; and, of course, Baltic Mining Co. v. Massachusetts, 231 U.S. 68 [1913]; Cheney Bros. Co. v. Massachusetts, 246 U.S. 147 [1918]; General Ry. Signal Co. v. Virginia, 246 U.S. 500 [1918]. And see Report of Mass. Committee on Corporations, note 44, *supra*, pp. 289–297.

in *Baltic Mining Co. v. Massachusetts, supra*; and that case was also cited with approval by a unanimous Court in *Kansas City, Fort Scott & Memphis Ry. Co. v. Botkin, supra*, at 231, 233, 234, 235; in *Crescent Oil Co. v. Mississippi, supra*, at 137; and by a divided Court in *Hump Hairpin Mfg. Co. v. Emmerson, supra*, at 294.

It is true that a different opinion prevails now. In *Alpha Portland Cement Co. v. Massachusetts, supra*, at 218, and in *Cudahy Packing Co. v. Hinkle*, 278 U.S. 460, 466 [1929], a divided Court expressed disapproval of the *Baltic* case. And in the case at bar, the Court declares that both the *Baltic* case and the *General Railway Signal* case are overruled. But neither the *Alpha Cement*, nor the *Cudahy* case, is directly in point here. In the former the corporation was engaged solely in interstate commerce (p. 211); in the latter (p. 467) the tax was measured, as in *Air-Way Electric Appliance Corp. v. Day*, 266 U.S. 71 [1924], by the authorized, as distinguished from the issued, capital stock. The distinction was called attention to in *Roberts & Schaefer Co. v. Emmerson, supra*, at 54; *New York v. Latrobe, supra*, at 424; *International Shoe Co. v. Shartel, supra*, at 433–4. Nor is the disapproval of the *Baltic* and *General Railway Signal* cases controlling. There, too, the measure was authorized stock.

The reason for overruling the earlier decisions is doubtless that more fully expressed at this term, in *Farmers Loan & Trust Co. v. Minnesota*, 280 U.S. 204, 209 [1930], when in overruling *Blackstone v. Miller*, 188 U.S. 189 [1903] — another important tax case — the Court said: "The inevitable tendency of that view [the rule of *Blackstone v. Miller*] is to disturb good relations among the States and produce the kind of discontent expected to subside after establishment of the Union . . . . The practical effect of it has been bad . . . ." [51] I do not question the propriety of the Court's overruling, in cases of this character, any decision which experience and reconsideration prove to have been mistaken.[52] Compare

[51] Similarly, the rule declared in Flint v. Stone Tracy Co., 220 U.S. 107, 161–2 [1911], also an important tax case, was disregarded by a divided Court in Quaker City Cab Co. v. Pennsylvania, *supra*, at 406–12, and Macallen Co. v. Massachusetts, *supra*, at 628, 636.

[52] Compare Taney, C. J., in The Passenger Cases, *supra*, at 470: "After such opinions, judicially delivered, I had supposed that question to be settled, so far as any question upon the construction of the Constitution ought to be regarded

Washington v. Dawson & Co., 264 U.S. 219, 238 [1924]; *Di Santo v. Pennsylvania*, 273 U.S. 34, 42–3 [1927]. For, the position of this Court in cases involving the application of the Constitution, is wholly unlike that of the highest court of England, where the doctrine of *stare decisis* was formulated.[53] "We must never forget, that it is a *constitution* we are expounding." *M'Culloch v. Maryland*, 4 Wheat. 316, 407 [1819]. We must never forget that the Federal Constitution, unlike an Act of Congress or the Constitution of a State, cannot be easily amended. We must never forget that what is called interpreting the Constitution is a function differing materially from that of passing upon the questions ordinarily arising at common law or in equity and that the function is rarely comparable to mere interpretation of a statute.

The decision of constitutional questions involves occasionally merely the correct reading of some provision of the Constitution. But the cases which have most engaged the attention of the Court since the adoption of the Fourteenth Amendment and the great development of interstate commerce, present no dispute as to the meaning of words or clauses. They deal with the application of admitted constitutional limitations to the varying and illusive facts of life.[54] Life implies growth. Only change is abiding. In order to reach sound conclusions in such cases, we must strive ceaselessly to bring our opinions into agreement with facts ascertained. We must never forget that the judgment of men is fallible, being influenced inevitably by their views as to economic, social and political policy.[55] Our effort to reach sound conclusions will be futile

---

as closed by the decisions of this court. I do not, however, object to the revision of it, and am quite willing that it be regarded hereafter as the law of this court, that its opinion upon the construction of the Constitution is always open to discussion when it is supposed to have been founded in error, and that its judicial authority should hereafter depend altogether on the force of the reasoning by which it is supported."

[53] See Arthur L. Goodhart, "Case Law in England and America," 15 Cornell Law Quarterly 173, 188, 193 [1929].

[54] Compare Frankfurter and Landis, The Business of the Supreme Court (1927) Ch. VIII, pp. 317, 318; also "The Business of the Supreme Court at October Term, 1928," 43 Harvard Law Review, 33, 53 [1929].

[55] Compare Benjamin N. Cardozo, The Nature of the Judicial Process (1921) 167–77; Ray A. Brown, "Due Process of Law, Police Power, and the Supreme Court," 40 Harvard Law Review 943, 961, 967 [1927]; "Police Power — Legislation for Health and Personal Safety," 42 Harvard Law Review 866, 867, 872 [1929]; Percy H. Winfield, "Public Policy in the English Common Law," 42 Harvard Law Review 76, 101–2 [1928].

if we substitute formulas for reasoning. Formulas block the paths to truth and wisdom. *Stare decisis* is always a desideratum, even in these constitutional cases. But in them, it is never a command.[56] For we may not close the mind to the lessons of experience and abdicate the sway of reason.

In my opinion, however, experience reinforces the reasoning behind the well established constitutional doctrine which permits States to impose the tax here in question. I find nothing in reason or experience to warrant our overruling a well-founded practice of three-quarters of a century.

In preparing this opinion, Brandeis studied Gerard C. Henderson's *The Position of Foreign Corporations in American Constitutional Law*, which had been published in 1918 and is today considered a classic. Brandeis' notes from the book cover eleven handwritten pages. Among other passages, he copied out the following ones, which can be traced to his opinion. At page 8: "General phrases embodied in a constitution are often little more than mandates and guides for judicial law making. As raw material for this law making, judges must use the social institutions and concrete legal relations with which they are familiar. The dynamic element in the development of a principle of constitutional law is therefore generally to be found in a changing economic background." At page 21: A reference to the identification, made by Jefferson among others, of "incorporation with monopoly," followed by the assertion that it "hardly needed argument that one sovereign could not give a monopoly in the territory of another sovereign." At page 35: Another reference to the same view, which condemned corporations "as encroachments on the citizen's natural right to freely exercise his faculties in trade and commerce." At page 50: The statement that throughout our history the task of the Court had been to examine "the political and economic nature of corporate groups" and then to apply the Constitution to them. But corporations had changed radically, though the "name remained the same," and "precedents have a way of attaching themselves to names rather than to things." At page 66: ". . . Marshall regarded the exercise of every corporate franchise as 'restrictive of individual rights' . . . ." At page 117: "Not only is commerce between the

---

[56] For some instances in which this Court has overruled prior decisions, see Washington v. Dawson, 264 U.S. 219, 236, 238, notes 17 and 21 [1924], and Di Santo v. Pa., 273 U.S. 34, 43, note 4 [1927].

states, as the court has so often said, a practical conception, drawn from the course of business, but the extent of the state's power over interstate commerce must be determined with an eye to a 'practical adjustment' of national and local authority." Brandeis also noted many references to early statutes and cases. It must not be supposed, however, that the Henderson book, though dedicated to Brandeis, was simply a reflection of the Justice's views, or that Brandeis' position was derived from it. Henderson had presented a historical and comparative, economic and legal analysis of a problem broader than the one immediately facing Brandeis in the *Stratton* case. With some of Henderson's recommendations, and perhaps with some of his conclusions, Brandeis might have disagreed. Brandeis drew on Henderson for statutory and case references, and for confirmation or striking formulations of his own conclusions.

By March 6, Brandeis, without apparently having so far used the services of his law clerk, had completed and received back from the printer a five-page draft of his dissent. He gave it to his law clerk, Harry Shulman, later Sterling Professor of Law, and at the time of his death in 1955, Dean, at Yale Law School, with this note: "This will give you the line of argument. Don't bother about the form, which has already been much changed." In this draft, the facts were fully set forth. It was customary procedure with Brandeis to hammer out a satisfactory statement of facts before he went on to anything else. The argument that the tax was based on economic truths was sketched in, and its supporting documentation briefly indicated. Brandeis did the same with the Commerce Clause and Due Process arguments. But, at this stage, first things came first. The economic facts of life here preceded rather than, as in the end, followed the legal ones. The concluding passage, which urged the Court to discard the *Cudahy* case and return to the *Baltic* decision, was finished in its essentials. The suggestion that the *Cudahy* case might be distinguishable because it dealt with a tax measured by authorized rather than issued stock was as yet omitted. For the rest, this version was somewhat briefer, and perhaps a bit blunter; and on the whole more eloquent. But the sense was not changed by subsequent revisions. These tended merely toward precision and elaboration, with the result that the end product loses something of unity and thrust. The last few sentences in this early draft were as follows:

We must never forget that what is called interpreting the Constitution involves but rarely the mere reading of the document. The constitutional questions which have most engaged the attention of the Court since the adoption of the Fourteenth Amendment and the great development of interstate commerce, deal with the application of constitutional limitations to the insistent,

ever varying and illusive facts of life. In deciding such questions the views of
the Court as to economic, social and political policy must often be a determining factor. The knowledge and the wisdom of man is finite, experience is his
teacher. To bring this Court's opinions into agreement with facts ascertained
must ever be its aim. Only by so doing will sound conclusions be reached.
And our efforts to reach them will be futile unless we bear ever in mind that
only change is abiding.

Shulman — as his own voluminous notes show — was set to gathering the detailed documentation which fills the footnotes of the final
opinion. He doubtless reported to Brandeis from time to time as the
mountain of specific references grew. Brandeis sent draft after draft
to the printer, constantly expanding his arguments and incorporating
Shulman's work as it came to him. The fruit of all this labor — the opinion as printed here — was dated for delivery on April 14, 1930. But it
must have been ready and been circulated about a week earlier.

There were two returns agreeing with Brandeis. Holmes said: "I
agree — I doubt the wisdom of making the opinion so long, interesting as it is." The second was from Stone, but it was probably delayed,
coming in a few days after Holmes', since it appears to refer to a recir-
culation of Sutherland's opinion, which had meanwhile been received,
and to which a subsequent note from Holmes also refers. Sutherland
had amended his opinion principally to comment on the suggestion
that the *Cudahy* case might be distinguishable. Brandeis let this idea
drop rather lightly just before the passage urging that the doctrine
of the *Baltic* case be revived. Sutherland very justly wished to point
out that the decision in *Cudahy* would have gone the same way if
issued rather than authorized stock had been the measure of the tax,
and that McReynolds had just about said as much. Sutherland also
added the following sentence to his contention that the power to tax
was the power to destroy, and that consequently a tax which would
be bad if large could not be upheld because it was small: "The courts
do not possess the benevolent power to compare and contrast infringe-
ments of the Constitution, and condemn them when they are great
and condone them when they are not." And for the benefit of the
Reporter, he noted: "The Chief Justice took no part in the considera-
'tion or decision of this case. Mr. Justice Sanford participated in its
consideration and expressly agreed to the foregoing opinion."

Chief Justice Taft, being in ill health, had resigned on February 3,
1930. (He died March 8.) Previously, he had not sat since December 9,
1929, and had therefore not heard the argument of the *Stratton* case.
Charles Evans Hughes, the new Chief Justice, had taken his seat on
February 24. He too had not heard the case and could not participate

in it. He wrote Brandeis: "I am not in this case, but I thank you for letting me see this opinion." Sanford did hear the case and was no doubt present at the conference at which it was decided. And he was available to receive Sutherland's first circulation of February 24; presumably he indicated assent to it. But on March 8, 1930, Sanford also died. His successor, Owen J. Roberts, was seated on June 2.

Stone's return read: "I join you. I am sorry I let that comment on the Airways [sic] Case by McR. in the Cudahy Case get by me. I am also sorry that you give currency to the supposed distinction between direct and indirect burdens on page 4. See my comment in the Di Santo Case, 273 U.S. 39, p. 44. If Justice Sutherland relies on Sanford's vote, I think he should mention the fact that Sanford had not received your opinion." Sutherland's amended opinion also provoked a note from Holmes: "You probably have noticed the humbug at the bottom of p. 5 of Sutherland's recirculated 98. We say the power to tax is not the power to destroy while this Court sits and that therefore that argument against the power to tax fails. A tax that does not tend to destroy is not unconstitutional. We do not 'condone' slight infractions. We say that moderate taxes are not infractions." Finally, there was a letter from Stone, dated April 11, 1930. This would appear to have been a second thought. It must have gone out after the return, if only by a matter of hours, since it asked for a change in the opinion on the back of which Stone had said, "I join you," and so forth. Stone now wrote:

I have studied very carefully your opinion in *Stratton* v. *St. Louis Southwestern Ry.*, and I am prepared to join you if you feel like making a slight modification of your opinion in your paragraph six on pages 21 and 22 and following. [That was the place where Brandeis alluded to the authorized as against issued stock distinction.]

It is true, as Justice Sutherland points out in his recirculated opinion, that Justice McReynolds, in *Cudahy Company* v. *Hinkle*, 278 U.S. at page 467, said "whether, because reckoned upon authorized and not upon actual common stock, the challenged legislation fails to require like fees for equal privileges within the doctrine of *Airway* [sic] *Electric Corporation* v. *Day*, 266 U.S. 71, we need not now consider." Justice McReynolds put out of consideration the equal protection clause, it is true, but nevertheless by his opinion he brought the case within the due process clause expressly on the ground that the tax was measured by authorized, as distinguished from issued stock. At page 465 he points out that this was the "characteristic feature" of *Looney* v. *Crane Co.* [245 U.S. 178 (1917); a case decided after *Baltic*, in which a tax without a maximum was struck down], and says that that case controls the Cudahy case unless the $3,000 limitation applies. He then proceeds to show that if the tax is otherwise bad the $3,000 limitation does not save it, and takes occasion to slap the Baltic Mining Company and the Atlas [Alpha] Portland Cement cases on that ground alone. We are now dealing with a new combination not within the reasoning of his case, namely, a tax measured by issued stock, and property and business within the state and the sole and narrow question is whether the minimum tax makes it a tax on issued capital and whether the tax on issued capital is bad.

Although Stone dictated it, and read and signed it after it was typed, this letter was surely sent in haste. McReynolds' opinion in *Cudahy* is cryptic and possibly ambiguous, but it simply will not lend itself to Stone's reading of it. There is no such phrase as "characteristic feature" used on page 465 with reference to the authorized stock measure which was before the Court in *Looney v. Crane Co.* Indeed, there is no such phrase used at all on page 465; or anywhere else in the opinion. The *Looney* case, McReynolds says, declared the tax unconstitutional because it fell on property outside the jurisdiction of the taxing State. This is not a ground which allows of a distinction between taxes measured by total authorized stock, representing in part non-existent property located nowhere, and one measured by issued stock, representing actual extraterritorial holdings. This is rather a ground that renders the distinction irrelevant, and McReynolds duly so notes. McReynolds "slapped" the *Baltic* case, as Stone said, because there the fact that the tax carried a maximum limit was considered decisive. It should not be, McReynolds held, and upset a tax which also had a maximum. And he did not "slap" the *Alpha Portland Cement* case; he referred to it as having undermined the *Baltic* doctrine.

The trouble was that Stone had been with McReynolds in *Cudahy*, and since he was now about to join Brandeis, he was particularly anxious to see that case distinguished. His letter went on to say: "Justice Sutherland's opinion does not rest the case on the denial of equal protection any more than did the Cudahy case. Therefore, the quoted passage of Justice McReynolds does not conclude those who were unwise enough to support the Cudahy case." And then: "I hope you will feel like putting in a brief paragraph covering this point."

It would seem that if Sutherland *had* rested the *Stratton* case on the Equal Protection Clause, those who had joined in *Cudahy* but were now in dissent might, possibly, have found comfort in "the quoted passage of Justice McReynolds." How Stone made it out the other way is not clear. In any event, it appears that at the time, Stone, no more than McReynolds, or than Brandeis in dissent, thought of the distinction between an authorized and an issued stock measure as the significant factor in *Cudahy*. On February 16, 1929, Stone wrote to Brandeis:

In your dissent in No. 278, Cudahy Packing Co. v. Hinkle, you take a sustainable position and present it with great force. But the other position, so far as it relates to making capital used outside the state a measure of the tax imposed within the state is also a workable rule. In one way it is capable of more definite and certain application, for it seems to me that under the rule you lay down as the tax becomes larger it is always open for the taxpayer to come here to have us pass on the question whether the tax is too large or too substantial to come within the doctrine of the Cheney case [*Cheney Bros. Co. v. Massachusetts*, 246 U.S. 147 (1918); a decision following *Baltic* and upholding a tax with a maximum]. See also what I said about the Air-Way case in Roberts and Schaefer v. Emmerson, 271 U.S. 50 [1926], at the bottom of page 53. These considerations, and my general disposition not to dissent unless I feel strongly on the subject, lead me to stand by my vote, although I can say very frankly that I could not affirm that your position is in any sense unsound.[28]

Roberts & Schaefer Co. v. Emmerson dealt with an authorized capital stock tax imposed on a domestic corporation doing intrastate business. Stone said that the *Air-Way Electric Appliance* case, which involved a foreign corporation, was not applicable.

His position in *Cudahy* was not the only indication that, prior to *Stratton*, Stone did not quite see eye to eye with Brandeis in these cases. Just before *Cudahy*, the Court, in *Quaker City Cab Co. v. Pennsylvania*,[29] held that a gross receipts tax falling only on corporations and not on individuals or partnerships, though valid under the Commerce Clause, violated the Equal Protection Clause, because it discriminated against corporations. Brandeis, of course, dissented. This tax, he wrote, embodied an anti-corporation policy, for which there was ample historical precedent. Then, in language foreshadowing the *Stratton* opinion, and indeed in some sentences which he repeated verbatim in the *Stratton* dissent, Brandeis indicated why many "intelligent, just-minded and civilized persons," were convinced that "the rapidly growing aggregation of capital through corporations constitutes an insidious menace to the liberty of the citizen." [30] A letter from Stone dated May 25, 1928, announced agreement with Brandeis, but objected to the passage just quoted. "You have so many stronger reasons for your conclusions, fully expressed in your opinion," Stone wrote, "that the overelaboration of this weaker one, to my mind, weakens the whole opinion. It will suggest to many minds that this is the real germ of your opposition." (Well it might!) Stone disliked to ask for any change "in so admirable a document," but he did hope that Brandeis might omit or modify the paragraph in question.[31] Brandeis did neither, and Stone did not join him, but wrote a short paragraph of his own. Stone's letter contrasts with the return from Holmes, who agreed "rejoicingly," failed to see the need for his own brief dissent, except as it might "exhibit your thoroughness in sockodologizing," and added: "I really grieve that the Court should tie things up as it is doing." [32]

There was actually no good objective reason why Stone should have felt embarrassed by the *Cudahy* case to the extent of being led to play fast and loose with it. It is widely suspected that the robes of Supreme Court Justices are inhabited by human beings, who have — indeed one hopes they have, since not all do — a normal flexibility of mind and at least the normal receptiveness to new insights. It is to Stone's credit that though his mind had been left in equilibrium (and in such an event the pull of the majority is and should be the stronger) by Brandeis' rather cursory dissent in *Cudahy*, he should a year later have been persuaded by the powerful opinion in *Stratton*. And one would think there was no need to try to create a spurious appearance of consistency. But Brandeis, though he had no inconsistency of his own to apologize for, was not unsympathetic to the pious fraud — an ancient lawyer's weakness — of the disingenuous distinction. He had been known to perpetrate one or two on his own, and was to do so again, before very long, as we shall see, when the chance to avoid *Cudahy* finally came. Of course, it would have been legitimate to point out that, on its exact facts, and in the strictly technical sense, *Cudahy* was different, though on any fair understanding of its reasoning, it ruled the *Stratton* case. This much Brandeis had already suggested. Now he was prepared also to accede to Stone's request for a further "brief paragraph."

After he had received Holmes' and Stone's returns, Brandeis inserted a couple of sentences at the appropriate place, saying that *Cudahy* was not controlling. Again, for Stone's benefit, he changed a reference to direct burdens on commerce to read, "Those burdens which are commonly called direct . . . ." And he added two other sentences, prompted by Holmes' note, to his refutation of the "humbug" about the power to tax being the power to destroy. "Our reports," he wrote, "abound with decisions, under the Interstate Commerce Clause and the Due Process Clause, in which the permissible is to be distinguished from the prohibited only by the difference between a little and too much." And: "To uphold this tax is not to condone a slight infraction, but to hold that a moderate tax of this character is not an infraction."

This revision of Brandeis' opinion, which included also a number of merely formal changes, apparently never went to the printer. At any rate, Brandeis' file shows no clean print of it. The reason the opinion was abandoned is that someone — and there is no indication that it was Brandeis — now discovered a jurisdictional imperfection in *Stratton*. It appeared that the case should have been heard below by a three-judge federal court. In fact, it had come up on appeal on the basis of an order entered by a single federal judge, which had been reviewed by the Circuit Court of Appeals. Neither party had raised the jurisdictional issue, and so a reargument was ordered. One is tempted to surmise that it was Hughes, the new Chief Justice — necessarily disqualified on the merits, though judging by the record of his past service on the Court, perhaps tending toward agreement with Brandeis — [33] to whom this way out occurred. Its discovery must in any event have come as a relief; for the Court was surely in an awkward position. A 4–3 division on the merits, with a new Chief sitting and not participating and another new judge to come, is an invitation to a petition for rehearing, which in its turn is then hard to resist, since a full court can provide a new majority. In 1870 the Court had had a well-remembered and quite unpleasant experience with a case which it chose to go ahead and decide under somewhat similar circumstances. A full court shortly thereafter reversed the decision.[34] Of course, *Stratton* could simply have been held to the next term, but the majority may have been unwilling to take this course. Be that as it may, the case was reargued in October 1930, and the following month a unanimous Court, Hughes writing, dismissed it for want of jurisdiction.[35]

That disposition was not, however, the end of *Stratton* in the Supreme Court. Lawyers for the railway heeded the jurisdictional lesson the Chief Justice had taught them and went back to have their case tried before a three-judge federal court. They won, as they had in the earlier proceedings, and the state brought the case up on appeal once more. It was argued on the merits in December 1931. But in vain, though a full court was available till January 12, 1932, when Holmes retired. The Court ordered reargument on the question of whether even a three-judge federal court had jurisdiction, and this issue was argued promptly on January 11. There is no telling which way the decision might have gone on the merits, but it is not impossible that Hughes and Roberts were willing to avoid *Cudahy* and that Holmes' retirement left an equally divided court. In any event, the new jurisdictional point — like the first one — was real enough, and by February the case was once again dismissed, Stone writing for a unanimous Court. Illinois law, it seemed, provided a way for contesting the tax in the state courts. Consequently, initial recourse to the federal courts was foreclosed. For the state should, if possible, be given a first chance to pass on objections to its tax. There might in the end be no need for federal intervention.[36]

Having assimilated their second jurisdictional lecture, counsel for the railway now went to the state courts, and there once again achieved victory. The Supreme Court of Illinois, one member dissenting, followed the *Cudahy* ruling and declared the tax unconstitutional.[37] The state tried to bring the case to the Supreme Court once more. But the avenue of an appeal, which it was mandatory for the Supreme Court to hear, was now closed. On each of the previous two times up, a lower federal court had, in striking down the Illinois tax, declared a state statute unconstitutional and had enjoined its enforcement. Thus, in the judgment of Congress, which makes the basic rules governing the Court's jurisdiction, a very important and urgent issue had been raised. Its prompt resolution was crucial to the smooth workings of our dual system of government, for state laws must not be allowed to remain in a condition of suspended animation — invalid and unenforceable, but not certainly so; and if they are to be declared definitely invalid by a federal court, that court should be the highest. Hence the mandatory appeal. But when a state court, as had happened this time, itself upholds an alleged federal right and invalidates its own statute, adjudication by the United States Supreme Court is a less urgent and even a less crucial necessity. No direct clash between state and federal institutions has taken place. In this posture, therefore, the *Stratton* case could be heard only if the Court itself elected to grant the discretionary writ of certiorari, by means of which the Court chooses from the many ordinary cases pressed upon its limited attention the ones it deems important enough to hear and decide at any given term. The considerations that enter into the grant or denial of the writ of certiorari are varied and they are by no means restricted to the question of whether the case was correctly or incorrectly decided below. In this instance, the writ was denied.

Denial of the writ of certiorari in the *Stratton* case ended the matter as far as the Illinois tax was concerned. The adverse decision of the Illinois court stood. But it stood neither approved nor disapproved. There had been no pronouncement on the merits by the Supreme Court. And as far as Brandeis was concerned, the fight had not ended. While the *Stratton* case was still having its jurisdictional tribulations, Holmes held for a unanimous Court that a state retained the power to require, as a condition upon the grant of permission to enter and do intrastate business, that a foreign corporation obtain a domestic charter. This ruling affected the *Cudahy* doctrine, for by becoming a domestic corporation, the formerly foreign corporation would presumably lay itself open to capital stock taxes measured in just about any old way.[38] In 1937, only three years after the Court had seen the last of *Stratton*, Brandeis had the satisfaction — though only by the employment of the thinnest of technical distinctions — of "slapping" the *Cudahy* case, as Stone might have said. The opportunity came in *Atlantic Refining Co. v. Virginia.*[39]

Virginia imposed an entrance fee on foreign corporations desiring to do intrastate business. It was measured by authorized capital stock and rose to a maximum of $5,000. This tax had been upheld soon after the decision in *Baltic Mining Co. v. Massachusetts,* pursuant to the doctrine enunciated in that case.[40] The Atlantic Refining Company, which was now just proposing to enter and do business in Virginia, was required to pay the maximum tax, and contested it on the ground that since *Cudahy,* the ruling following *Baltic* was no longer binding. Brandeis, in a relatively brief opinion, upheld the tax. In summary fashion he rehearsed the arguments he had made in his *Stratton* opinion, without, however, dwelling at any length on the economic truths on which, as he said in *Stratton,* the tax rested. Brandeis also touched on the question raised by the authorized, as opposed to an issued, stock measure. He brushed aside the equal-protection point which had been made in the *Air-Way Electric* case. Finally he came to *Cudahy.* The difference between that case and this one, he said, was that here the tax, or entrance fee as he now chose to call it, was exacted from a company about to enter the state. In *Cudahy* it was imposed on companies already in the state and doing business there. That was a decisive difference.

There is this much to be said for Brandeis' distinction with respect to *Cudahy,* and it is not much: In terms of the reasoning of the *Baltic* case, though not necessarily of the cases following it, entry fees might be distinguishable, since a tax was deemed bad if, in order to avoid it, a company would have to quit both its intra- and interstate activities. A company would have to do so if the two branches of its business had become inseparable; and that can scarcely have happened at the time when an entry fee is exacted. But nothing in *Cudahy* so much as suggested this point. *Baltic* was there plainly overruled on a ground applicable to entry fees as much as to subsequent taxes. To be sure, entry fees, if imposed only once, are less burdensome than a yearly tax. But the size of the burden was also irrelevant under *Cudahy.* And not all franchise taxes fall due every year, while some entry fees may.[41] Nevertheless, the stratagem of this distinction was sufficient to obtain for Brandeis a unanimous Court. He snatched it from the jaws of another 4–3 division, reminiscent of *Stratton,* and he might well not have got it if he had insisted on overruling *Cudahy.*

The *Atlantic Refining* case was first argued in October 1936. At that time four members of the majority in *Cudahy* were still on the Court — McReynolds, Sutherland, Butler, and Van Devanter. Stone was ill for the first part of that term and did not hear the argument. Hughes disqualified himself when the case was finally decided. His reasons are not apparent. Presumably he was disqualified when the case was first argued as well. That left a seven-man Court, on which the four horsemen of *Cudahy Packing Co. v. Hinkle* made a majority. And they had every intention of enforcing their will. Brandeis at that time prepared a short dissent. But the considerations against a 4–3 decision under such circumstances, which have been mentioned in connection with the first hearing of the *Stratton* case, could now be invoked with even greater force. For this was the period when the Court was under severe attack for upsetting New Deal measures by narrow majorities. Perhaps these considerations prevailed. We know only that the case was reargued at the beginning of the following term, in October 1937. By this time, Stone was well and in his seat, and Van Devanter, who had retired on the last day of the previous term, had been replaced — if so pallid a word can describe the event — by Mr. Justice Black. A new majority was thus obtained, and Brandeis was able to write for the Court. Among the returns which have been preserved are the following: "I agree," from Roberts; "I concur in this fine opinion," from Cardozo; "Please note that I take no part. But I may say that I think you have dealt with the case most effectively," from Hughes. Stone borrowed one of Holmes' favorite coinages: "It is sockodological," he wrote. McReynolds said: "I am unable to agree." [42] Brandeis' file shows no returns from Sutherland or Butler. In the end there was silence; from these two, and from McReynolds also.

Such was the campaign of many battles, of marches and counter-marches, skirmishes, delays, diversionary moves, tests of endurance, and defeats, which Brandeis waged to a somewhat dubious victory. The effort and the perseverance were on an heroic scale. One may wonder whether they weren't in disproportion to the stakes. It was not likely that the social policy expressed by capital stock taxes would be much furthered through the exaction from multimillion dollar corporations of one, or even of forty-seven, two- or five-thousand-dollar fees. This was not a very effective way to support state exchequers or to deter corporate bigness. The further history of "the seemingly endless problems," as the late Mr. Justice Jackson called them, "raised by efforts of the several states to tax commerce as it moves among them," [43] confirms this judgment. The states have resorted to other taxes of similar practical effect, but of greater yield; taxes, as Brandeis pointed out, which were being upheld even while modest unapportioned capital stock taxes were declared invalid. There are apportioned taxes on net income,[44] and apportioned capital stock taxes,[45] and taxes on property.[46] Controversy rages over gross income taxes.[47] But there is not much ado about small flat capital stock taxes. And that not necessarily because Brandeis' victory in 1937 was a compromised one, but because the need for such taxes is not felt.

Was Brandeis then tilting at windmills? If so, he did it more than once; for this campaign, in which the effort seems so disproportionately mountainous in comparison with the objective, was far from atypical. But Brandeis could not have mistaken the size or importance of the objective. He knew full well that five-thousand-dollar taxes would not curb industrial giantism. He fought and he wrote partly because he thought that education would do so, and because he believed that one of the high functions of the Court was to educate. He fought and he wrote partly because, as he saw it, it was not for him to say that a given road toward a worthy social goal would eventually prove useless and did not deserve to be kept open. Brandeis was patient and confident, and he took the long view. He was content to ease the way, by compromises and by large fights about little results, for future struggles and for future more significant victories. He was, Alvin Johnson once said, "a serenely implacable democrat." [48]

VIII

Herbert Spencer and the Commerce Clause

In January 1937 the President of the United States, having recently been reëlected by an overwhelming vote, voiced to his advisers what was then his dominant preoccupation. He said, and said repeatedly: "The time for action with respect to the Supreme Court really cannot be postponed, and unpleasant as it is, I think we have to face it." [1] Mr. Roosevelt did act. His recommendation to Congress was called a plan to pack the Supreme Court, and it was called a plan to unpack it. It was not enacted, and thus the Court missed being altered — as altered it would have been, though one cannot tell for certain just what new psyche it would have assumed. Twenty years later, the law has changed and changed greatly, both in subject matter and in answers to old problems. This sort of development has always been with us. But the Court has not changed. Its powers and its functions and its place in the national life are intact. It might very easily not have been so. The year 1937 was a close call for the institution.

If one asks what brought the Court to the dire straits of 1937, the clear answer, valid and not improved upon by all that has been written since in elaboration, is found in words spoken by Holmes only some three years after his accession and more than thirty years before the event. The Court, in 1905, through Justice Rufus W. Peckham, a Cleveland appointee, held that a New York statute establishing a ten-hour workday for bakers was unconstitutional.[2] ("You asked me about Peckham," Holmes wrote to Felix Frankfurter on March 28, 1922. "I used to say his major premise was God damn it. Meaning thereby that emotional predilections somewhat governed him on social themes. A good man, faithful, of real feeling — and a master of Anglo-Saxon monosyllabic interjections.")[3] Dissenting, Holmes wrote: "This case is decided upon an economic theory which a large part of the country does not entertain . . . . The Fourteenth Amendment does not enact Mr. Herbert Spencer's Social Statics." [4] The fact was that at the turn of the century, and then on through the twenties and early thirties — though of course not uniformly, not without detours and exceptions — what had been, in the main, the dissenting views of Justice Stephen J. Field in the post-Civil War generation, became the law of a majority of the Court, and the Social Statics of Mr. Herbert Spencer were written into the Constitution. This is the sin for which the Court nearly paid in 1937, and of which it has since well and truly purged itself.[5]

Laissez faire became constitutional doctrine chiefly through the Due Process Clause of the Fourteenth Amendment. As has been suggested in connection with the *Arizona Employers' Liability Cases*, it was through that clause that the monumental conceptualism of freedom of contract as between employer and employee was perpetrated. In deference to that freedom, the Court struck down minimum wage laws, and interfered with efforts to organize, and thus improve the position of, labor. The Due Process Clause, and sometimes the Equal Protection Clause, carrying the virus of the same philosophy, were interposed as well against other measures aiming to introduce some order into situations of social and economic chaos.[6] But Herbert Spencer also intruded into the Constitution in more indirect ways. Thus his influence was felt in adjudications under the Commerce Clause. In one aspect, the Court's maltreatment of that clause appears as its gravest transgression.

When it struck at legislation by means of the Due Process Clause, the Court decreed that neither sovereignty in our dual system, state or federal, could do certain things; that no free government should. This raised a clear-cut issue, plainly met, as Holmes met it. When it applied the Commerce Clause, the Court did not on the face of things deny all governmental power; it said only that, in a given instance, the wrong government had acted. In this fashion, it invoked another value, namely, the viability of our federal system. But actually the Court was all too often vindicating the same social and economic theories as in its Due Process Clause decisions. And it did not really leave one of our two systems of sovereignty free to deal with matters it had withdrawn from the jurisdiction of the other. "Instances have not been wanting," Professor Felix Frankfurter wrote in 1937, "where the concept of interstate commerce has been broadened to exclude state action, and narrowed to exclude Congressional action. Such complementary decisions are not dictated by federalism; they are functions of a laissez-faire philosophy."[7] Formally, such complementary decisions held that a nation constituted in the duality of federalism was, for that reason alone, helpless to solve certain problems. Thus, by taking it in vain, the Court brought into disrepute the fair and hopeful idea of federalism, which had survived a great war to become one of our principal exports. By comparison, the evil of the Court's due-process holdings may seem ephemeral.

A striking and particularly distressing illustration of the kind of gap or no man's land of power that the Court was wont to create in the name of federalism was the situation with respect to child labor, alluded to in a previous chapter. Another — among several dramatic ones early in the New Deal era — was provided by the crisis in the coal industry.

The Court held, in several contexts, that a state cannot arbitrarily exclude from its market goods manufactured in a sister state.[8] "Neither the power to tax nor the police power may be used by the state of destination with the aim and effect of establishing an economic barrier against competition with the products of another state or the labor of its residents."[9] These words were written by Cardozo for a unanimous Court in 1935, and the fact of his authorship alone is proof that here is a proposition which, though one or another of its particular applications may be debatable, genuinely derives from the necessities of a working federalism. But to lay the states open to competition in this way was to affect drastically, in practice if not in theory, their ability to regulate wages, prices, and conditions of labor within their jurisdiction. For the state that increased its costs of production drove its products out of the free national market. A working federalism required, therefore, a complementary rule permitting the federal government to regulate what the states, for good and sufficient reason, could not be allowed to deal with effectively. Yet the Court held that the Commerce Clause, which rendered state regulation of child labor ineffective in the manner described, did not authorize Congress to fill the gap by excluding from interstate commerce certain articles manufactured with the aid of child labor.[10] And the Court held that the Commerce Clause, which, by the same token, made it practically impossible for any single state to regulate prices or wages in its coal industry, conferred no power on Congress to enforce a national wage and price policy.[11] Thus appalling vacuums were created.

In cutting off federal intervention with respect to child labor, coal mining, and the like, the Court professed to be enhancing the power of the states, reserving exclusively to them the function of prescribing conditions (of course, the club of the Due Process Clause was always held in ready reserve) for the production and marketing of goods within their borders. From the point of view of federalism, this was lodging the wrong exclusive power in the wrong place. The Court again misplaced power and created a somewhat different but scarcely less serious gap by contracting state and enlarging federal authority in circumstances where the latter could only prove inefficient, if not futile. Thus, when Pennsylvania instituted a licensing procedure in an attempt to put an end to frauds perpetrated against its immigrant inhabitants by ticket agents selling overseas transportation, the Court drew the line. Pennsylvania, it held, was transgressing on the powers of Congress. These ticket agents were engaged in interstate and foreign commerce, and they were therefore immune from state licensing or regulation.[12]

Pennsylvania had diagnosed and had met a need peculiar to itself and perhaps one or two other states. It was very unlikely that South Carolina or Nebraska, for example, considered such legislation urgent. For that reason, it was exceedingly unlikely also that Congress, which like all human institutions must practice economy of effort, would deem it necessary to achieve the end Pennsylvania desired by a nationally applicable measure. It is the blessing of the federal system — which the Court chose to withhold — that state governments, representing their people and not a remote central authority, exist to seek solutions for problems which are of importance locally, but would necessarily rank low on a national scale of priorities. Even if Congress had found the time to enact comprehensive legislation — what a wasteful way that would have been to fill Pennsylvania's need! To be sure, Congress might have simply validated the Pennsylvania law, and thus avoided the foolishness of national administration of essentially local legislation.[13] But Pennsylvania is not the only state with particular local problems affecting interstate commerce. If Congress should enter the business of putting its imprimatur on such state statutes as this one, it would never see the end of it. Congress would be transformed into an irresponsible private bill factory.[14]

An earlier and perhaps less extreme example of the Court's robbing the country of the fruits of federalism by pointless expansion of exclusive federal power is *Lemke v. Farmers Grain Co.*[15] It was less unlikely that Congress would in fact assume the function conferred upon it by this case, and it would have been less wasteful for Congress to perform it.[16] Nevertheless, the rigid line drawn in *Lemke* was also at war with the true nature of federalism. For the system should permit an overlapping of power and tolerate an area in which practical judgment rather than hard and fast theory dictates the allocation of competences between state and nation; an area in which state and nation might assist each other toward common ends and states might devise variations suitable to their conditions upon major themes of national policy written by Congress. The North Dakota statute in question in the *Lemke* case provided for inspection, grading, and weighing of grain sold by farmers within the state, and for ensuring that fair prices were paid. The Court found that practically all grain sold in North Dakota was intended for interstate shipment. The sales that North Dakota had presumed to regulate were therefore held to be in interstate commerce, and immune from any and all state regulation.

Shafer v. Farmers Grain Co.,[17] was a sequel to the *Lemke* case. In holding the statute invalid in *Lemke*, Day, who spoke for the Court, emphasized two of its features. One was that buyers of wheat were not simply required to grade and weigh it in accordance with state regulations or under state supervision, but were required to obtain a state license, and were not permitted to buy unless they had such a license. The second, even more significant in Day's mind, was that prices were fixed. Thus, Day said, the state was assuming the power to exclude persons from doing interstate business, and it was setting the price of goods moving in interstate commerce. Such interference was wholly inadmissible. With Day's emphasis in mind, North Dakota enacted a second statute. Buyers were no longer required to be licensed as such, though it remained mandatory for them to have grain they bought graded under state license. This change might well be considered merely formal. But the earlier price-fixing provision was also eliminated, and this made a substantial difference, even though the new statute, like the old, enacted what was on the whole a close regulatory scheme.

Reviewing the new statute in the *Shafer* case, the Court, this time speaking through Van Devanter, made short shrift of the changes and simply applied its earlier holding. The opinion is notable for an incredibly mechanical statement of the issue, which Van Devanter permitted himself. Two rules, Van Devanter said, were invoked in this case. The first was that a state could, under the Constitution, affect interstate commerce indirectly and remotely. The other was that a state statute which necessarily operated directly on, or burdened, interstate commerce was invalid, regardless of its purpose. "These rules," Van Devanter blandly commented, "although readily understood and entirely consistent, are occasionally difficult of application, as where a state statute closely approaches the line which separates one rule from the other. As might be expected, the decisions dealing with such exceptional situations have not been in full accord. Otherwise the course of adjudication has been consistent and uniform." [18] The word "otherwise" is no stranger to comic locutions. But, surely, it has seldom, even in legal literature, been employed more hilariously. Yet Van Devanter was better than this. These sentences reflect more on his candor than on his intelligence.

Brandeis, throughout his career on the Court, was a firm supporter of national authority. Thus he participated, and on occasion led, in the fullest expansion of the Interstate Commerce Commission's power to override the local and safeguard the national interest in transportation.[19] And it was Brandeis who, though there was no applicable federal legislation, forbade the states to exclude interstate motor traffic from their highways on the sole ground that it lacked commercial justification, as when a new bus or truck line sought to enter an area adequately served by existing ones. Only Congress was capable of taking the larger view necessary for the framing of such a policy, Brandeis held.[20] Moreover, in a somewhat dubious line of cases, he deemed it an unconstitutional burden on interstate commerce for states to require railroads to defend personal injury suits in a capriciously chosen and inconvenient forum.[21] And he dissented, of course, in the child labor and coal cases mentioned earlier.

Nationalist though he was in appropriate circumstances, Brandeis had the statesman's natural abhorrence for vacuums of power. And he had a profounder insight into, and therefore greater regard for, the values of federalism than most of his colleagues and than many of his predecessors and successors. Hence he was generally wary of restricting state regulatory power. "What those fellows don't understand," Brandeis once said, referring to his brethren, "is that recognition of federal powers does not mean denial of State powers. I have not been against increase of federal power, but curtailment of State power." [22]

Brandeis dissented in the *Lemke* case, as he was to do in the later Pennsylvania ticket-agent case. The North Dakota statute, he said in his rather brief opinion in *Lemke*, was intended to protect local farmers from frauds practiced on them by local buyers. The means chosen were suited to the purpose. It was unnecessary to decide whether or not the sales of grain which North Dakota had regulated were in interstate commerce. This was the only inquiry the Court had made. But for Brandeis it was irrelevant. Even if the sales were held to be in interstate commerce, he said, the state should not be precluded from acting, in the absence of a conflicting Congressional policy.

When *Shafer* came along, about a year and a half after *Lemke*, Brandeis wrote the opinion here printed. He did so, apparently, before there was a majority opinion. This was not a dissent, but rather a memorandum aiming to persuade. For an effort at persuasion seemed worthwhile. Brandeis had been joined in dissent in *Lemke* by Holmes and Clarke. By the time *Shafer* was first argued, on May 4, 1923, Clarke had been replaced by Sutherland. But Day, who had written *Lemke*, had also left. And so had Pitney, another member of the *Lemke* majority. A new majority, made up of the two remaining dissenters in

Lemke, and of Sutherland, Butler, and Sanford, the new Justices who were uncommitted to that decision, was thus possible. Taft had been with the majority in *Lemke,* but except for that fact, the situation must have seemed to Brandeis similar to that in *Sonneborn Bros. v. Cureton,* in which his effort at persuasion was just then coming to a successful conclusion. As it turned out, however, Taft's allegiance to the *Lemke* decision made a vast difference.

Brandeis' memorandum addressed itself to matters not touched upon in the ultimate opinion of the Court, because they could become decisive only if one held that the North Dakota statute was not a direct burden on commerce. If, as the Court eventually said, it was such a burden, that was conclusive against it. If not, and if, as Brandeis was prepared to assume, the transactions in question were nevertheless in interstate commerce, yet subject not only to federal controls, but also to harmonious state regulations, then another issue became crucial. For, by Act of August 11, 1916,[23] Congress had also regulated the grading of grain sold in interstate commerce. Any conflicting or interfering state law would therefore have to fall, since, obviously, where federal power exists and is exerted, it must be paramount, and the Constitution so provides practically in so many words.

As Brandeis pointed out, there was no conflict. The North Dakota statute adopted the federally established grading system, making it its own. There remained, in this connection, only a question whether the statute might not violate a negative federal policy, implicitly formulated by Congress when it limited the exercise of its own regulatory power. For Congress had provided for grading and inspection only at major markets, not at rural ones, such as those in North Dakota. That was the point of the North Dakota statute. But had Congress, by stopping short of full exertion of its power, made a conscious choice between stages in the movement of grain in interstate commerce which it believed should be regulated, and those which it thought should not be? If so, and if North Dakota was doing what Congress had deliberately declined to do, that brought about a conflict with federal policy no less than action inconsistent with an affirmative Congressional requirement. But the meaning of the silence of Congress, of its self-restraint, was not to be assumed; it had to be ascertained by examining legislative intent.

It was, of course, conceivable that freedom from regulation in certain areas cognate to ones Congress was regulating should be an essential element of a comprehensive policy. Congress, as lawyer's shorthand has it, may want to "occupy the field," and deal with parts of it now, parts of it later and in the light of experience, and parts of it not at all. But that last intention — to become seized of a problem to the exclusion of state authority and to decree by silence that the best solution for it was inaction — bore the burden of proof in Brandeis' mind; especially since finding that Congress had "occupied the field" was another handy device for producing unwarranted no man's lands of power, wastelands in which was heard only the soft tread of Herbert Spencer. The first, and anguished, dissent of Brandeis' career was written against the willful creation of such a wasteland.[24] Brandeis could divine no Congressional intent that should cause the Court to create one in the *Shafer* case.

The first half of Brandeis' memorandum described in intimate and lucid detail the situation with which North Dakota had undertaken to deal. Brandeis discussed the importance of standardized and honest grading. Wheat was no longer, as in the past, sold solely upon inspection of samples, but largely by description and designation according to grades. Standard grades had at first been established by convention. Legislation followed gradually. National uniformity in grading was, of course, desirable, and it was to achieve it that Congress had acted. Standard grades were like weights and measures; they provided a common language for the business. But the application of standard grades was much more complicated than the application of ordinary weights and measures. Congress, by licensing inspectors, had met this problem part way, but only at terminal markets, of which North Dakota had none. Most North Dakota grain was shipped to such markets, where it was then inspected. But the shipments took place after the farmer had sold his grain to middlemen; it was they who shipped and resold, and it was their interest that was safeguarded by terminal-market inspection. The grading that determined the price the farmer got was done locally and was not subject to federal inspection. North Dakota had acted to guard against fraud and unfairness at this point. It had taken up where Congress had left off.

This half of the opinion is a marvelous demonstration of Brandeis' ability to penetrate an intricate business situation with the expertness of one directly engaged in it, and to lay bare, for the densest layman to see, the exact spot at which the shoe pinched. Throughout his active life, at the Bar and on the Bench, Brandeis displayed this talent for acquiring a clear and full understanding into the hows and whys of the conduct of affairs. And it was a talent of great range, equal to unraveling the mysteries of the most disparate branches of human enterprise: the grain business in *Shafer;* railroading, at the Bar and repeatedly on the Court, till it became a specialty;[25] the garment industry at the Bar;[26] valuation of public utilities;[27] the mortgage business; [28] coöperatives; [29] the ice business; [30] and more of all varieties. [31] Brandeis "believed in taking pains," [32] infinite pains, and when he set out to become familiar with a business, he exhausted all possible sources of information. In connection with the *Shafer* opinion, which was prepared mainly during the summer of 1923, while he was at his cottage at Chatham on Cape Cod, Brandeis sent his law clerk, William F. McCurdy, later Professor of Law at the Harvard Law School, to interview appropriate officials of the Department of Agriculture and the Federal Trade Commission. McCurdy reported in writing. Brandeis had McCurdy gather and send to Chatham countless published, and some unpublished, reports and materials collected from both agencies. Congressional hearings, reports, and other documents were thoroughly canvassed. All summer, as the picture came into focus in Brandeis' mind, new questions and new requests for materials flowed from Chatham to McCurdy in Washington. But that was not all. It happened that the family business, then headed by Brandeis' brother Alfred, dealt in grain: "A. Brandeis & Son, Receivers and Shippers of Grain, Louisville, Ky." Brandeis sent Alfred a clipping from the *Daily Market Record* for July 18, 1923, showing quotations at different markets ("Please return," Brandeis noted on the clipping). Brandeis was uncertain about some of the abbreviations. A letter from Alfred, dated August 2, 1923, cleared up these doubts ("1 D N S ch to fcy" turned out to mean, as Brandeis had suspected, "No. 1 Dark Northern Spring wheat choice to fancy"), along with a few other matters, on which "the general talk" of "grain circles" — Alfred's authority — could throw light. Thus, with no effort spared, was the grain business learned.

The second half of the *Shafer* opinion is all law. Brandeis dwelt rather more elaborately than may seem necessary on the question whether any of the North Dakota statute's provisions violated the Due Process Clause. But he was writing before the Court had spoken, and he knew his brethren. If they had been persuaded that the statute was invulnerable under the Commerce Clause, that it did not conflict with Congressional policy, and that Congress had not occupied the field, they might have at least tried to resort to the one remaining weapon — and that was due process.

SUPREME COURT OF THE UNITED STATES

No. 271. — October Term, 1923.

George F. Shafer, etc.,	Appeal from the District
vs.	Court of the United
Farmers Grain Company of	States for the District
Embden et al.	of North Dakota.

[October —, 1923]

Memorandum by Mr. Justice BRANDEIS.

Pursuant to United States Grain Standards Act, August 11, 1916, c. 313, Part B, 39 Stat., pp. 482–485, Part C, p. 486, the Secretary of Agriculture promulgated official grades for wheat. Thereafter, on November 7, 1922, North Dakota adopted, by an initiative measure, its Grain Grading Act. The latter statute makes the federal standards the official grades for wheat in that State; prohibits any person from purchasing wheat by grade unless it shall have been inspected and graded by an inspector licensed under either the federal or the state law; prohibits any persons from operating a public grain warehouse, unless he shall have secured for himself (or an employee) a state license as inspector, in addition to the state license for the warehouse; and requires all persons buying or shipping for profit grain bought on credit to file bonds to secure the value thereof. The state supervisor of grades, weights and measures, by whom inspectors' licenses are to be granted, is given power to revoke or suspend them for failure to comply with their conditions. Violation of any provision of the Act is made a misdemeanor.

To enjoin enforcement of the North Dakota statute this suit was brought in the federal court for that State. The plaintiffs are owners of many grain elevators within North Dakota which they operate as public warehouses. The defendants are state officials. The elevators are used mainly in the business of buying wheat grown in the neighborhood, and later shipped in interstate commerce for sale or consignment by grade. In this business grain elevators, like railroads, are an indispensable instrumentality. The only ground on which plaintiffs seek relief is that the statute violates rights guaranteed by the Federal Constitution. They contend that the statute deprives them of liberty and property without due process of law; that its provisions conflict with those of the United States Grain Standards Act; that it invades a field of regulation already occupied by Congress; and that, independently of federal legislation, it directly burdens and obstructs interstate and foreign commerce. District Judge Miller granted a restraining order upon the filing of the bill. An application for a preliminary injunction, heard on bill and answer by three other judges, was granted on the day of the hearing. The case is here on appeal under Section 266 of the Judicial Code. No opinion has been filed by the lower court. The injunction is sweeping in character and is not limited to transactions in interstate commerce. To appreciate the contentions made by counsel it will be necessary to examine the federal and the state statutes in detail. But, before doing so, it is desirable to consider usages of the trade. These will explain the occasion for the legislation and its application.

The value of wheat varies, at any time and in every market, according to quality and condition, and the admixture of foreign material, in the particular lot. Formerly, purchases of wheat were made solely upon inspection of the lot or by sample. This was true of sales made by dealers as well as of those made by farmers. Now, wheat is sold largely by description, the quality and condition being designated by grades. Most transactions on the exchanges — like trading in futures — are necessarily by grade. In many transactions off the exchanges — like the purchase of wheat "to arrive" and the sale of "cash" wheat to distant markets — the contract is usually for standard grades.[1] Even where the purchase is made upon inspection of the lot, as from the farmers' wagon in a country market[2] the grade determines the price in large measure. For in

[1] Chicago Board of Trade v. United States, 246 U.S. 231 [1918]; Munn v. Illinois, 94 U.S. 113, 131 [1877]. Report on the Grain Trade (Federal Trade Commission), Vol. I, pp. 175–77 [see also Vol. II, p. 77]; Vol. II, pp. 59–167; Vol. I, pp. 178, 184; Vol. II, pp. 295–322; Vol. V. pp. 27–43.

[2] A country market is one to which the farmer customarily brings his grain by wagon or truck. At these places are located country elevators or other warehouses. Terminal markets are roughly all markets other than country markets. They are

country markets the parties trade with reference to current prices at the applicable terminal market for the assumed grade.[3] Wheat in elevators is commonly graded; partly in order to be applicable on contracts, partly because the wheat of different buyers is customarily binned together.

Standard grades rested, at first, solely upon convention. Local boards of trade fixed them to govern transactions among their members. Then, provisions concerning grades so fixed were commonly embodied, either by express reference or by implication, in contracts of members with others.[4] Later, in some States, standards were fixed by legislation; and they thus became rules of law.[5] Naturally, the standards established in the several markets varied.[6] By

---

the markets to which grain is shipped from the country market; usually by rail or water. Report on the Grain Trade, Vol. II, p. 329. A primary terminal market is one — like Chicago — to which grain moves predominantly direct from country markets. A secondary terminal market is one — like New York — to which grain moves predominantly from primary terminal markets. There are in the United States about 35 terminal markets [each of] which handles more than 5,000,000 bushels of grain annually. Congressional Record, Vol. 53, p. 10,505; Senate Hearing on U.S. Grain Standards Act, May 19, 1916, pp. 35, 64. The Federal Trade Commission (Report on the Grain Trade, Vol. II, p. 19), basing its selection on the volume of business, names 17 terminal markets, of which 10 are primary, namely: Minneapolis, Chicago, Duluth, Kansas City, St. Louis, Omaha, Milwaukee, Cincinnati, Indianapolis, Peoria; and seven secondary: Buffalo, New York, Baltimore, Philadelphia, Boston, Toledo and Louisville. The Department of Agriculture has selected 38 cities (including the above) for the location of its administrative offices concerned with terminal marketing. Bulletin, May 1, 1923.

[3] Report on the Grain Trade, Vol. I, pp. 175–206; Vol. III, p. 17.

[4] Report on the Grain Trade, Vol. II, pp. 295–319.

[5] Grades were first established by legislation in Illinois pursuant to Article XIII, Section 7 of the Constitution of 1870. See Public Laws (April 25), 1871, Section 13, pp. 762, 766–7; 1873 (April 15), p. 189; 1907 (May 24), pp. 491-494; R.S. 1915–16, c. 114, sec. 161, p. 2106. Kentucky authorized the Louisville Board of Trade to establish standard grades and appoint inspectors, Acts of 1879–80, c. 1285, sec. 11 (April 28, 1880), p. 1291 [Vol. I]; Carroll's Kentucky Statutes (1922), sec. 4791. State grades were established in Missouri in 1889; Act of June 22, 1889, sec. 44, p. 133; 1907 (April 12), sec. 7666, p. 295; Rev. Stat. 1919, sec. 6039; Washington in 1895 (March 19), c. CIX, sec. 29, pp. 253, 263; 1909 (March 15), c. 137, p. 519; Remington Comp. Stat. (1922), sec. 6989. [Kansas in 1891 (March 6), c. 248, p. 394.] Kansas Gen. Stat. 1905, sec. 3385; 1907 (March 2), c. 222, sec. 36, pp. 341, 353. Oklahoma in 1899, [c. XXVII, Sec. 43], Compiled Stat. (1921), sec. 11096. Wisconsin in 1905, c. 19, sec. 38. North Dakota in 1909 (March 12), c. 135; Compiled Laws (1913), sec. 3103; 1917 (March 15), c. 56, p. 63; [1918, c. 14; 1919, c. 138]. Oregon in 1917 (February 19), c. 333, sec. 12, pp. 691, 694. Idaho in 1917 (March 12), c. 24; 1919 (March 6), c. 152, sec. 24, pp. 484, 490. Montana in [1915, c. 93]; 1919 (March 13), c. 209, sec. 20, pp. 502, 507; Rev. Code (1921), sec. 3580.

[6] Senate Hearing on U.S. Grain Standards Act (Grain Grade Amendment), May 19, 1916, pp. 34–35; Congressional Record, Vol. 53, p. 10,505.

reason of these variations, values and prices in the different markets were not strictly comparable; and quotations were confusing. Moreover, the several local standards were, themselves, unstable; for in leading markets the requirements of quality and conditions were changed from time to time.[7] An even more potent cause of uncertainty lay in the fact that in every market the rules embodying the requirements of the several grades were couched in terms so vague as to leave much to the discretion of the individual inspector.[8] Thus the function of establishing standards was, in practice, confused with the very different function of applying them. The resulting embarrassment was greatest when the trading was between markets located in different States. It seriously threatened the export trade.[9] To remove these uncertainties, and thus facilitate transactions in interstate and foreign commerce, Congress enacted the United States Grain Standards Act.

Standard grades for grain resemble standard weights and measures. The purpose of each is to provide a common language for business transactions. The need of standard grades for grain had been considered by Congress for thirteen years prior to 1916.[10] The task of establishing them was one of great difficulty.[11] Large ap-

[7] Congressional Record, Vol. 53, p. 10,547. Hearing on U.S. Grain Standards Act (Grain Grade Amendment), January 24, 1916, p. 442. Report on the Grain Trade, Vol. II, p. 78.

[8] Senate Hearing on U.S. Grain Standards Act (Grain Grade Amendment), January 24, 1916, pp. 434, 440, 443, 456, 463; May 19, 1916, pp. 7, 34, 35. "Mr. Duvel. In the present markets we have . . . a multiplicity of grades in the different markets, and a lack of definiteness of grades in the same market. A great many of our grade rules say that the grain should be reasonably dry and reasonably clean, but in all the years I have been working on this proposition I have yet to get anybody to outline to me or to specify what is reasonably dry or reasonably clean."

[9] Congressional Record, Vol. 53, p. 10,504; Senate Hearing on U.S. Grain Standards Act (Grain Grade Amendment), May 19, 1916, pp. 37, 38; compare Report on Grain Trade, Vol. II, p. 296.

[10] See Congressional Record, Vol. 36, p. 941; Vol. 37, p. 178; Vol. 38, pp. 3976–3981, 4469; Vol. 40, pp. 141, 1527, 7826–7829, 7832, 8666; Vol. 41, pp. 858, 1016; Vol. 42, pp. 140, 166, 187, 224, 245, 1000, 3773; Vol. 43, pp. 928, 1344, 1560, 1661, 1668, 1680, 1709, 1712; Vol. 44, p. 130; Vol. 45, pp. 10, 352; Vol. 46, p. 3511; Vol. 47, p. 104; Vol. 48, pp. 4958, 9734, 11000, 11001; Vol. 49, pp. 1717, 2471, 2479; Vol. 50, p. 53, Appendix, pp. 141–142; Vol. 51, pp. 4548, 4719, 4901, 5023, 5904, 6100, 6740, 7543–7557, 8824; Vol. 52, pp. 949–959, 3984.

[11] Prior to 1916 the investigation had included the study of about 50,000 samples of wheat. Senate Hearing on the U.S. Grain Standards Act, January 24, 1916, pp. 440, 422. See also Annual Reports of the Secretary of Agriculture (Year Books), 1907, p. 59; 1908, p. 65; 1909, pp. 84–85; 1910, pp. 63–64; 1911, pp. 67–68; 1912, pp. 134–135; 1913, p. 73; 1914, pp. 30–31; 1916, pp. 4, 9–10.

propriations for that purpose had been made, from time to time.[12] It was recognized that the grades to be established must be definite, in order to eliminate the wide discretion theretofore exercised by inspectors; that they must be so framed that they can remain stable, despite annual fluctuations in the character of the crops and occasional commercial emergencies in the trade; that the grades must meet the needs of farmer, dealer and consumer; and that they must be just to all concerned. To comply with these requirements, knowledge of all relevant facts was essential. No adequate collection of data existed. Investigation had to be made into the conditions governing the production, the marketing, the qualities and the use throughout the United States of each kind and variety of the several grains; and on some subjects conditions prevailing in foreign countries had to be ascertained and considered. It was necessary, among other things, to conduct extensive scientific experiments. When all relevant facts had been ascertained, there remained the exercise of judgment involved in formulating workable grades. This part of the task was eventually undertaken in conjunction with farmers, dealers and millers, after public hearings. The difficulties to be overcome before the grades could properly be formulated were so serious that when the 1916 Act was passed the Secretary was not yet ready to promulgate those for wheat;[13] al-

---

[12] Prior to the passage of the U.S. Grain Standards Act of 1916 Congress had, from time to time, appropriated a total of $485,420 (together with an unspecified share of an appropriation for the general expenses of the Bureau of Plant Industry in 1908 of $896,266) for investigations leading to standard grades for grain. See Act of June 30, 1906, c. 3913, 34 Stat. 669, 681 (grain grades $15,000); Act of March 4, 1907, c. 2907, 34 Stat. 1256, 1267 (grain grades $40,000); Act of May 23, 1908, c. 192, 35 Stat. 251, 257 (grain grades: unspecified share of an appropriation of $896,266 for general expenses of Bureau of Plant Industry); Act of March 4, 1909, c. 301, 35 Stat. 1039, 1045 (grain grades $52,440); Act of May 26, 1910, c. 256, 36 Stat. 416, 422 (grain grades $51,020); Act of March 4, 1911, c. 238, 36 Stat. 1235, 1242 (grain grades $57,080); Act of August 10, 1912, c. 284, 37 Stat. 269, 276 (grain grades $55,640); Act of March 4, 1913, c. 145, 37 Stat. 828, 835 (grain grades $65,000); Act of June 30, 1914, c. 131, 38 Stat. 415, 422 (grain grades $76,320); Act of March 4, 1915, c. 144, 38 Stat. 1086, 1092 (grain grades $72,920); Act of August 11, 1916, c. 313, 39 Stat. 446, 453 (grain grades $88,770) [Accompanied Grain Standards Act].

[13] By order issued March 30, 1917, tentative grades were established effective for certain classes of wheat July 1, 1917, and for others August 1, 1917. Office of Markets, etc., Service and Regulatory Announcements No. 22. These grades were later revised after extensive hearings. See Service and Regulatory Announcements No. 29, issued November 17, 1917; No. 32 issued March 5, 1918; No. 33, issued April 15, 1918; No. 34, issued May 21, 1918; No. 35, issued June 26, 1918; No.

though the preliminary investigations had been pursued by the Department of Agriculture continuously since 1901,[14] and in 1912 power had been conferred to publish (but not make compulsory) standard grades.[15]

An examination of the classes and grades finally established for wheat enables one to appreciate the complexity of the task which had to be performed. Five distinct classes of wheat are recognized. Each class is divided into several sub-classes.[16] Of each sub-class there are several varieties. Thus, in North Dakota three of these classes of wheat are grown in volume.[17] The varieties are many. Of its leading crop, Hard Red Spring Wheat, there are three sub-classes: Dark Northern Spring, Northern Spring, and Red Spring. Whether a lot of grain falls within one or the other of these sub-classes depends, in the main, upon the percentage in it "of dark, hard, and vitreous kernels." [18] Of each sub-class there are six grades. Whether a lot falls within one or another of the first five grades is determined partly by the test weight per bushel; partly by the percentage of moisture; partly by the percentage of damaged kernels; partly by the percentage of heat damage; partly by the percentage of wheat of other classes; partly by the percentage of other cereal grains; and partly by the percentage of foreign mat-

---

36, issued June 21, 1918; No. 48, issued May 8, 1919; No. 54, issued June 26, 1919; No. 62, issued May 29, 1920.

[14] Senate Hearing on U.S. Grain Standards Act, May 19, 1916, p. 79.

[15] Senate Hearing on U.S. Grain Standards Act, May 19, 1916, p. 7.

[16] Handbook of Official Grain Standards, U.S. Department of Agriculture, Bureau of Agricultural Economics, Revised September, 1922.

[17] Hard Red Spring, Hard Red Winter and Durum. See Handling the Farmer's Grain, by Frank R. Durant, June 1, 1922, pp. 7, 9.

[18] Handbook of Official Grain Standards:

"HARD RED SPRING WHEAT. — This class shall include all varieties of Hard Red Spring wheat, and may include not more than 10 per cent of other wheat or wheats. This class shall be divided into three subclasses, as follows:

"SUBCLASS (A) DARK NORTHERN SPRING. — This subclass shall include wheat of the class Hard Red Spring, consisting of 75 per cent or more of dark, hard, and vitreous kernels. This subclass shall not include more than 10 per cent of wheat of the variety Humpback.

"SUBCLASS (B) NORTHERN SPRING. — This subclass shall include wheat of the class Hard Red Spring consisting of less than 75 per cent and more than 25 per cent of dark, hard, and vitreous kernels. This subclass shall not include more than 10 per cent of wheat of the variety Humpback.

"SUBCLASS (C) RED SPRING. — This subclass shall include wheat of the class Hard Red Spring consisting of not more than 25 per cent of dark, hard, and vitreous kernels. This subclass shall also include wheat of the class Hard Red Spring, consisting of more than 10 per cent of the variety Humpback."

ter other than cereal grains. The sixth class, called sample grade, has still other distinguishing characteristics.[19]

The United States Grain Standards Act declares (Sections 2 and 3) that grades so fixed and established shall be known as the official grain standards of the United States. But Congress did not undertake to make these standards applicable to all transactions in grain within the United States. Its provisions govern only such transactions as involve shipment, or delivery for shipment in interstate or foreign commerce of grain which is sold, offered for sale or consigned for sale by grade. Interstate or foreign transactions in grain otherwise than by grade, and those by grade which do not involve shipment or delivery, are not affected by it. (Section 4.) Nor are dealings in grain which are wholly intrastate. It is only because the North Dakota Grain Grading Act adopts the federal standard grades that these are controlling in intrastate transactions. Thus, by coordinate federal and state action a uniform system of grades became, so far as applicable, rules of law for North Dakota governing intrastate, interstate and international transactions in wheat by grade.

There remained the further task of applying these standards. To

[19] Handbook of Official Grain Standards:

HARD RED SPRING WHEAT. — Grade requirements for —
(a) *Dark Northern Spring*, (b) *Northern Spring*, (c) *Red Spring*.

Grade No.	Minimum test weight per bushel.	Moisture.	Maximum limits of —						
			Damaged kernels.		Foreign material other than dockage.			Wheats of other classes.	
			Total	Heat damage.	Total	Matter other than cereal grains.	Total	White and Durum, singly or combined.	
	Lbs.	Pct.	Pct.	Pct.	Pct.	Pct.	Pct.	Pct.	
1	58	14.0	2	0.1	1	0.5	5	2	
2	57	14.5	4	.2	2	1.0	10	5	
3	55	15.0	7	.5	3	2.0	10	10	
4	53	16.0	10	1.0	5	3.0	10	10	
5	50	16.0	15	3.0	7	5.0	10	10	
Sample [a]	....								

[a] Sample grade shall be wheat of the subclass Dark Northern Spring or Northern Spring, or Red Spring, respectively, which does not come within the requirements of any of the grades from No. 1 to No. 5, inclusive, or which has any commercially objectionable foreign odor except of smut, garlic, or wild onions, or is very sour, or is heating, hot, infested with live weevils or other insects injurious to stored grain, or is otherwise of distinctly low quality, or contains small, inseparable stones, or cinders.

(1) The wheat in grades Nos. 1 to 4, inclusive, shall be cool and sweet.
(2) The wheat in No. 5 shall be cool, but may be musty or slightly sour.
(3) The wheat in grade No. 1 Dark Northern Spring and grade No. 1 Northern Spring may contain not more than 5 per cent of the Hard Red Spring wheat variety Humpback.

apply standard weights and measures is a matter so simple as not to require special administrative machinery.[20] To apply grain standards is a matter of difficulty. The accurate determination of the grade is made upon inspection of a representative sample.[21] Even the mere taking of a sample cannot appropriately be done by the untrained; and to properly pass upon it requires knowledge, skill and great care.[22] Special equipment is, also, indispensable.[23] Congress refused to have the federal Government furnish the inspection service.[24] It provided, however, for supervision by the Secretary of Agriculture of such inspection as is required by the federal Act. Under the system so established the inspector is not, in any sense, an employee of the federal Government. He is an independent person whose compensation is ordinarily paid wholly by those for whom he makes the inspection or to whom he furnishes certificates of inspection. In order to ensure the requisite qualifi-

[20] Standard weights, measures and grades established by other federal laws are in some instances compulsory, that is, they are the exclusive standards in all, or some, transactions or under some conditions; while for other articles the legal standards which are established are optional. Thus, the standards for the following articles are compulsory: The gauge for sheet and plate iron and steel, Act of March 3, 1893, c. 221, sec. 1, 27 Stat. 746; grades for apples, Act of August 3, 1912, c. 273, sec. 2, 37 Stat. 250; barrels for fruit or other dry commodities, Act of March 4, 1915, c. 158, sec. 1, 38 Stat. 1186; barrels for lime, Act of August 23, 1916, c. 396, sec. 2, 39 Stat. 530; climax baskets for fruits and vegetables, Act of August 31, 1916, c. 426, sec. 3, 39 Stat. 674; screw threads, Acts of July 18, 1918, c. 156, sec. 1, 40 Stat. 912; March 3, 1919, c. 96, 40 Stat. 1291; March 23, 1920, c. 106, 41 Stat. 536; March 21, 1922, c. 113, 42 Stat. 469. For the following articles the legal standards established are not declared to be exclusive or compulsory: Units of electrical measure, Act of July 12, 1894, c. 131, sec. 2, 28 Stat. 101, 102; barrels for apples, Act of August 3, 1912, c. 273, sec. 4, 37 Stat. 251; grades of cotton, Acts of August 11, 1916, c. 313, 39 Stat. 479; May 23, 1908, c. 192, 35 Stat. 256–7. As to powers of the Bureau of Standards, see Act of March 3, 1901, c. 872, sec. 2, 31 Stat. 1449.

[21] See Report on the Grain Trade, Vol. II, pp. 305–6, 309–312. The term inspection and grading is used under the federal Act as including also the issue of a certificate of the grade. Dept. of Agriculture, Office of the Secretary, Circular No. 70, issued August 15, 1920, Regulation 2, Sec. 15.

[22] To aid in furnishing the necessary instruction the Department of Agriculture has conducted grain-grading schools in connection with agricultural colleges. Report of Chief of the Bureau of Markets, September 23, 1919, p. 31; October 9, 1920, p. 23.

[23] The set of equipment deemed essential at country elevators consists of 16 articles; and 6 others are deemed desirable. Service and Regulatory Announcement, No. 47, pp. 20–21, May 29, 1919. U.S. Dept. of Agriculture, Bureau of Markets. Compare Report of Chief of Markets, October 9, 1920, p. 23. The equipment deemed essential for the determination merely of dockage consists of seven articles. Farmers' Bulletin 1118 [see pp. 9–10], Bureau of Markets, March, 1920.

[24] See Senate Hearings on U.S. Grain Standards Act, May 19, 1916, p. 30 and note 10, *supra*.

cations, inspectors are licensed by the Secretary of Agriculture under regulations issued by him. Competency is determined by examinations; proper performance of duties is sought to be assured by official supervision; and for correction of errors in inspection provision is made by appeals. The first appeal is to the federal district supervisor, of whom there are 38. From his decision a further appeal may be taken to a specially called board.[25] (Sections 6, 7, and 8.) Congress sought to ensure disinterestedness on the part of inspectors by a provision (Section 7) which declares that no one shall be licensed as inspector who is "interested, financially or otherwise, directly or indirectly, in any grain elevator or warehouse, or in the merchandising of grain, nor shall he be in the employment of any person or corporation owning or operating any grain elevator or warehouse."

The inspection required by the federal Act is confined to that which results from the prohibition of the shipment or delivery for shipment in interstate or foreign commerce of uninspected grain sold, offered for sale or consigned for sale by grade. (Section 4.) Grain is so shipped in interstate and foreign commerce from many thousand places. The number of inspectors holding federal licenses is about 424. Most of these are massed in 24 places. There are only 142 points in the United States at which grain inspectors licensed under the federal Act are located.[26] Still these few licensees are able to render to the trade the grading service required under the federal Act, because of two provisions contained in it. (Section 4.) By the first, grain to which the Act applies need not be inspected at point of shipment, if the inspection is made at the place to, or through, which the grain is shipped. By the second provision, the grain may likewise be so shipped without inspection from one place where there is no federal licensee to another place where there is none, "subject to the right of either party to the transaction to refer any dispute as to the grade of the grain to the Secretary of Agriculture, who may determine the true grade thereof."

[25] Regulations of the Secretary of Agriculture under the United States Grain Standards Act, Dept. of Agriculture, Office of the Secretary, Circular No. 70, pp. 7–33, issued Aug. 15, 1920; amended June 26, 1922; May 12, 1923; June 7, 1923. For the year ending June 30, 1922, the total number of appeals from wheat grading was 25,592. In 9,214 (i.e., 36 per cent.) the appeals were sustained. Report of Chief of Bureau of Markets, etc., October 5, 1922, p. 21.

[26] Bureau of Markets, Service and Regulatory Announcements, No. 64, issued July 9, 1920.

But transactions in which grain "sold, offered for sale, or consigned for sale by grade" is "shipped or delivered for shipment in interstate or foreign commerce" [Section 4] constitute only a small part of the aggregate number of sales of grain by grade within the United States. Most sales by grade do not involve, at the time when made, any shipment or delivery for shipment in interstate or foreign commerce. A very large part of them are sales of wheat which never leaves the State in which it was grown. The federal law does not purport to license inspectors to grade grain in intrastate commerce. Moreover, at the tens of thousands of country markets where wheat is so dealt in by grade, there is no inspector licensed under the federal law who could perform the service. Competent, disinterested persons cannot be induced to apply for federal licenses at country markets. The fee received for inspection is necessarily small. The earnings possible at such places would rarely justify private persons in taking up there, independently, the profession of inspector. How to supply for these many transactions at the country markets trustworthy inspection service for which the federal Act makes no provision was the problem which confronted the people of North Dakota.

The need for such inspection service was deemed pressing in North Dakota. Practically all the wheat is sold by grade. There is no terminal market within the State. The farmer's sale is commonly made at the country market. The purchaser is usually the local elevator concern. It is "a sort of public market place, where the farmers come with their grain for the purpose of selling the same, and where the purchaser, a party in interest, acts as marketmaster, weighmaster, inspector and grader of the grain." *W.W. Cargill Co. v. Minnesota*, 180 U.S. 452, 464 [1901]. The differences between the market price of the several grades is so great that accuracy in grading is a matter of vital interest. The distinction between the several grades is a matter of nicety. Farmers rarely possess the knowledge, experience, skill and equipment necessary to enable one to grade accurately. True, nearly 90 per cent. of the North Dakota wheat is ultimately shipped in interstate commerce; and when so shipped, it is usually inspected and graded under the federal law at destination or en route. But, in most instances, the shipment is not made by the farmer or on his account. It is made by the elevatorman — the purchaser from the farmer. Ordinarily it is only this purchaser who will benefit by a later federal inspection raising the grade. Thus, the grading which determines the price paid to the farmer rests with the elevatorman who is himself the buyer.[27] Grading done under these circumstances, without public supervision, must occasionally be unfair. That there should develop a widespread belief on the part of farmers that it was often so, is natural. In North Dakota such belief has, for years, been intense, widespread and persistent. The demand for trustworthy inspection service in cases where none could be had under the federal system became imperative. To supply it directly through inspectors employed by the State was precluded by the cost which such a provision would involve; for there are nearly 700 widely scattered country markets in North Dakota. In 1919 the legislature undertook, among other things, to supervise grading by requiring that buyers of grain be licensed as inspectors. The validity of the statute then enacted was challenged and [the statute was] held void in *Lemke v. Farmers Grain Co.*, 258 U.S. 50 [1922].

Instructed by that decision the people of North Dakota sought by the initiative measure here in question to ensure, in another way, honest grading at country elevators. It is a commercial necessity that every elevator have connected with it some person experienced in grading. For unless wheat is graded at the elevator, the operator can neither properly store that of the different owners in-common bins, nor can he safely buy any. To secure fairness in the grading, the 1922 Act provided for careful supervision of that actually being done at the elevator. It put under official supervision the person who is employed at the elevator to do the grading. The operator of a grain elevator had long been required to hold a license as public warehouseman. The 1922 statute added the requirement that either he, or an employee, must hold, also, a license

[27] Report on the Grain Trade, Vol. I, p. 35. The terminal markets for North Dakota wheat are Duluth and Minneapolis. Report on the Grain Trade, Vol. I, pp. 130–145; Vol. II, pp. 29–31, 41, 140–158. A small percentage is shipped by the farmer direct to terminals on consignment, Cong. Rec., Vol. 53, p. 10,628; a small percentage is shipped by the farmer to the terminal after storage in a country elevator; and a small percentage is sold in the country market to North Dakota mills. Report on the Grain Trade, Vol. I, pp. 94–107, 153. See also Cong. Rec., Vol. 53, pp. 10,775, 10,782. The weighted average price of Dark Northern Spring wheat in cash sales at Minneapolis during the week of June 30–July 6, 1923, was No. 1, $1.18; No. 2, $1.13; No. 3, $1.10. U.S. Dept. of Agriculture, Weather, Crops and Markets, issue of July 14, 1923, p. 49.

as inspector and grader of grain. And it prohibited all persons from purchasing by grade grain which had not been graded by either a federal or a state licensee. New administrative provisions believed to be necessary to secure due performance of the licensees' duties and payment for produce bought on credit were added.

In the attack upon this statute many questions were raised which do not require decision. Thus, we need not enquire into the validity of those provisions by which power to establish standard grades for grain was provisionally conferred upon the state supervisor. For that power is granted only in so far as the Secretary of Agriculture shall fail to establish grades; and grades for wheat (the only product here involved) had been established by the Secretary before this statute was enacted. We need not consider the validity of any provision as applied to purchases made by others than elevator concerns. For the plaintiffs are all owners and operators as public warehousemen of elevators located within the State; and they sue as such. We need not consider in detail what regulations the state supervisor of grades could legally establish. For this suit was commenced before he had prescribed any. The main questions for decision are whether the requirement that operators of public elevators be equipped with the warehouseman's and inspector's licenses, and whether the prohibition of purchases by grade of uninspected grain, invade rights guaranteed plaintiffs by the Federal Constitution. That they do, and that for this, and other reasons the statute is void, is asserted on four grounds.

First. It is contended that the statute deprives plaintiffs of liberty and property without due process of law. There is no claim that the State's police power may not be exerted to protect sellers, as well as buyers, against frauds.[28] Compare *House v. Mayes*, 219 U.S. 270 [1911]; *Lemke v. Farmers Grain Co., supra*, at 63. The objections insisted upon relate to specific conditions and restrictions which

---

[28] Section 4 prescribes the duty to establish grades "for the purpose of preventing fraud and wrongful handling of grain, seed and other farm products, and protecting the producers of the same in connection with the marketing thereof" and "in a general way [to] investigate and supervise the marketing of same with a view of preventing unjust discrimination, unreasonable margins of profit, confiscation of valuable dockage, fraud and other unlawful practices."

The preamble of the statute (Section 1) states that the enactment is: "For the purpose of encouraging, promoting, and safe-guarding agriculture, commerce and industry, and preventing confiscation of dockage, unjust discrimination, fraud and extortion in the marketing of all kinds of grain, . . ." etc.

the statute is said to impose upon the conduct of the business of buying wheat. The claims most strongly urged are that under this statute buyers of wheat must be licensed; that dockage must be specifically paid for or returned to the seller; that the state supervisor is empowered, by means of the margin clause, to fix the price at which wheat may be bought; and that such regulations violate the Fourteenth Amendment. Whether regulation of that character would do so we need not consider. For the statute, properly construed, contains none of these provisions.

The statute does not require that buyers of wheat be licensed. It requires that public grain elevators be equipped with a licensed inspector of grain (Section 12).[29] Many classes of persons habitually engaged in buying wheat are free to conduct their business without having a grain inspector's license. This is true of interior brokers, track buyers, scoop shovellers, solicitors for terminal dealers, feeders, retailers, country mills and other converters.[30] Plaintiffs are required to have such a license, not because they are buyers of grain, but because they are public warehousemen of grain. If their elevators are not so equipped, they may not be operated even if devoted exclusively to storage of grain for others. It is for operating a public grain elevator without an inspector's license, not for purchasing grain without the license, that a prosecution would have to be brought.

The assertion that the statute requires dockage [31] to be specifi-

---

[29] Section 12. ". . . And it shall be unlawful for any person or persons, corporation or association to operate a public warehouse . . . without first securing a [inspector's] license from the Supervisor of Grades, Weights and Measures . . ."

Section 5. ". . . Any person may buy any such product by sample or by type or under any name, description or designation which is not false or misleading and which name, description or designation does not include in whole or part the terms of any official grade or grain standard established or recognized by this act . . . ."

Section 7. ". . . Any person may without a license and according to provisions of the United States Grain Standards Act and the rules and regulations promulgated thereunder by the Secretary of Agriculture, buy by grade any grain, seed, or other agricultural products that have been graded as provided by this act."

Section 12, which prohibits unlicensed persons from grading grain and requires those operating elevators to secure an inspector's license, expressly provides "that this section shall not prohibit any such person from buying such agricultural products if they have first been lawfully graded or provided he buys them by samples as otherwise provided for herein."

[30] For the extent to which such other persons buy wheat, see Report on the Grain Trade, Vol. I, pp. 95–99.

[31] Dockage is not defined or mentioned in the federal law. But it has been de-

cally paid for or returned to the seller rests upon a misapprehension. The direction in Section IV that "the value of dockage shall be considered and the buyer shall not be permitted to retain the same without just compensation" applies only when grades of grain are established by the state supervisor; and that section confers upon him power to fix grades only when they have not been established under the federal Act.[31a] The Secretary of Agriculture had established grades for wheat more than five years prior to the enactment of the statute here in question. These federal grades (re-

---

fined by the instruction to federal licensed inspectors, by departmental announcements and the practice thereunder. "Dockage includes sand, dirt, weed seeds, weed stems, chaff, straw, grain other than wheat, and any other foreign material which can be removed readily from the wheat by the use of appropriate sieves, cleaning devices, or other practical means suited to separate the foreign material present. It also includes undeveloped, shriveled, and small pieces of wheat kernels removed in separating the foreign material, when these wheat kernels or small pieces cannot be removed from the dockage by proper rescreening or recleaning. If they are recovered they go back with the clean wheat and are not considered as dockage. The quantity of dockage is calculated in terms of percentage, based on the total weight of the grain including the dockage. The dockage is stated in terms of whole percentum and is added to the grade designation; for instance, No. 1 Hard Winter, Dockage 1 per cent, or No. 1 Hard Winter, Dockage 3 per cent. If the dockage does not amount to 1 per cent it is disregarded. Fractions of a percentum are not stated." In grading wheat under the federal grades the licensed inspector makes his determination, with certain exceptions, on the basis of clean wheat — on a "dockage free" basis. In other words, the dockage in the wheat is removed before the test weight of the wheat, the amount of damaged kernels, the admixture of other classes of wheat and the amount of rye and other cereal grains are determined. U.S. Department of Agriculture, Bureau of Markets, Service and Regulatory Announcement No. 54, issued June 26, 1919, pp. 6, 7. Compare No. 36, issued June 21, 1918, p. 13; No. 26, issued October 10, 1917, pp. 10–12. See also Farmers' Bulletin, No. 1118, "Dockage Under the Federal Wheat Grades," issued March, 1920; and Farmers' Bulletin, No. 1287, "Foreign Material in Spring Wheat," issued December, 1922.

[31a] Section 4 begins with the provision:

"It shall be the duty of the State Supervisor of Grades, Weights and Measures to fix and establish as soon as may be after the enactment hereof . . . ."

The section ends with the provision:

"In establishing such grades, weights and measures, the value of dockage shall be considered and the buyer shall not be permitted to retain the same without just compensation. He shall pay the fair market value for same or separate it and return it to the producer."

But the same section provides:

"that whenever the Secretary of Agriculture of the United States has established grades, weights and measures, or any standards of quality and condition of any grain, seed and other agricultural products under the United States Grain Standards Act, such grades, standards of quality and conditions, weights and measures shall become the grades, standards of quality and conditions, weights and measures of this state. . . ."

The other references to dockage in Sections 1, 4, 6 and 7 are merely provisions to secure honest inspection and grading by state licensees.

vised) are still in force. We have no occasion to consider what the situation would be if the Secretary had not acted.

Nor does the statute empower the state supervisor to fix, by means of the margin,[32] the price to be paid for wheat. The claim that the statute confers upon the state supervisor power to fix the margin at which wheat may be bought, rests upon two general provisions of the statute concerning the duties of the state supervisor. Neither of them authorizes him to fix directly or indirectly the price to be paid for wheat. One (Section 4) declares that he

"shall [among other things] in a general way investigate and supervise the marketing of same [farm products] with a view of preventing unjust discrimination, unreasonable margins of profit, confiscation of valuable dockage, fraud and other unlawful practices . . . ."

The duty so imposed upon the state supervisor to enquire into margins is part of that general survey and supervision of business practices commonly undertaken by governments to prevent unfair practices. To enable the state supervisor to perform this duty the public warehouseman must keep a record of the names and addresses of his warehouses, elevators or mills; of the prices paid for agricultural products, and the grades given; of the prices received and the grades received at the terminal market and within the State; and must furnish the information to the Supervisor of Grades, Weights and Measures upon written request. (Section 10.) To this end also, in case of any dispute as to grades, weights or measures between the farmer and the purchaser (if the latter is operating a public warehouse), a sample shall be taken from the farm product and shall be sent to the Supervisor of Grades, Weights and Measures; and he shall determine the grade, weight or measure under such rule and regulation as he may establish. (Section 11.) [33] Power and duty to investigate, however comprehensive, do not imply a power to fix prices.

[32] Margin is the difference between the current price for the grade in the terminal market and the price paid for the grade in the country market. The term is used sometimes to include the total "spread" between the gross selling prices at the two markets — thus including besides the net profit and all operating expenses also freight to the terminal market. When so used it is the equivalent of "gross margin." More commonly it is used as the spread after deducting freight to the terminal market. Report on the Grain Trade, Vol I, p. 187.

[33] Section 10. "And it shall be the duty of every public warehouseman in this state to keep a record of the names and addresses of their respective warehouses,

The other provision relied upon to support the assertion that the state supervisor may fix margins is Section 17 which declares that:

"All of the duties and obligations which were formerly performed by the State Inspector of Grades, Weights and Measures, and all of the obligations placed upon him by law, are hereby transferred and made part of the duties of the Supervisor of Grades, Weights and Measures."

The argument is that because the Act of 1919 [c. 138, §2] directed the state supervisor "to establish a reasonable margin to be paid producers of grain by warehouses, elevators and mills . . . " and because that statute was not in terms repealed, its provision for establishing margins is thereby incorporated into the 1922 statute here in question. What conditions and restrictions the statute imposes and what powers it confers upon the state supervisor of grades, weights and measures, are questions of state law. Where the statute of a State "is reasonably susceptible of two interpretations, by one of which it would be clearly constitutional and by the other of which its constitutionality would be doubtful, the former construction should be adopted." *Carey v. South Dakota*, 250 U.S. 118, 122 [1919]. Unless compelled by unequivocal language we should, in the absence of controlling decision, decline to give the statute a construction which would render it void. *Knights Templars' Indemnity Co. v. Jarman*, 187 U.S. 197, 205 [1902]; *Douglas v. Noble*, 261 U.S. 165, 169 [1923]. The whole 1919 statute had been held void in the *Lemke* case. It is not mentioned in the later act. We may not assume that the people of North Dakota intended to defy the power of this Court by re-enacting the margin provision which had just been held unconstitutional.

Objection is also made to the general provision (Section 5) which declares that:

"No person thereafter shall buy by grade any such farm product,

---

elevators or mills; the price paid for agricultural products, the grades given; the price received and the grades received at the terminal markets or within the state, which information shall be furnished to the Supervisor of Grades, Weights and Measures upon written request."

Section 11. "In case of any dispute as to grades, weights or measures, between the producer and the purchaser, operating a public warehouse, elevator or flour mill, handling agricultural products, then a sample shall be taken from such farm product, and shall be sent to the Supervisor of Grades, Weights and Measures, and the proper grade, weight or measure shall be determined by him under such rules and regulations as he may establish."

unless it shall have been inspected and graded by an inspector licensed under the provisions of this act, or under the provisions of the United States Grain Standards Act . . . ."

This prohibition against purchasing by grade uninspected grain does not unreasonably restrict the right of the plaintiffs to deal in grain. It is applicable not only to public warehousemen but to all persons except farmers buying from one another. It is applicable also whether the buyer holds an inspector's license or does not. Ample provision is made by which inspection can be secured. The license to an inspector is issued without the exaction of any fee. Any, and every, person who is competent to perform the inspection service may be so licensed. The statute expressly declares that anyone engaged in buying grain, if competent to grade, may be licensed; and that one operating an elevator (among others) can, as of right, secure a license for himself, his buyer or other employee.[34]

Still other requirements are imposed upon plaintiffs. As holders of inspectors' licenses they must honestly and correctly weigh grains inspected and fix the grades and dockage thereof according to law.[35] As public warehousemen they must file with the state supervisor a bond in at least $5,000 for the faithful performance of prescribed duties.[36] No other bond is required of them specifically

[34] Section 6. "The State Supervisor of Grades, Weights and Measures shall issue a license to grade to any person engaged in soliciting, buying, weighing and inspecting or grading grain, seeds or other agricultural products, or to the buyer or agent of a privately or publicly owned warehouse, elevator or flour mill handling agricultural products, provided such buyer, solicitor or agent shall pass such reasonable examination as to his competency as may be prescribed by the State Supervisor of Grades, Weights and Measures . . . ."

[35] Section 7. "Each person receiving such license shall cause same to be conspicuously posted at his place of business . . . ." Section 6. "The condition of such license shall require such person to honestly and correctly fix grades and dockage of grain and seed inspected at their respective places of business and to honestly and correctly weight the products so inspected and graded according to the provisions of this act and the rules and regulations made hereunder."

[36] Section 9. ". . . [the State Supervisor of Grades, Weights and Measures] shall require the proprietor, lessee or manager of any such public warehouse, elevator or flour mill, or any individual buying or shipping grain for profit in this state, who does not pay cash in advance for the grain so bought, to file with him a bond, running to the state, with good and sufficient surety in an amount sufficient to cover the value of all farm products bought and not paid for in cash and in addition thereto, he shall require a bond from such public warehouse in a penal sum of not less than five thousand dollars, as in his discretion he may deem fit for the faithful performance of their duties as public warehousemen, and the compliance with all of the laws of this state in relation thereto."

as warehousemen. But if plaintiffs buy grain and do not pay cash in advance, they, like every other buyer of farm products, are required to file a bond sufficient in amount to cover the value of all so bought on credit. The requirement of bonds from persons so engaged in quasi-public employment is common. Compare *Payne v. Kansas*, 248 U.S. 112 [1918]. We cannot say that there was no justification for such a protective measure in North Dakota.[37] The amount of the bond is to be fixed by the state supervisor. We may not assume that the state supervisor will exact bonds unreasonable in amount. All these requirements are clearly reasonable. Even if any one of them were objectionable, that would not invalidate the Act. For each is separable from its main provisions.

Finally, it is claimed that the Due Process Clause is violated because, while possession of the inspector's license is indispensable to carrying on plaintiffs' business, the state supervisor is empowered to suspend or revoke it without giving to the licensee notice and opportunity to be heard. (Section 7.) The statute provides that the license may be revoked or suspended if the licensee is incompetent, careless, or dishonest;[38] but it does not confer power to do this without notice and opportunity to be heard. On the contrary it provides that the license shall not be revoked or suspended without investigation; and that the licensee may, if dissatisfied with the state supervisor's decision, have his order reviewed by the District Court for the county. Moreover, the statute contemplates that the state supervisor, like other heads of executive departments, will prescribe rules and regulations. (Sections 3, 6.) Such rules would naturally provide for notice to a licensee whose conduct is under investigation. It is not to be assumed that the legislature intended to confer upon an administrative officer arbitrary power; or that he will exercise arbitrarily the powers actually vested in him. *Douglas*

---

[37] Compare Report on the Grain Trade, Vol. I, p. 96. Minnesota Gen. Laws, 1913, c. 432, p. 630; Nebraska Compiled Statutes (1922), sec. 7225; Alabama Gen. Acts, 1915, c. 160.

[38] Section 7. "The State Supervisor of Grades, Weights and Measures may suspend or revoke any license issued by him under this act whenever after investigation he shall determine that such licensee is incompetent or has knowingly or carelessly graded grain improperly or has short-weighed or has taken for his own use valuable dockage without compensation, or has issued any false certificate of grading or has violated any of the provisions of this act or of the United States Grain Standards Act . . . ." The licensee may have the supervisor's action reviewed by the county District Court.

v. Noble, supra, at 165, 170; *Hall v. Geiger-Jones Co.*, 242 U.S. 539, 554 [1917]; *Plymouth Coal Co. v. Pennsylvania*, 232 U.S. 531, 545 [1914]; *New York ex rel. Lieberman v. Van de Carr*, 199 U.S. 552, 562 [1905].

Second. It is contended that the statute necessarily conflicts with the United States Grain Standards Act; since most of the North Dakota wheat, although sold within the State, actually enters, at some time, into interstate commerce. The contention is unsound.

The basic provisions of the state statute are, in substance, these. No person shall purchase uninspected grain by grade; nor shall anyone operate a grain elevator as public warehouseman unless it is equipped with an inspector's license. The basic provision (Section 4) of the federal Act is this:

"No person thereafter shall ship or deliver for shipment in interstate or foreign commerce any such grain which is sold, offered for sale, or consigned for sale by grade unless the grain shall have been inspected and graded by an inspector licensed under this Act and the grade by which it is sold, offered for sale, or consigned for sale be one of the grades fixed therefor in the official grain standards of the United States . . . ."

Obviously there is no direct conflict between these substantive provisions of the federal and the state legislation. The state statute does not undertake to restrict in any way the right to ship or to deliver for shipment in interstate or foreign commerce, or to sell, or to offer for sale, or to consign for sale in interstate or foreign commerce. Its requirement of inspection does not apply to the purchase of any wheat which has been inspected under the federal law; and the requirement is limited to those transactions in which a sale is consummated within the State before a shipment or delivery for shipment in interstate or foreign commerce begins. The requirement of inspection under the federal law applies only to shipments or deliveries for shipment in interstate or foreign commerce. There is no provision in it which can conceivably be construed as conferring the right to purchase within the State by grade uninspected wheat, whenever the purpose or intention of the purchaser is to ship or deliver it, at some time thereafter, in interstate or foreign commerce. Nor is there in the federal Act any provision denying to the State power to regulate its public warehouses by prescribing that they shall be equipped with an inspector's license, even if used also for interstate and foreign commerce. Compare *Brass v. North Dakota ex rel. Stoeser*, 153 U.S. 391, 396 [1894]; *W. W. Cargill Co. v. Minnesota, supra,* at 470.

The argument of plaintiffs is that, since wheat bought by a country elevator will, in most cases, be later inspected under the federal law, conflict will arise, because inspectors frequently disagree in grading the same lot of wheat. But inspection of a carload at the terminal market is not, usually, inspection of the same lot of wheat which the farmer delivered to the country elevator. A lot commonly loses its identity when it enters the country grain elevator, because it is not separately binned. Moreover, the federal Act does not prohibit double inspection, even where wheat remains in the same car with bulk unbroken.[39] Nor does that Act give to the grading of a licensed inspector conclusive effect under any circumstances. His cetificate of grade is not even made evidence of the facts found by him.[40]

Nor is there any conflict between the state legislation and subsidiary provisions of the federal Act. An attempt is made to establish a conflict by reference. To this end Sections 3107 and 3113 of the North Dakota Compiled Laws of 1913 are invoked. These sections require a public elevator to give a storage receipt for grain which shall entitle the holder (on terms named) to demand at his option delivery of an equal quantity of the same grade either at the local elevator or at the terminal market in another State. The argument is that under the North Dakota Grain Grading Act a licensed

[39] The federal Act, as construed by the Department of Agriculture, requires a new inspection of the same lot of wheat, whenever a new shipment in interstate commerce is entered upon. As to "in" and "out" grading, see Service and Regulatory Announcements, No. 17 (issued December 21, 1916), pp. 29, 30; No. 18 (issued January 27, 1917), p. 12; No. 26 (issued October 10, 1917), p. 29; No. 42 (issued December 1, 1918), p. 9. It is a common practice of millers, dealers and receivers of grain in the terminal markets to supplement, or check, by their own inspection that made by the federal licensee. And by reason of such re-inspection premiums are often established which enhance the market value of a particular lot within the standard grades. Report on the Grain Trade, Vol. II, pp. 295–319; particularly pp. 297–300, 309. Thus the Daily Market Record for July 18, 1923, gives the quotation for that day's sales of No. 1 Dark Northern Spring Wheat: for "ordinary to good," $1.03¼ to $1.08¼ per bushel; for good to choice, $1.09¼ to $1.17¼; for choice to fancy, $1.18¼ to $1.28¼.

[40] The findings by the Secretary of Agriculture as to grade are made, under some circumstances, *prima facie* evidence of the true grade in courts of the United States, provided the parties in interest had the opportunity of being heard by him. [Section 6.]

warehouseman must bind himself to comply with all the laws of the State in relation to that employment (Section 9); that while these sections of the Compiled Laws are not therein specially referred to, they must be deemed to be incorporated (since they have not been expressly repealed); and that they are inconsistent with the prohibitions contained in Section 4 of the federal Act. Several answers to this argument suggest themselves. It is enough to say that acceptance from a State of a license conditioned generally to obey its laws does not bind the licensee to comply with a statute which is not a law because it is repugnant to the Federal Constitution. *W.W. Cargill Co. v. Minnesota, supra,* at 468.

The contention that the dockage and margin provisions of the state statute will result in conflict, rest, as shown above, upon a misapprehension of their character and effect. If there were any doubt as to the entire consistency of the federal and state systems of inspection it would be resolved by "the settled rule [of construction] that a statute enacted in execution of a reserved power of the State is not to be regarded as inconsistent with an act of Congress passed in the execution of a clear power under the Constitution, unless the repugnance or conflict is so direct and positive that the two acts cannot be reconciled or stand together." *Missouri, Kansas & Texas Ry. Co. v. Haber,* 169 U.S. 613, 623 [1898].[41]

Third. It is contended that Congress occupied the field by the United States Grain Standards Act. The argument is that thereby Congress indicated its intention to prohibit the States from regulating in any way the marketing of wheat destined for shipment in interstate or foreign commerce; and that, hence, the North Dakota Grain Grading Act is void, even if each of its provisions is consistent with those of the federal law. It will be assumed that Congress has the power to freely impose, even upon purely intrastate transactions, regulations concerning the marketing of any class of merchandise of which the larger part is destined for shipment, at some time, in interstate or foreign commerce. We are thus relieved from

[41] Sherlock v. Alling, 93 U.S. 99 [1876]; Smith v. Alabama, 124 U.S. 465, 482 [1888]; Reid v. Colorado, 187 U.S. 137, 149 [1902]; Crossman v. Lurman, 192 U.S. 189, 199–200 [1904]; Asbell v. Kansas, 209 U.S. 251, 257 [1908]; Missouri Pacific Ry. Co. v. Larabee Flour Mills Co. 211 U.S. 612, 623 [1909]; Missouri, Kansas & Texas Ry. Co. v. Harris, 234 U.S. 412, 419 [1914]; Atlantic Coast Line R.R. Co. v. Georgia, 234 U.S. 280, 293–94 [1914]; Illinois Central R.R. Co. v. Public Utilities Commissions, 245 U.S. 493, 510 [1918].

determining the exact point in the history of wheat grown in North Dakota and shipped to the Minnesota terminal markets at which it can be said to have entered interstate commerce. But marketing of grain is not one of those functions national in character which at every stage, and in all its branches, can be appropriately subjected to uniform regulation throughout the United States. Such marketing includes buying, storing, transporting, treating and selling. Of these five stages in marketing, four are performed mainly intrastate, either at the country market or at the terminal market. Conditions affecting most of these stages in marketing differ widely in the several surplus grain States.[42] Recognizing this fact, Congress carefully circumscribed the field of its regulation through the United States Grain Standards Act to grain shipped or delivered for shipment in interstate or foreign commerce which is sold, offered for sale or consigned for sale by grade. To no other grain, and to no other stage in the marketing of that grain, does the federal Act apply. It makes no provision concerning the purchase by grade intrastate of grain destined later for shipment or delivery for shipment in interstate or foreign commerce. It makes no provision concerning the sale intrastate of grain received on interstate shipments. It makes no provision concerning either storage or treatment at the country elevator, or at the terminal elevator, of grain moving in interstate commerce. The omission of such provisions furnishes reason to believe that Congress intended to leave the States free to regulate, under their police power, those stages in the transactions although they might constitutionally be deemed a part of interstate commerce. It was not necessary, in order to preserve the States' police power over these stages, that there should be an express authorization by Congress, like that made in the Webb-Kenyon Act. *Clark Distilling Co. v. Western Maryland Ry. Co.*, 242 U.S. 311 [1917]. Compare *Merchants Exchange v. Missouri*, 248 U.S. 365, 368 [1919].

Whether Congress occupied the field and thus precluded regulation by the States is a question of statutory construction. The "intent to supersede the exercise by the State of its police power as

[42] How different conditions governing country marketing of wheat on the Pacific Coast are from those prevailing in North Dakota and the neighboring States is illustrated by the fact that in California, Oregon and Washington most wheat is handled, not in bulk by elevators, but in sacks by ordinary warehouses. Report on the Grain Trade, Vol. I, pp. 57–59.

to matters not covered by the Federal legislation is not to be inferred from the mere fact that Congress has seen fit to circumscribe its regulation and to occupy a limited field." *Savage v. Jones,* 225 U.S. 501, 533 [1912]. Here the federal Act bears conclusive evidence that such was not its intent. It makes provisions concerning state grain inspection departments — then existing or thereafter to be established — and makes specific reference to inspectors to be licensed under state law.[43] The Federal Grain Standards Act, like the Federal Food and Drugs Act of June 30, 1906, c. 3915, 34 Stat. 768, left the States free to provide appropriate regulation under the police power. *Savage v. Jones, supra; Armour & Co. v. North Dakota,* 240 U.S. 510 [1916]; *Weigle v. Curtice Bros. Co.,* 248 U.S. 285 [1919]; *Hebe Co. v. Shaw,* 248 U.S. 297 [1919]; *Corn Products Refining Co. v. Eddy,* 249 U.S. 427 [1919].[44]

Fourth. Finally, plaintiffs contend that the North Dakota Grain Grading Act is void independently of federal legislation, because it directly burdens or obstructs interstate and foreign commerce. To sustain this contention it must either be established that the marketing of wheat is a function national in character which requires at all stages and in all its branches uniform regulation throughout the United States (so that any state regulation whatsoever would be void) or it must appear that specific requirements of the state statute would in fact directly burden or obstruct interstate or foreign commerce.

That marketing of wheat is not a national function of that char-

[43] Section 7. ". . . No person authorized or employed by any State, county, city, town, board of trade, chamber of commerce, corporation, society, partnership, or association to inspect or grade grain shall certify, or otherwise state or indicate in writing, that any grain for shipment or delivery for shipment in interstate or foreign commerce, which has been inspected or graded by him, or by any person acting under his authority, is of one of the grades of the official grain standards of the United States, unless he holds an unsuspended and unrevoked license issued by the Secretary of Agriculture: *Provided,* That in any State which has, or which may hereafter have a State grain inspection department established by the laws of such State, the Secretary of Agriculture shall [except as in such section provided] issue licenses to the persons duly authorized and employed to inspect and grade grain under the laws of such State."

When Congress enacted the United States Grain Standards Act there existed systems for state inspection and grading of grain in eight States; and, in others, there was legislation which regulated, in other ways, the inspection and grading of grain.

[44] Compare Service and Regulatory Announcements, U.S. Department of Agriculture, Office of Markets and Rural Organization: No. 15, pp. 13, 14, issued December 6, 1916; No. 48, p. 2, issued May 8, 1919.

acter has already been shown. Indeed, plaintiffs' contentions that
the North Dakota statute is invalid rest throughout upon the fact
that the conditions affecting the wheat crop of the State are peculiar. The assumption is that, since 90 per cent. of its marketed
wheat is destined to enter, at some time, into interstate commerce,
therefore, sales of wheat within North Dakota although completed
within the State are to be treated as part of an interstate movement. But the percentage of the grain grown in the several States
which ultimately enters interstate or foreign commerce differs
widely as to each kind of grain; and the percentage of each kind
which is so marketed differs in each State widely from year to
year.[45] The diversity of conditions affecting the grain trade is
such that it can be regulated appropriately only through diversity
of treatment of those stages in the operation which like buying at
country markets are local in character.

It remains to consider whether any specific requirement of the
state statute renders it obnoxious to the commerce clause. None
of its provisions purports to regulate interstate or foreign commerce. None imposes upon commerce a direct tax, charge, or
other burden. The effect of the statute upon interstate and foreign commerce, if any, is indirect. No doubt, even such indirect
effect may invalidate a state statute, if the effect is such that legitimate interstate or foreign commerce is in fact unduly obstructed. See *Union Pacific R.R. v. Public Service Comm. of Missouri*, 248 U.S. 67 [1918]. But unless it is shown that obstruction
will result, a state statute which is passed in the exercise of the
police power and which influences such commerce only indirectly,
will be sustained. *Southern Railway Co. v. King*, 217 U.S. 524,
533–34 [1910]; *Seaboard Air Line Ry. v. Blackwell*, 244 U.S. 310
[1917]. Here the facts alleged fail to show that such obstruction
will result; and facts of which we take notice show affirmatively
that it will not. Compare *Pierce Oil Corporation v. Hope*, 248 U.S.
498 [1919].

The requirement that wheat purchased by grade must be graded
by a licensed inspector does not obstruct the commerce; because

[45] Thus, while 90 per cent. of the marketed North Dakota wheat leaves the
State at some time, probably very little of its marketed corn does so. And while
most of the North Dakota wheat crop is marketed interstate, most of that grown
in Minnesota is marketed within its borders. [See Report on the Grain Trade, Vol.
I, p. 149.]

ample provision is made for securing the inspection without appreciable expense.[46] The requirements that grain elevators (an indispensable instrumentality of the interstate commerce) be licensed as public warehousemen, that they be equipped with a licensed inspector, and that they keep a record of transactions which shall be subject to examination by the state supervisor of grades, weights and measures, do not unduly obstruct interstate or foreign commerce. The licenses may be had by any competent and trustworthy person. The inspector's license is issued without the payment of any fee. The fee charged the public warehouseman is clearly reasonable.[47] *Pure Oil Co. v. Minnesota*, 248 U.S.

[46] Similar state statutes were sustained in the following cases, among others: (a) Inspection laws as applied to merchandise destined for, or shipped to, other States. Sligh v. Kirkwood, 237 U.S. 52 [1915]; Diamond Glue Co. v. United States Glue Co., 187 U.S. 611, 616 [1903; fee required from foreign corporation as condition of doing business within State]. Compare Turner v. Maryland, 107 U.S. 38 [1883]; Crescent Oil Co. v. Mississippi, 257 U.S. 129 [1921]. (b) Inspection of pure food laws as applied to merchandise received from other states or moving in interstate commerce. Pure Oil Co. v. Minnesota, 248 U.S. 158, 162 [1918; oil and gas]; Hebe Co. v. Shaw, *supra*; Weigle v. Curtice Brothers Co., *supra*; Armour & Co. v. North Dakota, *supra*; Savage v. Jones, *supra* [livestock feed]; Patapsco Guano Co. v. North Carolina, 171 U.S. 345 [1898; fertilizer]; Plumley v. Massachusetts, 155 U.S. 461 [1894]. In Corn Products Refining Co. v. Eddy, *supra*, at 438, the statute was sustained even as to goods received from another State and sold in the original packages.

[47] No less burdensome regulations of indispensable instrumentalities of commerce have been sustained in many cases — e.g., of grain elevators in Brass v. North Dakota ex rel. Stoeser, *supra*; W. W. Cargill Co. v. Minnesota, *supra*; Merchants Exchange v. Missouri, *supra*.

The public warehouseman's fee could not average more than $33. It may not exceed one dollar for each 1,000 bushels capacity. [Section 8.] The average capacity of North Dakota elevators is about 33,000 bushels. Obviously, this small fee would not deter anyone from engaging in the business of public warehouseman, nor could the resulting *pro rata* charge upon interstate transactions in wheat deter anyone from entering into them. The annual cost to the elevator of the license is one-tenth (1/10) of a cent per bushel of capacity. The average turnover of North Dakota elevators is four. The average cost to them of the license fee per bushel of grain handled would thus not exceed one-fortieth (1/40) of a cent per bushel handled.

Moreover, the statute names only the maximum fee. That imposed may be much less. The amount is limited by the needs of the service. There are about 2,200 public elevators in North Dakota. If necessary, $72,600 could thus be raised from license fees. But the State provided for paying part of the expense out of other revenues, making a direct appropriation for the purpose.

The *pro rata* charge averages even less than one-fortieth (1/40) of a cent per bushel. For a large majority of the North Dakota elevators, about 74 per cent, are engaged also in side-lines. That is, they also transact other businesses than handling grain. The volume of this side-line business should be included in estimating the *pro rata* charge imposed by the license fee. Federal Grain Commission, Report on the Grain Trade, Vol. 1, p. 172. The average percentage of income

158 [1918]. The keeping of appropriate records of business transactions is a common provision in the regulation of quasi-public
businesses. Nor is commerce unduly obstructed by the requirement of a bond where farm products are purchased on credit. Compare *Payne v. Kansas, supra.* Moreover, it does not appear that
plaintiffs will ever have occasion to give such a bond.

The provisions mainly relied upon to establish the proposition
that the requirements of the North Dakota Grain Grading Act
obstruct interstate and foreign commerce are the alleged dockage
and margin clauses, and the alleged requirement that buyers of
wheat be licensed. As shown above, there is in this statute no requirement that buyers be licensed; and the provisions relating to
dockage and to margins do not impose upon plaintiffs any obligation which could conceivably obstruct commerce. In these respects the initiative measure of 1922 differs fundamentally from
the statute passed in 1919, which was held void in the *Lemke* case.
The later statute eliminated all of the features of the earlier which
were there held to be objectionable. Neither the decision nor the
opinion in the *Lemke* case is in any respect inconsistent with the
conclusions here stated.

Brandeis' opinion, or memorandum, as he called it, dated October
1923, was ready for circulation when the Court convened for the new

---

on capital (excluding borrowed money) invested in country elevators in the 14
leading grain-growing States east of the Rocky Mountains was in 1915–16, 20.73
per cent; in 1916–17, it was 32.33 per cent; in 1919–20, it was 25.33 per cent.
The average percentage earned in 1919–20 by the North Dakota non-line elevators
was 31.34 per cent. See Profits of Country and Terminal Grain Elevators, 67th
Cong., 1st Sess., Sen. Doc. No. 40, pp. 8–10. The customary charge in North Dakota for the mere elevation of grain at the country market is two cents. The elevation of grain by country elevators for account of the farmers involves unloading
from the wagon the grain hauled in by the farmer, its weighing, elevation into a
bin, and storage either until all the farmers' grain has been hauled, or the quantity
in the particular bin is sufficient for a carload; and finally loading the grain into
cars for shipment. Federal Trade Commission Report on the Grain Trade, Vol. I,
pp. 62, 120–124, 151, 157.

Section 16. "There is hereby appropriated for the purpose of carrying out the
provisions of this act out of any of the general funds of the State Treasury, the
sum of ten thousand dollars, together with all moneys in the State Treasury known
as the State Grain Grading Fund, and all fees for licenses collected under the provisions of this act shall be turned into the State Treasury and designated as the
North Dakota Grain Grading Fund and when so turned in and designated, it
shall be appropriated and available for the purpose of carrying out all of the provisions of this act."

term beginning that month. We do not know for certain what use Brandeis made of the opinion. But it is relevant in this connection to recall one of the things Brandeis appreciated about Chief Justice Taft. Taft would use his influence to hold up a case till Brandeis had a chance to mount — on paper — one of his weighty efforts at persuasion, and he was then willing to bring the case up for discussion once more. That had happened, at the previous term, with *Southwestern Tel. Co. v. Public Service Commission*,[33] which was argued a few months before *Shafer*. *Southwestern Telephone* was a tremendously complicated utility valuation case. Brandeis referred to it in confidential conversation as illustrating the fact that there was "a better atmosphere for discussion" under Taft than there had been in Chief Justice White's day. He said that he had told the conference, "I'll report on that, if you want me to." Taft had asked that he do so "and I took months to prepare a memo [it was a huge one, with an appendix almost as big as the memo itself], printed it and had it circulated . . . as a basis for discussion." There had been those who were impatient, but through Taft and Van Devanter, "the thing was held up until my report was in. We then had a whole day set aside for discussion. And it was a thorough discussion. Some didn't grasp the facts and hadn't thoroughly mastered the memo, but it was a new method in the consideration of issues."[34] It seems a reasonable surmise that, having spent the summer preparing a similar memorandum in *Shafer*, Brandeis also circulated it, and that discussion also followed.

In the *Southwestern Telephone* case, Brandeis failed to make his views prevail. He published them as a separate opinion, concurring in the result, but dissenting from the Court's reasoning. Brandeis had no greater luck with *Shafer*, though he may have shaken some of the brethren. The case was held through the 1923 term and was reargued at the following term, in March 1925. In May of the same year, it came down with Van Devanter's opinion. By then there had been another change in personnel. Stone had replaced McKenna in time to hear the argument and participate in *Shafer*. But no dissenting opinion by Brandeis was published. It was merely noted that "Mr. Justice Brandeis dissents." (No one else joined him.)

Brandeis may have felt that he had spoken once on the subject in *Lemke*, and that no purpose would be served by doing so again. Holmes often said that he did not like to record dissenting views more than once on any single issue. Or Brandeis may have thought that to dissent at length was to highlight the case unduly, and to make it appear as an extension of the *Lemke* holding, rather than only a routine reapplication of it, which had no additional significance in itself.[35] For these reasons, or perhaps for other or supplementary ones, Brandeis' opinion was withheld.

Beginning in the late thirties, the tide of adjudication turned with respect to measures of social and economic regulation. Laissez faire was read out of the Due Process Clause of the Fourteenth Amendment.[36] And it was read out of the Commerce Clause as well. There came a great closing of gaps and filling of vacuums. Such decisions as those in the child labor case on the one hand, and in the Pennsylvania ticket agent case on the other, were overruled.[37] Other decisions were more quietly swept under the rug. These included *Shafer*, and its predecessor, *Lemke*.[38] In sum, state, and especially federal, power was allowed to range much more freely. But this spring cleaning did not solve all problems; it simply made room for the real, the hard ones.

In his dissent in 1905 in the *Lochner* case, in which he pointed the accusing finger at the chief villain in our story, Herbert Spencer, Holmes said: "I think that the word liberty in the Fourteenth Amendment is perverted when it is held to prevent the natural outcome of a dominant opinion. . . ." But he added immediately: "unless it can be said that a rational and fair man necessarily would admit that the statute proposed would infringe fundamental principles as they have been understood by the traditions of our people and our law." [39] That is a statement which poses as many problems as it solves. Holmes and Brandeis themselves each had occasion to strike down statutes about which, others might say, rational men could fairly differ.[40]

Difficult issues also continued to bedevil the application of the Commerce Clause to state social and economic regulations. Laissez-faire preconceptions (resulting in extreme and rigid lines drawn against state power) to the side, there is room for differences of opinion about how much overlapping of functions can be permitted, and about the point at which the free play of particular state interests begins to tend dangerously toward Balkanization of the economy. Judgments are hard, being based largely on prophecy. As recently as 1949, the Court struck down a New York regulation of milk processing, against the well-taken protest of Mr. Justice Black that a gap was being created, since "it is inconceivable that Congress could pass uniform national legislation capable of adjustment and application to all the local phases of interstate activities that take place in the 48 states." [41] Added to this protest were the very substantial doubts of Mr. Justice Frankfurter.[42]

Since the body of federal legislation is now many times what is was in the twenties and early thirties, much of the controversy today rages over whether state statutes conflict with Congressional legislation, and whether the latter was intended to "occupy the field." [43] These — as

Brandeis' *Shafer* opinion suggests — are properly issues of fact; and if men were clairvoyant angels (and no laws were needed), there would presumably be such a thing as a pure and simple issue of fact. As it is, judgments are often close, and they often depend on whether a Justice's national outlook or his sympathetic understanding of local problems prevails in a given case.[44] Again, the sweeping away of the debris of laissez faire has cleared the decks for the real difficulties. Holmes and Brandeis were also known to hold, sometimes in debatable cases, that Congressional action had foreclosed state legislation.[45] It was Holmes who once had occasion to write: "When Congress has taken the particular subject-matter in hand coincidence is as ineffective as opposition. . . ."[46]

The doctrine of Congressional "occupation of the field" is currently in the public eye as it relates to internal security legislation. In the spring of 1956, in *Pennsylvania v. Nelson*,[47] a divided Court struck down state legislation parallel to the federal Smith Act. It should be noted that this case and a similar one, which on the same ground invalidated the same state's alien registration act in 1941,[48] are not of a kind with those discussed so far. The common security, national defense, foreign affairs, control of aliens — these are the primary provinces of the general government; these matters before all others it was created to deal with, and on them the states retain, if at all, only the most tenuous of holds. Here there are no local interests of any respectable weight as against the preponderant federal concern. The problems are, to all intents and purposes, indivisible, and the hard issues that are present in Commerce Clause cases are, therefore, scarcely reached.

The Court's attitude, as exemplified by the *Nelson* case, is foreshadowed by Brandeis' dissent in *Gilbert v. Minnesota*,[49] written in 1920, in the aftermath of the First World War. In a closely similar context, Brandeis said: "The responsibility for the maintenance of the Army and Navy, for the conduct of war and for the preservation of government, both state and federal, from 'malice domestic and foreign levy' rests upon Congress. It is true that the States have the power of self-preservation inherent in any government to suppress insurrection and repel invasion; and to that end they may maintain such force of militia as Congress may prescribe and arm. But the duty of preserving the state government falls ultimately upon the Federal Government. And the superior responsibility carries with it the superior right. The States act only under the express direction of Congress."[50]

IX

"Things Go Happily with Taft"

In at least two cases discussed in earlier chapters — both of considerable importance in their time and for many years following — it is as certain as such things can be (in a third it is quite likely and in a fourth possible) that, but for Brandeis and his persuasive unpublished opinions, the results would have been the opposite of those ultimately announced. In *United Mine Workers v. Coronado Co.* the Sherman Act would have been applied on the record as it then stood, and in *Sonneborn Bros. v. Cureton* the original-package doctrine would have been reëstablished as a much-strengthened barrier against state taxation. In each of these cases, it is plain that the unanimous acceptance of Brandeis' result (not the ideal result necessarily, but one that offered a chance of success), and indeed, its acceptance at all, was possible only because Chief Justice Taft was persuaded, and because he was able to prevail on other brethren to permit themselves also to be persuaded. Thus it is evident that, unlikely as it might have seemed, there developed, soon after Taft's accession, a useful working relationship between him and Brandeis. It would be wrong to assume that Taft and Brandeis could be united any more closely than by a drawbridge over a wide gulf. But it is undeniable nevertheless that from their relationship there emanated at times a potent influence for reason, consistency, and restraint.

Taft's initial attitude toward Brandeis was, of course, one of deep distrust. In 1910 Brandeis had been the aggressive counsel for Louis R. Glavis in the so-called Ballinger-Pinchot conservation controversy, provoked by Glavis' charges of misconduct in the Department of the Interior. This had been a first-class row in the Taft administration, and Brandeis had directly involved the President himself. Taft considered Brandeis' actions unfair if not unethical. In 1916 Taft opposed Brandeis' confirmation. He signed the petition of protest of the past presidents of the American Bar Association. Privately he wrote that Brandeis was "a muckraker, an emotionalist for his own purposes, a Socialist . . . a man . . . of much power for evil. . . ." And falling, oddly enough, into a habit Brandeis himself indulged in correspondence, that of using German phrases: "When you consider Brandeis' appointment, and think

that men were pressing me for the place, *es ist zum lachen. . . .*" But —
and this tells much of how service on the Court brings most men out
of themselves — it was not long after he reached the place to which
he had always aspired that Taft was able to write: "I have come to
like Brandeis very much indeed."

The common ground on which the two met was that of complete
and high-minded devotion to the Court and its work. This is not to
say that they conceived of the Court's function in identical terms. But
each in his way cared selflessly for its past and for its future. Their first
contact after Taft's appointment concerned their joint interest in ex-
pediting the flow of business in the federal court system. When he
wrote that he had come to like Brandeis, Taft added this reason: "He
thinks much of the court and is anxious to have it consistent and strong,
and he pulls his weight in the boat." This was the essential thing, up-
permost in Taft's mind. In the letter the brethren sent to Day on his
retirement, which Taft drafted, there is praise for Day's "loyalty to the
Court and its traditions." [1] Taft — though he may have expected otherwise — did not find Brandeis lacking in this respect. One anxiety of
Taft's in the Court's behalf, amounting at times almost to an obsession
and not shared by Brandeis to any such degree, centered on the avoidance of dissents and particularly of close divisions. In this connection,
Taft was surely impressed by Brandeis' forbearance in the *Child Labor
Tax Case* and his moderation in *United Mine Workers v. Coronado Co.*
And in *Sonneborn Bros. v. Cureton*, he doubtless saw Brandeis on the
side of having the Court appear "consistent and strong."

Brandeis for his part — after the experience of Chief Justice White's
declining years — appreciated Taft's efforts to speed up disposition of
cases, and his concern for the quality of the Court's work. He referred
to Taft's "open mind," at least in some matters; to his willingness to
listen to reason; and to the good effect this had on the others. He considered him a "cultivated man" and enjoyed talking to him. "Things
go happily in the conference room with Taft," he said. "The judges go
home less tired emotionally and less weary physically than in White's
day." And: "When we differ we agree to differ, without any ill feeling.
It's all very friendly."

Of course, Brandeis retained his reservations, and according to his
lights, so did Taft. "He is a first rate second rate mind," Brandeis once
said. And at another time: "He is the Taft we thought he was." Taft
continued to look askance at Brandeis' "social economics," and in 1926,
when faced with an elaborate dissent by Brandeis (and another by
Holmes and another by McReynolds) in a case that had aroused strong
feelings in him, he could still explode privately that "McReynolds and

Brandeis . . . have no loyalty to the court . . . and wish to stir up dissatisfaction . . . ." But, his biographer says, "Taft must have regretted [these words] if he ever glanced back through the copies of his letters." [2]

A letter from Taft to Brandeis, dated December 23, 1922 (*Sonneborn Bros. v. Cureton* was then under advisement), is characteristic, both in tone and content, of the dealings between the two men. It is confirmed by numerous shorter returns scratched on the backs of circulated opinions. "Dear Justice Brandeis," Taft wrote, "I congratulate you on your opinion in the North Carolina R.R. Tax cases. It is admirable, compact, forcible and clear. It relieves me greatly to get rid of such a case so satisfactorily. I thank you for your promptness." [3] There followed a couple of agreeable suggestions for changes in the opinion, which Brandeis accepted. Then: "In the Day letter [from the Court to Day on the occasion of his retirement] I have adopted your suggestions and under the influence of Brothers Holmes and McKenna, I have moderated some of the superlatives and come nearer the truth as you will see when I send it to you for your signature." Finally, after a Christmas pleasantry, there was a postscript: "By the way, I am disturbed by McReynolds' opinion in the Curtis Publishing Co.'s case. As he has put it, it seems to me that he is weighing evidence in making his conclusions as if we were a jury or a chancellor. What do you think of it?" [4] This case involved review of findings of fact by the Federal Trade Commission, one of McReynolds' pet peeves.[5] The Court's function normally would have been to do no more than pass on the sufficiency of the evidence supporting the administrative findings. McReynolds seemed to be doing more, and Brandeis joined Taft in a short opinion expressing the doubt suggested in the letter.[6]

The postscript just quoted alludes to a problem — McReynolds — that Brandeis and Taft together were able to deal with successfully from time to time. McReynolds, as Brandeis once remarked, had a lawyerlike understanding of jurisdictional issues. For the rest, his opinions were either brutally slashing, or more frequently, offhand, as when he wrote for the first majority in *Sonneborn Bros. v. Cureton*, and nearly always arbitrary and undiscriminating. McReynolds was not one to be reasoned with, and he would listen least of all to anything coming from Brandeis. He was given, as Brandeis wrote in dissent from one of his worst excesses, to reaching conclusions by "unfounded assumption which crumbles at the touch of reason." [7] Taft thought him selfish, prejudiced, and possessed of "a continual grouch." [8] A *Naturmensch*, Brandeis explained, paraphrasing Holmes, who had called him "a savage, with all the irrational impulses of a savage"; a man of

tender affections and correspondingly strong hates. Brandeis was one
of his hates. Pitney had evidently been one also. McReynolds "used to
say the cruellest things" to Pitney, Brandeis commented.[9] Clarke had
been another. McReynolds even went to the length of not signing
the customary letters from the Court to Clarke on his resignation and
to Brandeis on his retirement.[10] Taft, abetted by Van Devanter, his
close friend and "mainstay," [11] was able somehow to cope with Mc-
Reynolds, to take him in hand, in Brandeis' phrase. And it was through
Taft that the influence of Brandeis' knowledge and views, which the
other brethren, with whom Brandeis was on perfectly cordial terms,
felt directly at one time or another, could be brought to bear on Mc-
Reynolds. It happened in *Sonneborn Bros. v. Cureton*. And it happened less than a year later in *Railroad Commission v. Southern Pacific Ry.*,[12] decided in the spring of 1924. Later still, under different
circumstances, something similar occurred in *American Railway Express Co. v. Kentucky*.[13]

The *Southern Pacific* case concerned the Transportation Act of 1920.
Congress had long since lodged comprehensive federal regulatory power over the nation's railroads in the Interstate Commerce Commission.
By the 1920 Act, it had broadened that power still further.[14] There
was admittedly little room left for the states to make regulations of
their own affecting interstate railroads. But, again admittedly and by
specific proviso,[15] there was some room left, so long as the I.C.C. did
not assert its own jurisdiction. The issue in *Railroad Commission v.
Southern Pacific Ry.* was how much is a little; a question of delicate
judgment particularly unsuited to McReynolds' talents.

California had ordered three interstate railroads coming into Los
Angeles and maintaining separate terminals to build and use a single
union station at a certain location, and while they were about it, to
eliminate dangerous grade crossings within the city limits. The local
interests that the order was aimed to promote are plain. The railroads
maintained that they were being put to an expense of upwards of $25
million, and that only the I.C.C., one of whose functions it was to try
to keep the railroads solvent by controlling both their income and
their outgo, had jurisdiction to make such an order. An opinion by Mc-
Reynolds so held, and annulled the California order. The opinion con-
sisted of a statement of facts, followed by four-and-a-half pages of
straight quotation from the federal statute, followed by three paragraphs in which union terminals were characterized as "not a mere
local facility," the breadth of the authority vested in the I.C.C. was
emphasized, and the surmise was ventured that the I.C.C. could not
perform its task "if the State Commissions may issue orders like the

one here under consideration, where the subject matter is of general importance." There was a proviso in the federal statute saving some power to the states, to be sure, but it was "subordinate to the fundamental purposes of the Act and must be so construed."

McReynolds had dealt with the issue by blotting it out. He had said — if he had said anything at all, and of course, the Bar and the federal and state authorities concerned could not be expected to assume that he had said nothing — that there was no regulatory function whatever preserved to the states. For it was the basic premise of the federal statute that interstate railroads and everything affecting them were "of general importance." The question was whether some matters, and which ones, also touched local interests so seriously that state regulation would, in the absence of supervening action by the I.C.C., be tolerable. Brandeis wrote the dissent printed below. It recited in detail the powers formerly exercised by the states, which the 1920 Act had now, by express provision, lodged exclusively in the federal Commission. The power to order the elimination of grade-crossings and the erection of terminals, previously conceded to the states, was not one of these. A specific statement by the chairman of the House Committee on Interstate and Foreign Commerce, who managed the bill, indicated that the omission was intentional. Of course, if the national interest was adversely affected, the I.C.C. could intervene, and its authority would then be paramount. But there had been no such intervention here.

SUPREME COURT OF THE UNITED STATES

Nos. 283, 284, 285. — October Term, 1923.

Railroad Commission of the State of California, Petitioner,	
283 vs.	
Southern Pacific Company and Southern Pacific Railroad Company.	
Railroad Commission of the State of California, Petitioner,	On Writs of Certiorari to
284 vs.	the Supreme Court of the
The Atchison, Topeka & Santa Fe Railway Company.	State of California.
Railroad Commission of the State of California, Petitioner,	
285 vs.	
Los Angeles & Salt Lake Railroad Company.	

[January 7, 1924]

Mr. Justice BRANDEIS, dissenting.

Prior to Transportation Act 1920, the States could, in the exercise of the police power, require interstate railroads to eliminate dangerous grade crossings either by relocation of tracks or otherwise,[1] *Erie Railroad Co. v. Public Utility Commissioners*, 254 U.S. 394 [1921]; and could, likewise, require them to provide adequate passenger stations. *Minneapolis & St. Louis R.R. Co. v. Minnesota*, 193 U.S. 53 [1904]. See *Wisconsin, Minnesota & Pacific R.R. Co. v. Jacobson*, 179 U.S. 287 [1900]; *Chicago & Northwestern Ry. Co. v. Ochs*, 249 U.S. 416 [1919]. That Act introduced limitations upon the States' police power. It set a limit upon requiring interstate railroads to make expenditures, by regulating the issue of securities. Section 20a. It set a limit upon requiring them to make low rates, by prohibiting any which would unduly

---

[1] The order here in question provided for the elimination of 23 grade crossings. The Railroad Commission found that they were dangerous and that the establishment of the union station was essential to their elimination. [Petition for Writ of Certiorari, pp. 102–04, Railroad Commission v. Southern Pacific Ry., 264 U.S. 331 (1924).]

discriminate against or burden interstate commerce. Section 15a. It prevents extensions or abandonment of lines by interstate carriers without first obtaining a certificate of convenience and necessity from the Interstate Commerce Commission. Paragraph 18 of Section 1. It conferred emergency powers over railroad property and routing. Paragraphs 15 and 16 of Section 1. But except for the control so provided, and the limitations resulting therefrom, the Act does not, in my opinion, affect the States' police power as applied either to grade crossings or to the furnishing of adequate terminals.

The Act contains no provision which deals specifically either with the elmination of grade crossings or with the establishment of terminals. Nor do I find a grant to the Interstate Commerce Commission of any power, general or special, which precludes the continued exercise of the States' police power over grade crossings and terminal facilities of interstate carriers, subject to the control above referred to. The relocation of tracks involved is obviously not an extension or abandonment of line within the meaning of Paragraph 18 of Section 1. See *Texas v. Eastern Texas R.R. Co.*, 258 U.S. 204 [1922]. The erection of the union station is not a joint use of terminals and tracks within the meaning of Paragraph 15 of Section 1. The great detail with which Transportation Act 1920 enumerates and describes every new or enlarged power conferred upon the Commission, prohibits our extending, by implication, its functions to other subjects. See *Peoria & Pekin Union Ry. Co. v. United States*, decided this day [263 U.S. 528 (1924)]. That Congress did not intend to take away the power of the States over depots was definitely stated by the Chairman of the Comittee on Interstate and Foreign Commerce when explaining the bill to the House of Representatives. In so doing, he gave persuasive reasons for the committee's recommendation.[2]

---

[2] Mr. Esch: "The committee in framing the bill has sought not to encroach upon such [the police] powers. The matter of depots and joint use of depots is practically in the jurisdiction of the State commissions, and all but one of the States have such commissions. In such small matters the detail should be left within the jurisdiction of the State authorities, who know the situation, know the conditions, and know how best to meet the needs. There is, however, a provision in this bill providing for the joint use of terminals." Cong. Rec., Vol. 58, Part 9, p. 8579 (November 15, 1919). See also Vol. 58, Part 8, p. 8310 [November 11, 1919]; and statement of Senator Cummins, Chairman of the Senate Committee, Cong. Rec., Vol. 59, Part 1, p. 143 (December 4, 1919).

The new departure in policy inaugurated by Transportation Act 1920, *Railroad Commission of Wisconsin v. Chicago, Burlington & Quincy R.R. Co.*, 257 U.S. 563, 585 [1922]; *The New England Divisions Case*, 261 U.S. 184, 189 [1923]; *Dayton–Goose Creek Ry. Co. v. United States*, decided January 7, 1924 [263 U.S. 456, 477–78], is the policy of ensuring adequacy in transportation service. It is not the policy of taking away the States' police power. That power was to be preserved unabridged in scope; but it was made subject to such control, by order of the Interstate Commerce Commission, as may be necessary to ensure adequate transportation service and otherwise to protect interstate commerce. This is shown, among other things, by the proviso therein contained at the end of Paragraph 17 of Section 1.[3]

In my opinion, Transportation Act 1920 affords no justification for judicial interference with the action of the state commission. The federal commission has made no order which can conceivably affect the matter here involved.

Nor does any fact appear, either by a finding of the lower court or otherwise, which would require the Interstate Commerce Commission to make any order, unless some carrier should seek to issue securities. It cannot be said, as a matter of law, that the erection of a union station at the cost of thirty million dollars will necessarily discriminate against or burden interstate commerce. For aught that appears, the carriers affected are prosperous, and the improvement directed by the state commission may afford the least expensive (if not the only appropriate) means of eliminating the dangerous grade crossings and of providing adequate terminals.

Speaking of the case later, Brandeis said that he had told Taft that he "couldn't stand for" McReynolds' opinion. There was too much in it that would "bother us in the future." Van Devanter, Brandeis went on to say, "worked with McReynolds and made changes, and the Chief asked me whether that will remove my sting. The corrections weren't adequate, and finally the Chief took over the opinion and put out what

[3] Act of February 28, 1920, c. 91, sec. 402, 41 Stat. 456, 477: *"Provided, however,* That nothing in this Act shall impair or affect the right of a State, in the exercise of its police power, to require just and reasonable freight and passenger service for intrastate business, except in so far as such requirement is inconsistent with any lawful order of the Commission made under the provisions of this Act."

is now the Court's opinion and I suppressed my dissent, because, after all, it's merely a question of statutory construction and the worst things were removed by the Chief." [16] (Even before Taft took over, Holmes had been uncertain whether it was worth dissenting in the case. He had returned to Brandeis' opinion: "I agree with this and only am not quite sure whether it is best to dissent." Holmes may have felt that dissent might unduly emphasize the case.)

Having, like *Sonneborn Bros. v. Cureton*, been delivered from rather than by McReynolds, the decision in *Southern Pacific* became a different matter. Taft's opinion trod carefully. Taft emphasized the expense involved, and the fact that relocation of main tracks and changes in the handling of interstate traffic would be necessary. He pointed out that building the new terminal was not necessarily tied in with elimination of the dangerous grade-crossings; a state order directed mainly at the grade-crossing problem might well be held valid. No doubt other functions were also saved to the states by the 1920 Act. [17] In any event, the city of Los Angeles had in the meantime itself brought the dispute before the I.C.C. It would be best to let it run its course there. On these qualified grounds, Taft upset the California order.

Nevertheless, this was not one of Taft's most felicitous opinions, and events proved how much wiser it would have been to have accepted Brandeis' result and let the state order stand. As it was, it took a good many more years to straighten out the matter of the Los Angeles union terminal. In 1929, after proceedings before the I.C.C., Taft, again writing for a unanimous Court, held that the I.C.C. had no authority to compel erection of a union terminal. That had been the conclusion of the I.C.C. itself. It could only approve or disapprove such a project, the Commission had held, if the railroads themselves proposed it or the state ordered it. [18] The state then made another order, which had I.C.C. approval, and Hughes in 1931 (McReynolds dissenting) held that the new state order as approved was unobjectionable. [19] Thus, in 1931, an effort to obtain a union terminal which had been initiated in 1916 finally came to fruition. Brandeis' disposition in 1924 would have ensured the same outcome while avoiding several years' delay; although, to be sure, Taft's opinion made eventual erection of the union terminal possible at all without a new Act of Congress, which would have been necessary if McReynolds' opinion had prevailed in 1924.

American Railway Express Co. v. Kentucky [20] was another occasion when McReynolds felt the touch of Brandeis' reason. This time McReynolds responded to treatment, and it was he who handed down the opinion of the Court.

The case was an outgrowth of the consolidation, at the time of the

First World War, of the railway express business. The American Railway Express Company — formed for this purpose — acquired the Kentucky business of the Adams Express Company, and all of that company's property in Kentucky. American paid by issuing part of its own capital stock to Adams. Nothing was said in the transfer agreement about American's assuming obligations and liabilities which Adams had outstanding in Kentucky. Adams had all along been a New York corporation, and it remained in existence as such. It owned, of course, the stock given it by American, and it had other assets, all in New York. But in Kentucky it disappeared, and a judgment rendered against it could not be executed there. Its creditor — the state itself, as it happened — thereupon sued American, which had taken over the business and property in the manner described and was engaged in operations in Kentucky. A lower Kentucky state court gave judgment against American, and the Kentucky Court of Appeals affirmed. American claimed that to render this judgment against it on a debt it had not assumed was to deprive it of property without due process of law, contrary to the Fourteenth Amendment.

The case was decided in the Supreme Court in February 1927, together with a companion case, in which the same issue had arisen in Virginia, owing to another of American's acquisitions, and in which that state had reached the same result.[21] McReynolds' opinion ran to five pages. The requirements of procedural due process, he said — a fair hearing — had been satisfied. The Kentucky court had applied its unwritten common law. The application might be debatable or even erroneous; but even if it were, it would not for that reason violate the Due Process Clause, else every question of state law would raise a federal constitutional issue. A due process question would be present only if the state court's decision could be said to be arbitrary and capricious, "or obviously contrary to the fundamental principles of justice." [22] That was not the case here. When the Adams company removed itself from Kentucky, it created a serious difficulty for creditors trying to collect their prior existing debts. In these circumstances, there was no unfairness in holding American liable.

It is most improbable today that the Court, exercising its discretionary power to choose the cases it will hear, would take jurisdiction in such a case as *American Railway Express*; it is even less likely that if the case somehow reached the Court, there would be any difficulty in disposing of it by affirming the Kentucky judgment. But this was 1927. Sutherland and Butler, without writing, noted dissent from Mc-Reynolds' opinion. It took two full years to dispose of the case. And the Court at one point concluded that the Kentucky judgment had indeed deprived the American company of property without due process of law.

The case was heard for the first time on January 29, 1925, and it was discussed at the conference on February 23. Brandeis carried into this conference a page of notes, preserved in his file, citing authorities in support of the Kentucky judgment. We do not know what happened at this juncture, but research in preparation for the writing of an opinion was in progress in the Brandeis office. This would suggest that the consensus at conference had been that the Kentucky judgment violated the Due Process Clause. In any event, a reargument was ordered for the following term. It took place in November 1925, when the companion case, eventually decided together with *American Railway Express*, was also heard. Before the reargument, Brandeis had reached the writing stage in the preparation of the opinion printed below. At this time, he called it a memorandum. Nothing appears to have happened for the rest of the term, though no doubt the case was discussed again. Early in the October term 1926 Brandeis made some revisions in his opinion. He now labeled it a dissent. Thus we know that the Court had decided against Kentucky. But by February 1927, only a few months later, Brandeis' view had prevailed and McReynolds' opinion for the Court came down.

What McReynolds' position had been earlier we do not know. However, considering that Holmes and Stone very probably sided with Brandeis all along, and that Taft or Sanford or even Van Devanter may have wavered, it is not likely that a majority for the other result could have been formed without McReynolds. It is more probable that the opinion going against the Kentucky judgment should have been assigned to McReynolds and that he should have changed his mind, than that it should have gone first to Sutherland or Butler, for example, and then been taken away and given to McReynolds. Had either Sutherland or Butler prepared an opinion of the Court, he would surely have been tempted to publish it as a dissent.

In any event, McReynolds wrote with knowledge of Brandeis' views; for, in his summary fashion, he adopted the reasoning of Brandeis' opinion. On the basis of what we know of the relationships between Brandeis and McReynolds and between Taft and Brandeis, it seems fair to surmise that Taft was the agent through whom Brandeis' reasoning was rendered palatable to McReynolds. Be that as it may, *American Railway Express* is another case in which Brandeis' earnest and documented argumentation changed the result to which the predilections of a majority of the brethren would otherwise have led.

With ample citation of cases, Brandeis' opinion assimilated the common law rule adopted by the Kentucky court to decisions by other common law courts in cognate situations. The problem — it came up not infrequently and in several contexts — was to achieve a fair adjustment between the rights of the purchaser of an existing business and those of the seller's prior creditors. The good faith expectations of the purchaser had to be taken into account, but in this case it could hardly be assumed that American did not foresee that the going concern it was acquiring might have creditors. Placed in its setting, that is, in the framework of the law generally applicable to similar situations, the Kentucky judgment appeared as anything but unreasonable. Indeed, other state courts, faced with the very same issue as a result of other acquisitions by the American company, had come to the same conclusion as the Kentucky court. All this is in essence very much what McReynolds wrote. It differs in that it is set out more explicitly, and above all, in that it is documented. As, in other cases, he demonstrated the reasonableness of state action by explaining it in terms of economic or social conditions — the legislative facts — so Brandeis here sustained Kentucky's decision by founding it in the mold of the common law.

SUPREME COURT OF THE UNITED STATES

No. 5. — October Term, 1926.

| American Railway Express Company, Petitioner, vs. Commonwealth of Kentucky. | On Certiorari to the Court of Appeals of Kentucky. |

[   ]

Mr. Justice BRANDEIS, dissenting.

The Adams Express Company is a joint-stock association organized under the laws of New York. For many years it carried on the express business in Kentucky, with the consent of that State; had property there used for the purpose; and incurred obligations there in the course of that business. On June 30, 1918, it transferred its Kentucky business and all its property within that State to the American Railway Express Company, taking in exchange a part of the latter's capital stock. The Adams had then outstanding obligations and liabilities incurred in Kentucky and to be satisfied there, including one to the Commonwealth. The contract of sale to the American made no provision for discharging these liabilities. Because of this transfer of assets, an execution which issued on the judgment recovered against the Adams in a Kentucky court was returned *nulla bona*. The judgment remaining unsatisfied, this suit for the amount was brought in a Kentucky court against the American, and a judgment entered against it in the trial court was affirmed by the highest court of the State, 190 Ky. 636 [1920].

That court based the liability of the American upon the ground that, as a matter of substantive unwritten law, the trust fund doctrine applies to a case where the purchaser takes over all the business and assets of a company within a State and gives as sole consideration a part of its capital stock, which is held outside the State. It holds immaterial the fact that the seller retains other assets subject to execution in some other State which are ample to pay all its debts. It is urged by the American Company that this decision deprives it of property without due process of law. We may not consider whether the rule of substantive law declared is good. *Arrowsmith v. Harmoning*, 118 U.S. 194, 196 [1886]; *Patterson v. Colorado*, 205 U.S. 454, 460, 461 [1907]. Our sole function is to determine whether the rule applied is so clearly unreasonable, unjust or arbitrary as to contravene the Fourteenth Amendment.

Under the trust fund doctrine, it had long been widely held that where one corporation buys all the property of another and makes payment therefor by giving in exchange only its capital stock, the buyer is liable for the debts of the seller to the extent of the assets acquired.[1] The additional step taken by the Kentucky

[1] The rule is generally stated as given above. In many of the cases involving its application, however, it has been in evidence that the stock consideration was distributed by the buying corporation directly to the stockholders of the selling corporation. Tompkins v. Augusta Southern R.R., 102 Ga. 436 [1897]; Chicago, S.F. & C. Ry. v. Ashling, 160 Ill. 373 [1895]; Shadford v. Detroit, etc. Ry., 130 Mich. 300 [1902]; Vicksburg and Yazoo City Telephone Co. v. Citizens' Telephone Co., 79 Miss. 341 [1901]; Hurd v. New York & C. Steam Laundry Co., 167 N.Y. 89 [1901]; McIver v. Young Hardware Co., 144 N.C. 478 [1907]. Compare Chase v. Michigan Telephone Co., 121 Mich. 631 [1899]; Kentucky Distilleries, etc. Co. v. Webb's Ex'c'r, 181 Ky. 90 [1918]; Okmulgee Window Glass Co. v. Frink, 260 Fed. 159 [1919]. In such cases the purchasing corporation takes the assets of the

court was to apply this general rule to a case where the property transferred constituted, not all the seller's property, but all within the State, and where the stock received in payment was held outside the State. It recognizes that to deny to the domestic creditor the only redress possible within the State would, where the claim is small, be tantamount to a denial of all redress. See *Barrow Steamship Co. v. Kane*, 170 U.S. 100, 109 [1898], quoting from *Railroad Co. v. Harris*, 12 Wall. 65, 83–84 [1871]. The difficulty of pursuing the remedy in a foreign State is made the basis of the liability of the buying corporation, just as the difficulty of levying on stock makes the buying corporation liable when all the assets of the selling corporation are transferred.

The trust fund doctrine, like the law of fraudulent conveyance, is a manifestation of the fundamental principle that the owner's right to dispose of property is limited by his duty to devote it, so far as necessary, to the payment of his existing unsecured creditors. The essence of the limitation is that the right of disposition may not be so exercised as unduly to hinder or delay creditors of the owner. Under the law of fraudulent conveyance, invalidity of the transfer is often established without showing fraud in fact. In many situations it is sufficient to show that creditors were un-

---

selling corporation with knowledge that they are being diverted and on well-established trust principles ought to be held. In other cases the courts, holding the buyer, have emphasized the "substantial identity" of the two corporations. Hibernia Insurance Co. v. St. Louis & N.O. Transportation Co., 13 Fed. 516 [1882]; Brum v. Merchants Mutual Ins. Co., 16 Fed. 140 [1883]; Collinsville Nat. Bank v. Esau, 74 Okla. 45 [1918]. But in many cases neither of these features has been present, and the decision must rest upon the fact that the stock paid, even though held by the debtor corporation, is not a satisfactory subject of execution by the creditors. United States Capsule Co. v. Isaacs, 23 Ind. App. 533 [1899]; Altoona v. Richardson Gas & Oil Co., 81 Kan. 717 [1910]; Jennings, Neff & Co. v. Crystal Ice Co., 128 Tenn. 231 [1913]. Compare Chicago, I. & S.R.R. v. Taylor, 183 Ind. 240 [1915]; Louisville, N. A. & C. v. Boney, 117 Ind. 501 [1888]; Berry v. Kansas City, F. S. & M. R. Co., 52 Kan. 759, 774 [1894]. For the case of the transfer of assets by a partnership to a corporation, see Du Vivier & Co. v. Gallice, 149 Fed. 118 [1906]. See, in general, 3 Cook, Corporations (8th ed. 1923) §§ 672, 673; 7 Fletcher, Cyclopedia Corporations §§ 4756–4758 (1919).

The form of the transaction does not affect the right of the creditor to obtain relief by some method of procedure through some channel against the buyer-transferee. The transaction may be in the form of a consolidation, a merger, a reorganization, or a reincorporation. It may not fall technically within any one of those categories. Whether a creditor may proceed directly at law against the second corporation, whether he may bring a direct action in equity to reach the transferred assets, whether he must first reduce his claim against the selling corporation to judgment and bring action upon that — these questions of method may depend upon the form of the transaction.

duly hindered.[2] Whether a hindrance is undue depends upon the circumstances. The question is ordinarily determined by weighing its effect upon the conflicting social and economic desirables — on the one hand, freedom in the disposition and acquisition of property; on the other, faithful performance of obligations incurred and preservation of the means of enforcing them.

The fact that a transfer attacked involved removal from the State of all the property of the debtor which could be reached there in satisfaction of the claim of a domestic creditor, has often been deemed a controlling factor in determining that the transfer should be set aside as an undue hindrance to creditors. In all these cases, the greater difficulty and expense of conducting litigation in a State other than that of the creditor, was clearly the reason why this factor was deemed controlling, but the courts have assigned various grounds for giving that factor effect. Some have said that the transfer may have been intended to hinder and delay creditors, and may have had that effect, regardless of the existence of property in another State.[3] Some that, in deciding whether the creditor's legal remedy has been exhausted, the existence of property of the debtor subject to execution in another State, or the liability of a co-obligor enforceable in another State, is immaterial.[4]

The obvious difficulties and expense incident to the collection of claims by legal process in a foreign State have, in other connections, given rise to exceptional rights in domestic creditors. The contemplated removal of the defendant's property from the jurisdiction is a common ground for the issuance of an attachment.[5] The

---

[2] McVicker v. American Opera Co., 40 Fed. 861 [1889]; Thomson v. Crane, 73 Fed. 327 [1896]; Sims v. Gaines, 64 Ala. 392, 396–397 [1879]; Burnwell Coal Co. v. Setzer, 203 Ala. 395, 396 [1919]; Barber v. Wilds, 33 App. D.C. 150, 155 [1909]; Kelley Co. v. Pollock & Bernheimer, 57 Fla. 459, 464 [1909]; Marmon v. Harwood, 124 Ill. 104, 110 [1888]; Salzenstein v. Hettrick, 105 Ill. App. 99, 102 [1902]; Rolfe v. Clarke, 224 Mass. 407 [1916]; Wood v. Eldredge, 147 Mich. 554, 564 [1907]; Marks, Rothenberg & Co. v. Bradley, 69 Miss. 1, 11 [1891]; Cook v. Johnson, 12 N. J. Eq. 51 [1858].

[3] Baker v. Lyman, 53 Ga. 339 [1874]; Harding v. Elliot, 91 Hun (N.Y.) 502 [1895]; First State Bank, etc. Co. v. Walker, 187 S.W. (Tex. Civ. App.) 724, 726 [1916].

[4] Alford v. Baker, 53 Ind. 279 [1876]; O'Brien v. Stambach, 101 Ia. 40 [1897]; Rohrer v. Snyder, 29 Wash. 199 [1902].

[5] Mack & Co. v. McDaniel, 4 Fed. 294 [1880]; Walker v. Welch, 13 Ill. 674 [1852]; Mingus v. McLeod, 25 Ia. 452 [1868]; Montgomery v. Tilley, 1 B. Mon. (Ky.) 155 [1840]; Bates Machine Co. v. Norton Iron Works, 113 Ky. 372, 377–

fact that the respondent is removing his property from the jurisdiction may be the controlling factor in determining whether a writ of *ne exeat* shall issue.[6] In the ancillary administration of decedents' estates, and in ancillary receiverships, removal of the assets from the jurisdiction is commonly denied until provision is made for the payment, in full or *pro rata*, of the claims of domestic creditors.[7] This consideration is frequently controlling in administering the assets of foreign corporations.[8] And the same consideration has led to the suggestion that the repeal of a State statute providing for suits against foreign corporations would be an impairment of the obligation of contracts made with such corporations during the existence of the statute.[9]

Regardless of the locality of the debtor's property, transfers have been held to be fraudulent conveyances, although made for value, where the consideration received in exchange was of such a nature as to constitute an impediment to its application by compulsory process toward the satisfaction of creditors' claims.[10] This

---

378 [1902]; Grigsby Construction Co. v. Colly, 124 La. 1071 [1909]; Stock v. Reynolds, 121 Mich. 356 [1899]; Philadelphia Investment Co. v. Bowling, 72 Miss. 565 [1895]; Lyons v. Mason, 4 Coldw. (Tenn.) 525 [1867]; Dillingham v. Traders' Insurance Co., 120 Tenn. 302 [1907].

In Kentucky the statute contains the further ground for an attachment:

"In an action for the recovery of money due upon a contract, judgment, or award, if the defendant have no property in this State subject to execution, or not enough thereof to satisfy the plaintiff's demand, and the collection of the demand will be endangered by delay in obtaining judgment or a return of no property found." Ky. Civ. Code. §194. See Burdett v. Phillips & Bro., 78 Ky. 246 [1880]; Downs v. Ringgold, 101 Ky. 392 [1897]; Goepper & Co. v. Phoenix Brewing Co., 115 Ky. 708 [1903].

[6] Dean V. Smith, 23 Wis. 483, 487 [1868].

[7] Ancillary administration of estates: Mitchell v. Cox, 28 Ga. 32 [1859]; Coombs v. Carne, 236 Ill. 333 [1908]; Newell v. Peaslee, 151 Mass. 601 [1890]; Middleby's Estate, 249 Pa. 203 [1915].

It has been held that statutory provisions regulating the administration of insolvent estates are applicable when the estate of a non-resident is insolvent within the non-domiciliary State, although it may be amply solvent elsewhere. Gilchrist v. Cannon, 1 Coldw. (Tenn.) 581, 586 [1860]; Laws of Tennessee, 1838, c. 111 [Tenn. Acts 1837–38, p. 171].

[8] Ancillary receiverships: Frowert v. Blank, 205 Pa. 299 [1903]; Smith v. St. Louis Mutual Life Ins. Co., 6 Lea (Tenn.) 564 [1880]. In applying this principle in insolvency proceedings against a foreign corporation, the same court has said: "It is sufficient to say that it is not the duty of the court to inquire into this matter [assets in another State]. We must deal with the foreign corporation as we find it here." Voightman & Co. v. Southern Ry. Co., 123 Tenn. 452, 459 [1910].

[9] D'Arcy v. Mutual Life Ins. Co., 108 Tenn. 567, 571–575 [1902].

[10] Mallow v. Walker, 115 Ia. 238, 246 [1901]; Ludlow Savings Bank & Trust Co. v. Knight, 92 Vt. 171, 173–174 [1917]. See Hall & Farley v. Alabama Ter-

attitude might well be adopted toward an exchange of all the property of a solvent corporation for stock in another.[11] The property received in exchange, although in some cases equal in value, may not be equally available to creditors for the satisfaction of debts by compulsory process. Whether it was this consideration which led the Kentucky court to limit the rule to the case where the exchange of the debtor's property was for stock in a corporation, or whether the fact of the exchange of stock was deemed by the court to bring the case within the rule commonly applied where there is a consolidation, we need not consider.

The sale by the Adams of its Kentucky business and the transfer to the American of all its property within that State was a transaction out of the ordinary course of business. Knowledge on the part of the buyer that the going business was likely to have creditors may be imputed; and likewise knowledge that persons resident there would be hindered and delayed in obtaining payment, if all property within the State is transferred without making provision for satisfying obligations there incurred. Therefore, the transferee can not claim immunity as a *bona fide* purchaser for value.[12]

For the reasons stated, the application of the trust fund doctrine made in this case, even if unsound, cannot be deemed an unreasonable restraint upon alienation or the creation of a liability by an arbitrary judicial act. It was at most a new application or extension of established principles. The decision of the Court of Appeals of Kentucky involves far less of an innovation than many extensions of liability introduced by courts which have later received widespread judicial approval. For instance, the liability declared in *Northern Pacific Ry. v. Boyd*, 228 U.S. 482 [1913]; the liability, introduced by *Pasely v. Freeman*, 3 T.R. 51 [100 Eng. Rep. 450 (1789)], for intentional deceit by one who was under no defined duty to speak and in nowise profited; the liability, introduced by *Lumley v. Gye*, 2 E. & B. 216 [118 Eng. Rep.

---

minal & Improvement Co., 143 Ala. 464, 481 [1904]; Seger's Sons v. Thomas Bros., 107 Mo. 635, 641 [1891]; Billings v. Russell, 101 N.Y. 226, 231 [1886]; Comstock v. Bechtel, 63 Wis. 656, 663 [1885].

[11] See Jennings, Neff & Co. v. Crystal Ice Co., 128 Tenn. 231, 237–238 [1913].

[12] Bertholdt v. Holladay-Klotz Land & Lumber Co., 91 Mo. App. 233, 238 [1901]; Young v. McIver Hardware Co., 144 N.C. 478, 489–490 [1907]; Williams v. Commercial National Bank, 49 Ore. 492 [1907]; Jennings, Neff & Co. v. Crystal Ice Co., 128 Tenn. 231, 236 [1913]; Amsden v. Fitch, 67 Vt. 522, 525 [1895].

749 (1853)], of a third person who induced a breach of contract; the liability, introduced by *Rylands v. Fletcher*, L. R. 3 H. L. 330 [1868], for damages caused by escape of dangerous objects brought upon the land.

The fact that the appellate courts of several other States have reached independently the conclusion that the American Railway Express Company was liable, under similar circumstances, for the domestic debts of its predecessors in business,[13] may not convince us that the rule enunciated is sound. But it should make us hesitate to declare that the judgment of the Court of Appeals of Kentucky is so unreasonable and arbitrary as to amount to a taking of property without due process of law.

[13] See American Ry. Express Co. v. Downing, 132 Va. 139 [1922]; American Ry. Express Co. v. Snead, 96 Okla. 278 [1923]; Peters v. American Ry. Express Co., 256 S.W. (Mo. App.) 100 [1923]. Compare Grice v. American Ry. Express Co., 248 S.W. (Tex. Civ. App.) 82 [1923]; Gibson v. American Ry. Express Co., 195 Ia. 1126 [1923]. In two States it has been held that no such liability arose. McAlister v. American Ry. Express Co., 179 N.C. 556 [1920]; Brown v. American Ry. Express Co., 128 S.C. 428 [1924], distinguishing Brabham v. Southern Express Co., 124 S. C. 157 [1922].

X

Holmes

Very few Supreme Court judges in our history have ever become household names. Very few have been accompanied through their careers by the sort of popular image of themselves, constituted of fact merging into legend, which is the shadow of great men in other walks of public life. To this generalization, Justice Holmes, certainly in the last twenty years of his life, was an exception. So, to a lesser extent, was Brandeis; chiefly, and at the end of his career wholly, in his own right, but at first in some degree because his name was coupled with that of Holmes. They were the dissenters, the liberals, as the labels had it, in an institution which during the period of their tenures was the citadel of conservatism. The fact underlying this popular coupling of the two names was that Holmes and Brandeis did indeed very frequently arrive at the same results in conspicuous cases. But there was also an element of fiction; it lay in an implied equation of the processes of the Court with those of other institutions of government, in the assumption that a frequent coincidence of views between two such men as Holmes and Brandeis must be compounded, as it would be in the case of two Senators, for example, of similarities in basic outlook, of friendship, of leadership and followership, and even of a certain amount of back-scratching.

No less a figure than Chief Justice Taft, who knew better, writing in a fit of pique to Henry L. Stimson in 1928, could say: "I am very fond of the old gentleman [Holmes], but he is so completely under the control of Brother Brandeis that it gives to Brandeis two votes instead of one." [1] This was fiction. Of course the two men were friends, although there was an enormous contrast between them in cast of mind and personality; and of course they held some important principles in common. In April 1916, during the fight about Brandeis' confirmation, some nonsense to the effect that Brandeis did not believe in a written constitution came to the ear of T. W. Gregory, Wilson's Attorney General, who was busily at work trying to obtain a favorable vote in the Senate. Gregory brought this to Brandeis' attention, and the latter urged that such rumors be traced to their source. "My views in regard to the Constitution," he added, "are as you know very much those of Mr. Justice Holmes."[2] There was never a time in the later career of either man when Brandeis might have needed to retract this qualified commitment. But the arresting thing about the common results they so frequently reached was the difference in the routes by which Holmes and Brandeis each got there. For this reason, the fact that they came together as they did sheds much light on the nature of the issues involved, on the Court's function as the two men saw it, and on the process of deciding. This is to say that the differences between Holmes and Brandeis are infinitely more interesting and more fruitful to explore than the similarities.

Both Holmes and Brandeis generally resisted the imposition of constitutional barriers against measures of social and economic regulation enacted in their wisdom by state and federal legislatures. But of Holmes, Max Lerner has acutely observed: "His judicial philosophy of leaving the legislature alone came from a deeper philosophy of leaving the cosmos alone."[3] Nothing could have been less true of Brandeis, who was an improver, an experimenter, and a sober optimist about long-range prospects for bettering the lot of man in society. Continuing where they had left off in a conversation they had evidently had on this disparity in their outlooks, Holmes once wrote to Brandeis: "Generally speaking, I agree with you in liking to see social experiments tried but I do so without enthusiasm because I believe it is merely shifting the pressure and that so long as we have free propagation Malthus is right in his general view."[4]

Again, although it is more than somewhat question-begging to state the issue as broadly as this, it may be said that, in context of the free-speech cases of their day, both Holmes and Brandeis were generally astute to resist encroachments on individual liberty urged in the name of order and security. But, once more, Holmes' devotion to the free market place of ideas was largely a function of his desire to let the cosmos alone, of his skepticism concerning the ultimate truth of any idea. "If in the long run" — so goes one of his celebrated dicta — "the beliefs expressed in proletarian dictatorship are destined to be accepted by the dominant forces in the community, the only meaning of free speech is that they should be given their chance and have their way."[5] For Brandeis, that was not the meaning of the First Amendment. Free speech was a faith rooted in deeply held ethical and moral values, which he believed it was the function of the state to promote. The Founders, he wrote in *Whitney v. California*,[6] "valued liberty both as an end and as a means. They believed liberty to be the secret of happiness and courage to be the secret of liberty." Similarly, for Holmes, wiretapping was "dirty business"; *merely* dirty business. For Brandeis freedom from wiretapping, privacy, was an immutable value which, when his back was to the wall, he could find in the Constitution, and to the defense of which he was impelled by the inclination of his temperament to admire and seek to induce in men such qualities as valor, self-reliance, and dignity.[7] Holmes, to be sure, subscribed to these values as well, but always in context of his all-encompassing skepticism. And he could not see government as their active promoter.

To Brandeis, the state was an instrument for the achievement of the highest good. In some areas this meant for him legislative freedom to experiment. But in others the state was morally bound to adhere to unchanging values, whose attainment was its ultimate end. It is to be doubted, on the other hand, whether for Holmes, with his persistent strain of positivism, the state, the territorial club, as he called it, was in this sense anything but a morally neutral fact; a prerequisite to the good life, yes, but quite helpless to create it.[8] In a letter to Harold J. Laski, written late in 1930, Holmes alluded to this disparity between himself and Brandeis: "I told him [Brandeis] long ago that he really was an advocate rather than a Judge. He is affected by his interest in a cause, and if he feels it he is not detached . . . ." But Holmes hastened to add that "his interests are noble, and as you say his insights profound." [9] Much earlier, speaking of other men, Holmes had expressed in letters to Felix Frankfurter a thought which must have struck him as well in connection with Brandeis: "It seems as if the gift of passionate enthusiasm were racial. It is a great one." And: "It seems as if an exquisite moral susceptibility were the gift of many Jews." [10]

There were other differences, as well, between the two judges, not of so lofty a nature, perhaps, as the one discussed above, but of considerable importance just the same. Some of these are laid bare by the history of *Bullock v. Florida*,[11] an otherwise undistinguished little case.

A lower Florida court had issued a decree authorizing the sale on foreclosure of a bankrupt railroad to a purchaser who proposed to dismantle it for its scrap value. The state thereupon obtained from the Supreme Court of Florida a writ of prohibition voiding so much of the lower court's decree as had authorized dismantling. The Supreme Court of the United States was asked to vacate this writ of prohibition, on the ground that it amounted to forcing operation of the railroad at a loss and thus to a deprivation of property without due process of law.

The case was argued early in December 1920. It was disposed of a little more than a month later, Holmes writing the unanimous opinion of the Court. After setting out the facts, Holmes noted that no one questioned the jurisdiction of the lower Florida court to issue its order permitting sale on foreclosure to a buyer who proposed to dismantle. The order had no other technical flaw either; nor did it run counter to the provisions of any statute. It followed, therefore, that the Supreme Court of Florida had upset so much of the order as permitted dismantling for the sole reason that it took a different view than did the lower court of the obligation of a public utility such as this railroad to continue operations at a loss. But, Holmes continued, unless they had undertaken a duty to the contrary, contractual in nature, people who had put their money into a railroad did not have an obligation to go on running it at a loss. The fact that they had accepted a charter from the state and had exercised by its authority the power of eminent domain did not change matters. "Suppose that a railroad company should find that its road was a failure, it could not make the State a party to a proceeding for leave to stop, and whether the State would proceed would be for the State to decide. The only remedy of the company would be to stop, and that it would have a right to do without the consent of the State if the facts were as supposed. Purchasers of the road by foreclosure would have the same right."[12]

The perceptive reader who follows Holmes' opinion along this far is led almost inevitably to look for a reversal of the Florida Supreme Court's writ of prohibition and for a reinstatement of the lower court's decree, which asserted for the purchaser on foreclosure a right Holmes recognizes as legitimately his. But the perceptive reader had best read on, for Holmes turns around to defeat his expectations. The last two paragraphs of the opinion are as follows:

But the foreclosure was not a proceeding *in rem* and could confer no rights except those existing in the mortgagor. A purchaser at the sale would acquire all such right as the mortgagor had to stop operations, whatever words were used in the decree, and, whatever the words, would get no more. The prohibition excluding from the decree the words purporting to authorize dismantling the road did not cut down the future purchaser's rights, any more than did the presence of those words enlarge them. Therefore the action of the Supreme Court is not open to objection under the Constitution of the United States, although it may be that it hardly would have been taken if the authority to dismantle had not sounded more absolute than it could be in fact, considering the nature of the proceeding. Without previous statute or contract to compel the company to keep on at a loss would be an unconstitutional taking of its property. But the prohibition does not compel the company to keep on, it simply excludes a form of authority from the decree that gives the illusion of a power to turn the property to other uses that cannot be settled in that case.

As the State voluntarily made itself a party to the foreclosure suit before the decree went into effect, as indeed the decree never has, it might seem that the State ought to be bound in a way that otherwise it would not be. But if in a revisory proceeding the higher State Court says that the State should not be bound and that the decree was wrong in this particular, that is a local question with which we have nothing to do. The result is that although the State Court may have acted on questionable or erroneous postulates there is nothing in its action that calls for a reversal of its judgment.

> *Writ of Error dismissed.*
> *Writ of Certiorari granted.*
> *Judgment affirmed.*

The expectations to which the first part of Holmes' published opinion gives rise, and which are defeated by the last two paragraphs ending in affirmance of the Florida Supreme Court's writ of prohibition, were fully met by an earlier version of the opinion. In this draft, the place of the two paragraphs just quoted was taken by a concluding passage supporting the opposite result; that is, reversal of the Florida Supreme Court's judgment. The passage read as follows:

Possibly less objection would have been made to the decree [of the lower Florida court, ordering the foreclosure sale] if its language as to dismantling had not seemed to convey an absolute authority. But it operated only as between the parties and transferred to the purchaser the right of the company and no more. At least if the State had not made itself a party whatever rights it had against the company it would have had against the purchasers. On the other hand no one denies that whatever rights the company had could be sold. The reason why the decree was objected to was the notion that even if the company was going at a loss it was bound to keep on until the State sanctioned its ceasing to do what the State could not require it to do, coupled, perhaps, as we have suggested, with an impression that the decree was conferring new rights. Without previous statute or contract, to compel the company to keep on would be an unconstitutional taking of its property. We do not perceive why the State should not be bound by a decree to which it was a party before the decree went into effect, which it has not done yet. If not, it can institute such proceedings as it is advised, but meantime it cannot complain of a sale of the railroad with whatever right to dismantle it the vendor had, and that is all that the foreclosure decree meant or could mean.

> *Writ of Error dismissed.*
> *Writ of Certiorari granted.*
> *Judgment reversed.*

Holmes circulated his opinion in this form shortly after the argument. Brandeis returned as follows: "I like your saving clause in the last par." — meaning no doubt the sentence in which Holmes allowed that Florida might yet in appropriate further proceedings seek to force continued operation of the road — "but see pp. 3–4." Pages 3–4 bristled

with Brandeis' angular handwriting: ". . . it is not suggested," Holmes
had written, "that any statute forbids the decree that was made" by
the lower court in Florida; that any statute "expressly" forbids, Brandeis inserted. And where, in the next sentence, Holmes spoke of a duty
to carry on operations as "not based upon statute," Brandeis inserted
"any express provision" of statute. Coming to the heart of the case,
Brandeis noted in the margin: "There is no right to compel operation at a loss — because that involves putting in new money. But it
does not follow that because it cannot be operated today, except at
a loss, the judgment (a prophecy) of the wise may not be that in a
reasonable time it will not [*sic!*] be possible to operate at a profit. The
mere fact that, at public sale, X will not buy charged with the obligation to operate now — is not proof." On Holmes' assertion that a
railroad company which found its road a failure had a right to stop
"without the consent of the State," and "could not make the State a
party to a proceeding to stop," Brandeis commented: "This cannot be
stated as a general proposition — See People vs. Col. Title & Trust
Co., 178 Pac. 6" [65 Colo. 472 (1918)]. In that case, the Colorado
Supreme Court upheld a statute vesting in the state Public Utilities
Commission exclusive jurisdiction to do precisely what Holmes had
said no railroad company need wait for the state to do; namely, give
it permission to cease operations. Finally, in the margin next to the
sentence, "Without previous statute or contract, to compel the company to keep on would be an unconstitutional taking of its property,"
Brandeis asked: "Can this be stated generally? Are you sure that isn't
a Fla. question? See State v. Dodge City, 53 Kan. 377" [1894] — holding that a railroad may not be dismantled without state permission.

Possibly before receipt of Holmes' draft, perhaps later (but not
much later, for as was usual with an opinion assigned to Holmes, events
moved rapidly), Brandeis started in long-hand to write a dissent. It
dealt at greater length with the issue as he put it in his return to
Holmes. To reverse the Florida Supreme Court's judgment, Brandeis
wrote, it was necessary to hold "that although those who construct a
railroad under a state charter thereby devote the property to a public use, the Federal Constitution implies . . . a condition, paramount
to the right of the State, to the effect that the owners may dismantle
the railroad and dispose of the junked material . . . because [the
railroad] cannot be operated at a profit. I find nothing in the Federal
Constitution which compels the Supreme Court of Florida to imply
such a condition; and I find much in the common law to the contrary." The common law Brandeis referred to was that by which an
appropriate expression of an owner's intent could irrevocably dedi-

cate his property to public use as a highway. He cited two early Supreme Court cases: *Cincinnati v. Lessees of White,* and *Barclay v. Howell's Lessee.*[13] "The railroad," he said, "is, of course, a form of highway." The owner of a highway right-of-way had no obligation to keep it in repair. But he could not remove the material with which it was fitted for use. By the same token, a railroad could not be dismantled without consent of the state. To be sure, Brandeis continued, the owner could not be obliged "to operate the property at a loss . . . and where it is clear that there is no prospect of being [able] to operate it without incurring a loss a Court may well apply the principle by which land is held to revert to the dedicator when the intended use becomes impossible . . . or the use is abandoned by the public." (This was the "prophecy" which he mentioned in his return to Holmes.) "But it is for the courts of a State, not for this Court, to determine how and by what tribunal it shall be determined that a further use has become impossible. And as the enquiry affects directly the interests of the public, the determination can be made only in a proceeding to which the State is in some form a party."

On the issue which this dialogue outlines, there was to be in this case no full meeting of minds between Holmes and Brandeis. Holmes accepted Brandeis' result. But most of the statements that Brandeis found objectionable, including Holmes' flat declaration of a constitutional right in the final paragraph of the early draft of his opinion, remained, though the eventual disposition of the case rendered them dicta. Actually, however, the difference of opinion was narrower than it appeared. Brandeis, of course, was not claiming for the state an absolute right to force continued operation at a loss.[14] And only a few terms later, Holmes, without, apparently, so much as a private murmur of protest, joined Brandeis and a unanimous Court in holding that a street railway company could, under some circumstances at least, be prevented from abandoning an unprofitable operation.[15]

It was characteristic of Holmes that his generalizations in this case should have made the gap between him and Brandeis appear to be wider than, on the record of future actions, it was. Not infrequently Holmes' "forms of words," as he liked to call them, seemed more sweeping than he really intended them to be, or than — refusing to descend from the eminence of subtle silent premises and reservations on which he was poised — he could be made to see that they would seem. "He doesn't realize," Brandeis once said of him, "that others haven't his precipitate of knowledge — they don't know as he knows — and secondly he doesn't sufficiently consider the need of others to understand . . . . Philosophically he would admit the difference between truth and consent of others to truth — but he does not regard the difference in practice."[16]

Thus it cannot be said that the history of *Bullock v. Florida* exposes any broad disagreement between Holmes and Brandeis concerning the social obligations that the holders of property owe to the state. Yet Holmes and Brandeis did differ on questions of the rights of property, and this case suggests it. There was between them a difference of, for lack of a better word, tendency, of the way each leaned in close cases. And it was sometimes decisive. For both, so long as a due process clause remained in the Constitution and was applied to substantive as well as procedural matters, there came an extreme point at which they deemed it to be the Court's duty to protect property rights against infringement by the state.[17] But — perhaps simply because he had been born earlier, perhaps because he nearly always was out of sympathy with, and often did not care to understand, in practical terms, the social purpose behind state action — the point tended to come sooner for Holmes than for Brandeis. Then, instead of being content to let the legislature alone, as he did the cosmos, Holmes required the legislature also to keep hands off the cosmos. This difference between Holmes and Brandeis is discernible in a series of obligation of contract cases involving new burdens sought to be imposed by growing cities on established public transportation companies. Holmes and Brandeis were on opposite sides in these cases.[18] It came to a head, almost exactly two years after *Bullock v. Florida*, in *Pennsylvania Coal Co. v. Mahon*.[19]

When, some decades earlier, the Pennsylvania Coal Company had sold to Mahon's predecessors the land on which his home now stood, it had expressly reserved to itself title to, and the right to remove, any coal that might be found under the lot in question. Acting pursuant to its right so stipulated, the coal company now gave notice that it was about to mine under Mahon's house. At Mahon's behest, the Pennsylvania courts enjoined the company from proceeding, on the ground that to do so would violate a recent statute forbidding the mining of coal in such a way as to cause the subsidence of any human habitation, public building, public passage-way, or public service facility. The coal company took the case to the United States Supreme Court, where it was powerfully argued in its behalf by John W. Davis. If the company could be prevented from mining, Davis contended, its remaining property right in the coal became quite theoretical; indeed, no more serviceable "than was Shylock's right to his pound of flesh."[20]

Therefore, the argument ran, Pennsylvania had taken the company's property without paying compensation and had thus violated the Due Process Clause of the Fourteenth Amendment.

Holmes, who spoke for the Court, declared the Pennsylvania statute unconstitutional. In the circumstances before him, he could not see a substantial public interest which Pennsylvania might legitimately wish to protect in this fashion. The state had merely chosen to enrich one private party at the expense of another. That could not be done without providing some compensating benefit to the losing party. As for the undoubted public interest that would arise in the case of public buildings, roads, or other facilities, Pennsylvania would have to safeguard it by exercising its right of eminent domain and paying for its taking of the coal company's property. For, as John W. Davis had argued, and as Holmes agreed, this was a taking, not a regulation.

Brandeis, though he stood alone, dissented. There had, in his view, been no taking, "merely the prohibition of a noxious use"[21] of property. In the sense used by Holmes, every regulation was a taking. The issue was simply whether the regulation could be supported on the basis of its reasonable relation to an identifiable public interest. And the public interest in the maintenance of private dwellings as well as public buildings was plain. The Court's conclusion, Brandeis said, seemed to rest on the assumption that there had to be "an average reciprocity of advantage" as between the owner of the regulated property and the community; and the further assumption that in this case such reciprocity was lacking. But, in Brandeis' opinion, that was irrelevant where the state's power was invoked not to make an adjustment between two conflicting private interests, but to safeguard the public interest. In the latter instance, the owner of the regulated property received "the advantage of living and doing business in a civilized community."[22]

Holmes' position in the *Mahon* case caused some surprise and dismay among his admirers. But Holmes stood his ground. He was "not greatly impressed" by an editorial in the *New Republic* holding that Brandeis had shown "the superior statesmanship." Its author, Holmes wrote Laski, was Dean Acheson, Brandeis' law clerk of two terms back, who in supporting his former boss had expressed his disagreement with "admirable politeness." And the term "statesmanship" was an "effective word" — but it needed "caution in using it."[23] Brandeis, Holmes complained to both Pollock and Laski, had made too much of his idea of "average reciprocity of advantage." Brandeis had suggested that Holmes used it as a general rationale. But in fact, Holmes maintained, he meant it as a formula explaining only certain cases, not all.[24] From Pollock, Holmes got a diffident but sympathetic reply, rounded off with this pleasant frivolity: "That the destruction of this or that dwelling house taken by itself is necessarily a bad thing is very far from obvious: I know many by sight which I would gladly see devoured by a mine, a dragon or anything else . . . ." [25]

Holmes' admirers need not have been quite so surprised at the tendency Holmes displayed in the *Mahon* case. Brandeis wasn't. He had had a clear inkling of it earlier. One link in the chain of Brandeis' reasoning in his dissent in the *Mahon* case was the proposition that regulations of property depriving the owner of the only use to which the property could profitably be put had previously been upheld. For this proposition he cited the old case of *Mugler v. Kansas*,[26] decided in 1887 by Mr. Justice Harlan the Elder. In that case the Court had upheld a state prohibition on the manufacture and sale of intoxicating liquors, applied without the payment of compensation to an existing manufacturing concern. "I always have thought," Holmes wrote Laski after the *Mahon* case was decided, "that old Harlan's decision in Mugler v. Kansas was pretty fishy." [27] That Holmes had always thought so Brandeis had very good reason to know. Early in his judicial career, just after the First World War, Brandeis had written two opinions upholding the federal prohibition statutes, based on the war power, which preceded the Eighteenth Amendment.[28] The Court had had trouble with these cases. In one of them there was to the end only a bare majority for Brandeis' view. Holmes, as Brandeis once told the story, had originally been for striking down the statutes, although eventually he went along. Brandeis, in one of the cases in particular, made much, as he naturally would have, of the decision in *Mugler v. Kansas*.[29] "A mighty fishy decision," Holmes wrote him. But he added that he was "merely whispering in your ear, not suggesting that you make any changes. You have done nobly and I felicitate you on getting away with it." [30] In conversation after the *Mahon* decision, Brandeis, recalling this episode, commented that Holmes' well-known impatience with prohibition, a social experiment he had perhaps less sympathy with than any other, might be thought to explain his distaste for *Mugler v. Kansas*.[31] But that, Brandeis well knew, was not the heart of the matter. The uneasiness with the *Mugler* case was grounded in the same tendency which prevailed with Holmes in *Pennsylvania Coal Co. v. Mahon*, and which nearly prevailed in *Bullock v. Florida*.

More strikingly than it illustrates the difference of tendency in dealing with property rights, the Holmes-Brandeis debate occasioned by *Bullock v. Florida* highlights another difference between the two judges; one of method more than of principle, yet one affecting principle and results. This difference has been the subject of much comment, most perceptively by Holmes and Brandeis themselves.

Holmes' mind operated with abstractions which he brought to bear on affairs. As he said himself, he believed that "the chief end of man is to form general propositions — adding that no general proposition is worth a damn." [32] In theory, the admonition doubtless had as much weight with Holmes as the belief itself. But it cannot be said that Holmes regularly acted on it. It was quite otherwise with Brandeis. On questions such as those concerning regulation of property, Brandeis' thought was rooted in experience of affairs, and in the feel for affairs where experience was lacking.

"I hate facts," Holmes said; and, "I hate them except as pegs for generalizations"; and of Brandeis, he said a little patronizingly, which was quite unusual, "To be familiar with business is a great (secondary) advantage." [33] In his best disarming manner, Holmes wrote to Felix Frankfurter in July 1923: "I have just received a typewritten report of the U.S. Coal Commission. Brandeis would be deep in it at once. I turn to Sainte-Beuve." [34] And, again to Felix Frankfurter, in December 1925: "If I wanted to be epigrammatic I should say that he [Brandeis] always desires to know all that can be known about a case whereas I am afraid that I wish to know as little as I can safely go on . . . . Think not that I don't appreciate the power that his knowledge gives him." [35]

Brandeis, for his part, telling of a famous incident of which Holmes also spoke to his correspondents,[36] said: "It's perfectly amazing that a man who has had no practical experience to speak of, and no experience at statesmanship, should be so frequently right as to matters that have significance only in their application. I have told him so — how amazing it is. And once told him that if he really wants to 'improve his mind' (as he always speaks of it), the way to do it is not to read more philosophic books — he has improved his mind that way as far as it can go — but to get some sense of the world of fact. And he asked me to map out some reading — he became much interested — and I told him that I'd see, get some books, [but] that books could carry him only so far, and that then he should get some exhibits from life. I suggested the textile industry, and told him in vacation time he is near Lawrence and Lowell and he should go there and look about. He became much interested — although he said he was 'too old.' I told him he was too old to acquire knowledge in many fields of fact but not too old to realize through one field what the world of fact was, and to be more conscious and understanding of it. With his mind as an instrument, there wasn't anything he couldn't acquire. And so he undertook to do the textiles — but very unfortunately it was the time when Mrs. Holmes was very sick, and he had her on his mind, and studying became a duty instead of, as I hoped, a new interest and possibly, therefore, a relaxation. And so he reported to me, very apologetically, in the fall his inability to pursue the study." [37]

Brandeis recognized, of course, that it was precisely his systematic and powerfully developed set of ideological abstractions that gave to Holmes' work its extraordinary coherence. "It's all been thought out," Brandeis once said. "His work is a chemical composition and not a conglomerate. He has said many things in their ultimate terms, and as new instances arise they just fit in." [38] But there were times when a new instance would simply not just fit in. One such intractable instance was *Portsmouth Co. v. United States*,[39] a case involving a claim against the federal government for a "taking" of private land by firing coast-artillery over it, which Holmes decided for the claimant a week before he handed down his opinion in the *Mahon* case. As in *Bullock v. Florida*, the issue here also was enmeshed in difficulties of procedure and of what Brandeis, in that case, called the prophecies of the wise concerning future conditions. Holmes could summon no patience with these complications. Brandeis, in dissent, was joined by, of all people, Sutherland. Taft, though he stuck by Holmes, wrote Brandeis: "You shake me considerably . . . ." [40] Another such instance, coming a term later, was *Chastelton Corp. v. Sinclair*,[41] which put in issue the continued validity, in 1922, of the District of Columbia's wartime rent control act. Holmes spoke for the Court, dealing, very wisely, to be sure, with the war powers question. Brandeis agreed in part, but was constrained to write a separate opinion, insisting on the relevance of a factual nicety that Holmes had brushed aside.

In *Bullock v. Florida*, also, Holmes' abstractions were not sufficiently pliable to bend to all the facts. But in this case, though Holmes again would not bend, it was possible to divert him. Brandeis failed, for the time being, at least, to bring Holmes around to the view that a constitutional right to discontinue operations could not be given effect as a general proposition, because its existence had to depend on varying particular circumstances, of which the state should be the judge. But he did succeed in persuading Holmes that the Florida Supreme Court's writ of prohibition, no matter what grounds that court had based it on, left everyone's rights in *statu quo*, and that there was, therefore, no reason to upset it. This was the point Brandeis made in an unpublished dissent.

Brandeis — and this was a very unusual occurrence with him — did not send to the printer his long-hand draft dealing more directly with the issue of when a public utility may discontinue operations without the state's consent. He abandoned that draft and fell to writing the dissent printed here. And he went about doing this also in unusual fashion. He attacked it at the midriff. He drafted first what became the third paragraph of his opinion, following the statement of the facts. He then, in two quick successive drafts, constructed the rest of the dissent around this paragraph.

SUPREME COURT OF THE UNITED STATES

No. 262. — October Term, 1920.

W. S. Bullock, Judge of the Circuit Court of the Fifth Judicial Circuit of the State of Florida and William F. Hood, Trustee, Petitioners, *vs.* The State of Florida upon the Relation of the Railroad Commission of the State of Florida, et al.	On writ of Certiorari to the Supreme Court of Florida.

[   ]

Mr. Justice BRANDEIS, dissenting.

As I see it, a constitutionally correct judgment of the Supreme Court of Florida is being set aside on a writ of certiorari because this court holds reasoning in the opinion to be unsound. The supervisory power of this court does not extend so far.

The essential facts are few: In an inferior State court the mortgagee of a railroad brought suit against the mortgagor to foreclose. The defendant made no contest. That court inserted in the decree a provision purporting to authorize the purchaser at foreclosure sale to dismantle the railroad; and the sale was held. Before confirmation the inferior court heard the State in protest against this dismantling provision; and announced its decision to confirm the sale on terms which included that clause. The State then brought in the Supreme Court of Florida this proceeding to

prohibit the confirmation of the sale in so far as the decree authorized dismantling the railroad; the Supreme Court of Florida issued the writ of prohibition so limited.[1] This court was asked to
set aside that judgment of the Supreme Court of Florida on the
ground that it violates the Due Process Clause of the Fourteenth
Amendment.

This court holds that the mortgagee is entitled to have sold on
foreclosure the mortgagor's whole interest in the property; and
only that. This court also holds that the decree on foreclosure as
entered by the inferior State court does not affect the right, if any,
of the State, to have the mortgaged property continued in use
for railroad purposes; and that the State may, in spite of the sale
under the decree, assert and enforce by other appropriate proceeding its alleged right to have such use continued. With these
two propositions the judgment of the Supreme Court of Florida
is in entire harmony. How then can it be said that the judgment
of the Supreme Court of Florida deprives the mortgagee of prop-

---

[1] The judgment was: "Application having been made to the Court for the issuance of a peremptory writ of prohibition in this cause, and the Court having
approved the form of such writ, it is ordered by the Court that the Clerk do forthwith issue the peremptory writ of prohibition in this cause in the form approved
by the Court." The writ, omitting the preamble, was in the following form: ". . .
the Court having determined that the said demurrers are severally ill-founded and
that said decree, in so far as it authorized a dismantling of said railroad, a sale of
its property as junk and a discontinuance of its operation as a common carrier,
was beyond the jurisdiction of said Circuit Court and said demurrants having failed
to avail themselves of the opportunity allowed them to plead over;

"It is now considered by the Court that the Circuit Court of the Fifth Judicial
Circuit of the State of Florida in and for Marion County and W. S. Bullock, as
Judge of said Court, be and they are hereby prohibited from approving or con-
firming the sale made under the decree entered on the 24th day of December,
1917, in a certain cause pending in said Court wherein William S. Hood as Trustee
is complainant and Ocklawaha Valley Railroad Company, a corporation, is defendant, and authorizing or decreeing the dismantling, taking up, or removing
any of the rails or tracks of said Ocklawaha Valley Railroad Company, and from
exercising any further jurisdiction in said cause relating to the junking of said
property.

"This writ, however, applies only to that portion of the final decree which was
found to be in excess of the jurisdiction of the Court, which portion is hereby
eliminated, but all other portions of the final decree remain in full force and effect
so that such final decree should read as shown by the attached copy, with the
parts in brackets eliminated, with full power and authority in the Circuit Court
in which the decree was entered to deal in all respects with the matter, except that
he shall not, and is hereby prohibited from undertaking, by decree, order, or otherwise, to authorize the dismantling of said railroad . . . ."

"Witness the Honorable Jefferson B. Browne, Chief Justice of the Supreme
Court of the State of Florida, and the Seal of said Court, at Tallahassee, this
eleventh day of December, A.D. 1919."

erty without due process of law? Its judgment does not purport to adjudge whether or not the mortgagor, the mortgagee and the purchaser had the right to dismantle the railroad; nor whether the State had the right under any circumstances to have the mortgaged property left in a form so that it could continue to be used as a railroad; nor does the judgment prohibit the mortgagor, the mortgagee or the purchaser from dismantling the railroad, and the judgment does not otherwise adjudge any of these matters. The owner of the mortgaged property had after entry of the judgment of the Supreme Court of Florida as full right, if any, to dismantle the railroad as he had before its entry. All that the judgment does is to prohibit the inferior court from expressly authorizing the purchaser to deprive the State, without due process of law, of a property right which it claims to have. Put at its lowest, the decree of the inferior court cast a cloud upon the alleged right of the State to have the mortgaged property left in its then form or condition — a form which could not be changed without in effect destroying, in advance of appropriate adjudication, the alleged right of the State to have the property continue to be devoted to the public use.

Whether the inferior court when it cast this cloud upon a right asserted by the State exceeded its jurisdiction or the powers properly exercisable in a foreclosure suit; whether the inferior court could properly, after the sale had been made, admit the State "as a party" to protest against such cloud being cast upon its alleged right; and what the effect, if any, was of so admitting the State at that stage of the litigation; these were all matters of local law and procedure reviewable by the highest court of the State. The Supreme Court of Florida, the appellate tribunal, decided that the inferior court exceeded its jurisdiction in so casting a cloud upon the alleged right of the State and in granting an authority to dismantle, a matter which, in that proceeding, it had no power to pass upon; and it prohibited such action on the part of the inferior court. As the question whether the inferior court did exceed its jurisdiction by so incorporating the dismantling clause in a decree of foreclosure is obviously a matter of local law, the decision thereon of the highest court of a State must be accepted by us as conclusive.

Whether or not upon the facts as they appeared to the inferior court when it entered its decree, the State had a right to have the mortgaged property left in a form so that it could continue to be used as a railroad is a question confessedly not before us in this proceeding. We have, therefore, no occasion to consider it now; and no power to determine it on this writ of certiorari.

We do not know whether or not Brandeis circulated this opinion. It seems a safe assumption that Holmes saw it and that the two talked. On or immediately after Christmas, 1920, Holmes circulated the following:

No. 262. — Bullock vs. Florida.

Memorandum by Mr. Justice HOLMES.

Further reflection leads me to doubt the correctness of the opinion circulated. If it be plain, as there said, that the rights and only the rights of the mortgagor are transferred by the foreclosure and that those rights would be transferred without any language in the decree as to selling the road for one purpose or another, and equally would be transferred in the form prescribed by the Supreme Court, how can it be said that any constitutional right is impaired? It is a mere fight about words. I incline to think that the opinion is still under the influence of the fallacy there adverted to, that the authority conveyed is absolute, instead of being confined to mortgagor and mortgagee. It is true that the State voluntarily made itself a party, and it might be thought that if it saw fit to do so, no matter how late, while the decree was in the power of the Court, it should be bound by the decree and could not deprive the seller of rights that by its joinder became adjudicated against it, which otherwise they would not be. But this is in the nature of an appellate proceeding and if the higher Court says that the State should not be bound and that the decree was wrong, that is a local question of procedure, with which we have nothing to do, if I am right in thinking that the effect of the sale will be the same whichever form of words is employed.

Please let me hear your views in time for action.
December 25, 1920.

There is in Holmes' memorandum the sense of the Olympian's brusque disengagement from a battle that has suddenly appeared unworthy. He has discovered that "it is a mere fight about words," and he washes his hands of it. The problem now was to bring the Court around. A note from Holmes to Brandeis indicates that Holmes, at least, thought there was some chance that the case would be assigned to someone else, to be written in the sense in which Holmes had first done it. The note, which was dated January 4, 1921, accompanied a near-final draft of Holmes' changed opinion. ". . . I feel a little confused," Holmes said, "by my effort to avoid throwing the case on to someone else and don't feel satisfied — and yet hardly know what more to say or do."

Holmes circulated to the rest of the Court as well as to Brandeis the draft which went with the note just quoted. Its last sentence read: "The result is that although the State Court acted on questionable or erroneous postulates there is nothing in its action that calls for a reversal of its judgment." This was a little too much for Brandeis. He inserted, "may have" after the words, "State Court." His return read: "This is very good. Yes — but 'may have' should be inserted on p. 4. We have no right — as I see it — to express an opinion on that." Van Devanter returned: "Inclined to come in, but will wait to hear what others have to offer. A few feeble suggestions in the margin which are thought to be in keeping with your purpose." Van Devanter's suggestions may not have been momentous, but they were not feeble. This opinion was to strike neutral ground between opposite views, represented, no doubt, by himself on the one hand and Brandeis on the other; and Van Devanter, like Brandeis, had it in mind to make sure that the concluding — and decisive — sentences were truly neutral. Holmes suggested that the lower Florida court, whose decree the Florida Supreme Court had modified, had granted an authority to dismantle "more absolute than it could be in fact" — "considering the nature of the proceeding," Van Devanter inserted. McReynolds returned a bon mot: "This seems to save the substance to the mortgagee and the form to the Supreme Court. I agree." Clarke agreed, but wished some of the statements in that part of the opinion which had remained unchanged might be shaved down a bit. "I fear," he said, "that, in its present form, [the opinion] may be seized upon as a justification for taking up temporarily unprofitable branch lines to the great inconvenience and loss of many communities." [42]

On these returns, if Van Devanter and Brandeis could be held, there was a court. Holmes, custodian of the neutral ground, accepted the "may have" Brandeis asked for, and he took Van Devanter's suggestion. He ignored Clarke. The unchanged tone of the balance of the opinion presumably carried the day with the other brethren — or at least secured their silence. Brandeis once remarked — not very long after this case had come down: "Holmes is very powerful when he changes his mind — with others." [43]

APPENDIX

NOTES

Justices Who Sat with Brandeis

HUGO LA FAYETTE BLACK (1886–   )

Mr. Justice Black attended the public schools of his native Clay County, Alabama, and the University of Alabama Law School. In 1910 and 1911 he was police judge in Birmingham, and for three years, starting in 1914, he was public prosecutor in the same city. Following army service in the First World War, he returned to law practice. In 1926 he was elected to the Senate from Alabama, serving until his appointment to the Supreme Court by President Roosevelt in 1937.

PIERCE BUTLER (1866–1939)

Butler came to the Court, by appointment of President Harding, from an important corporation (heavily railroad) practice in St. Paul, Minnesota. He was born on a Minnesota farm of Irish immigrant parents and was educated at Carleton College. His legal education was obtained in the old-fashioned way: he read law in the office of a senior member of the Bar. He served on the Bench from 1923 until his death in 1939. Butler promptly joined in steadfast partnership with the group whose other members were Justices Van Devanter, McReynolds, and Sutherland. However, he did occasionally strike out on his own, as in his insistence on rigorous observance of the Fourth Amendment's prohibition against "unreasonable searches and seizures." Butler was a man of power and passion, a formidable individual and individualist. There was truth about his physical presence, about the quality of his mind, and about his temperament in the appellation, "Fierce" Butler.

BENJAMIN NATHAN CARDOZO (1870–1938)

Cardozo, Chief Judge of the New York Court of Appeals — always an important, and often, as in the years of his tenure, a truly great court — was appointed to the Supreme Court by acclamation as the fitting successor to Holmes. The President who gladly yielded to the clamor was Herbert Hoover. Cardozo, whose forebears were members of a pre-Revolutionary Sephardic Jewish settlement, was tutored by Horatio Alger, and was graduated from Columbia College at the age of nineteen. He also attended the Columbia Law School, but took no degree in law. In 1914, after some two decades of practice, Cardozo began his career on the highest court of the state, becoming Chief Judge in 1927. He was quickly and widely recognized as a great common-law judge, his reputation being much enhanced by his extra-judicial writings, which are philosophical inquiries into the nature of law and of the judicial process. Cardozo, seated on the Supreme Court in March 1932, did not serve long. He was absent because of illness after December

10, 1937, and died the following year. Despite the brevity of this tenure, he made his mark in Washington as he had in Albany. Among his writings are: *The Nature of the Judicial Process* (1921); *The Growth of the Law* (1924); *The Paradoxes of Legal Science* (1928); and *Law and Literature* (1931).

JOHN HESSIN CLARKE (1857–1945)

In 1914 President Wilson appointed Clarke, engaged in a successful corporation and railroad practice in Cleveland, to a federal district judgeship in Ohio. Two years later, not long after the Brandeis appointment, Wilson promoted Clarke to the Supreme Court. Born in Ohio of an Irish immigrant father and educated there at Western Reserve University, Clarke had been active in Democratic politics and had run a losing race for the Senate against Mark Hanna in 1903. On the Bench he often aligned himself with Brandeis — but not in the civil liberties cases which came to the Court in the aftermath of the First World War. In 1922, though still relatively young, Clarke resigned in order, as he said, to devote himself to the advancement of the cause of the League of Nations. But there appear to have been other reasons as well. On September 13, 1922, after he had tendered his resignation but before it had become effective, Clarke wrote Brandeis: "I became convinced that I should die happier if I should do all that it is possible for me to do to promote the entrance of our Government into the League of Nations, than if I continued to study applications for writs of certiorari and to devote my time and strength to determining whether a drunken Indian had been deprived of his lands before he died or whether the digging of a ditch in Iowa was *constitutional* or not. The triviality of more than half of the work I was doing became insupportable to me."

WILLIAM RUFUS DAY (1849–1923)

Day took a bachelor's degree at the University of Michigan and two years after graduation entered practice at Canton, in his native state of Ohio. Like so many men of his generation, he did not take a law degree. Soon after he settled at Canton, Day formed the friendship with William McKinley which was to have a profound influence on his career. Day was McKinley's legal and political adviser. He declined the office of Attorney General when McKinley became President, but soon came to serve him as first assistant to an ailing Secretary of State, John Sherman, briefly as Secretary of State himself, and finally as chairman of the United States Commission for the negotiation of peace with Spain. In 1899 Day succeeded William Howard Taft as judge of the United States Court of Appeals for the Sixth Circuit, and in 1903 was promoted by President Theodore Roosevelt from that fertile mother of Justices to the Supreme Court. He retired in ill health in 1922. As is so often — most often — the case, the course he steered on the Court cannot fairly be characterized in a word or a sentence; but he was more likely to agree with a Van Devanter or a White than with Holmes or Brandeis. He was a man of lively temperament, and small in stature. Having in mind one of Day's sons, who was a six-footer, Holmes once remarked: "A block off the old chip."

FELIX FRANKFURTER (1882–   )

Mr. Justice Frankfurter was born in Vienna, attended the New York City public schools, including the City College, and took his LL.B. at the Harvard Law School. After service under Henry L. Stimson in the office of the United States Attorney in New York and in the War Department, he returned to the Law School as a member of its faculty, remaining there, with an interruption for wartime government service and another for a year at Oxford, until his appointment to the Supreme Court by President Roosevelt in 1939. Among his books are: *The Case of Sacco and Vanzetti* (1927); *The Public and Its Government* (1930); *Law and Politics* (Archibald MacLeish and Edward F. Prichard eds., 1939); and *Of Law and Men* (Philip Elman ed., 1956).

OLIVER WENDELL HOLMES (1841–1935)

Son and namesake of the Autocrat of the Breakfast-Table, Holmes was a member of the Harvard College class of 1861. Soon after graduation, he went south with a Massachusetts regiment to join the Army of the Potomac. Three times wounded, he was mustered out in the summer of 1864. After taking a degree at the Harvard Law School, Holmes entered practice, which he was able to combine with considerable activity as a legal scholar. Holmes published his epoch-making book, *The Common Law* (1881), before he was forty. Shortly thereafter, he accepted an appointment to the faculty of the Harvard Law School, but a few months later withdrew to become Associate Justice of the Supreme Judicial Court of Massachusetts. He sat on that court for nearly twenty years, from 1883 until his appointment by President Theodore Roosevelt to the Supreme Court of the United States. During the last three years of his tenure in Massachusetts, Holmes was Chief Justice. He began his service in Washington in December 1902, and retired in January 1932. Three years later, at the age of ninety-four, Holmes died. He was, of course, one of the towering figures of his time, a many-colored Renaissance Man not to be enclosed within the conventional boundaries of the legal profession or of any other discipline he might have chosen. It has been remarked that no other man of comparable intellect and spirit has been a judge in the United States, or for that matter among English-speaking peoples.

CHARLES EVANS HUGHES (1862–1948)

For Hughes, as for Taft, the Chief Justiceship of the United States was the crowning office in a singular career of public service. The son of an immigrant Welsh Baptist preacher, Hughes was born in Glens Falls, New York. After graduation from Brown University and Columbia Law School, he commenced practice in New York City. Hughes achieved great prominence in the state in 1905 as the result of an investigation of insurance companies, which he conducted as counsel to a legislative committee. He was elected Governor the following year and reëlected in 1908, remaining in office until October 1910, when he took his seat as Associate Justice of the Supreme Court of the United States by appointment of President Taft.

TENURES OF JUSTICES WHO SAT WITH BRANDEIS

WHITE, C.J.
Seated
March 12, 1894
Dec. 19, 1910
(as C.J.)
Died
May 19, 1921

MCKENNA
Seated
Jan. 26, 1898

HOLMES
Seated
Dec. 8, 1902

DAY
Sworn In
March 2, 1903

VAN DEVANTER
Seated
Jan. 3, 1911

PITNEY
Seated
March 18, 1912

MCREYNOLDS
Seated
Oct. 12, 1914

BRANDEIS
Seated
June 12, 1916

CLARKE
Seated
Oct. 9, 1916

Resigned
Sept. 18, 1922

SUTHERLAND
Seated
Oct. 2, 1922

Retired
Dec. 31, 1922

SANFORD
Seated
Feb. 19, 1923

Retired
Nov. 18, 1922

BUTLER
Seated
Jan. 2, 1923

TAFT, C.J.
Seated
Oct. 6, 1921

Retired
Jan. 5, 1925

STONE
Seated
March 2, 1925

Absent after
Dec. 9, 1929
Resigned
Feb. 3, 1930

HUGHES, C.J.
Seated
Feb. 24, 1930

Died
March 8, 1930

Retired
Feb. 25, 1957

Retired
Jan. 18, 1938

REED
Seated
Jan. 31, 1938

Retired
Feb. 13, 1939

Retired
Feb. 1, 1941

Resigned
July 31, 1945

ROBERTS
Seated
June 2, 1930

Retired
June 2, 1937

BLACK
Seated
Oct. 4, 1937

Died
Nov. 16, 1939

Retired
Jan. 12, 1932

CARDOZO
Seated
March 14, 1932

Absent after
Dec. 10, 1937

Died
July 9, 1938

FRANKFURTER
Seated
Jan. 30, 1939

Died
April 22, 1946

Retired
July 1, 1941

Hughes left the Court in the summer of 1916 to submit — with reluctance and misgivings — to one of the very few genuine drafts of a presidential candidate known to American politics. After his defeat by Woodrow Wilson, Hughes returned to the Bar and was soon immersed in a large corporate practice. As for other leaders of the Bar, private practice for Hughes did not exclude the assumption of certain public responsibilities. He undertook to protest the expulsion of five Socialist members of the New York Legislature in 1920, and he argued a case in the Supreme Court for the United Mine Workers. In 1921 he became President Harding's Secretary of State and carried on for President Coolidge, resigning in 1925. Hughes once more resumed practice in New York, but in 1928 he accepted an appointment as Judge of the Permanent Court of International Justice. Two years later, President Hoover brought him to the Chief Justiceship. He retired in 1941 at the age of seventy-nine. Hughes led the Court, as not all Chief Justices have done. He invested with the authority of his own person the uncertain perquisites of the office of *primus inter pares*, and he did it at a time of crisis, when even the center of the storm could not remain quiet.

JOSEPH McKENNA (1843–1926)

McKenna was born in Philadelphia and was taken to California as a boy. He attended Catholic seminaries intending to enter the priesthood, but turned to law after graduation from Benicia Collegiate Institute. McKenna served four terms in the House, becoming a friend of William McKinley's. President Benjamin Harrison named him to the United States Circuit Court of Appeals for the Ninth Circuit in 1892. Five years later McKenna resigned to become McKinley's Attorney General, an office which he retained only a few months. By President McKinley's further appointment, he was seated on the Supreme Court in January 1898. McKenna retired in 1925 and died the following year. A little, bearded, birdlike man, McKenna had occasional flashes of insight into the nature of the new social and economic problems that came, more and more during his tenure, to be at the core of constitutional issues; but he was just as capable of having no insights.

JAMES CLARK McREYNOLDS (1862–1946)

President Wilson took McReynolds for his Attorney General in 1913, although he did not know him, presumably because McReynolds was a Southern Democrat with an established reputation as a trust-buster. McReynolds, a Kentuckian, was educated at Vanderbilt University and at the University of Virginia Law School and practiced successfully in Nashville, Tennessee, until he was called in 1903 to serve a Republican administration as Assistant Attorney General in charge of enforcement of the Sherman Anti-Trust Act. For four years McReynolds conducted some celebrated prosecutions under that Act. Then he moved to New York to resume practice. He was in Wilson's cabinet for little more than a year before he came to the Supreme Court, by Wilson's appointment, in October 1914. And there he remained, an American primitive, resisting all or nearly all that was not as he had known it, until his retirement in 1941. The least, but also the most, that can be said of his performance was said by Solicitor General Philip B.

Perlman in the course of the Court's proceedings in McReynolds' memory: "It was not James Clark McReynolds who changed. It was the times, the country, the prevailing constitutional views and the Supreme Court that changed." To this may be added that McReynolds was a man of numerous and abrasive personal idiosyncrasies.

MAHLON PITNEY (1858–1924)

Pitney, the son of a judge and himself a member of the state and federal judiciaries through the largest part of his career, was born in Morristown, New Jersey. Following graduation from Princeton (then the College of New Jersey), he read law and entered practice in his native city. Active in Republican politics, he served in the state Senate and in the national House. In 1901 he was appointed to the New Jersey Supreme Court. When President Taft promoted him to the Supreme Court of the United States in 1912, Pitney had been on the Bench continuously for upwards of ten years, the last four as Chancellor of New Jersey. Though only sixty-four, he retired in ill health in December 1922. "He had not wings," Holmes said of him. "And why, oh why," Holmes complained in a letter to Laski, "must Mr. Justice Pitney ask questions which even to a callow youth like myself betray a dubious familiarity with economics?" But, as Holmes and Brandeis both recognized, Pitney had rare intellectual honesty and, within his limitations, the capacity to rise or be helped to rise above his intellectual and emotional beginnings.

STANLEY FORMAN REED (1884–   )

Mr. Justice Reed was educated at Kentucky Wesleyan College, at Yale, and at the Law Schools of the University of Virginia and of Columbia University. In 1929, President Hoover called him from practice in Maysville, Kentucky, to be General Counsel to the Federal Farm Board. He moved to a similar position with the Reconstruction Finance Corporation in 1932 and three years later became Solicitor General of the United States. In that capacity, he argued for the government many of the important New Deal cases. He was President Roosevelt's second appointment to the Supreme Court, taking his seat in January 1938. He retired in February 1957.

OWEN JOSEPHUS ROBERTS (1875–1955)

Born in Philadelphia, Roberts was educated at the University of Pennsylvania and at its Law School. Following graduation in 1898, he entered upon what was to become the large and varied practice of a leader of the Bar. Until 1919, Roberts found it possible to combine this practice with regular teaching at his Law School. In 1924 he was retained as a Special Counsel for the United States to prosecute cases arising out of the Teapot Dome scandal. He was still involved in aspects of this litigation when President Hoover appointed him to the Supreme Court in 1930. Roberts resigned in July 1945. In 1948 he returned to the Pennsylvania Law School as Dean, and in 1951 he gave the Holmes Lectures at Harvard Law School, which are published as *The Court and the Constitution* (1951). It fell to Roberts, on a Court in crisis in the thirties, to be swing man between wings popularly identified as rigidly conservative and rigidly liberal. In 1937, it was

Roberts who, in the words of the current witticism, made the switch in time that saved nine. This switch in a celebrated case was often ascribed to ordinary if shrewd political motives. It has since been made clear that while Roberts' change of position may have demonstrated his limitations — those of an able but narrow practitioner — it sprang from no ulterior, "temporal" purpose.

EDWARD TERRY SANFORD (1865–1930)

When President Harding raised him to the Supreme Court in 1923, Sanford had been a United States District Judge for fifteen years, having been appointed by President Theodore Roosevelt in 1908 after a year's tenure as an Assistant Attorney General of the United States. Sanford was born in Knoxville, Tennessee, and was educated at the University of Tennessee, at Harvard, and at Harvard Law School. He served on the Supreme Court until his death in 1930. "Mr. Justice Sanford," Thomas Reed Powell once remarked, "had both a deference toward government and a deference toward Mr. Chief Justice Taft, and these two inclinations were not always harmonious."

HARLAN FISKE STONE (1872–1946)

Stone, President Roosevelt's choice as twelfth Chief Justice of the United States, had been introduced to the national scene by President Coolidge, who brought the former law-school dean from a partnership in a large Wall Street law firm to the Attorney Generalship to clean up after Harry Daugherty and the Teapot Dome. Stone, a native of New Hampshire, was educated at Amherst and Columbia Law School. Through most of his private career, he combined teaching at his Law School with practice. He was Dean from 1910 to 1923. His incumbency as Attorney General was not prolonged; Coolidge in 1925 raised him to the Supreme Court. Stone became Chief Justice upon Hughes' retirement in 1941. He was stricken in open court just after delivering a dissenting opinion on April 22, 1946, and he died that evening. In the late twenties and in the thirties, Stone aligned himself fairly consistently with Holmes and Brandeis and then with Brandeis and Cardozo, and he lived to participate in the vindication of many of their views. It is generally recognized that Stone lacked as Chief Justice the qualities which distinguished his predecessor. But it also seems certain, on the basis of his entire period of service, that Stone will remain one of the major constructive figures in the Court's history.

GEORGE SUTHERLAND (1862–1942)

Born in England, Sutherland was raised in Utah and educated at Brigham Young Academy (now University) and briefly at Michigan Law School, where he took no degree. Practice in Utah brought Sutherland to local prominence, and in 1900 he was elected to the House of Representatives. In 1904 he won a seat in the Senate and remained there until his defeat in a race for a third term in 1916. The same year saw his election to the presidency of the American Bar Association and his establishment in practice in

Washington. Nor did Sutherland quit Republican politics. He was active in 1920 in securing the nomination of his old Senate friend, Warren G. Harding. Sutherland took his seat on the Supreme Court, by appointment of President Harding, in 1922. He retired, together with the era of which he was the most articulate representative, in 1938. Sutherland, Van Devanter, McReynolds, and Butler were a unit. The Four Horsemen, they were called; and there was a fifth — Herbert Spencer and his *Social Statics*. It may be, indeed it seems quite likely, that their intellectual leader was Van Devanter. But Sutherland had a fluent pen, and it is not unfair to think of him as their spokesman.

WILLIAM HOWARD TAFT (1857–1930)

The twenty-seventh President and tenth Chief Justice of the United States (and the only man ever to hold both offices) was born in Cincinnati and was educated at Yale and the Cincinnati Law School. Before he was thirty, this scion of a prominent family was a judge of the Superior Court of Ohio, and three years later he was Solicitor General of the United States. In 1892 he began an eight-year tenure as a judge of the United States Circuit Court of Appeals for the Sixth Circuit. During this period, Taft was often mentioned for vacancies on the Supreme Court; and he himself looked hopefully to a place on that Bench. President McKinley, however, named a reluctant Judge Taft principal officer of the United States Philippine Commission in 1900; shortly thereafter Taft became the first civilian governor of the Islands. From this position, Theodore Roosevelt called him to his cabinet as Secretary of War in 1904. In the meantime Roosevelt had offered, and Taft, on account of the work he felt was unfinished in the Islands, had declined, the coveted place on the Supreme Court. In 1908 Taft ran as his friend Roosevelt's chosen successor for the Presidency. In this highest office Taft was, for the first time in his public career, less than a success, and he was of course beaten in 1912. He retired to a professorship of law at Yale, and, at last, was appointed Chief Justice by Harding in 1921. He became ill and was absent from the Court after December 9, 1929, and died a few months later. Taft's values were very much those of his close and esteemed friend, Van Devanter, and of McReynolds and Sutherland and Butler. Yet he was capable of striking out constructively on his own. He took a broad view of the federal power over commerce, and he wrote a notable dissent in favor of upholding a minimum-wage statute. As Chief Justice, Taft was a prime mover in speeding the flow of litigation through the federal court system and in lightening the burden of cases for the Supreme Court itself.

WILLIS VAN DEVANTER (1859–1941)

Born in Indiana and educated at DePauw University and at Cincinnati Law School, Van Devanter moved to Cheyenne, Wyoming, in 1884. Here he practiced law and took part in politics. He served briefly as Chief Justice of the territorial Supreme Court and as first Chief Justice of the new state. Having emerged into national Republican politics, he held office for some years under President McKinley as Assistant to the Attorney General of the United States, in charge of legal matters in the Department of the Interior.

In 1903 Theodore Roosevelt appointed Van Devanter judge of the United States Circuit Court of Appeals for the Eighth Circuit. Seven years later, President Taft raised him to the Supreme Court. Van Devanter retired in 1937, making way for the first of President F. D. Roosevelt's appointments. Van Devanter's outlook was formed on the last frontier, among men who, as Chief Justice Stone remarked in paying tribute to his memory, held to "the philosophy that that government governs best which governs least, a philosophy not without its effect upon Justice Van Devanter's appraisal of the functions of government under the restraints of a written constitution." Others on the Court of Van Devanter's time spoke more often and more loudly for this philosophy and for the doctrines which made of it, for a day, constitutional law. But there is much testimony that this able and subtle student, who had also the qualities of a diplomatist, wielded a decisive influence. He wrote slowly and with difficulty. But he spoke authoritatively and lucidly in conference, and he labored indefatigably.

EDWARD DOUGLASS WHITE (1845–1921)

White, whose appointment as Chief Justice by President Taft in 1910 was deemed quite a gesture in binding up the remaining wounds of civil war, was born in Louisiana and enlisted in the Confederate army at the age of sixteen. He had been educated in Jesuit colleges before the war. After he was mustered out he read law, and then proceeded to combine practice with Democratic politics. Following a brief judicial career on the Supreme Court of Louisiana, White was elected United States Senator in 1890. In 1894 he took his seat as Associate Justice of the Supreme Court by appointment of President Cleveland. It was from this position that Taft raised White to the Chief Justiceship, which he retained until his death in 1921. His Civil War experience, it has been remarked, inclined White perhaps to a strongly national view in Commerce Clause matters. His course otherwise is not unjustly characterized as erratic, and his opaque style yields few clues to a coherent philosophy. He was a big, powerful man, the very picture of a Chief Justice; but he made no great mark as a leader of the Court.

Notes

I. *Atherton Mills v. Johnston*

1. See Raymond G. Fuller, *Child Labor and the Constitution* (1923).
2. Act of September 1, 1916, 39 Stat. 675.
3. 247 U.S. 251 (1918).
4. 40 Stat. 1138.
5. 259 U.S. 20 (1922).
6. See Fair Labor Standards Act of 1938, 52 Stat. 1060.
7. 259 U.S. 13 (1922).
8. 297 U.S. 288, 341 (1936).
9. 297 U.S. at 346.
10. 259 U.S. at 15.
11. See Pennsylvania v. West Virginia, 262 U.S. 553, 611 (1923) (dissent); Chastelton Corp. v. Sinclair, 264 U.S. 543, 550 (1923) (dissent).
12. See United States v. Johnson, 319 U.S. 302, 305 (1943); Coffman v. Breeze Corp., 323 U.S. 316, 324 (1945); C.I.O. v. McAdory, 325 U.S. 472, 475 (1945).
13. 239 U.S. 33 (1915).
14. See Alpheus Thomas Mason, *Brandeis — A Free Man's Life* 558 (1946).
15. 249 U.S. 86 (1919).
16. 276 U.S. 332 (1928).
17. United States v. Constantine, 296 U.S. 287, 297 (1935).
18. United States v. Butler, 297 U.S. 1, 78 (1936).
19. Sonzinsky v. United States, 300 U.S. 506 (1937).
20. United States v. Constantine, 296 U.S. 287, 298–99 (1935). The quotations in the text omit citations.
21. 274 U.S. 357, 372 (1927) (concurring).
22. Brandeis-Frankfurter Conversations, manuscript in the Library of Harvard Law School.
23. 195 U.S. 27 (1904).
24. United States v. Doremus, 249 U.S. 86 (1919).
25. Brandeis-Frankfurter Conversations, manuscript in the Library of Harvard Law School.
26. Brief for the United States as Amicus Curiae, No. 16, at 4, Atherton Mills v. Johnston, 259 U.S. 13 (1922).
27. 259 U.S. 44, 72 (1922).
28. United States v. Darby, 312 U.S. 100 (1941).
29. United States v. Kahriger, 345 U.S. 22, 37, 38 (1953). But cf. United States v. Sanchez, 340 U.S. 42 (1950) (federal marijuana tax unanimously upheld).
30. Milwaukee Publishing Co. v. Burleson, 255 U.S. 407, 417, 433 (1921).

II. *St. Louis, Iron Mountain & Southern Ry. v. Starbird*

1. 243 U.S. 592 (1917).
2. 34 Stat. 584 (1906); see Adams Express Co. v. Croninger, 226 U.S. 491 (1913).
3. 243 U.S. at 607.
4. 18 How. 511, 515 (1856).
5. See Motion of Defendant in Error to Dismiss or Affirm, and Brief of Argu-

ment in Support Thereof, No. 275, at 2–3, St. Louis, Iron Mountain & Southern Ry. v. Starbird, 243 U.S. 592 (1917).

6. See Brief of Defendant in Error, No. 275, at 39 *et seq.*, St. Louis, Iron Mountain and Southern Ry. v. Starbird, 243 U.S. 592 (1917).

7. Gooch v. Oregon Short Line, 258 U.S. 22 (1922).

8. Brandeis-Frankfurter Conversations, manuscript in the Library of Harvard Law School.

9. See, *e.g.*, Dahnke-Walker Co. v. Bondurant, 257 U.S. 282, 293 (1921) (dissenting); King Manufacturing Co. v. Augusta, 277 U.S. 100, 115 (1928) (dissenting).

10. See, *e.g.*, American Surety Co. v. Baldwin, 287 U.S. 156 (1932); Wuchter v. Pizzutti, 276 U.S. 13, 25 (1928) (dissenting); Whitney v. California, 274 U.S. 357, 372 (1927) (concurring); Missouri, Kansas and Texas Ry. v. Sealy, 248 U.S. 363 (1919); see also Southern Ry. v. Kentucky, 274 U.S. 76, 86 (1927) (dissenting).

11. Louisville & Nashville R.R. v. United States, 242 U.S. 60 (1916); Detroit United Ry. v. Michigan, 242 U.S. 238 (1916); Owensboro v. Owensboro Water Works Co., 243 U.S. 166 (1917).

12. The Carmack Amendment had itself been amended to provide that in the event damage to freight was attributable to the carrier's negligence or delay, "no notice of claim . . . shall be required as a condition precedent to recovery." First Cummins Amendment, so-called, 38 State. 1197 (1915). It is, in any event, probable that Brandeis would have conceded that the *Starbird* case was correctly decided on the merits. In an opinion of his own at the following term, he went somewhat out of his way to cite Day's opinion in this case. Missouri, Kansas and Texas Ry. v. Ward, 244 U.S. 383, 386 (1917).

13. New York Central R.R. v. Winfield, 244 U.S. 147, 154 (1917).

14. Adams v. Tanner, 244 U.S. 590, 597 (1917).

15. 96 U.S. 1 (1877).

16. See Felix Frankfurter, *The Commerce Clause under Marshall, Taney and Waite* 106 (1937).

17. See Pullman Co. v. Kansas, 216 U.S. 56 (1910).

18. See Frankfurter, *op. cit. supra* at 102, 107.

19. 270 U.S. 438 (1926).

20. See Alfred McCormack, "A Law Clerk's Recollections," 46 *Columb. L. Rev.* 710, 715–16 (1946); see also Alpheus Thomas Mason, *Harlan Fiske Stone; Pillar of the Law* 219–20 (1956). Stone's memorandum is quoted from a manuscript in the Library of Harvard Law School.

21. 248 U.S. 525 (1919).

22. Wright v. Central of Georgia Ry., 236 U.S. 674 (1915).

23. Holmes Papers, Library of Harvard Law School.

24. 247 U.S. 105 (1918).

25. Holmes Papers, Library of Harvard Law School.

26. See Erie R.R. v. Stone, 244 U.S. 332, 335 (1917); Southern Pacific Co. v. Stewart, 248 U.S. 446, 449 (1919); Baltimore & Ohio R.R. v. Leach, 249 U.S. 217, 218 (1919).

27. See New York *ex rel.* Bryant v. Zimmerman, 278 U.S. 63, 67 (1928); Illinois Steel Co. v. Baltimore & Ohio R.R., 320 U.S. 508, 511 (1944).

28. 252 U.S. 341 (1920).

29. Brandeis Papers, Library of Harvard Law School.

III. *Strathearn S.S. Co. v. Dillon*

1. Augustus N. Hand to Brandeis, May 28, 1927; November 21, 1931. Manuscripts in the Library of the Law School of the University of Louisville.

2. 252 U.S. 348 (1920).

3. 248 U.S. 185 (1918).

4. See Note, 7 *Miami L.Q.* 400 (1953).

5. See A.M. Bickel, "The Doctrine of Forum Non Conveniens as Applied in the Federal Courts in Matters of Admiralty," 35 *Corn. L.Q.* 12, 19–26 (1949).

6. 248 U.S. at 195.

7. 248 U.S. at 201, 202.

"Underlying the Court's reasoning is the belief that the language of the 1947 amendment is so clear that it would require creative reconstruction [to apply it in a certain fashion]. On more than one occasion, but evidently not frequently enough, Judge Learned Hand has warned against restricting the meaning of a statute to the meaning of its 'plain' words. 'There is no surer way to misread any document than to read it literally . . . .' Of course one begins with the words of a statute to ascertain its meaning, but one does not end with them. The notion that the plain meaning of the words of a statute defines the meaning of the statute reminds one of T. H. Huxley's gay observation that at times 'a theory survives long after its brains are knocked out.'" Frankfurter, J., dissenting in Massachusetts Bonding & Ins. Co. v. United States, 77 S. Ct. 186 (1956).

8. Neilson v. Rhine Shipping Co., 248 U.S. 205, 213 (1918).

9. Dillon v. Strathearn S.S. Co., 248 U.S. 182 (1918).

10. Iowa v. Slimmer, 248 U.S. 115, decided December 9, 1918; Tempel v. United States, 248 U.S. 121, decided December 9, 1918; United States v. Spearin, 248 U.S. 132, decided December 9, 1918; Luckenbach v. W. J. McCahan Sugar Refining Co., 248 U.S. 139, decided December 9, 1918; MacMath v. United States, 248 U.S. 151, decided December 9, 1918.

11. Iowa v. Slimmer, *supra* n. 10, argued April 15, 1918.

12. Tempel v. United States, *supra* n. 10.

13. 248 U.S. 215, 248, argued May 2, 3, 1918, decided December 23, 1918.

14. Turner v. United States, 248 U.S. 354, argued November 13, 14, 1918, decided January 7, 1919. See also these Brandeis opinions: Chicago, Rock Island & Pacific Ry. v. Maucher, 248 U.S. 359, argued December 17, 18, 1918, decided January 7, 1919; Missouri, Kansas & Texas Ry. v. Sealy, 248 U.S. 363, argued December 18, 1918, decided January 7, 1919; Merchants Exchange v. Missouri, 248 U.S. 365, argued December 19, 1918, decided January 7, 1919.

15. See Mason, *Brandeis — A Free Man's Life*, 353, 365–76 (1946).

16. See Belle Case La Follette and Fola La Follette, 1 *Robert M. La Follette*, 336–37, 346–47, 475 (1953).

17. The quotations are derived from an article by Robert M. La Follette published in April 1915, from which excerpts are given in the La Follette biography, *op. cit. supra* n. 16, at 521–22. See also *id.* at 500, 520–36; *A Symposium on Andrew Furuseth* (Silas B. Axtell ed., n.d.); Paul S. Taylor, *The Sailors' Union of the Pacific* (1923); Arthur S. Link, *Woodrow Wilson and the Progressive Era* 61–63 (1954). For indication of Furuseth's friendship with Brandeis, see letter from Mae E. Waggaman, Furuseth's secretary, to Silas B. Axtell, in *A Symposium on Andrew Furuseth* at 35–37. See also Paul A. Freund, "Mr. Justice Brandeis," in *Mr. Justice* 97, 101 (Dunham and Kurland ed. 1956).

18. See J. Francis Paschal, *Mr. Justice Sutherland* 71–72 (1951).

19. Petition for Writ of Certiorari and Brief in Support of Petition, No. 392, at 11, Sandberg v. McDonald, 248 U.S. 185 (1918).

20. 248 U.S. at 197.

21. 252 U.S. 348, 354–55 (1920).

22. Jackson v. S.S. Archimedes, 275 U.S. 463 (1928).

23. See, *e.g.*, Charles P. Curtis, "A Better Theory of Legal Interpretation," 3 *Vand. L. Rev.* 407 (1950); Felix Frankfurter, "Some Reflections on the Reading of Statutes," 47 *Colum. L. Rev.* 527, 538–39 (1947); Max Radin, "Statutory In-

terpretation," 43 *Harv. L. Rev.* 863 (1930); but cf. James M. Landis, "A Note on 'Statutory Interpretation,' " 43 *Harv. L. Rev.* 886 (1930).

24. See Robert H. Jackson, "The Meaning of Statutes: What Congress Says or What the Court Says," 34 *A.B.A.J.* 535 (1948); 8 *F.R.D.* 121 (1949).

25. 41 Stat. 1007 (1920).

26. Lauritzen v. Larsen, 345 U.S. 571 (1953).

27. 345 U.S. at 593.

IV. *Arizona Employers' Liability Cases*

1. See Thomas Reed Powell, "Collective Bargaining before the Supreme Court," 33 *Pol. Sci. Q.* 396, 407 (1918).

2. See *Hearings before the Committee on Interstate Commerce of the Senate pursuant to S. Res. 98*, 62nd Cong., Dec. 1911, Part XVI, at 1166. See also Brandeis' dissenting opinion in Truax v. Corrigan, 257 U.S. 312, 354, 368 (1921).

3. 208 U.S. 412 (1908).

4. Bunting v. Oregon, 243 U.S. 426 (1917). See also Radice v. New York, 264 U.S. 292 (1924) (women's night work).

5. Adkins v. Children's Hospital, 261 U.S. 525 (1923); see Thomas Reed Powell, "The Judiciality of Minimum-Wage Legislation," 37 *Harv. L. Rev.* 545 (1924); cf. Wilson v. New, 243 U.S. 332 (1917) (interstate railroad wages).

6. See Brandeis' dissent in New York Central R.R. v. Winfield, 244 U.S. 147, 154 (1917).

7. Compare The Employers' Liability Cases, 207 U.S. 463 (1908), with Second Employers' Liability Cases, 223 U.S. 1 (1912).

8. 250 U.S. 400 (1919).

9. 243 U.S. 188 (1917).

10. 243 U.S. at 196–97, 201, 202, 203, 205.

11. Hawkins v. Bleakly, 243 U.S. 210 (1917).

12. Mountain Timber Co. v. Washington, 243 U.S. 219 (1917).

13. See Thomas Reed Powell, "The Workmen's Compensation Cases," 32 *Pol. Sci. Q.* 542, 565 (1917).

14. 250 U.S. at 433.

15. See 2 *Holmes-Pollock Letters* 15 (M. DeW. Howe ed. 1941).

16. Holmes Papers, Library of Harvard Law School.

17. Compare Coppage v. Kansas, 236 U.S. 1 (1915), with Wilson v. New, 243 U.S. 332 (1917).

18. Brandeis-Frankfurter Conversations, manuscript in the Library of Harvard Law School.

19. *Ibid.*

20. See 2 *Holmes-Pollock Letters* 113, 150.

21. 236 U.S. 1 (1915); see Adair v. United States, 208 U.S. 161 (1908) (opinion to the same effect by Justice Harlan the Elder).

22. 245 U.S. 229 (1917).

23. 254 U.S. 443 (1921); 38 Stat. 730 (1914).

24. See David M. Levitan, "Mahlon Pitney — Labor Judge," 40 *Va. L. Rev.* 733 (1954).

25. Brandeis-Frankfurter Conversations, manuscript in the Library of Harvard Law School.

26. 257 U.S. 312 (1921).

27. Brandeis Papers, Library of Harvard Law School.

28. See 1 *Holmes-Laski Letters* 389 (M. DeW. Howe ed. 1953).

29. See 2 *Holmes-Pollock Letters* 22.

30. Brandeis-Frankfurter Conversations, manuscript in the Library of Harvard Law School.

31. Ward & Gow v. Krinsky, 259 U.S. 503 (1922); Madera Co. v. Industrial

Commission of California, 262 U.S. 499 (1923); Cudahy Co. v. Parramore, 263 U.S. 418 (1923).

32. See Sandberg v. McDonald, 248 U.S. 185, 202 (1918).

33. 250 U.S. at 434, 435, 436, 438, 439.

34. 234 U.S. 548 (1914); 34 Stat. 584 (1906).

35. Brandeis-Frankfurter Conversations, manuscript in the Library of Harvard Law School.

36. See, *e.g.*, German Alliance Insurance Co. v. Kansas, 233 U.S. 389 (1914); Walls v. Midland Carbon Co., 254 U.S. 300 (1920).

37. 250 U.S. at 451, 452.

38. See 64 Ohio L. Bull. 335, 337 (1919).

39. Morehead v. New York *ex rel.* Tipaldo, 298 U.S. 587, 635 (1936). This case was overruled within the year in West Coast Hotel Co. v. Parrish, 300 U.S. 379 (1937).

V. *United Mine Workers v. Coronado Co.*

1. See Title III, Transportation Act, 1920, 41 Stat. 456, 469; Railway Labor Act, 44 Stat. 577 (1926).

2. See Archibald Cox, *Cases on Labor Law* 20 (1954).

3. 26 Stat. 209 (1890). Federal courts for a time derived authority also from the Interstate Commerce Act, 24 Stat. 379 (1887); see *In re* Debs, 158 U.S. 564 (1895).

4. See Edward Berman, *Labor and the Sherman Act* 3–98 (1930).

5. 208 U.S. 274 (1908).

6. 245 U.S. 229 (1917).

7. 208 U.S. at 284–85.

8. 208 U.S. at 304–05.

9. American Banana Co. v. United Fruit Co., 213 U.S. 347, 354 (1909).

10. See, *e.g.*, Dunbar, "Government by Injunction," 13 *Law Quarterly Rev.* 347 (1897). Compare the later remarks in the same vein by Senator George Warton Pepper in 49 *A.B.A. Rep.* 174 (1924).

11. Truax v. Corrigan, 257 U.S. 312, 368 (1921).

12. See, *e.g.*, Gregory, "Government by Injunction," 11 *Harv. L. Rev.* 487 (1898); Fauntleroy, "Government by Injunction," 69 *Central L. J.* (1909). See *supra* n. 10. See Felix Frankfurter and Nathan Greene, *The Labor Injunction* 141 (1930).

13. 38 Stat. 730 (1914).

14. Quoted from the *American Federationist* in Frankfurter and Greene, *The Labor Injunction* 143.

15. 254 U.S. 443 (1921).

16. American Steel Foundries v. Tri-City Central Trades Council, 257 U.S. 184 (1921).

17. 274 U.S. 37 (1927).

18. See Frankfurter and Greene, *The Labor Injunction* 197–98.

19. 47 Stat. 70 (1932).

20. 257 U.S. 312 (1921); see also Adair v. United States, 208 U.S. 161 (1908); Coppage v. Kansas, 236 U.S. 1 (1915).

21. See Senn v. Tile Layers Protective Union, 301 U.S. 468 (1937); see also Lauf v. E. G. Shinner & Co., 303 U.S. 323, 330 (1938).

22. National Labor Relations Board v. Jones & Laughlin Steel Corp., 301 U.S. 1 (1937).

23. Apex Hosiery Co. v. Leader, 310 U.S. 469 (1940).

24. United States v. Hutcheson, 312 U.S. 219 (1940); see Charles O. Gregory, *Labor and the Law* 253–88 (1949); Nathaniel Nathanson and Willard Wirtz,

"The Hutcheson Case: Another View," 36 *Ill. L. Rev.* 41 (1941); Frank C. Newman, "Comment," 29 *Calif. L. Rev.* 399 (1941).

25. Compare Allen Bradley Co. v. Local Union No. 3, 325 U.S. 797 (1945), with Hunt v. Crumboch, 325 U.S. 821 (1945); cf. United States v. Brims, 272 U.S. 549 (1926).

26. See Giboney v. Empire Storage & Ice Co., 336 U.S. 490 (1949); International Brotherhood of Teamsters, Chauffeurs, Warehousemen and Helpers, Local 309 v. Hanke, 339 U.S. 470 (1950). Of course, state action is limited by federal preëmption of most of the field of labor relations, as it touches interstate commerce.

27. United States v. United Mine Workers and John L. Lewis, 330 U.S. 258 (1947).

28. See Labor Management Relations Act, 1947, 61 Stat. 136, Sections 10 (j), 10 (l); 208, 61 Stat. at 146, 149–50, 155–56.

29. 259 U.S. 344 (1922).

30. ". . . In the opinion of the court there is no reason on earth why reasonable men with a due regard for right, and each having due respect and consideration for the other's opinion, should not arrive at a conclusion in this case . . . . Now . . . you are advised that this court is of the opinion that the facts in this case justify you in the conclusion overwhelmingly that it was the policy and therefore the agreement for years of this national organization to prevent mining of nonunion coal for the unlawful purposes named in this complaint that it might not come into competition with union-mined coal . . . . Now, that is the judgment of this court and if it were my duty to decide it, I would decide it here. Now, you are not bound by my opinion. I have a right to give you my judgment, however, you are the sole and exclusive judges of the facts . . . ." Transcript of Record, pp. 3233–34, United Mine Workers v. Coronado Co., 259 U.S. 344 (1922).

31. United Mine Workers v. Coronado Co., 258 F. 829, 847 (1919).

32. See Merlo J. Pusey, 1 *Charles Evans Hughes* 388–89 (1951).

33. Brandeis-Frankfurter Conversations, manuscript in the Library of Harvard Law School.

34. 247 U.S. 251 (1918).

35. Dean Acheson to Alexander M. Bickel, December 7, 1955.

36. *Ibid.*

37. *Ibid.*

38. See, *e.g.*, Port of Seattle v. Oregon R.R., 255 U.S. 56 (1921).

39. See, *e.g.*, Wan v. United States, 266 U.S. 1 (1924), a chilling description of the third degree.

40. See, *e.g.*, International News Service v. Associated Press, 248 U.S. 215, 248 (1918); Pennsylvania v. West Virginia, 262 U.S. 553, 563 (1923).

41. 254 U.S. at 488; cf. Dorchy v. Kansas, 272 U.S. 306 (1926).

42. See Richard Hofstadter, *Social Darwinism in American Thought* 30–66 (rev. ed. 1955).

43. Brandeis-Frankfurter Conversations, manuscript in the Library of Harvard Law School.

44. *Ibid.*

45. *Ibid.*

46. See Henry F. Pringle, 2 *The Life and Times of William Howard Taft* 967 (1939).

47. 259 U.S. at 408; cf. National Labor Relations Board v. Jones & Laughlin, 301 U.S. 1, 39, 40 (1937).

48. See United Brotherhood of Carpenters and Joiners v. United States, 330 U.S. 395 (1947).

49. Cf. Section 303 of the Taft-Hartley Labor Management Relations Act, 1947, 61 Stat. 136, 158.

50. Compare Brandeis' views on the social responsibilties of unions, expressed before his accession to the Bench. See Mason, *Brandeis — A Free Man's Life*

142–43, 294–315 (1946); "Mr. Justice Brandeis, Competition and Smallness: A Dilemma Re-examined," 66 *Yale L. J.* 69, 76–77 (1956). See also Felix Frankfurter, "The Coronado Case," 31 *New Republic* 328 (1922).

51. United Leather Workers v. Herkert, 265 U.S. 457 (1924). Cf. National Association of Window Glass Manufacturers v. United States, 263 U.S. 403 (1923); but cf. United States v. Brims, 272 U.S. 549 (1925).

52. Coronado Co. v. United Mine Workers, 268 U.S. 295 (1925).

53. See Berman, *Labor and the Sherman Act*, 121, 128, 303–04 (1930).

54. See, *e.g.*, National Labor Relations Board v. Jones & Laughlin, 301 U.S. 1, 39, 40 (1937); Santa Cruz Fruit Packing Co. v. National Labor Relations Board, 303 U.S. 453, 465 (1937).

VI. *Sonneborn Bros. v. Cureton*

1. 9 Wheat. 1 (1924).

2. "Our national free intercourse is never in danger of being suddenly stifled by dramatic and sweeping acts of restraint. That would produce its own antidote. Our danger, as the forefathers well knew, is from the aggregate strangling effect of a multiplicity of individually petty and diverse and local regulations . . . .

"I do not suppose the skies will fall if the Court does allow Arkansas to rig up this handy device for policing liquor . . . but in doing so it adds another to the already too numerous and burdensome state restraints of national commerce . . . ." Jackson, J., concurring in Duckworth v. Arkansas, 314 U.S. 390, 401–02 (1941).

3. "When the Supreme Court decides whether an exercise of state police or fiscal power is an unconstitutional regulation of interstate commerce . . . it must form its judgment without the aid of any language in the Constitution . . . . Yet unless the Court in some way settled such disputes there would be recurrent clashing and not a little resulting chaos . . . . The judicial task . . . is for the most part a task of statesman-like umpiring of a game without any explicit rules. The considerations which determine decision are more often an understanding of practical situations, an appraisal of practical needs and a choice between competing policies than they are an interpretation of constitutional phraseology or a knowledge of legal lore." Thomas Reed Powell, "Umpiring the Federal System, 1922–1924," 40 *Pol. Sci. Q.* 101, 101–02 (1925); see also Thomas Reed Powell, "Indirect Encroachment on Federal Authority by the Taxing Powers of the States. VIII," 32 *Harv. L. Rev.* 902, 930 (1919).

4. 262 U.S. 506 (1923).

5. 12 Wheat. 419 (1827).

6. 8 Wall. 123 (1869).

7. See Frankfurter, *The Commerce Clause Under Marshall, Taney and Waite* 37 (1937).

8. 249 U.S. 389 (1919).

9. 252 U.S. 444 (1920).

10. 256 U.S. 642 (1921).

11. 251 U.S. 95 (1919).

12. See Paul J. Hartman, *State Taxation of Interstate Commerce* 107–13 (1953).

13. 258 U.S. 466 (1922).

14. See Foote & Co. v. Maryland, 232 U.S. 494 (1914); but cf. Phipps v. Cleveland Refining Co., 261 U.S. 449 (1923). Brandeis' law clerk, William G. Rice, put up a vigorous argument against this distinction. He noted on a draft of the opinion which had been given to him for comment: "In the Graves case a small charge would be valid despite its being a 'direct burden' on interstate commerce, because it would be held an exercise of the 'police power' — just as state laws regarding prevention of combustion or explosion would be valid. The size

of the charge merely keeps it out of this special exception (according to 'direct burden' language)."

15. 262 U.S. at 522.

16. Brandeis-Frankfurter Conversations, manuscript in the Library of Harvard Law School.

17. After Woodruff v. Parham had, once before, rejected it in state tax cases, the original-package formula had survived, though in a condition of somewhat suspended animation, in cases dealing with regulatory statutes. See Leisy v. Hardin, 135 U.S. 100 (1890), from which Congress promptly extracted the sting by supervening legislation. 26 Stat. 313 (1890); see In re Rahrer, 140 U.S. 545 (1891). See Malcolm P. Sharp, "Movement in Supreme Court Adjudication — A Study in Modified and Overruled Decisions III," 46 *Harv. L. Rev.* 593, 604–10 (1933). For a current attitude toward the distinction between fiscal and regulatory measures, see Freeman v. Hewit, 329 U.S. 249, 253 (1946). But cf. Thomas Reed Powell, "More Ado about Gross Receipts Taxes," 60 *Harv. L. Rev.* 710, 715 (1947).

18. See Thomas Reed Powell, "Contemporary Commerce Clause Controversies over State Taxation," 76 *U. of Pa. L. Rev.* 773, 783–84 (1928); 37 *Harv. L. Rev.* 157 (1923); 33 *Yale L. J.* 321 (1923).

19. See Thomas Reed Powell, "Umpiring the Federal System, 1922–1924," 40 *Pol. Sci. Q.* 101, 114 (1925).

20. See Hooven & Allison Co. v. Evatt, 324 U.S. 652 (1945); Baldwin v. G. A. F. Seelig, Inc., 294 U.S. 511 (1935).

21. See McGoldrick v. Berwind-White Co., 309 U.S. 33 (1940); see also Hart Refineries v. Harmon, 278 U.S. 499 (1929); Minnesota v. Blasius, 290 U.S. 1 (1933); Wiloil Corp. v. Pennsylvania, 294 U.S. 169 (1935); International Harvester Co. v. Department of Treasury, 322 U.S. 340 (1944); Independent Warehouses, Inc. v. Scheele, 331 U.S. 70 (1947).

22. Compare, *e.g.*, Chicago v. Willett Co., 344 U.S. 574 (1953), with Bode v. Barrett, 344 U.S. 583 (1953).

23. 254 U.S. 113, 119–20 (1920).

24. "The tax now under consideration . . . bears no semblance of a property tax, or a franchise tax in the proper sense; nor is it an occupation tax except as it is imposed upon the very carrying on of the business of exporting merchandise. It operates to lay a direct burden upon every transaction in commerce by withholding, for the use of the State, a part of every dollar received in such transactions." 245 U.S. 292, 297 (1917).

25. 245 U.S. at 297–98.

26. Cheney Bros. Co. v. Massachusetts, 246 U.S. 147 (1918); Northwestern Mutual Life Insurance Co. v. Wisconsin, 247 U.S. 132 (1918); U.S. Glue Co. v. Oak Creek, 247 U.S. 321 (1918).

27. Peck & Co. v. Lowe, 247 U.S. 165 (1918); Thames & Mersey Ins. Co. v. United States, 237 U.S. 19 (1915); United States v. Hvoslef, 237 U.S. 1 (1915); Cornell v. Coyne, 192 U.S. 418 (1904); Fairbank v. United States, 181 U.S. 283 (1901); Turpin v. Burgess, 117 U.S. 504 (1886); Pace v. Burgess, 92 U.S. 372 (1876).

28. 31 *Harv. L. Rev.* 321, 572, 721, 932 (1918); 32 *Harv. L. Rev.* 234, 374, 634, 902 (1919).

29. See, *e.g.*, Sprout v. South Bend, 277 U.S. 163 (1928); Interstate Transit Inc. v. Lindsey, 283 U.S. 183 (1931); Pacific Telephone Co. v. Tax Commission, 297 U.S. 403 (1936).

30. See, *e.g.*, State of Washington v. Dawson, 264 U.S. 219, 236 (1923) (dissenting); Jaybird Mining Co. v. Weir, 271 U.S. 609, 619 (1926) (dissenting); Di Santo v. Pennsylvania, 273 U.S. 34, 43 (1927) (dissenting); Burnet v. Coronado Oil & Gas Co., 285 U.S. 393, 407 (1932) (dissenting).

VII. *Stratton v. St. Louis Southwestern Ry.*

1. *Hearings before the Committee on Interstate Commerce of the Senate pursuant to S. Res. 98*, 62d Cong., Dec., 1911, Part XVI, at 1156, 1166, 1174.

2. Brandeis to Paul U. Kellogg, November 7, 1920. Manuscript in the Library of the Law School of the University of Louisville.

3. Bernard Flexner, *Mr. Justice Brandeis and the University of Louisville* 3, 50 (1938).

4. Ray Stannard Baker to Brandeis, November 11, 1931. Manuscript in the Library of the University of Louisville.

5. Brandeis to Harold J. Laski, September 21, 1921. Manuscript in the Library of Yale Law School.

6. Paul A. Freund, "Mr. Justice Brandeis," in *Mr. Justice* 97 (Dunham and Kurland ed. 1956).

7. Whitney v. California, 274 U.S. 357, 375 (1927).

8. Olmstead v. United States, 277 U.S. 438, 479 (1928).

9. As Paul A. Freund has pointed out (see Freund, *op. cit. supra*, n. 6, at p. 97, n. 19), the phrase occurs in Brandeis' testimony before the Interstate Commerce Commission in 1910, when he appeared to argue against an advance in railroad freight rates. S. Doc. 725, 61st Cong., 3d Sess., Vol. 9, p. 5256. Brandeis also used the phrase as the title of Chapter VIII of his *Other People's Money*, published in 1913. The correspondence, in 1934, between Brandeis and his publisher, the Viking Press, as a result of which the title, *The Curse of Bigness*, was chosen, is preserved in the Library of the Law School of the University of Louisville.

10. 285 U.S. 262, 280 (1932).

11. 288 U.S. 517, 541 (1933). For a discussion of these and like cases, see "Mr. Justice Brandeis, Competition and Smallness: A Dilemma Re-examined," 66 *Yale L. J.* 69 (1956).

12. 285 U.S. at 310, 311. Cf. Holmes, J. dissenting in Truax v. Corrigan, 257 U.S. 312, 344 (1921).

13. 288 U.S. at 549, 565, 567, 568–69, 580.

14. See Bank of Augusta v. Earle, 13 Pet. 519, 589 (1839); Paul v. Virginia, 8 Wall. 168 (1869); Gerard C. Henderson, *The Position of Foreign Corporations in American Constitutional Law*, 36–49, 101–11 (1918).

15. See, *e.g.*, Insurance Co. v. Morse, 20 Wall. 445 (1874); Barron v. Burnside, 121 U.S. 186 (1887). For a later case see Terral v. Burke Construction Co., 257 U.S. 529 (1922). See Elcanon Isaacs, "The Federal Protection of Foreign Corporations," 26 *Col. L. Rev.* 263 (1926).

16. See Pensacola Tel. Co. v. Western Union Tel. Co,. 96 U.S. 1 (1877); Crutcher v. Kentucky, 141 U.S. 47 (1891).

17. Western Union Telegraph Co. v. Kansas, 216 U.S. 1 (1910); Pullman Co. v. Kansas, 216 U.S. 56 (1910); Ludwig v. Western Union Telegraph Co., 216 U.S. 146 (1910).

18. 231 U.S. 68 (1913).

19. Compare Looney v. Crane Co., 245 U.S. 178 (1917); International Paper Co. v. Massachusetts, 246 U.S. 135 (1918), with Cheney Bros. Co. v. Massachusetts, 246 U.S. 147 (1918); General Railway Signal Co. v. Virginia, 246 U.S. 500 (1918). See also Western Gas Construction Co. v. Virginia, 276 U.S. 597 (1928). See Thomas Reed Powell, "Indirect Encroachment on Federal Authority by the Taxing Powers of the States. II," 31 *Harv. L. Rev.* 572, 594–618 (1918); Note, 51 *Harv. L. Rev.* 508 (1938).

20. 278 U.S. 460 (1929).

21. 268 U.S. 203 (1925).

22. Compare Memphis Gas Co. v. Stone, 335 U.S. 80 (1948); and Interstate

Oil Pipe Line Co. v. Stone, 337 U.S. 662 (1949), with Spector Motor Service Inc. v. O'Connor, 340 U.S. 602 (1951); and Railway Express Agency, Inc. v. Virginia, 347 U.S. 359 (1954); see Thomas Reed Powell, "Contemporary Commerce Clause Controversies Over State Taxation," 76 *U. of Pa. L. Rev.* 773, 791–93 (1928).

23. 268 U.S. at 218.

24. 266 U.S. 71 (1924).

25. *E.g.*, Cheney Bros. Co. v. Massachusetts, 246 U.S. 147 (1918); General Railway Signal Co. v. Virginia, 246 U.S. 500 (1918).

26. 278 U.S. at 467.

27. Ozark Pipe Line Corp. v. Monier, 266 U.S. 555, 567 (1925); see also Texas Transport Co. v. New Orleans, 264 U.S. 150, 155 (1924).

28. Brandeis Papers, Library of Harvard Law School.

29. 277 U.S. 389 (1928).

30. 277 U.S. at 410.

31. Brandeis Papers, Library of Harvard Law School. The same sort of difficulty cropped up as well in connection with Brandeis' dissent in Liggett Co. v. Lee, 288 U.S. 517, 541 (1933), in which Stone did not join. See Mason, *Harlan Fiske Stone: Pillar of the Law* 349–50 (1956).

32. Brandeis Papers, Library of Harvard Law School.

33. Cf. Kansas City, F.S. & M. Ry. v. Kansas, 240 U.S. 277 (1916); Lusk v. Kansas, 240 U.S. 236 (1916) (opinions by Hughes, J.).

34. Compare Hepburn v. Griswold, 8 Wall. 603 (1870), with The Legal Tender Cases, 12 Wall. 457 (1871). See Charles Fairman, "Mr. Justice Bradley's Appointment to the Supreme Court and The Legal Tender Cases," 54 *Harv. L. Rev.* 977, 1128 (1941). But cf. Baizley Iron Works v. Span, 281 U.S. 222 (1930). This case was argued on January 8, 1930, before Hughes was seated, and decided on April 14, 1930, after Sanford had died. McReynolds wrote for a majority of four. Holmes, Brandeis and Stone dissented. A fortuitous jurisdictional way out is not always available.

35. Stratton v. St. Louis Southwestern Ry., 282 U.S. 10 (1930).

36. Stratton v. St. Louis Southwestern Ry., 284 U.S. 530 (1932).

37. St. Louis Southwestern Ry. v. Stratton, 353 Ill. 273, 187 N.E. 498 (1933); *cert. denied*, 291 U.S. 673 (1934).

38. Railway Express Agency, Inc. v. Virginia, 282 U.S. 440 (1931); see Note, 44 *Harv. L. Rev.* 1111 (1931).

39. 302 U.S. 22 (1937).

40. General Railway Signal Co. v. Virginia, 246 U.S. 500 (1918). See also Western Gas Construction Co. v. Virginia, 276 U.S. 597 (1928).

41. Cf. Lincoln Life Insurance Co. v. Read, 325 U.S. 673 (1945).

42. Brandeis Papers, Library of Harvard Law School.

43. Railway Express Agency, Inc. v. Virginia, 347 U.S. 359, 360 (1954).

44. See, *e.g.*, Underwood Typewriter Co. v. Chamberlain, 254 U.S. 113 (1920); Bass, Ratcliff & Gretton, Ltd. v. State Tax Commission, 266 U.S. 271 (1924).

45. See, *e.g.*, Hump Hairpin Mfg. Co. v. Emmerson, 258 U.S. 290 (1922); Atlantic Lumber Co. v. Commissioner, 298 U.S. 553 (1936); Ford Motor Co. v. Beauchamp, 308 U.S. 331 (1939); International Harvester Co. v. Evatt, 329 U.S. 416 (1947).

46. See, *e.g.*, Cudahy Packing Co. v. Minnesota, 246 U.S. 450 (1918); Pullman Co. v. Richardson, 261 U.S. 330 (1923); see Thomas Reed Powell, *Vagaries and Varieties in Constitutional Interpretation*, 202–04 (1956).

47. See, *e.g.*, Western Live Stock v. Bureau of Internal Revenue, 303 U.S. 250 (1938); Freeman v. Hewit, 329 U.S. 249 (1946); Joseph v. Carter & Weekes Stevedoring Co., 330 U.S. 422 (1947); see Thomas Reed Powell, "More Ado

about Gross Receipts Taxes," 60 *Harv. L. Rev.* 710 (1947); Note, 56 *Yale L. J.* 898 (1947).

48. Alvin Johnson to Brandeis, Nov. 11, 1936. Manuscript in the Library of the Law School of the University of Louisville.

VIII. *Shafer v. Farmers Grain Co.*

1. See Samuel I. Rosenman, *Working with Roosevelt* 153 (1952).

2. Lochner v. New York, 198 U.S. 45 (1905). Cf. Bunting v. Oregon, 243 U.S. 426 (1917); Adkins v. Children's Hospital, 261 U.S. 525 (1923).

3. Holmes to Felix Frankfurter, March 28, 1922. Manuscript in the Library of Harvard Law School.

4. 198 U.S. at 75.

5. See Paul A. Freund, *On Understanding the Supreme Court* 7–22 (1949); Robert Stern, "The Commerce Clause and the National Economy, 1933–1946," 59 *Harv. L. Rev.* 645, 883 (1946).

6. See, *e.g.*, Adams v. Tanner, 244 U.S. 590 (1917); Burns Baking Co. v. Bryan, 264 U.S. 504 (1924); Tyson & Brother v. Banton, 273 U.S. 418 (1927); Louisville Gas Co. v. Coleman, 277 U.S. 32 (1928); Frost v. Corporation Commission, 278 U.S. 515 (1929); Liggett Co. v. Lee, 288 U.S. 517 (1933); Railroad Retirement Board v. Alton R.R., 295 U.S. 330 (1935).

7. See Frankfurter, *The Commerce Clause Under Marshall, Taney and Waite* 76 (1937); see also Powell, *Vagaries and Varieties in Constitutional Interpretation* 84 (1956).

8. *E.g.*, Leisy v. Hardin, 135 U.S. 100 (1890); Schollenberger v. Pennsylvania, 171 U.S. 1 (1898).

9. Baldwin v. G. A. F. Seelig, Inc., 294 U.S. 511, 527 (1935).

10. Hammer v. Dagenhart, 247 U.S. 251 (1918).

11. Carter v. Carter Coal Co., 298 U.S. 238 (1936).

12. Di Santo v. Pennsylvania, 273 U.S. 34 (1927).

13. Cf. *In re* Rahrer, 140 U.S. 545 (1891); Clark Distilling Co. v. Western Maryland Ry., 242 U.S. 311 (1917); but cf. Washington v. Dawson & Co., 264 U.S. 219 (1924).

14. See Note, 27 *Col. L. Rev.* 573 (1927).

15. 258 U.S. 50 (1922).

16. Cf. United States v. Rock Royal Co-operative, Inc., 307 U.S. 533 (1939).

17. 268 U.S. 189 (1925).

18. 268 U.S. at 199.

19. See, *e.g.*, Railroad Commission of Wisconsin v. Chicago, B. & Q. R.R., 257 U.S. 563 (1922); Texas & Pacific Ry. v. Gulf, Colorado & Santa Fe Ry., 270 U.S. 266 (1926); Napier v. Atlantic Coast Line R.R., 272 U.S. 605 (1926); Midland Valley R.R. v. Barkley, 276 U.S. 482 (1928).

20. Buck v. Kuykendall, 267 U.S. 307 (1925).

21. Davis v. Farmers Co-operative Co., 262 U.S. 312 (1923); Michigan Central R.R. v. Mix, 278 U.S. 492 (1929). But cf. St. Louis, Brownsville & Mexico Ry. v. Taylor, 266 U.S. 200 (1924).

22. Brandeis-Frankfurter Conversations, manuscript in the Library of Harvard Law School.

23. 39 Stat. 482 (1916).

24. New York Central R.R. v. Winfield, 244 U.S. 147, 154 (1917).

25. See Mason, *Brandeis — A Free Man's Life* 177–214, 315–51 (1946); see, *e.g.*, New England Divisions Case, 261 U.S. 184 (1923); St. Louis & O'Fallon Ry. v. United States, 279 U.S. 461, 488 (1929) (dissent).

26. See Mason, *op. cit. supra* n. 25, at 289–315.

27. See, *e.g.*, Southwestern Tel. Co. v. Public Service Commission, 262 U.S.

276, 289 (1923); Pacific Gas & Electric Co. v. San Francisco, 265 U.S. 403, 416 (1924) (dissent).

28. See Louisville Gas Co. v. Coleman, 277 U.S. 32, 42 (1928) (dissent).

29. See Frost v. Corporation Commission, 278 U.S. 515, 528 (1929) (dissent).

30. See New State Ice Co. v. Liebmann, 285 U.S. 262, 280 (1932) (dissent).

31. See, *e.g.*, Pere Marquette Ry. v. French & Co., 254 U.S. 538 (1921).

32. See Felix Frankfurter, "Mr. Justice Brandeis," 55 *Harv. L. Rev.* 181, 183 (1941).

33. 262 U.S. 276 (1923).

34. Brandeis-Frankfurter Conversations, manuscript in the Library of Harvard Law School.

35. Compare Public Utilities Commission v. Attleboro Co., 273 U.S. 83, 91 (1927), which *was* an extension of the holding in the Lemke case, or at least a new application of it, and in which Brandeis did write a dissent.

36. See, *e.g.*, Nebbia v. New York, 291 U.S. 502 (1934); West Coast Hotel Co. v. Parrish, 300 U.S. 379 (1937).

37. United States v. Darby, 312 U.S. 100 (1941); California v. Thompson, 313 U.S. 109 (1941). See N.L.R.B. v. Jones & Laughlin Steel Corp., 301 U.S. 1 (1937); Wickard v. Filburn, 317 U.S. 111 (1942).

38. See Townsend v. Yeomans, 301 U.S. 441 (1937); Milk Control Board v. Eisenberg Farm Products, 306 U.S. 346 (1939); Parker v. Brown, 317 U.S. 341 (1943); Cities Service Gas Co. v. Peerless Oil & Gas Co., 340 U.S. 179 (1950); see also remarks of Frankfurter, J., concurring in Phillips Petroleum Co. v. Wisconsin, 347 U.S. 672, 687 (1954): "It may well be that if the problem in the *Attleboro* case [which followed the *Shafer* case, see *supra*, n. 35] came before the Court today, the constitutional doctrine there laid down would not be found compelling." To the extent, however, that in contracting state power, they suggested the expansion of federal power, both the Lemke and Shafer cases have been cited with approval. See Currin v. Wallace, 306 U.S. 1, 10, 11 (1939); Mulford v. Smith, 307 U.S. 38, 48 (1939); United States v. Rock Royal Co-operative, Inc., 307 U.S. 533, 568–69 (1939).

39. 198 U.S. at 76.

40. See, *e.g.*, Pennsylvania Coal Co. v. Mahon, 260 U.S. 393 (1922); Nashville, Chattanooga & St. Louis Ry. v. Walters, 294 U.S. 405 (1935); Thompson v. Consolidated Gas Co., 300 U.S. 55 (1937).

41. Hood & Sons v. Du Mond, 336 U.S. 525, 545–46 (1949).

42. 336 U.S. at 564.

43. See George D. Braden, "Umpire to the Federal System," 10 *U. Chi. L. Rev.* 27 (1942); Note, 60 *Harv. L. Rev.* 262 (1946).

44. Compare, *e.g.*, Cloverleaf Butter Co. v. Patterson, 315 U.S. 148 (1942), and Hill v. Florida *ex rel.* Watson, 325 U.S. 538 (1945), with California v. Zook, 336 U.S. 725 (1949), and United Automobile, Aircraft & Agricultural Implement Workers of America v. Wisconsin Employment Relations Board, 351 U.S. 266 (1956).

45. See, *e.g.*, Napier v. Atlantic Coast Line R.R., 272 U.S. 605 (1926). But cf. Dickson v. Uhlmann Grain Co., 288 U.S. 188 (1933).

46. Charleston & W.C. Ry. v. Varnville Furniture Co., 237 U.S. 597, 604 (1915).

47. 350 U.S. 497 (1956).

48. Hines v. Davidowitz, 312 U.S. 52 (1941).

49. 254 U.S. 325, 334 (1920).

50. 254 U.S. at 338. Citations omitted.

IX. *Railroad Commission v. Southern Pacific Co.*
American Railway Express Co. v. Kentucky

1. 260 U.S. ix (1922).
2. Taft's views, referred to in the text, and the quotations attributed to him are from 1 & 2 Pringle, *The Life and Times of William Howard Taft* 470–514, particularly 510–14, 952–53, 970–71, 1025 (1939). The case in connection with which Taft remarked that "McReynolds and Brandeis . . . have no loyalty to the court, etc." was Myers v. United States, 272 U.S. 52 (1926). See also Mason, *Brandeis — A Free Man's Life* 254–82, 470, 489, 538, (1946). Quotations and views attributed to Brandeis in these passages in the text are from the Brandeis-Frankfurter Conversations, manuscript in the Library of Harvard Law School.
3. The case referred to is Southern Ry. v. Watts, 260 U.S. 519 (1923).
4. Brandeis Papers, Library of Harvard Law School.
5. Cf. Federal Trade Commission v. Gratz, 253 U.S. 421 (1920); Federal Trade Commission v. Klesner, 274 U.S. 145, 159 (1927); Federal Trade Commission v. Claire Co., 274 U.S. 160, 175 (1927).
6. Federal Trade Commission v. Curtis Publishing Co., 260 U.S. 568, 582 (1923).
7. Washington v. Dawson & Co., 264 U.S. 219, 231 (1924).
8. 2 Pringle, *op. cit. supra* at 971.
9. Brandeis-Frankfurter Conversations, manuscript in the Library of Harvard Law School.
10. 260 U.S. v (1922); 306 U.S. v (1939).
11. See 2 Pringle, *op. cit. supra* at 971.
12. 264 U.S. 331 (1924).
13. 273 U.S. 269 (1927).
14. 41 Stat. 456 (1920). See Railroad Commission of Wisconsin v. Chicago, Burlington & Quincy R.R., 257 U.S. 563 (1922); The New England Divisions Case, 261 U.S. 184 (1923); Texas & Pacific Ry. v. Gulf, Colorado & Santa Fe Ry., 270 U.S. 266 (1926).
15. 41 Stat. 477 (1921).
16. Brandeis-Frankfurter Conversations, manuscript in the Library of Harvard Law School.
17. Cf. Western & Atlantic R.R. v. Georgia Public Service Commission, 267 U.S. 493 (1925); Lehigh Valley R.R. v. Commissioners, 278 U.S. 24 (1928).
18. Interstate Commerce Commission v. Los Angeles, 280 U.S. 52 (1929).
19. Atchison, Topeka & Santa Fe Ry. v. Railroad Commission, 283 U.S. 380 (1931); see Note, 80 *U. Pa. L. Rev.* 1001 (1932).
20. 273 U.S. 269 (1927).
21. American Railway Express Co. v. Royster Guano Co., 273 U.S. 274 (1927).
22. 273 U.S. at 273.

X. *Bullock v. Florida*

1. See Pringle, 2 *The Life and Times of William Howard Taft* 969–70 (1939).
2. Mason, *Brandeis — A Free Man's Life* 495 (1946).
3. See Max Lerner, *The Mind and Faith of Justice Holmes* xxxv (1943).
4. Holmes to Brandeis, April 20, 1919. Manuscript in the Library of the Law School of the University of Louisville.
5. Gitlow v. New York, 268 U.S. 652, 673 (1925).
6. 274 U.S. 357, 375 (1927).
7. Olmstead v. United States, 277 U.S. 438 (1928). See 2 *Holmes-Pollock Letters* 222.
8. See Lon L. Fuller, *The Law in Quest of Itself* 106–10, 117–18 (1940);

Henry M. Hart, Jr., "Holmes' Positivism — An Addendum," 64 *Harv. L. Rev.* 929 (1951). But cf. Mark De Wolfe Howe, "The Positivism of Mr. Justice Holmes," and "Holmes' Positivism — A Brief Rejoinder," 64 *Harv. L. Rev.* 529, 937 (1951).

9. Holmes to Laski, December 11, 1930. Holmes Papers, Library of Harvard Law School.

10. Holmes to Felix Frankfurter, June 15, 1912; August 14, 1916. Holmes Papers, Library of the Harvard Law School.

11. 254 U.S. 513 (1921).

12. 254 U.S. at 521.

13. 6 Pet. 431 (1832); 6 Pet. 498 (1832).

14. Cf. Railroad Commission v. Eastern Texas R.R., 264 U.S. 79 (1924).

15. Fort Smith Traction Co. v. Bourland, 267 U.S. 330 (1925).

16. Brandeis-Frankfurter Conversations, manuscript in the Library of Harvard Law School.

17. See, *e.g.*, Brandeis' opinions in Nashville, C. & St. L. Ry. v. Walters, 294 U.S. 405 (1935) (Stone and Cardozo, JJ., dissenting), and Thompson v. Consolidated Gas Corp., 300 U.S. 55 (1937).

18. *E.g.*, Detroit United Ry. v. Michigan, 242 U.S. 238 (1916); Northern Ohio Traction Co. v. Ohio, 245 U.S. 574 (1918); Covington v. South Covington Street Ry. Co., 246 U.S. 413 (1918).

19. 260 U.S. 393 (1922).

20. 260 U.S. at 395.

21. 260 U.S. at 417.

22. 260 U.S. at 422.

23. See 1 *Holmes-Laski Letters* 473–74.

24. See 1 *Holmes-Laski Letters* 466; 2 *Holmes-Pollock Letters* 109.

25. See 2 *Holmes-Pollock Letters* 111–12.

26. 123 U.S. 623 (1887).

27. See 1 *Holmes-Laski Letters* 473.

28. Hamilton v. Kentucky Distilleries Co., 251 U.S. 146 (1919); Jacob Ruppert v. Caffey, 251 U.S. 265 (1920).

29. 251 U.S. at 301–02.

30. Brandeis Papers, Library of the Harvard Law School.

31. Brandeis-Frankfurter Conversations, manuscript in the Library of Harvard Law School.

32. See 2 *Holmes-Pollock Letters* 13.

33. See 2 *Holmes-Pollock Letters* 13; *Holmes-Laski Letters* 205, 810, 1135.

34. Holmes to Felix Frankfurter, July 12, 1923. Holmes Papers, Library of Harvard Law School.

35. Holmes to Felix Frankfurter, December 3, 1925. Holmes Papers, Library of Harvard Law School.

36. See 2 *Holmes-Pollock Letters* 13; 1 *Holmes-Laski Letters* 204–05.

37. Brandeis-Frankfurter Conversations, manuscript in the Library of Harvard Law School.

38. Brandeis-Frankfurter Conversations, manuscript in the Library of Harvard Law School.

39. 260 U.S. 327 (1927).

40. Brandeis Papers, Library of Harvard Law School.

41. 264 U.S. 543 (1924).

42. Holmes Papers, Library of Harvard Law School.

43. Brandeis-Frankfurter Conversations, manuscript in the Library of Harvard Law School.

Table of Cases

Index

In the following table, cases listed in CAPITALS are those in which unpublished opinions are given in full. Cases listed in *italics* are discussed in some detail. Those listed in ordinary type are merely cited. References are to pages and, where appropriate, to end notes pertaining to the page references immediately preceding them.

Table of Cases

Index

PHOENIX BOOKS
in Political Science and Law